THE DREAM OF A NEW SOCIAL ORDER

POPULAR MAGAZINES IN AMERICA 1893–1914

THE DREAM OF A NEW SOCIAL ORDER

POPULAR MAGAZINES IN AMERICA 1893–1914

Matthew Schneirov

COLUMBIA UNIVERSITY PRESS
NEW YORK

COLUMBIA UNIVERSITY PRESS
NEW YORK CHICHESTER, WEST SUSSEX

Library of Congress Cataloging-in-Publication Data

Schneirov, Matthew.
The dream of a new social order : popular magazines in America, 1893–1914 / Matthew Schneirov.
p. cm.
Includes bibliographical references (p.) and index.
ISBN 0-231-08290-8
1. American periodicals—History. 2. Journalism—Social aspects—United States. 3. Popular culture—United States. I. Title.
PN4877.S36 1994
051'.09034—dc20 *94-12534*
CIP

Casebound editions of
Columbia University Press books
are printed on permanent
and durable acid-free paper.

Printed in the United States of America
c 10 9 8 7 6 5 4 3 2 1

IN MEMORY OF MY PARENTS,
MAURICE SCHNEIROV AND RUTH SCHNEIROV

CONTENTS

ACKNOWLEDGMENTS

There is one person who took an interest in this manuscript when it was in an early stage and was instrumental in seeing it through to completion. Professor John Markoff encouraged the completion of this project, saw its promise, and provided detailed and insightful criticisms on each chapter. I am indebted to him for the role of mentor he has played in my professional development.

I would also like to thank professors Anthony Mendonça, Daniel Regan, Allen Spencer, José Moreno, and Larry Glasco, who read and commented on much of this book. I am indebted to Professor Wendy Griswold for her generous words of praise and helpful criticism. Professors Martin Sklar, Charles Hanna, and Michael Schudson also provided helpful comments on sections of this work. Thanks also the staff of the University of Pittsburgh Photographic Lab for their quality work in reproducing magazine photographs and illustrations and to the University of Pittsburgh Sociology Department for their generous financial support. Of course, thanks to the good people at Columbia University Press, especially Gioia Stevens.

Thanks for the gift of your friendship. Finally, I'd like to thank my brother Richard Schneirov for his helpful advice on historical sources, on understanding the Progressive era, for introducing me to the work of Martin Sklar, and for his own historical (not to mention personal) insights.

THE DREAM OF A NEW SOCIAL ORDER

POPULAR MAGAZINES IN AMERICA 1893–1914

Introduction: A Power and a Pleasure

Popular Dreams

During the late nineteenth century, novelist and veteran magazine editor William Dean Howells spoke of his fears and his hopes for America in his utopian novel *A Traveller from Alturia.* Writing shortly after the Homestead Steel strike of 1892 and during the great depression which began in 1893, Howells had his utopian traveler assert that the system of "competitive individualism" was not working, that America will "come out Europe in the end." The financial panic, the growing gap between the rich and the poor, violent class conflict and social disorder—each of these "teaches the middle class the insecurity of the old system. . . . At any rate it is not the very rich or the very poor who are leading reform in our direction, but it is such of the comfortable middle class as have got the light." [1] In the pages of this same magazine, which published a number of excerpts of Howells's novel, was a series of glowing articles on the 1893 World's Columbian Exposition in Chicago—popularly, the World's Fair in the "White City." Here with an excitement that can only be compared to the enthusiasm of a new religious convert, *Cosmopolitan* editor and publisher John Brisben Walker told his readers of the wondrous advances in science and technology that would revolutionize society and in an editorial outlined a new vision of a rationally planned industrial city. Not many years later *Cosmopolitan* and other popular magazines would exhibit the same enthusiasm in describing the wonders of the department store and the skyscraper, the new technology of the automobile and the camera, and the advances in the "flying machine."

By the first decade of the twentieth century most of the leading American popular magazines, now reaching millions of people on a regular basis, were espousing an ethic of social responsibility and solidarity—decrying public selfishness and corruption, and railing against political bosses, corrupt "plutocrats," and legislative bodies bought off by monied interests. For the first time, a national medium of mass communication had become a political force as magazine "muckraking" popularized a wave of reform movements across the country. The young journalists who pioneered muckraking saw themselves as more than journalists. They saw themselves as social prophets who sought to transmit to their readers their vision of an industrial society in which shared principles of social justice and responsibility would overcome greed and selfishness. In their view humans were social by nature, capable of being motivated by more than economic self-interest.

This book explores the cultural dreams of the American popular magazine during the 1890s and the first decade of the twentieth century. It explores this emerging culture in the context of the genteel culture expressed in the postbellum "family house magazines," *Harper's Monthly*, *Century*, *Scribner's*, and *Atlantic Monthly*. Our story will take us from this genteel culture—fearful of immigration, working-class unrest, and the emergence of a mass society—to the business and journalistic perspective of the new popular magazines, which presented themselves as "vital and timely." A central argument of this book is that popular magazines saw themselves as engaged in the "whirlpool of real life," expressing the "moving spirit of the times." Rather than defining "culture" in terms of the literary, artistic, and philosophical heritage of the Protestant middle and upper classes and emphasizing the boundary between this culture and various threats from the masses, popular magazines presented an image of vitality and energy that depended on a blurring of this boundary. Rather than attempting to preserve a preindustrial past, the new culture sought fulfillment in the future.

The phrase "dreams of a new social order" will be discussed in a number of places in this study, but for now it can be provisionally defined. The word *dream* appeared frequently throughout popular magazines and in ways that might strike the contemporary reader as surprising. "Captains of industry" like

John Rockefeller and Andrew Carnegie as well as scientists and inventors were described (at least before the muckraking period) as "dreamers." The Columbian Exposition in Chicago was a "wonderful frozen dream."

A dream is a psychological phenomenon that is the property not of groups but of individuals (unless you're a Jungian), but it may provide a useful metaphor in helping us to understand the cultural sphere. Dreams, as Freud characterized them, are wish-fulfillments, expressions of human desire. Moreover, they reside in the unconscious, speaking in a language of images rather than of words. So too, during the turn of the century, there was a growing awareness of the depths of the human psyche, of the nonrational sources of our beliefs and motivations as well as the nonrational behavior of "crowds" and other groups (especially the suggestibility of urban "mobs," urban consumers, and new types of readers). Some feared these forces, seeing only the disruptive effects of class conflict, crude materialism, and a society populated with immigrants who were not imbued with an ethic of "self control." Others began to embrace the energies of the city, the vitality of immigrant ghettos, the spirit of expansiveness in American industry, and even the new sense of boundless energy that many felt within themselves. This was the stuff of dreams—cultural dreams.

Cultural dreams are also projections of human desire onto the future, what some call "utopias." Popular magazines of the period were filled with these utopian projections. The dream of a society governed by experts and freed from the chaos of class conflict, poverty, political corruption and the business cycle, the dream of social justice, and the dream of a consumer wonderland of material abundance and technological mastery have all the fantastic and transcending qualities of dreams with the important addition that they are projected onto history, located in secular time. These dreams carry with them an expansive sense of possibility, a depiction, directly or indirectly, of individuals with an abundant source of energy, of the human power to harness the forces of nature and to rationally direct the social and economic forces of American society.

The "new social order" refers to the widespread perception (to be discussed throughout this book) that America was entering an important transition period, perhaps as important as the Civil War. *Cosmopolitan* editor and publisher John Brisben Walker was not alone in his characterization of postbellum American society as the "regime of competitive individualism" and not alone in expressing dissatisfaction with its extremes of wealth and poverty, unrestrained individualism and unregulated economic forces. It will be argued in this study that popular magazines helped to articulate a new culture for this new social order. Popular magazines, forerunners of modern mass communications, were central in the development of the new social order of corporate capitalism.

This book explores the cultural dreams of Americans through the pages of the first dominant discursive medium of mass culture in American history—the popular magazine. The focus of this study is on John Brisben Walker's and William Randolph Hearst's *Cosmopolitan* (not to be confused with the current modern *Cosmopolitan*). The word *dominant* refers to two characteristics of popular magazines. First, they were the only medium that reached a national audience on a regular basis and, second, they did not claim to represent a particular subculture, political party, or interest group, ideology or constituency. As a result, when an article or story or illustration appeared in one of the popular magazines, this fact already conferred on it a kind of substantiality, acceptability, or weightiness. Popular magazines, more than any other medium, seemed to represent "America" itself. We know that in any society marked by significant class divisions, not all ideas are given equal weight or legitimacy. This was certainly true of popular magazines. While there were few if any discussions of populism, the Knights of Labor, or the socialist movement (with the partial exception of the Hearst *Cosmopolitan*), popular magazines were important because they were, for a period, the only cultural form that seemed to represent the entire nation, thus conferring a kind of legitimacy on certain ideas and images by bringing them before a national audience.

Popular magazines, in other words, were important not only as vehicles for new cultural ideals but also as the first form of mass communications that reached a national audience. Twenty years before the "magazine revolution" of 1893, George William Curtis, editor of *Harper's Weekly,* observed that magazines had become "a power as well as a pleasure." [2] By the early twentieth century they were not only a regular form of entertainment, a source of pleasure for a national audience of readers, but a potent and powerful force in shaping the consciousness of millions of Americans.

The popular monthly magazines revolutionized mass communications between 1893 and 1914—the beginning of the First World War. They called themselves "general interest" because they were not intended for particular consumer subcultures or age groups and tried to appeal to a large audience of adult men and women. As a result of technological innovations such as the development of photoengraving and the rotary press, large-scale national advertising, and a group of editors and publishers who saw themselves as businessmen and journalists rather than literary patrons, a new era in magazine publishing began in 1893. This was the year S. S. McClure established *McClure's* to compete with the "quality" family house magazines—*Scribner's, Century,* and *Harper's Monthly* (published by the leading publishing houses). This was also the year that Frank Munsey cut the price of his magazine to ten cents—well below the cost of unit production—and made his profit through advertising. Others shortly imitated *Munsey's* business strategy. By 1901 *Munsey's* had a circulation that was double the combined circulations of *Harper's Monthly, Century,* and *Scribner's*.[3]

Magazine circulation tripled between 1890 and 1905 while the total circulation of newspapers only rose from 36 million to 57 million during the same period. By 1900 the total circulation of monthly magazines was 65 million or about three magazines for every four people.[4] The general interest monthly (in contrast to mail-order magazines, which were only a vehicle for advertisers) was characterized by its low price, its national readership and high circulation, its reliance on advertising for revenue (in contrast to subscriptions), and its somewhat topical content. These magazines carried a range of nonfiction articles as well as serialized novels and short fiction. Through the popular magazine, readers throughout the country were exposed to new literary and journalistic forms from muckraking journalism, science fiction, and the works of an entire generation of realist authors—Hamlin Garland, Stephen Crane, Conan Doyle, O'Henry, Jack London, Upton Sinclair, Booth Tarkington, Frank Norris, and Willa Cather, to name a few. In addition, the expertise of a new professional middle class and university-trained intellectuals reached a mass audience through the pages of popular magazines. It is certainly plausible to suggest that these magazines were the earliest expression of a national mass culture.[5]

The fact that these magazines were the first and, during this period, the only medium of communication to reach a national audience is significant. During this period there were no radio or film industries, no official state newspaper, no regular medium of information and entertainment that reached a national audience except for magazines. A study of these magazines can provide a case study of the formation of modern "mass" communications. Newspapers, even the New York publications of Hearst and Joseph Pulitzer, appealed to large groups of readers but in primarily local markets. This is not to say that the "new journalism" (especially the "sensational" journalism of Pulitzer and Hearst) was not significant in the development of "mass" culture. The relationship between nineteenth-century newspapers and the development of the popular magazine will be explored in subsequent chapters. There were certainly best-selling books, from the sentimental fiction that appealed to middle-class female readers as well as the "dime novel" tradition that reached a mass working-class audience, but these were not forms of print culture that reached a large audience in a regular, repeated manner week after week, year after year. Unlike other forms of print culture that reached a mass audience—such as the Sears catalog, mail-order magazines, and even the older, more established family house publications—the popular magazines had a broad national base of readers. They were neither limited to one subgroup or status group (as were the family house magazines) or intended for one limited purpose (as were the Sears catalog and mail-order magazines). Popular magazines, unlike these preexisting forms of print culture, became a regular form of information and entertainment to a broad segment of the American reading public. These magazines eventually established close connections to national reform movements and to centers of power in the business world and government.

Studies of Popular Magazines

In focusing on the cultural dreams of the middle class and on popular magazines as vehicles for these dreams, this study departs from an emphasis in much of the recent work on popular magazines and the culture of this period. The recent work of Jan Cohn, Richard Ohmann, and Christopher Wilson all focus on popular magazines as vehicles for a hegemonic culture that encouraged readers to "adjust" to new economic realities. Ohmann and Wilson explicitly rely on a "Western Marxist" paradigm that leans heavily on Italian Marxist Antonio Gramsci's theory of hegemony and to a lesser extent the Frankfurt School's critique of the "culture industry." Cohn was also influenced by many of the new developments in cultural studies primarily in her emphasis on the *Saturday Evening Post* as constructing an ideology rather than reflecting some other, more primary sphere of social life.

Richard Ohmann in "Where Did Mass Culture Come From?" utilizes Gramsci's concept of hegemony in arguing that the popular magazine was the first expression of a national mass culture in America.[6] He criticizes modernization theory's treatment of mass culture for concentrating on the choices made by consumers rather than the "desires and choices made by those who produce mass culture." Traditional Marxist theory is also deficient, according to Ohmann, because it assumes that readers are "poor suckers who passively do what they are told." Instead, Ohmann argues that the mass-circulation magazine arose as a result of the development of national advertising, which was in turn a response to the growing need for businesses with high fixed costs to reach out to a national market of consumers. Magazines were part of a "consumer culture" that "became a strategy for shaping people's social identities in leisure time, as consumers—a strategy for creating a new social order beyond the work place."

Magazine content reflected the new consumer culture, Ohmann maintains, in helping readers feel more at home in the new world of consumer capitalism. "Magazines helped ease the passage into industrial society for working people of moderate means just as, on the other side of the class divide, they helped capitalists make that society a less menacing environment for their project of development" (p. 99). Magazines contributed to ideological domination, he argues, not because of a conscious conspiracy but because of its "gatekeeping function." The need for magazine editors to hold on to large audiences for advertisers required that only those ideas and feelings that worked within "invisible hegemonic limits" could be admitted into the "arena of the discussible."

In the same vein, Christopher Wilson argues that mass-circulation magazines reflected the dominance of a new "managerial elite" who were outsiders to the Eastern literary establishment.[7] In contrast to the genteel editors of *Harper's Monthly* and *Century*, the new editors did not relate to their readers as members of a common subculture, as "companions." Instead they transformed the reading process through changes in format, the "voice" of the editor, design strategies, and "narrative devices." These changes resulted in magazines becoming "a primary institution by which a consumer rhetoric, confined originally to the service or sales economy, penetrated other spheres of American life–politics, contemporary affairs, even family life." Wilson documented the ways that George Horace Lorimer, Edward Bok (editor of the *Ladies' Home Journal*), and other editors developed a personalized editorial voice and used other methods to develop a "magazine personality." Magazines acquired professional staffs that "reduced magazine content to an 'idea' that could be farmed out to a writer, and then 'gotten across' to a reader." Wilson also discusses the appeal to female readers, who were beginning to be addressed in their role as directors of family consumption. Magazines transformed the reading process in directions that encouraged status consciousness and reliance on professional expertise. These changes, Wilson argues, were consistent with the development of corporate capitalism but not in accord with the "needs" of readers. "If anything these magazines suggest that the pitch to 'practicality' and masculinity masked a deepening of consumer dependency, a fragmenting of his supposed 'needs' " (p. 64).

Jan Cohn's case study of the *Saturday Evening Post* during the 1899–1936 period is a detailed account of changes and continuities in this magazine's content over the first three decades of the twentieth century.[8] Her thesis is that the magazine was largely an expression of its powerful editor, George Horace Lorimer, who set out to "create America." This phrase is meant to focus on the *Post*'s role in shaping the consciousness of Americans, in representing the nation as a "construct, idea or image." The *Saturday Evening Post* was not simply a vehicle for the dissemination of an ideology. It was, she argues "an artifact of that ideology." What was this ideology? The core of Lorimer's vision of America was embodied in his conception of the businessman. It was business, he believed, that was the hope of the future. But he had an expansive definition of the businessman which seemed to include most middle-class men, who had achieved "a fair amount of material success" without too much "ripe culture" or bookishness. The traditional values of common sense, thrift, diligence, and hard work that Lorimer preached were "rooted in nineteenth-century virtues." Even as the economy became more dependent on consumption, Lorimer's *Post* retained its traditional nineteenth-century values and became a symbol for a variety of conservative positions: anti-immigration, anti-union, antipoor.

In varying ways all three works focus on the popular magazine as actively shaping the consciousness of Americans, not passively reflecting something else. Moreover, there is some attention paid to the properties of the magazine as a cultural form. In other words, magazine articles and fiction are treated as something other than a collection of data to be pulled out without attention to the formal properties of "texts." All of this reflects developments in cultural sociology that are a step forward. But there is a clear impression in this body of work that magazines functioned as an agent of ideological domination, "preserving nineteenth-century values," "helping readers adjust to corporate capitalism," or producing a "deepening of consumer dependency." It is these conclusions that the present study calls into question.

While Cohn is scrupulous in limiting the applicability of her claims and in reminding the reader that they only apply to the *Post*, the impression is bound to be a misleading one. Other magazines with high circulations had a far more complex image and vision. Other editors exerted less of a direct influence and afforded more of an opportunity for diversity. Moreover, during the 1899 to

1914 period, even the *Post* may not have been quite as conservative as Cohn claims. It is only the longer time frame (which includes the *Post*'s anti-immigration campaign and anti-Bolshevik hysteria) that allows for a generalization that Lorimer created an image of America that was racist, sexist, and dominated by nineteenth-century individualist values.

Despite the repeated references to "nineteenth-century values" as a basis for comparison, there is no systematic study of nineteenth-century culture that could provide a basis for comparison. None of the above authors focused on the nineteenth-century magazines or nineteenth-century print culture as an object of systematic study. The problem becomes an acute one for Cohn because of her thesis that Lorimer's *Post* was a conservative continuation of nineteenth-century values. A sympathetic effort to understand what these magazines and their editors were trying to accomplish, from their own point of view, is largely missing in the previous work on the popular magazine.

Certainly Cohn's portrayal of Lorimer as a conservative agent of ideological domination cannot explain how the businessman-editor John Brisben Walker could regard himself as a kind of socialist and could see the businessman as an agent of progressive reform. It is well known that William Randolph Hearst also was sympathetic to many socialist ideas. Perhaps we ought to take more seriously the view, expressed by many businessmen during this period, that businessmen could become leaders in the larger society through the sponsoring of reforms in child labor and protective legislation, government regulation of railroads and other corporations, tax reform to ensure a more equitable distribution of wealth, an improvement in urban living conditions, and a variety of other reforms. These reforms would stabilize the relationship between government, corporations and the market, worker-employee relations, class and ethnic relations in America's industrial cities and establish an era of "cooperation." This is the view of progressive business leadership in social reform developed by Kolko, Wiebe, Weinstein, and Sklar.[9] So the "pro-business" emphasis that Cohn identifies is, in fact, far more complex and cannot necessarily be equated with conservatism. Quite a few businessmen, *Cosmopolitan*'s Walker and William Randolph Hearst especially, were hardly conservative in the sense of wanting to conserve the old social order of "competitive individualism." If we take their own intentions and rhetoric seriously, they sought to popularize elements of a new social order through the pages of their magazines.

Ohmann's essay remains provocative and useful in raising a variety of issues. He makes no claim to be basing his conclusions on systematic empirical research but instead wants to make a case for the importance of the popular magazine and for a Gramscian perspective as a useful way to approach the topic. But Ohmann's concept of hegemony is a rigid one that equates it with "ideological domination." Others have used the concept of hegemony to refer to a process, inherently complex and contested, that is never fully achieved precisely because of the need for mass culture to incorporate new social developments.[10]

Despite the claim to be presenting a more sophisticated Marxist treatment of culture, Ohmann winds up reducing culture to economic factors. He inaccurately presents the popular magazine as primarily a vehicle of consumer culture. As Theodore Greene has pointed out, the advertising business was not fully rationalized and could hardly dictate to magazines, the only national medium, in a highly competitive market. Editors were generally given considerable freedom by their publishers as long as circulations were increasing, and the effort to appeal to specific consumer markets was largely hit or miss. Editors had to rely on their "instincts" rather than reader surveys while writers could not rely on public relations departments for ready-made information or publicity. Only after 1917, with the development of the American Association of Advertising Agencies, did these firms develop systematic, standardized, and rationalized practices, utilizing market research to maximize economic returns. The popular magazine did not begin, at least, as simply a vehicle for national advertising.[11]

Overall, ideological effects seem to be determined by economic causes in the Ohmann analysis, resulting in something very similar to the mechanistic Marxist view that he started out criticizing. "Corporate capitalism," [12] the independent variable in Ohmann's thesis, was not an accomplished fact in the late nineteenth century, but, as Sklar has demonstrated, was a matter of intense dispute. The entire political-economic and legal framework for corporate capitalism emerged only after intense struggle and debate between various classes and interest groups on the national level as well as in the workplace.[13] Changes in the economy cannot be given an independent status as a causal agent and then used to explain cultural factors because economic change is never purely "economic" (i.e., divorced from larger social and cultural frameworks). It is difficult to imagine what an empirical study based on Ohmann's thesis would look like since he provides no theoretical space for discovering evidence of magazine content that did not contribute to ideological domination or "prepare readers for the passage into industrial society." Magazines became the ideal vehicle for national advertising, but they were also a national forum for an assortment of ideas—some from social reformers, others from journalists, editors, businessmen, and scientists. Indeed, as we will see, the wide assortment of ideas and utopian speculation that appeared in popular magazines is striking. Of course, as Ohmann argues, not all ideas could be admitted; there were "invisible hegemonic limits." But within these limits there was ample room for diversity.

Methodological Issues

In addition to *Cosmopolitan,* this study particularly examines two other popular magazines, *Munsey's* and *McClure's.* These three were the most important general interest monthlies during the first decade of the "magazine revolution" in terms of circulation as well as amount of advertising carried. Between 1895 and 1907, *McClure's* carried more advertising than any other magazine in the United States, even though it was not the circulation leader. By 1897, four years after *Munsey's* price reduction, *McClure's* had a circulation of 260,000, *Cosmopolitan* 300,000, and *Munsey's* 700,000. The leading magazine of the nineteenth century, *Century* had reached its peak circulation at 250,000. It was the top circulation magazine among the quality monthlies, which included *Harper's Monthly* and *Scribner's.* From 1904 to 1909, *Munsey's* ranked consistently second in circulation behind the *Saturday Evening Post.* After 1909 it fell to fifth or sixth place among magazines in terms of circulation. *Cosmopolitan* consistently ranked fifth or sixth in circulation until 1911 when its circulation increased to 750,000, second only to the *Saturday Evening Post. McClure's* circulation ranged from 375,000 to 500,000 during the 1904 to 1913 period (see appendix 1).

In addition to circulation and amount of advertising carried, these magazines provide a reasonable sample of the diversity among popular magazines.[14] During the 1890s, *Cosmopolitan* was the most explicitly utopian of the three, serializing the work of a number of utopian and science fiction authors as well as providing a forum for its prolific editor, John Brisben Walker, who used the occasions of industrial expositions to speculate on the city of the future and advocated in editorials a "new political-economic order." In addition, Walker's *Cosmopolitan* focused more than other popular magazines on educational reform, and Walker used the pages of *Cosmopolitan* to advocate a free correspondence university. Both *Cosmopolitan* and *Munsey's* emphasized the new cultural and political developments associated with the "new woman" even though Frank Munsey, unlike Walker, was not known as a progressive reformer. *McClure's* focused far more during this period (compared to the other two magazines) on Civil War stories and also provided a forum for some early prolabor articles by Hamlin Garland and others that broke clearly with the older genteel tradition. In addition, *McClure's* printed more fiction in the realist tradition than *Munsey's* and *Cosmopolitan*.

Despite these differences there were broad areas of commonality during the 1890s. All three focused on new scientific and technological developments, with glowing depictions of "captains of industry" and new industrial organizations and (as we will see in chapters 4 and 6) on advertising, illustrations, and half-tone photography. All three magazines departed in various ways from the genteel discourse of the family house magazines and sought timely, lively, and entertaining features. By November 1902, *McClure's* printed some of the first muckraking exposés. *Cosmopolitan* in 1905 was sold to William Randolph Hearst, who provided a forum for the left wing of the muckraking movement while *Munsey's* remained aloof from these political developments.

Munsey's remained consistent throughout the entire period in its focus on success and achievement, with articles on the wonders of the new department stores, automobiles, skyscrapers, and the lives of European monarchs. In addition, *Munsey's* carried numerous photographs of half-dressed "artists' models," pioneered in the very short, one-half page story ("storiettes"), and promoted itself as carrying more illustrations than any other magazine. It carried numerous "departments," a feature adapted from newspapers, and focused on the glamour of the upper-class urban lifestyle with articles on "Ball Giving in New York" and "The Palace Cottages of Newport." While there is no way of knowing the social composition of the readers, the level of literacy or "cultural competence" required to read *Munsey's* was considerably less than that of *Century*, *Cosmopolitan*, or *McClure's*. Many of its features were similar to the sensationalist New York dailies that consciously sought an audience that was not highly educated. In short, these magazines represent well the overall diversity of popular magazines—from *McClure's* middlebrow tone of making high culture accessible to the masses and its celebration of scientific discovery and exploration to *Cosmopolitan*'s international flavor and coverage of industrial expositions to *Munsey's* more lowbrow celebration of success and journalistic features on sports, music, and theater.

Theodore Greene's magazine periodization provides the rationale for choosing to focus on this period of popular magazine history. The magazines from 1893 to 1914 were run by journalists-entrepreneurs who operated in a largely competitive environment. Advertising agencies exerted only a limited influence, and efforts to reach specialized markets were sporadic and haphazard. After

World War I, large-scale organization became dominant in magazine publishing and advertisers exerted a far greater influence on format and content. Perhaps just as important, magazines during the later period were no longer the only form of national mass culture, and their importance was considerably reduced.[15]

There are a number of reasons for choosing *Cosmopolitan* for intensive study. Under the direction of John Brisben Walker, *Cosmopolitan* combined many of the features of the quality nineteenth-century magazines like *Century,* with *Munsey's* journalistic and "sensational" emphasis as well as *McClure's* focus on "great personalities" and scientific and technological achievements. Unlike *McClure's,* little has been written about this magazine and its publisher-editor. As a member of "the monied class" (Walker was an entrepreneur, industrialist, newspaperman, diplomat, and congressman), he departed in important ways from the genteel, upper-class concerns of his nineteenth-century predecessors. I will argue that Walker's championing of new technology, activist government, and education through the pages of his magazine reflected important changes in American upper-class culture that began to filter down to a broader audience. Another reason for focusing on *Cosmopolitan* is that after 1905, when William Randolph Hearst bought the publication, it became the home for the left wing of the muckraking movement. In contrast to *McClure's* middle-of-the-road positions, *Cosmopolitan* under Hearst's aegis—and through the work of some of the leading journalists in the country—printed a sensational and quasi-socialist version of the exposés of corruption that shook up the nation between 1903 and 1910. Hearst, of course, was notorious for the sensationalist "yellow journalism" of his newspapers, which appealed to a largely working-class and immigrant constituency. While much has been written about the entry of Hearst into the newspaper world, little has been said of the use of elements of the sensational newspaper style in the "middlebrow" world of the popular magazine.

My original intention was to read a sample of magazine articles and stories. I read cover to cover four issues of *Cosmopolitan* for the 1894, 1898, 1902, 1906, 1910, and 1914 years.[16] I soon discovered, though, that any limited sample would leave out too many important articles. As a result, I wound up reading or skimming every article and story between 1893 and 1914. Since an index is not available for *Cosmopolitan,* I developed a rough procedure for categorizing all the articles, dividing them into the following categories: (1) "Science, Technology, Exploration," (2) "Art and Literature," (3) "Politics and Current Events" (i.e., business, religion, politics, social reform, and the military), (4)

"Popular Entertainment" (including the theater), (5) "Sports, Recreation, and Health," (6) "International Royalty and American Upper-Class Life" (7) "Travel [foreign and domestic] and Nature," (8) "Fiction," and (9) "Self-Promotion and Editorials." Categorizing all the articles was especially useful for the chapters that focused explicitly on magazine content and provided a basis for rough comparisons between different periods of the magazine's history. Any article in *Cosmopolitan* from the 1893–1914 period that was not read was "skimmed." Title, author's name, and editorial comment (if applicable) were recorded.

Cosmopolitan before 1905 published a "Men, Women and Events" department and after 1905 a "Shop Talk" feature in which particular articles were promoted by the editor and in which the editor reported on what articles had elicited comment and controversy from readers. These departments became useful guides in selecting additional articles for detailed reading. I also used a magazine, *Review of Reviews,* which printed a feature called "Leading Articles of the Month," a summary of leading magazine articles. Another feature of this review magazine focused on particular popular magazine articles for critical commentary. This was useful in discovering which features of the three popular monthlies had attracted wider attention and comment. The *Review of Reviews* was founded by the English reformer William Stead who later established an American affiliate (also called *Review of Reviews* and edited by Dr. Albert Shaw). *The Bookman,* which was a more "highbrow" journal of literary criticism and cultural commentary, provided monthly discussions of American literary developments as well as magazine illustrations, photography, and new authors (its editor Thursten Peck wrote extensively for Walker's *Cosmopolitan*). Overall in the course of doing the research for this study, I moved toward a pragmatic and comprehensive approach to reading, focusing on specific questions that needed to be addressed and reading or skimming material in *Cosmopolitan* for every year of the study.

To guard against personal bias, other magazines were used for comparison. In this way there was some kind of check on using selected *Cosmopolitan* articles to make claims about popular magazines as a class. The material in *Munsey's* and *McClure's* provided a useful basis for judging the extent to which *Cosmopolitan*'s coverage and emphasis on particular issues were typical or idiosyncratic. These two magazines were not covered in as much detail as *Cosmopolitan,* although an effort was made to read thoroughly the distinctive articles, departments, and fiction in each. A similar sample was used for both magazines with four issues read cover to cover during the 1894, 1898, 1902, 1906, 1910, and

1914 years. Special attention was paid to the muckraking articles in *McClure's* by Ida Tarbell, Lincoln Steffens, and Ray Stannard Baker. In addition, *McClure's* focused (especially during its first decade) on new developments in science, technology, articles on explorations of the Arctic and Antarctic, wild animals, and so on. Ida Tarbell's biographies of Lincoln and Napoleon were read as well as much of the articles and fiction on the Civil War. The *McClure's* Index from 1893 to 1903 provided a useful guide to articles during these years, and many were read outside the original sample. In addition, issues of *McClure's* were skimmed in order to compare *McClure's* coverage and mix of articles with *Cosmopolitan* and *Munsey's* for selected topics and years, e.g., industrial expositions (1893), articles on the "new woman" (1890s), sports, and Civil War stories and articles, among others. In many cases, as with discussions of the automobile or the Spanish-American wars, all three magazines focused on the same topics during the same time period. In other cases, such as sensationalistic muckraking, *Munsey's* emphasis on athletics and popular music, or Walker's emphasis on foreign and "exotic" places, particular magazines had their own characteristics and emphases.

In addition to *McClure's* and *Munsey's,* a sample of articles were read in the *Woman's Home Companion,* one of the leading women's magazines. In order of detailed coverage, the *Women's Home Companion* would rank fourth on the list of popular magazines behind *Cosmopolitan, McClure's,* and *Munsey's.* This material provided a useful way of comparing the characterization of women and women's issues in the three general interest magazines with a magazine intended primarily for a female audience. It also allowed for some sense of whether the trends discovered in the three general interest magazines, beyond women's issues, applied to a more specialized publication. While the *Woman's Home Companion* material has not been the focus of this study, it was useful in comparing the general interest magazines with a more specialized magazine that reached as large if not a larger audience.

In addition to the popular magazines that are central to this study, I explored the major quality magazines for comparison. The *Readers Periodical Guide* and *Poole's* indexes were especially useful in locating relevant articles in *Harper's Monthly, Century, Atlantic Monthly,* and *Scribner's* on "amusements," photography and illustration, newspapers, civil service reform, and an assortment of other topics. For chapters 1 and 2, I have read George Curtis's "Easy Chair" department between 1873–1890 in *Harper's Monthly,* Richard Watson Gilder's "Topics of the Time" for 1885–1895 in the *Century,* and W. D. Howells's "Editor's Study" (also in *Harper's Monthly*). I have read extensively through issues of *Harper's Monthly* and the *Century* for the 1870 to 1890 period, and to provide a basis for comparison I examined the pages of the *Century* and *Atlantic Monthly* during the era of the popular magazine. The *Nineteenth Century Readers Guide to Periodical Literature* was also used to choose relevant articles in other nineteenth-century magazines.

Apart from the magazines themselves, I found other sorts of material valuable—for example, book-length autobiographies as well as autobiographical sketches and retrospectives by editors. S. S. McClure and Edward Bok each wrote autobiographies that discussed their magazine careers in detail. John Brisben Walker wrote extensively in his magazine about a range of political, scientific, and cultural issues. Published letters and essays by W. D. Howells, Ellery Sedgwick, George Curtis, Richard Watson Gilder, Richard Underwood Johnson, Henry Alden, Henry Seidel Canby, and others provided valuable insight into the nineteenth-century magazine editor. Leading contributors and staff members to popular magazines, particularly the "muckrakers," wrote accounts of their work, among which were the famous *Autobiography* of Lincoln Steffens, works by William Allen White, David Graham Phillips, Ida Tarbell, and others. I discovered early in the project that I needed to read some issues cover to cover in order to develop a sense of the "magazine reading experience." Of course, there is no way of reproducing the nineteenth- or early twentieth-century reading experience. Nevertheless, this was useful in helping me understand, at least intuitively, the appeal of certain magazines, to get a sense of a magazine's coherence, diversity, "flavor." It also seemed to me that other studies had relied too extensively on only one element of the magazine, either its muckraking or biographies or editorials and had therefore arrived at generalizations that were suspect. A major advantage of focusing on more than one feature of a magazine is the check it provides on such overly broad generalizations. Reading a wide range of articles and stories helped me to become sensitive to the complexities and potential contradictions within magazines—to understand how they can serve the interests of editors and publishers in a variety of ways as well as the pleasure of their readers. I have tried to provide what Geertz has called a "thick description,"[17] one that is sensitive to textual complexities and to the motivations of relevant actors.

This study does not focus on the *Saturday Evening Post,* the circulation leader from 1904 to the end of this period. A detailed study already exists of the *Post.* More importantly, the focus of many of those who have written about popular magazines has been on the two great Cyrus Hermann Curtis publications, the *Post* and the *Ladies' Home Journal.* This emphasis needs to be balanced by a treatment of some of the other leading general interest magazines. Moreover, George Horace Lorimer's *Post* began publication in 1899, well after Munsey's price reduction sparked the popular magazine "revolution." The *Post* achieved a position of dominance in the magazine world only during the later years of this period. The Walker and Hearst *Cosmopolitan* provide an interesting but, until now, not well-researched contrast. I have tried, though, to take into account Jan Cohn's and Theodore Greene's valuable work on the *Post* during this period in order to provide a frame of reference for my generalizations about *Cosmopolitan, McClure's,* and *Munsey's.*

New Approaches to Understanding Culture

I hope to contribute to the growing body of interdisciplinary work in cultural studies by examining the popular and quality magazines in a larger social and historical context. Michael Denning has argued that there is a need to integrate the analysis of cultural commodity forms with that of "the subcultures, class fractions, social movements that produce and consume them." [18] This is in large part what I have tried to do, while at the same time paying attention to the properties of the popular magazine as a cultural object.

I have tried to avoid the pitfalls of an overly "textual analysis" as well as an overly "external" interpretation of magazine content while learning from both approaches. On the one hand, structuralists have, in their critique of referential theories of language, focused exclusively on the text as a "signifying system" and how meaning is generated through the text's rules and assumptions. Their analysis requires a "bracketing of history." In other words, the relationship between meaning and the social environment in which it is produced and read is not part of the analysis. The valuable insight here is that the text must be taken seriously and units of meaning must be understood in a larger textual context—not abstracted from context and compared to some external referent.

The other theoretical position, exemplified by certain Marxist approaches, understands a social text, whether it is a magazine, film, book, or television show, as important only as an effect of some other cause, a reflection of class interests or technological developments. In the mechanistic version of Marxism, culture is part of the "superstructure." Interestingly enough, some non-Marxists have also retained the same assumptions about the derivative nature of cultural texts. In this case, though, they are often interpreted as "reflecting" not class or elite interests but changes in "social structure," which assume in the analysis a primary causal role.

This study departs from both theoretical approaches in a number of ways. First, the view that culture consists of ideas and beliefs that are to be explained in terms of the more "material" substructure of political economy neglects the extent to which "culture" can be thought of as having its own "mode of production." Cultural forms like magazines, books, films, and so on are produced in institutions with their own specific technologies and property relations. Culture consists of those quite "material" practices that are embedded in cultural institutions from movie studios to newsrooms, as well as those practices that are embedded in everyday life, from the activities of soap opera viewers to Madonna fans to readers of romance novels. A reductionist view of culture also excludes the possibility that some cultural forms during certain historical periods can play a crucial role in contributing to social transformation as well as social reproduction.

The challenge in any study of culture is to avoid, on the one hand, reifying culture so that "it" changes independent of human agency and, on the other hand, reducing culture and cultural institutions to reflexes of more primary social processes—to treat it as a dependent variable. In contrast to the structuralist or semiotic conception of culture, I have not assumed that culture has a life of its own independent of the "subjects" who produced it. Instead I have tried to take seriously the intentions of publishers, editors, and contributors about what they were trying to accomplish. Publishers and editors of the leading "genteel" magazines of the late nineteenth century had a clearly expressed political and cultural project. The popular magazine publishers and editors were a more diverse group in terms of social background, politics, and how they viewed the magazine enterprise. But here too it is necessary to examine carefully the beliefs and projects of the pioneers of this new cultural form. While it would be a mistake to reduce popular magazines to the intentions of their editors and publishers, it would also be a mistake to ignore them.

To summarize, in the structuralist analysis of culture, experience is reduced to meaning and virtually anything can be understood as a text, a signifying system. On the other hand, in various reductionist analyses of culture, social experience is more fundamental than meaning and determines it. I have focused on the magazine as a creative product of its publishers, editors, and contributors but at the same time as a product created in a larger social context. Moreover, I have also paid some attention (in chapter 3) to the popular magazine as an evolving cultural form borrowing from sensational and independent journalism, genteel magazines, and the mass market "story papers." In short, this study examines the popular magazine as a product of human action or agency within certain structural contexts and as a cultural form or "object." The approach taken here is similar to Wendy Griswold's "cultural diamond." The cultural diamond is a model for the study of any cultural object, focusing on the interactions between the cultural object, cultural producers, the audience, and the larger social context.[19]

I have learned from the semiotic and structuralist traditions that a "text" like the popular magazine or television or dime novels is not a passive reflection of some more primary domain of experience. Instead it is important to take into account the characteristics of the cultural form itself and the active role it plays in defining the categories through which people interpret their experience. But I have also learned from more recent developments in cultural studies that cultural texts must be understood in terms of the social contexts of production and reception.[20] The question, then, is not simply what can we learn about the American middle class as a result of reading their magazines, but how did these magazines refocus, re-present and transform the "lived culture" of middle-class men and women in ways that served editors, publishers, and larger social interests as well as in ways that resonated with various audiences of readers?

Mass Culture Theory

There is a tradition of "mass culture" scholarship that this study implicitly calls into question. Not only contemporary cultural critics but late nineteenth-century ones as well worried about the socially disruptive consequences of new forms of mass culture. In the late nineteenth century it was photography and illustration. Later it was the film industry that critics feared would degrade the critical capacities of the masses, stimulate wants and desires that could not be met, encourage emotionalism rather than reason, and lead viewers to want to escape from reality rather than come to terms with it. This genre of cultural criticism continues with diatribes against rock and rap music, videos, and whatever new development comes out of the culture industry. Ironically, cultural critics of the left as well as the right seem to agree that mass culture is harmful—only for somewhat different reasons. For cultural conservatives the importance of preserving standards and distinctions (between high and popular culture for example) is emphasized as a way of encouraging social order, stability, and respect for tradition. On the left, mass culture is thought to be intellectually debilitating and so undermines possibilities for transforming the social order.

One of the clearest explications of the "mass culture critique" by sociologists can be found in a collection of articles published in the 1950s. Quite a few of the critiques were clearly influenced by the Frankfurt School's work on the "culture industry" so that an examination of one such essay will provide an overview of a broader theoretical tradition. Dwight MacDonald, in "A Theory of Mass Culture," began by rejecting the designation of "popular culture" since "its distinctive mark is that it is solely and directly an article for mass consumption, like chewing gum." Mass culture unlike high culture, he maintained, is a commodity while high culture is a product of the creativity of an individual artist. High culture requires creative effort on the part of the spectator, while mass culture tells the spectator how to react and is "predigested." Also, unlike "folk art," which is an authentic, spontaneous, and autonomous expression of the people, mass culture is imposed from above. Mass culture is not only impersonal and mass-produced but is an instrument of political domination. It "breaks down the wall" of folk culture and presents to the masses "a debased form of high culture." Mass culture in totalitarian societies like the former Soviet Union is not a commercial product, but like its counterpart in the West it "exploits rather than satisfies the cultural needs of the masses" and is manufactured for mass consumption.[21]

Leo Lowenthal's content analysis of popular magazines reflects the same theoretical orientation. Lowenthal compared biographies in the *Saturday Evening Post* and *Collier's* for the 1901–1914, 1922–1930, 1930–1934, and 1940–41 periods. He discovered that "idols of production" predominated in the pre–World War I magazine biographies—heroes from productive life, business, industry, and the natural sciences. By the 1940–41 period, a very different picture emerged. The vast majority of biographical heroes were from entertainment and sports and only 2 percent were from the sphere of production. The heroes from the realm of leisure and entertainment he called "idols of consumption." While a host of criticisms can raised concerning his methodology (among which is the complete lack of attention to the magazine as a cultural form and a willingness to generalize about American culture as a whole based on a study of one magazine genre), what is more significant is Lowenthal's evaluation of his data.

> While we found that around 1900 or even 1920 the vocational distribution of magazine heroes was a rather accurate reflection of the nation's living trends, we observe that today the hero selection corresponds to needs quite different

> from those of genuine information. They seem to lead to a dream world of the masses who no longer are capable or willing to conceive of biographies as a means of orientation and education.[22]

For Lowenthal, mass culture and mass consumption are unmitigated disasters, producing a view of man as an "object of external forces" as well as a loss of autonomy and rationality.

MacDonald assumes that mass, folk, and high culture refer to distinct objects. Instead, much of the recent work in cultural studies suggests that the distinction is not merely a neutral and descriptive one. "High" culture, in the beginning of his essay, is equated with art—which is assumed to be a product of individual genius and an expression of transcendent and timeless truths. But works of "art" convey multiple meanings that are as independent of the artists' intentions as the products of "mass" culture. A book or painting or musical form may be considered art within one historical and social context and demoted to the merely popular in another. Exponents of a cultural form like rock music, once considered a crude expression of youthful rebellion, successfully made their case for rock music as "art" by highlighting its musical complexity and the virtuosity of its musicians, as well as the erudition of its critics.[23] Once-popular works like Edgar Allan Poe's detective stories in subsequent generations acquired the aura of a unique and timeless aesthetic work.[24] In short, it has proven to be an impossible task to define the characteristics of a distinct aesthetic object.[25]

MacDonald's comparison of mass and folk culture can also be usefully reexamined. According to one historian, the concept of folk culture emerged in the late eighteenth and early nineteenth centuries as part of the Romantic movement in which authentic folk traditions were seen as expressions of nature—the instinctive, unrefined, primitive virtues of the sturdy peasant. Another element in the discovery of folk culture by intellectuals was the development of early nineteenth-century national liberation movements in Europe, in which intellectuals formed alliances with peasants in order to defeat foreign domination. Revivals of traditional culture helped to legitimate these efforts. This is of interest for my purposes because it demonstrates that the concept of "folk" culture with its accompanying connotations of primitive, organic, and authentic was from the first an ideological formulation. Historical research has demonstrated that many of the "primitive" folk songs and folktales that were supposed to have survived unchanged since the Middle Ages were in fact of recent origin. Moreover, many of these oral traditions were influenced by developments in the larger culture, including the spread of literacy and commercial capitalism.[26]

In short, a major problem with these critiques is that "mass culture" is all of a piece. Little attention has been paid to the distinct characteristics of various cultural forms, how they differ, the range of meanings within each, how these cultural products are interpreted and used by readers or viewers. A more useful approach (consistent with the results of this study) has been suggested by Stuart Hall when he argued that there is no wholly authentic "popular" culture that is not influenced by the dominant culture. Moreover, commercial mass culture cannot be entirely manipulative and externally imposed.

> If the forms of provided commercial culture are not purely manipulative, then it is because, alongside the false appeals . . . there are also elements of recognition and identification, something approaching a recreation of recognizable experiences and attitudes, to which people are responding. The danger arises because we tend to think of cultural forms as wholly corrupt or authentic. Whereas, they are deeply contradictory; they play on contradictions, especially when they function in the domain of the 'popular.'[27]

The work of Fredric Jameson as well focuses on "mass culture" as a contested terrain that is never, at any one moment, wholly manipulative or authentic, that is the site of struggle over its meaning and uses.[28] Jargon-filled as it is, Michael Denning's definition of mass culture (clearly influenced by Stuart Hall and Jameson) is a useful one. Mass (or what he calls "popular" in this particular context) culture consists of "that contested terrain structured by the culture industries, the state cultural apparatuses, and the symbolic forms and practices of the subaltern classes."[29]

One reason it has taken so long to seriously study forms of mass culture is that a crude form of economic or technological determinism has impeded it. It has been assumed that the use of mass production methods or the commercial character of mass culture determines its meaning and effects. Rather than assuming what should be the object of study, I have explored the world of popular magazines in order to discover what they said, who produced and edited them, how they compared to other forms of print culture, and what these magazines meant for their readers.

The study is divided into three parts. Part one explores the world of the family house magazines of the 1865–1893 period. The publishers and editors of these magazines, many of whom were also active in the world of independent journalism, sought to improve the cultural taste of their readers and provide a forum for upper-class reformers within the Republican party who sought to remove politics from the control of political parties. Chapter 1 provides a sketch of the "mugwump" editors of *Atlantic Monthly, Harper's Monthly,* and especially Richard Watson Gilder of the *Century.* The genteel conception of culture is explored as well as their relationship to contributors and their audience. Chapter 2 focuses on the Victorian reader with a sketch of the social functions of didactic and imaginative literature in nineteenth-century America. The chapter concentrates on the political struggle over the rise of a "mass culture" and genteel fears concerning the commercialization of literature and changes in the reading process. Throughout these chapters the "cultural diamond" of the genteel magazine is explored—from the worldview and professional ideology of the cultural producers to the characteristics, real and imagined, of the readers, to an examination of the larger social context and the characteristics of the genteel magazine as a cultural object.

Part two explores the magazine revolution of the 1890s and the background and perspectives of the "cultural entrepreneurs" who created the popular magazine—Frank Munsey, S. S. McClure, and especially John Brisben Walker. In these two chapters, the characteristics of the popular magazine as a new cultural form are explored as well as the similarities and differences between these new magazines and their editors on the one hand, and the genteel tradition on the other.

Part three is an exploration of the content of popular magazines. Chapter 5 focuses on the popular magazine's therapeutic stance toward its readers in articulating a new cultural ideal of abundant physical, psychological, and spiritual energy through articles on sports, physical culture, nation building, and health. Chapter 6 explores the "dreams of progress," the way popular magazines introduced their readers to the spectacle of urban life, industrial expositions, and more generally to the wonders of science and technology. Finally, chapter 7 looks at two strands of magazine muckraking, the Hearst *Cosmopolitan* and the more restrained approach of *McClure's.*

But enough of this. To paraphrase Frank Munsey, the reader wants a good story, a story with "action, force and a tale that means something."[30] In this spirit of giving the customer what he wants, I invite the reader to join me, first in the upper-middle-class parlor where a copy of *Harper's Monthly* sits on the marble center table. This is the world of the gentle reader and the genteel editor. But shortly, like poor Dorothy in the Kansas tornado, we will be whirled into the exciting world of "human interest," a world of zealous crusaders against corruption, and jingoistic advocates of war; of optimistic faith in progress and nervous anxiety over health, of photographic realism and illustrations of artists' models. If this sounds familiar, perhaps it is because we still live in this world.

1

THE GOSPEL OF CULTURE AND THE VICTORIAN READER

CHAPTER ONE

The Family House Magazines and the Gospel of Culture

This chapter will focus on the "family house magazines" of the 1865–1893 period.[1] These were the magazines of the major publishing houses that reached the height of their reputation and circulation during this period. Until the "magazine revolution" of the mid-1890s, it was primarily *Harper's Monthly, Century, Scribner's*,[2] and *Atlantic Monthly* that educated middle-class Americans read and that helped to shape the thinking and tastes of a generation of readers. Moreover, these magazines were a major influence, as a positive model and as a point of departure, on the popular magazines of the early twentieth century. S. S. McClure worked on the staff of the *Century* before publishing and editing his own magazine, and many of the contributors and staff members of *Cosmopolitan, Munsey's*, and *McClure's* had been regular contributors to the family house magazines as well. During the 1890s many of the popular magazine editors thought of "the big three" as their main competitors in terms of readership and quality.

More importantly, these magazines were significant as the vehicle for the "mugwumps," [3] who espoused a cultural project that in many ways remains a part of the discourse of modern societies. As political reformers the mugwumps, in part through the pages of their magazines and in part through the newspapers that many of the same individuals edited, espoused a project of "liberal" [4] reform in which they sought to "improve" the quality of public life by removing government from the control of political parties and partisan politics.[5]

My main argument in this chapter is that the success and the eventual failure of the family house magazines can be understood in terms of their accommodation and resistance to what was later called "mass society" as well as mass culture. During the 1870s and 1880s what caused the greatest concern to the educated, Eastern upper class was the emergence of a mass democracy, especially the rise of the big city machines who owed their support to the immigrant and native working class.[6] Newspapers from E. L. Godkin's *Nation* (and the *New York Evening Post*) to George William Curtis's *Harper's Weekly* to Murat Halstead's *Cincinnati Commercial* espoused a nonpartisan, "educational" style of politics and an independent journalism. Their goal was to limit the influence of a growing immigrant working class in local and national politics through educating and "uplifting" the cultural level of their middle-class readers.

For the family house magazines (the focus of these two chapters), the reform of political institutions was not as significant as it was for the independent, nonpartisan newspapers. Instead, these magazines were intended to elevate the tastes of their middle-class readers so that they would be protected from the dangers that editors saw all around them—an excessive materialism, immorality in public life, a lack of good taste and good manners, and a mass print culture that focused the reader's attention on the transient, the timely, and the commonplace.

Publishers and editors of the family house magazines fought a constant battle against cultural developments that challenged their authority as arbiters of public taste. During this period "mass" culture was intimately connected to the production of consumer goods that dazzled consumers in the growing number of department stores and to the cheap reproduction of art works that were popular decorations in middle-class homes. The late nineteenth century also saw the development of a mass print culture in the form of mail-order catalogs, newspapers, dime novels, story papers, as well as new methods for reproducing photographs and illustrations. The growth of spectator entertainments from circuses to sports to vaudeville that attracted an assortment of classes and ethnic groups also caused concern.[7] These magazines sought to elevate middle-class tastes through exposure to great literature and art in order to protect the Protestant middle class[8] from the dangers of the "lower orders"[9] and to counteract their influence. But magazine editors also intended to indirectly contribute to the education and assimilation of the working class as well. After all, the middle class as teachers, ministers, writers, and professionals of various sorts were in contact with the industrial working class in various capacities.

Century and *Scribner's* were instrumental in the reproduction of works of art and in printing a distinctly American literature that reflected every region of the country. Moreover, they were forerunners of the popular magazines in their depoliticized tone, their reliance on scientific expertise, and their largely secular outlook. In their historical pieces (the *Century's* Civil War series was most important), these magazines contributed to the development of a national culture. By the 1880s the family house magazines were printing more fiction in the "realist" tradition, articles written from the perspective of social science and accepting a substantial number of pages of advertising. All of these changes anticipated the developments of the "magazine revolution" of the 1890s. But there were limits to how far editors would go in reaching out to new readers without threatening their core mission.

The Mugwumps and the Gospel of Culture

In George Santayana's famous essay, *The Genteel Tradition in American Philosophy,* the Harvard philosopher argued that American culture was plagued by a split between the practical drive for mastery and for bold action associated with business, and the "genteel" culture of intellectuals, writers, and artists who were more at home in the parlor and at the museum. This, Santayana argued, was a reflection of a deeper division in American culture between thought and action, theory and practice.

> The truth is that one-half of the American mind, that not occupied intensely in practical affairs, has remained, I will not say high and dry, but slightly becalmed: it has floated gently in the back-water, while, alongside, in invention and industry and social organization, the other half of the mind was leaping down a sort of Niagara Rapids. This division may be symbolized in American architecture: a neat reproduction of the colonial mansion—with some modern comforts introduced surreptitiously—stands beside the skyscraper; the American intellect inhabits the colonial mansion. The one is the sphere of the American man; the other, at least predominately, of the American woman. The one is all aggressive enterprise; the other is all genteel tradition.[10]

Santayana's article (adapted from a lecture given to a university audience in 1913) was a critique of this "genteel tradition"—the roots of which he traced back to Puritanism. For our purposes, though, his argument seems to be particularly salient in late "Victorian" America.

On the one hand, the 1865–1893 period was one of "aggressive enterprise"—the empire building of industrial entrepreneurs, called "the Gilded Age" by Mark Twain.[11] Inventions like the telegraph, telephone, typewriter, the electric light, the trolley, and the camera and technological advances in printing all transformed the way Americans (and, indeed, industrialized Europe) lived, thought, communicated, and perceived the world. Industrial production expanded at an unprecedented rate, leading to the outward symbols of wealth—huge luxury hotels, department stores, upper-class mansions in semi-secluded areas of cities, and monumental public buildings. Mass production allowed for the growth of consumer goods that reached a national market.

One historian has called the "Gilded Age" an age of "self consciousness." In the growing number of newspapers, magazines, books, and catalogs, Americans seemed to be expressing a desire to learn more about the world, about the emerging realities of class and ethnicity within their own country, about consumer goods, new scientific discoveries, and the way their society worked.[12] It is not surprising that authors and editors in commenting upon these changes expressed some ambivalence, a mixture of awe in the face of unprecedented changes within one generation and uneasiness about the consequences of these changes. Mark Twain observed in an essay that appeared in *Harper's Monthly* in 1890,

> The prevailing tone of old books regarding new ideas is one of suspicion and uneasiness at times and at other times contempt. By contrast, our day is indifferent to old ideas, and even considers that their age makes their value questionable, but jumps at a new idea with enthusiasm and high hope. . . . Nothing is today as it was when I was an urchin; but when I was an urchin, nothing was much different from what it had always been in this world.[13]

Charles Eliot Norton, former editor of the *North American Review,* observed in 1907 that there was a new generation of contributors to the *Atlantic Monthly* after the New England Transcendentalists had passed away.

> This was indeed an early symptom of the enormous change in every field of thought—intellectual, moral, spiritual, social, and material—during the past fifty years, which makes a wider division between the beginning of the half-

> century and its end than is to be measured by the mere tale of years. The change marks a new era in the history of civilization, and to an old man whose memories extend over the whole period, the difference between 1857 and 1907 seems like that between ancient and modern times.[14]

The "aggressive enterprise" of frontier taming and industrial empire building coexisted with a cultural program that emphasized contrasting (though not contradictory) values. Book and magazine publishers, editors and writers, university presidents, liberals in the Republican party expressed the "genteel" view through their published writing. Culture for this segment of the Northern upper class was an antidote to the materialism of modern life; it signified the timeless qualities of the spirit, the nonutilitarian activities of leisure, the sphere of home and family life.

The mugwumps were not in any way opposed to the dominant economic and political system, even though their rhetoric was often directed against the vulgarities of the industrial capitalists and their newly earned wealth. Few of them owned factories; most had inherited fortunes from the Eastern "mercantile houses." They were supporters of an upper-class program of "hard money" and the gold standard, low tariffs and (until the late nineteenth century) "laissez-faire" economics.[15] According to some historians mugwumps were "regional elites whose fortunes came from commercial, rather than industrial concerns." [16] Industrialists, in contrast to the older commercial interests, seemed to represent a new national elite unrestrained by the gentility of those who could trace their ancestry and wealth back to the American Revolution. "There's no doubt," said one of W. D. Howells's characters, "but money is to the fore now. It is the romance, the poetry of our age." [17]

But the greatest fears of the mugwumps were directed toward the working class and the new immigrants. An increasingly competitive mass-production economy often led to economic crises and efforts to reduce wages. By the late 1880s a growing working class was becoming increasingly organized and assuming a distinctly immigrant character. The upper class was also becoming more homogeneous, living in semi-secluded suburban areas, sending their children to exclusive schools, and attending expensive resorts. Violent labor conflict—as with the railroad strikes and riots of 1877 and the Great Upheaval of 1886—was often the result. It was hard to maintain America's uniqueness as a classless republic of self-made men under such circumstances. Along with growing class conflict, the surge of immigration from eastern and southern regions of Europe into American cities challenged the dominant meaning of "America." The "dangerous classes" and the "irresponsible crowds" presented an even greater challenge to the custodians of culture.[18] Instead, genteel publishers and editors believed that the dissemination of traditional culture through magazines and also through urban cultural institutions like museums and public libraries would improve the morality of American public life as well as the cultural standards of their middle-class audience.

The editors and publishers of the family house journals were also active in the world of independent journalism, took part in liberal reform within the Republican party, and were closely associated with the "old money" commercial interests of the Northern upper class. They were predominately men born between 1820 and 1845 who grew up in the East. They were Protestants (many from both liberal Protestant and Evangelical backgrounds) and Whig-Republican in political allegiance, who were influential in the world of magazine and book publishing, the lecture circuit, and university teaching and administration. Some were well-known poets, authors, and literary critics. Together they were instrumental in the establishment of many modern urban "cultural institutions"—museums, art institutes, concert halls, and libraries.[19] Most were university educated and had close links to the major Eastern educational institutions. They were advocates of social science and empirical inquiry, especially in the solution of social problems.[20]

Looking to England for cultural and intellectual leadership, they maintained a close connection with English authors and intellectuals. They were also aware of their status as "guardians of culture" and maintained contact with one another in informal clubs (for example, the "Author's Club," a regular gathering of writers and poets that met at the home of Richard Watson Gilder, editor of the *Century*). With enough members, clubs would often meet at hotels (or in Gilder's case at the *Century*'s offices). These were not only social gatherings and occasions for entertaining foreign guests but also at times forums for the exchange of papers, poetry, and of course the fellowship of like-minded folk. The Town and Country Club organized in 1849 included fifty-seven prominent Bostonians (Ralph Waldo Emerson and William Lloyd Garrison were members). Henry and William James, Oliver Wendell Holmes, Jr., William Dean Howells, and John Fiske were prominent members of "The Club" organized in 1868. The Cosmos Club was organized in 1878 by a prominent group of scientists. In other words, these editors and publishers were well aware of their membership in a select group—as well as of a sense of responsibility for disseminating a culture to wider segments of society.[21]

But it would be misleading to suggest that this "cultural program" existed apart from a political one. Most of the leading independent newspaper publishers, magazine editors and publishers, and university presidents were also active in the political movement to lessen the influence of political parties and "popular" politics. Much but not all of this activity took place within the Republican party and was connected to efforts to develop an independent wing of the party in order to promote civil service reform and to combat urban political machines, which represented the urban poor. Their political vision was one of a government of experts and the educated that transcended party affiliation. Challenging the dominance of the party system meant educating the public through the power of the new print media, both newspapers and magazines.

The era of partisan party politics beginning in the early nineteenth century and lasting until the late 1890s was characterized by extremely high turnouts and very competitive national elections. Parties were mass organizations that called out their constituents in marches, parades, and mass rallies that were often organized in a quasi-military manner. These mass events or "spectacles" were not only ways of demonstrating popular support for a candidate but were also popular leisure and recreational activities. In addition, they were rituals that required candidates to call upon the masses to confer on them their "symbolic approval." Linked to the powerful party system was a party press that acted as an agent of the parties. There was no clear line between news and opinion, and editors of the party-dominated press did not hesitate to use their papers to promote party politics. Until the 1870s and 1880s with the growth of independent newspapers, journalism was still of the "personal" variety; staffs were small, and it was quite common for editors to wear the hat of party activist as well as editor.[22]

The mugwumps' "gospel of culture" was closely related to the reform movement that culminated in the 1884 split within the Republican party over the nomination of James G. Blaine, who was associated with corrupt machine politics. The defection of the mugwumps may have been responsible for Democrat Grover Cleveland's election. Leading up to the "mugwump" movement was an educational effort in the growing independent press and the family house magazines. In the words of the liberal writer Jonathan Baxter Harrison, "The people who believe in culture, in property, and in order, that is civilization, must establish the necessary agency for the diffusion of a new culture. Capital must protect itself by organized activities for a new object—the education of the people."[23]

In 1877 the Tilden Commission, headed by lawyer-politician Samuel Jones

Tilden and dominated by liberal reformers, advocated that cities in New York state be governed by a "Board of Finance" selected by taxpayers and property holders. This measure, which would have required disfranchisement of some voters on the municipal level, was not well received.[24] But other reforms fared better, including civil service reform, which succeeded in passing the Pendleton Act of 1883 (the first federal civil service law) and ballot reforms that included the secret ballot. Overall the reformers wanted government on the municipal level to be divorced from partisan politics and run according to "sound business principles."[25]

According to McGeer, liberal reformers, advocates of a nonpartisan political style, had "their own network of journals."

> During the late 'sixties and early 'seventies, a group of newspapermen, mostly Republicans, began to reconsider their relationship to the parties. . . . Some of the foremost Republican papers in the country led the reconsideration of party ties: the *New York Tribune* of Horace Greeley and Whitelaw Reid, the *New York Evening Post* of William Cullen Bryant and later Horace White, E. L. Godkin, and Carl Schurz, Samuel Bowles's *Springfield Republican,* Horace White's *Chicago Tribune,* and the *Cincinnati Commercial* of Murat Halstead. Along with Godkin's *Nation* and George William Curtis's *Harper's Weekly,* these dailies formed the communications network that nurtured liberal reform within the Republican Party.[26]

In addition to the independent newspapers, "liberalism was best identified by its magazines" (*Harper's Weekly,* edited by George Curtis, the *North American Review* of Henry Adams and Allan T. Rice, and William Dean Howells's *Atlantic Monthly*). The social network of clubs formed by the mugwumps were forums for sharing poetry, essays, and literary work, but as reformers they also formed political networks for revitalizing the culture of the Northern upper class and educating the middle class for a new nonpartisan political style.[27] Some of these organizations included the National League of Republican clubs (formed in 1887 to oppose party bosses and educate voters) as well as the Young Men's Republican clubs, Lincoln Leagues, National Civil Service Reform League, and the New York Reform Club.[28]

The word *mugwump* has sometimes been used in the narrow sense of referring only to those that bolted the Republican party in 1884, while others have used it in the broader sense to refer to upper- and middle-class participants in the larger political and cultural movement of the post–Civil War period. In this and subsequent chapters I refer to "mugwumps" in the broader rather than restricted meaning.[29] The family house magazine played an important role as a communications vehicle for these genteel reformers throughout the East and Midwest who shared essentially the same values. As David Thelen has documented, mugwump businessmen and professionals in Wisconsin were active throughout the late 1880s in civil service reform, temperance, vice crusades, and educational reform.[30] Mugwump reformers were active in many cities, in other words, outside the Eastern seaboard, but the intellectual leaders of the movement wrote for the family house magazines and were part of the Eastern cultural establishment (the phrase "Victorian gentry" has been used by some to refer to the cultural elite of the Eastern seaboard).[31]

While there were significant commonalities in social background and beliefs among mugwump writers, editors, and reformers, there were also differences. Some were more interested in social reform, particularly civil service reform, while others were interested in the cultural project of elevating the tastes of middle-class readers. George Curtis wore both hats. As a writer and editor of literary magazines, he was a literary gatekeeper who helped to define what could legitimately be called culture. In his capacity as editor of *Harper's Weekly* (more of a newspaper than a magazine) and as a participant in reform organizations, he was a liberal reformer. Some individuals from mugwump social backgrounds who were generally sympathetic to the mugwump political and cultural projects did not join the mugwump split of the Republican party in 1884. Theodore Roosevelt and Henry Cabot Lodge were two examples of what some called "traitors to their class," who stood for an expansionist foreign policy, an active federal government, and espoused the "strenuous life." Both came from Eastern, old-money backgrounds but refused to bolt the Republican party in 1884.[32] By the late 1880s some mugwumps like Howells split with many of his colleagues in supporting the labor movement and moving in the direction of socialism. Within the literary world of genteel culture there were differences between the Boston Brahmin–oriented *Atlantic Monthly* group (with roots going back to Emerson, Unitarianism, and Transcendentalism) and the more recent group of scholars and authors connected to the New York publishing worlds of *Scribner's* and the *Century*.

The following were some of the editors, publishers, and intellectuals identified with the cultural and political program of the mugwumps. Richard Watson Gilder was the editor of *Century Illustrated Monthly* from 1881 until his death in 1909. While he regarded himself as a poet and contributed to many of the leading magazines of the period, he is primarily known for his work on the *Century*. He was born in 1844 (the youngest of the group) and wanted to become a minister (like his father, a Methodist minister). Later he decided to study law but had to drop out of college due to the death of his father and the need to support his family. As editor of the *Century*, Gilder published the work of the leading authors of the period, including Henry James, Mark Twain, William Dean Howells, Theodore Roosevelt, Charles Elliot Norton, and S. Weir Mitchell, among many others. Most of these people he met on a regular basis at *Century*'s plush New York offices. He was also one of the leading advocates of civil service reform and an advocate of housing reform in the 1890s. In addition to being the editor of *Harper's Weekly*, which focused on current political events, and writing "The Easy Chair" for *Harper's Monthly*, George Curtis was one of the most sought after speakers on the Lyceum circuit of the 1850s and later for university commencements.[33] Also during this period (1853 to 1857) Curtis was an editor and frequent contributor to *Putnam's Monthly*, which published some of the leading American authors as well as the usual assortment of sentimental fiction. He was the author of a number of popular travel books and novels. A New York critic polled his readers in 1884 about their favorite authors and discovered that Curtis placed sixth (above Henry James and Mark Twain).[34]

Other proponents of liberal party reform and the "gospel of culture" included E. L. Godkin, editor of the *Nation;* Charles Dudley Warner, novelist and editor; Richard Henry Stoddard, poet; Charles Elliot Norton, editor of *North American Review* for a short period and specialist in medieval literature and architecture; Thomas Bailey Aldrich, poet and editor of *Atlantic Monthly* between 1881 and 1890; Bayard Taylor, author and literary critic; and William Dean Howells, novelist and editor of *Atlantic Monthly* and, after 1886, author of "The Editor's Study" in *Harper's Monthly*.[35] The Eastern "cultural establishment" also included university presidents— Charles William Elliot of Harvard; Frederick A. P. Barnard of Columbia University; Noah Porter of Yale; James McCosh of Princeton; Andrew Dickson White of Cornell; and others. In this chapter I will focus on three of these men—novelist William Dean Howells (who was the editor of *Atlantic Monthly* from 1871 to 1881 and assumed an editorial position at *Harpers Monthly* in 1886—in which he was a leading advocate of "realism" in his "Editor's Study" feature), Richard Watson Gilder, and George Curtis.

The use of the word *Victorian* in connection with the culture of the mid- to late nineteenth century requires some explanation. It refers in part to the "transatlantic connection" between American and English "gentry," leading members of the cultural establishment of both nations. It is also meant to refer to the connections between the intellectual leaders of a large segment of the middle class and the wider stream of American culture. The mugwumps and their publications were an important vehicle for the dissemination of one strand of Victorian values. Daniel Howe in his essay "Victorian Culture in America" described American Victorianism as originating in the Protestant evangelical awakening of the 1830s and as essentially "bourgeois" or middle class. Victorian values were future-oriented, emphasizing delayed gratification, rational calculation of time and resources, self-improvement, and self-control. The ideal of Victorian culture, a culture based largely on the printed word, was the self-directed or "inner-directed" man, an individual whose character was fixed and not open to modification or external influence. Victorians viewed human nature as divided between the animal passions and the civilized, "higher" faculties of reason and sentiment. They valued competitiveness in religion, politics, and the economy, and rational order in social and intellectual life. The emphasis on order and on developing spatial and conceptual boundaries was expressed in the growing academic and professional specialization and in the "spatial structuring" of cities into public parks, civic buildings, private clubs, and public playgrounds.[36] The domestic sphere, the home was guarded by the middle-class woman and was thought of as the shock absorber for the rapid changes in the larger society. The home was to be a "moral nursery" for children, instilling in them the character that would allow them to succeed in a competitive world filled with temptations. It was to provide the businessman or wage earner with a "haven" of sincerity and unconditional love. Victorian culture, Howe argued, was not the property of one particular group or social class, although it was bourgeois in its origins. Instead we need to think of it as a structure of values that united many diverse groups within a common cultural community.[37] The Knights of Labor, which became the dominant organization of the working class, opposed the "wage system" but often spoke in the language of Evangelical Protestantism—a language shared by the Victorian middle class. Studies of artisan culture have shown how workers often adopted Victorian values and used them for their own purposes.[38]

The Editor's Easy Chair

What did it mean to be an editor of one of the quality middle-class magazines of the mid- to late Victorian period? What was their relationship to their contributors? What was their relationship to their audience? How did they view their profession and the magazines they edited? What was their relationship to the wider society—to movements of social, economic, and political reform?

George Curtis, editor of *Harper's Weekly*, and Richard Gilder, editor of the *Century*, were perhaps the two best representatives among major magazine editors of mugwump reform as well as leaders in the Eastern cultural establishment. Both were active in the mugwump campaign for civil service reform and advocated a more professional state bureaucracy, one that would be independent of party interests. Curtis was the leading activist among the mugwumps in the campaign against the corruption of the New York Tammany machine (in 1880 Curtis was named president of the New York Civil Service Reform League).[39] This campaign reflected the political philosophy of many of the editors of the upper-middle-class magazines—a suspicion of the party system not only because of its corruption but also because of its ties to the masses (or what Curtis called "the shouting rabble").[40] Gilder made a remarkable suggestion in the pages of the *Century* that party nominating conventions be held in halls "barely large enough to contain the delegates." As a result, he suggested, the conventions could become deliberative bodies and "exercise some judgment in the choice of candidates." [41]

While consistently aligning themselves with industrial capitalists in labor disputes, by the mid-1880s both Gilder and Curtis expressed alarm at the growth of the "trust." Gilder said that the trusts had startled America more than anything since the Knights of Labor.[42] Also, around the same time, the *Century* began to publish articles by Washington Gladden, Richard Ely, and other advocates of the Social Gospel, a liberal Protestant movement that tried to replace the "gospel of wealth" with a social ethic. Gilder supported the new American Economics Association (closely connected to the Social Gospel) which was formed in 1885 to combat the principles of orthodox political economy and advocate a more active economic role for government.[43] In 1894, Governor Roswell P. Flower appointed Gilder to a state commission for the investigation of New York City tenements where he held lengthy hearings and exposed a number of respectable property holders as owners of some of the worst tenements. He was a leading advocate of housing reform and was credited by the *New York Tribune* for his "unselfish zeal" in his efforts on the commission.

These gentry reform efforts were infused with a moralism that assumed that success should be the fruit of a virtuous life and institutions a reflection of the character of individuals. Gilder, in an editorial, worried "that dishonesty is one of the forces of worldly success." More ominously, he worried that "in the present constitution of society a lack of conscience may be an important, even a deciding, element of worldly success." When Andrew Carnegie argued in the pages of the *Century* (May 1890) that concentration of capital is an inevitable product of the laws of evolution, Gilder responded that the issue was primarily a moral one, the right of every American to have a fair chance.[44] In an 1884 editorial Gilder criticized the "reckless speculation" of business as well as the "economic mistakes of the poor" who "spend large sums on vulgar amusements."

Richard Gilder's view of culture and of art is of particular interest. He was an assistant under the first editor of *Scribner's,* Josiah Gilbert Holland (*Scribner's* became the *Century Illustrated Monthly* in 1881 after a dispute between the editors of *Scribner's* and the Scribner brothers who owned the magazine). Starting in 1875 and later as editor of *Scribner's-Century* in 1881, Gilder was largely responsible for the magazine's high literary and artistic reputation. *Scribner's-Century* eventually bettered its main competitor *Harper's Monthly* in the quality of its illustrations. New techniques of wood engraving, developed by *Scribner's* art director Alexander W. Drake, paved the way for contributions from some of the best American artists, including Thomas Eakins, W. M. Chase, Edwin Austin Abbey, and Winslow Homer. Gilder also carried throughout his editorial reign a series of articles on leading American artists and published the poetry (his own included) of the "genteel" American poets—including Richard Henry Stoddard, Bayard Taylor, and Edmund Clarence Stedman. Along with Gilder these poets articulated the genteel view of art as an expression of timeless truths through conformity to the laws of beauty. Gilder dissented from Holland's more religious view that art and literature had to explicitly serve moral purposes; instead Gilder argued that the beautiful is naturally good. It did not need to explicitly serve moral ends. In an editorial commenting on a series of articles on art education, Gilder argued for the importance of raising the public's taste for an understanding of great art.[45] In an era of materialism, Gilder believed that the appreciation of good art would serve to improve middle-class tastes and help his readers to transcend the mundane and commonplace world of commerce and consumption.

In a broader sense, Gilder and other mugwump advocates of the "gospel of culture" may have realized that religion was losing its hold on middle-class Americans and that high culture could partially replace religion as a transcendent ideal and as a civilizing force. Like religion, art could function as a social cement in its ability to unite diverse groups and classes in an activity that claimed to be separated from the profane world. Gilder and other American editors acknowledged their appreciation of Matthew Arnold, who argued for a concerted effort to instill in the middle class "the best culture of their nation." The problem, Arnold argued, was that the middle classes had a spirit and a culture that was "narrow, unattractive and harsh" and therefore would not be up to the important task of "assimilating the masses below them."[46]

Charles Dudley Warner (coauthor along with Mark Twain of *The Gilded Age,* author of numerous essays and travel books, frequent contributor to the family house magazines, and "Editor's Study" successor to Howells at *Harper's Monthly*) presented many of the same ideas in an 1872 article in *Scribner's.* Like Arnold he was interested in the relevance of "culture" to the laboring masses. The essay was meant as a response to what Warner believed was a widespread indifference, if not disdain, for learning and the arts—expressed in the question, "What Is Your Culture to Me?"[47] He acknowledged the widespread suspicion that culture ("that fine product of opportunity and scholarship which is to mere knowledge what manners is to a gentleman") was thought of as useless by the laborer as well as the farmer, the politician, and the shopkeeper. Warner's answer to the question presented by his title came early in the essay.

> There is no culture so high, no taste so fastidious, no grace of learning so delicate, no refinement of art so exquisite, that it cannot at this hour find full play for itself in the broadest fields of humanity, since it is all needed to soften the attritions of common life, and guide to nobler aspirations the strong materialistic influences of our restless society.

But Warner was not addressing a working-class audience in *Scribner's.* The real question was why the educated and cultured man did not view it as his responsibility to "make the world of the past, the world of his books, serviceable to his fellows?" Culture was too often, Warner argued, viewed as the property of the educated middle class. Instead, he suggested a program of cultural diffusion through books, newspapers, works of art. But more important than this is "the reconciliation of the interests of the classes" through sympathy and personal contact. As an example of such personal sympathy and contact, he mentioned the establishment in "one of our cities" of an all-purpose reading room, conversation room, and sewing room "where young girls who work for a living and have no opportunity for any culture, at home or elsewhere, may spend their evenings." There educated ladies would "pass the evening with them in reading or sewing or music." The argument, then, was for a type of engagement of the cultivated person with the laboring classes in contrast to the selfish desire to retain and preserve one's own accomplishments. The fruit of such an engagement would be a mitigation of class envy and class conflict.

In their editorials and private letters, Gilder and Curtis reflected the mugwump's alienation from evangelical religion. Under the editorship of Josiah Holland, its first editor, *Scribner's* had had a strong evangelical Christian flavor. While Holland was a religious liberal and no friend of religious sectarianism, he made it clear that he had to take into account his large number of religious readers (whom he believed to be primarily women) and also the fact that during the early 1870s the over two hundred religious weeklies were the preferred medium for advertisers. Under Gilder's influence the *Century*'s orientation became even more secular. Gilder himself, near the end of his career, went beyond religious liberalism and confessed his agnosticism.[48] Curtis, in his "Easy Chair" feature, criticized the dogmatism of evangelical Protestants more than a few times. Responding to an 1874 meeting of the Evangelical Alliance in which "the body arrayed itself against the Roman Catholic Church and infidelity," Curtis asked,

> But what is infidelity? Every religious reformer is denounced as an infidel. . . . The greatest of theologians and the greatest of scientific inquirers, if they are sincere, are equally seekers of the truth. They approach it differently but their purpose and spirit is the same. . . . It is a mistake to suppose that religious truth is in danger from the most searching investigation. All truth is sacred, and truth only is precious. And among the most devoted and unflinching seekers of truth are many whom popular opinion would stigmatize as infidel.[49]

This secular critique of religious dogmatism lends credence to the view of some historians that the mugwumps felt alienated from two of the major sources of power during the decades after the Civil War—the industrial elite and evangelical Protestantism.[50]

The "quality" magazine editor thought of himself as a steward or custodian of a revered cultural heritage and in part as a cultivator of new literary talent. The editor's relationship to contributors and readers was ideally congenial and at times patronizing but always based on the assumption that they were all part of a common subcultural community. Most revenue at this time came from subscriptions, not advertising, making it possible for editors to take for granted a stable readership. By the late nineteenth century, when revenue came primarily from advertising, readers would be packaged as commodities and essentially sold back to advertisers. But the genteel editor could still see his readers as personal friends, roughly sharing the same tastes and level of education. Given the nature of the content and the price (outside the reach of a working-class audience), this assumption was a plausible one.

W. D. Howells was the editor of *Atlantic Monthly* from 1871 to 1881. For five years from 1866 to 1871, he had served as an editorial assistant to James Thomas Fields. *Atlantic Monthly* originated in 1857 and for quite a period afterward became known as the home of the best of New England's literature. Howells was well aware of this tradition when he took over as editor: "During the nine years of its existence before my time it had the best that the greatest writers of New England could give it. First of these were, of course, Longfellow, Emerson, Hawthorne, Whittier, Holmes, Lowell, Mrs. Stowe, and Bryant." He recalled that there was little division of labor in the editorial office. He not only read the manuscripts and wrote all the "Literary Notices" for the magazine but also did most of the clerical work. In addition to his own literary work, he revised all the proofs, verified quotations, and wrote to contributors. Editing meant literally reading and revising—sometimes quite intrusive revising—of scores of manuscripts weekly. In his "Recollections of an *Atlantic* Editorship," Howells did not once boast of an editorial decision that increased circulation (not that this was irrelevant to his position). Instead it was likely that a dedicated and loyal readership was something he took for granted just as his publishers James Osgood & Co. (1871–1873), H. O. Houghton & Co. (1874–1877), and Houghton, Osgood & Co. (1878–1879) took for granted that Howells would be a good steward of the *Atlantic* literary tradition. His triumphs, instead, were discoveries of literary talent and a pride in attracting and keeping established names. As for his relationship to the contributors,

> It was all very intimate, that relation of editor and contributor. I do not mean as to personal acquaintance, for in the vast, the overwhelming majority of cases, it never came to that; but I mean the sort of metempsychosis by which I was put so entirely in their place, became so more than one with them, that any slight or wrong done them hurt me more than if it were done to me.[51]

Despite the reputation that many of the genteel editors had of cutting and revising the work of even the most prominent contributors, genteel editing was essentially passive in contrast to the popular magazine editors of a later generation.[52] It was an unheard-of practice to aggressively seek out new contributors, much less lure writers committed to other publications with higher payments. The tone of these magazines was largely consistent with the editorial voice.[53] A quick glance at an issue of *Harper's Monthly* will illustrate this point. The June 1874 issue of *Harper's Monthly* began with something called "Our Nearest Neighbor (First Paper)." There was a small illustration but no author's name. Not listing the name of the author was a common practice justified by the claim that the magazine was an expression of its editor, not the individual contributors. The first paper turned out to be a travel article on Mexico. It was followed sixteen pages later by an untitled short poem and another article entitled, "A Naturalist in the Heart of Africa," which concerned the travels of a western naturalist into the region of a group of cannibals in eastern Africa. This was followed by another poem and an article, "Collecting Salmon Spawn in Maine." The following feature was a ten-page poem, "Nymphidia: The Court of Fairy." Other articles included a biography of the poet Joseph Rodman Drake, "Army Organization" by Gen. George B. McClellan, and "Recollections of an Old Stager." Fiction was entirely of the sentimental school and included "My Mother and I," "A Love Story for Girls," "Mildred in Search of a Husband," and "'Tina.'"

None of the articles had an editor's introduction either of the article or the author, and most did not even list the name of the author. Information of this kind might have given the casual reader unfamiliar with *Harper's* some sense of what to expect and where to start reading. There was no self-promotion to inform the reader of future attractions. Except for the editorial features at the back of the magazine, there were no easily recognizable departments or sections, no way of determining a logical order in which one type of article might be expected to follow from another. There certainly wasn't a prose style that tried to "grip the reader," and it would be difficult to maintain that *Harper's Monthly* had a "vital personality" (a common phrase used to describe the popular magazines of the early twentieth century). In short, the assumption was of a leisurely reader who could take his or her time, who was curious about the world but did not expect to learn about current events from a magazine, and a reader who was already familiar with *Harper's Monthly* and magazines of the same type and did not have to be made familiar with it through active editorial intervention.

George Curtis's "Easy Chair" feature in *Harper's Monthly* was perhaps the clearest example of the genteel editorial voice. While Curtis was not the editor of *Harper's Monthly,* he was the editor of *Harper's Weekly* and his "Easy Chair" editorial feature ran in *Harper's Monthly* for nearly forty years. The tone of this regular monthly feature was one of a highly literate and genial conversation with a friend. Curtis addressed in his four- to six-page essay three or four topics, separated only by a space between the paragraphs. Some specific topics addressed during the 1870s were comments on English travel books, reviews of American opera performances, a response to a sermon entitled "Riches Have Wings and Fly Away" (which turned into a commentary on the immorality of speculation), the extent to which secret societies at universities presented a moral danger, reactions to various commencement addresses at major universities, amusing anecdotes concerning the Lyceum circuit during the 1850s or a canoeing trip with Henry David Thoreau, whether anything in America can compare to English Christmas pantomimes, the dangers of labor unrest, support for women's suffrage, comments on a biography of Dickens, suggestions for centennial celebrations, eulogies of famous Americans, and a discussion of Disraeli and the Tory party in England. These issues were almost always addressed in a reasoned rather than emotional manner (the labor question was somewhat of an exception), and the conversational tone meant that the reader never knew when a discussion of one topic would remind Curtis of a related issue. Curtis wasn't interested in arousing his readers, only entertaining, amusing, and in a nonpatronizing manner educating them. The personal tone of Curtis's "Easy Chair" should not be confused with the later effort to personalize the voice of the editor (which will be discussed in chapter 3). By and large, genteel editors remained anonymous. Most readers did not know the names of the editors of the magazines they read. The "Easy Chair" was never signed. Curtis referred in his essays to himself as "Easy Chair" or with the pronoun "we," and his readers addressed him in the same manner.

Richard Watson Gilder was responsible for many innovations in editorial policy that helped to transform the *Century Illustrated Monthly* into the leading American quality magazine by the mid-1880s. The *Century* was widely recognized for the quality of its woodcut illustrations as well as its historical and biographical articles.[54] In 1876 the magazine had spent $1,500 on drawings and engravings for one issue. In 1890 it spent about $8,000 for a single issue.[55] Beyond illustrations, Gilder was a more active editor than Howells had been at *Atlantic Monthly* or Fletcher Harper had been during the 1870s for *Harper's Monthly*. He was the first editor of a major magazine to change the policy of not printing authors' names.[56] In November 1884, at the suggestion of business manager Roswell Smith, Gilder launched a risky and expensive series on the American Civil War.[57] It included articles by Ulysses S. Grant (for which Gilder paid an enormous sum) and scores of firsthand accounts by soldiers and participants on both sides. The series lasted over three years and increased the circulation to 250,000.[58] Near the end of the Civil War series Gilder expressed his hope that the series would contribute to national unity.

> It is particularly desirable at this time, with a new generation rising up and coming to the front in the South, that the sentiment of nationality should be fostered and strengthened as it can alone be by a study of the political causes of the armed conflict which happily ended in the salvation of the leading nation of the world.[59]

Gilder also sought out a select group of writers who became regular contributors of biographies and articles of travel and adventure. He was partly responsible for the shift from serialized novels to short stories and for shorter, crisper articles—an accommodation to the less leisurely reading habits of the middle-class reader by the late nineteenth century. In contrast to *Harper's Monthly, Scribner's-Century* published primarily American authors and helped to develop American literary talent. Indeed, by the 1880s, publication in the *Century* was a prerequisite to literary success. Under Holland's editorship in the 1870s, fiction was of the sentimental variety, but by the 1880s under Gilder, local color, historical fiction, and some of the "new realism" began to appear. Under Gilder and Roswell Smith, advertising played a more prominent role than ever before in a quality magazine. While periodical advertising more than tripled during the 1880s, consumer-goods advertising appeared for the first time. Volume 35 (November 1887–April 1888) had 642 pages of advertising while volume 23 (November 1881–April 1882) had had 161.5 pages.[60] Nevertheless, Gilder remained within the tradition of genteel editing.

The genteel editors took the view that their readers needed to be protected from what might shock them as bad taste even if the editor himself could see the value in what could not be printed. Henry Alden, then editor of *Harper's Monthly,* explained to an author whose work he had blue-penciled, "My objections are based on purism (not mine, but our readers!) which is undoubtedly more rigid here than in England." [61] Edward Livermore Burlingame, editor of *Scribner's* after 1886, expressed a view of the family house magazine that was widely shared: "The buyer of a magazine buys a variety of literature. He may buy it for one thing, yet have another for which he also pays, thrust upon him. The buyer of a book, on the other hand knows or should know what he is getting in for." [62]

Gilder's timidity in breaking with genteel standards was part of his public role as editor and was not always carried through into his private activities.

Even in his public role he sometimes expressed frustration at the limitations imposed on him as editor. For example, Walt Whitman reported that Gilder was quite hospitable to him in private even when Whitman's reputation was at its lowest, but Gilder steadfastly refused to print his poetry for fear of upsetting his readers. Aldrich maintained a similar policy during his editorial reign at the *Atlantic Monthly,* barring articles on religion and controversial political and economic issues, again for fear of alienating his readers.[63] Writing in 1885, in a *Century* editorial, Gilder acknowledged the truth of some of the criticisms of the "family magazine."

> It cannot be denied that much of the world's most valuable literature, sacred and secular, could never reach the public through the pages of the 'family magazine.' . . . It behooves all concerned to see to it that the limitations of the popular periodical do not have a narrowing and flattening effect upon current periodical literature; do not put our best writers into a sort of literary bondage; do not repress originality and individuality either of style or of opinion.[64]

Gilder expressed encouragement at the decline of "oversensitive" readers who expected all shades of opinion to be expressed. He hoped that readers would help editors by being open-minded, sympathetic, and tolerant.[65]

The genteel editors, it seems, took a variety of stances toward their readers. Sometimes they were educators who aimed to elevate their readers taste; at other times editors saw their role as protectors of their readers' sensibilities and at still other times as reluctant guardians of the family circle (even though they were more tolerant themselves). The ideal reader might be one who was not oversensitive because he or she trusted the editor's judgment, but some manuscripts could not be published because accommodations would have to be made to these very readers. Alden implied that his editorial policy had to passively reflect his readers' tastes, yet at one time or another all of them desired to actively improve their readers' taste.

Each stance expressed a different public image. A self-image, as we know, is always formed in relation to an "other." The self-image is an interpretation of the other's response to us. A public image depends on the responses of various audiences. As self-professed literary figures, the editors saw themselves as men of culture who were not overly narrow-minded or prudish. They were primarily concerned with the responses of their fellow authors as well as the readers of their poetry, travel books, novels, and so on. As public figures who were often active in improving the moral standards of political leaders or elevating the tastes of the public through various cultural projects, they saw their mission as one of providing an antidote to the crass materialism of American society and raising their readers' artistic and moral standards. As professional editors responsible to business managers and publishers, they had to worry about not offending too many of their readers and thereby jeopardizing circulation. A balance had to be struck between their own "highbrow" and their readers' "middlebrow" culture, between a secondary audience of literary men who might criticize them for catering to middlebrow taste and their own readers who might not want to be challenged or upset.[66] A somewhat different kind of balance had to be struck between their own ideal of what a magazine should be and the compromises needed to maintain and increase circulation.

CHAPTER TWO

The Victorian Reader and the Political Economy of the Magazine

The Victorian Reader

By the 1870s it would not have been uncommon to find a copy of *Harper's Monthly* on a typical middle-class center table along with a Bible, a book or two of poetry, a stereoscope, a well-illustrated travel book, and perhaps a scrapbook. The genteel magazine, an outgrowth of the nineteenth-century publishing industry, was part of the reading world of middle-class Americans, a world that was central to the culture of Victorian America. What social functions did reading serve for Victorian Americans? How did magazine publishers and editors conceive of the reading process? How did these same arbiters of taste respond to changes in the reading public brought about by the commercialization of literature, academic and professional specialization, new developments in journalism, and the rise of a new visual culture based on the halftone method of illustration and magazine reproduction?

For Victorian Americans, starting with the decades of urban and commercial growth that preceded the Civil War, reading was a significant and memorable experience. Imaginative literature united not only Americans and the British in a common literary culture but also penetrated beyond the boundaries of class. Native works such as Harriet Beecher Stowe's *Uncle Tom's Cabin* (1852) or

English Victorian favorites had a following beyond the well educated. By the 1870s American school curricula became centered around English literature.[1] The pleasures of imaginative literature were many and often contradictory. Reading for middle-class Americans could provide an entertaining escape from the dominant social order while also reinforcing it. It was a supremely private and solitary activity yet one that often connected the reader to communities and traditions that provided a haven from isolation. It was associated, ideally, with reason and deliberation yet was also the object of suspicion for inciting the passions.

Bledstein in his account of the Victorian reading process emphasized the way the printed word reinforced dominant values. "Words created distances between people, distances a Mid-Victorian welcomed. At best, the printed page exemplified detachment, calm consideration, order, permanence, and responsibility for judgment, all Mid-Victorian virtues." [2] There was a formality to the printed word which, ideally, allowed the reader to consider rationally an author's argument or reread passages without the danger of succumbing to an emotional appeal. Eighteenth-century English literary conventions provided the reader with opportunities to consider the text through various narrative devices that suspended the action of the plot temporarily. Herman Melville's narrative intrusions that interrupt the *Pequod*'s journey in *Moby-Dick* was an example of such an effort to address the reader and provide him or her with a space to contemplate, reread, and react.[3]

The very process of fixing meaning into words and categories was a containment of potential chaos, a drawing of boundaries. The private and solitary nature of the reading process represented the antithesis of the dangerous and emotionally unstable crowd—the political rally, the popular amusements of the lower classes, or the many dangers represented by urban crowds of strangers. These virtues—formality, order, and privacy—were associated with the middle-class parlor, the space reserved for reading and entertaining, that region midway between the potentially uncontrollable and disordered public sphere and the more intimate and private regions of the home.

Reading could also unite the family and serve as a vehicle for character formation and self-improvement. Works of literature would often be read out loud, in the tradition of Bible reading, from father to daughter or among the entire family. Louisa May Alcott remembered her father reading aloud to her and her sisters as the most pleasant memory of her childhood. Lyman Beecher, the American minister and patriarch of the famous Beecher family, was one of the first prominent Americans to defend the propriety of reading imaginative literature as opposed to religious tracts. Fiction, he maintained, refined the emotions, elevated the sensibilities, and improved the tastes. His daughter Catherine remembered being introduced to "the poetry of my childhood"—Scott and Burns by her Aunt Mary and hearing the stories of Washington Irving and the poetry of Lord Byron read to her by her uncle and aunt.[4]

Reading and its pleasures might not always support and sustain the social order, or at least it might not be thought of as supportive. While words for the Victorian reader and author were ideally associated with calm, detached reason and "natural" sentiment, they might also be used in a less respectable manner. A contributor to the *Atlantic Monthly* remembered his youth, a few years before the Civil War, when some of the first dime novels were published.

> What boy of the sixties can ever forget Beadle's novels! To the average youngster of that time the advent of each of these books seemed to be an event of world consequence. . . . How the boys swarmed into and through stores and news-stands to buy copies as they came hot off the presses. . . . What silver-tongued orator of any age or land ever had such sympathetic and enthusiastic audiences as did the happy youths at those trysting places, who were detailed to read those wild deeds of forest, prairie, and mountain.[5]

While the author maintained that most of these early dime novels were morally respectable, he also acknowledged that "nearly every sort of misdemeanor into which the fantastic element enters, from train robbery to house burning, is laid to [dime novels]." What probably upset ministers and moralists was that these novels, inexpensive and cheaply illustrated, seemed to appeal to working-class readers. In addition, these books were not often read in the "family circle" where parental influence could be exerted. Instead, as the author described, they were often read by groups of young boys and sometimes girls, often out loud to one another, a process that increased the novels' emotional and sensual attractions and therefore their potentially subversive appeal.[6] Similar concerns were expressed for other forms of popular culture—for example, the theater with its special section for prostitutes and its unruly crowds that could shield the impressionable man or woman from surveillance.[7]

Reading might sustain traditions and memories, even while they were being undermined by rapid economic development. If more and more of nature as well as social relationships were being transformed into commodities and as a result uprooting old habits and folk traditions, at least within literature there could be a haven of revered memories, a link to the past. That link to the past might come through the content of an historical romance, for example, which might remind the reader of previous eras of history. Or memory might be revived through a sense of connection to the older generation who revered the same literature. Henry Seidel Canby, editor of the *Saturday Review,* in 1934 wrote a memoir of his youth in the late nineteenth century and of growing up in Wilmington, Delaware. This memoir provides a useful illustration of the importance of reading for the Victorian middle class. He and his generation, he remembered, were passionate readers. "Books to us were what the bard's chants were to the tribe—a recalling, an enriching, an extension of memory." In his parent's library were William Hickling Prescott, Sir Walter Scott, Grant's memoirs, Nathaniel Hawthorne, English poets from Gray to Byron and Longfellow to Whittier, William Shakespeare, Charles Dickens, *Uncle Tom's Cabin, Uncle Remus,* Howells, and Doyle's Sherlock Holmes—in other words, an assortment of English Victorian fiction and poetry as well as a smattering of American fiction. He remembered "the stories of Dickens richest in sentiment" and most of all the novels of Sir Walter Scott. The romances of Scott and, to a lesser extent, James Fenimore Cooper had a great influence on his generation. "And from these romances so alien to our bourgeois Quaker Town we drew an ethics for ideal conduct and in emotional stress." [8]

Canby's attraction to these romances was not only as an extension of memory, a link to other generations, but as an escape from small-town life. "We yearned . . . after heartiness and found it in these romances. Our small-town culture was drying up." [9] And yet Canby described reading as a supremely confident endeavor. By "confidence" Canby seemed not to be saying that reading gave him greater confidence in the progress of his own society, but that reading connected him to a cultural tradition he regarded as superior, and that he was confident in the perpetuation of that culture. Canby's commitment to the imaginative literature of his youth was in part a product of the intimate manner in which authors would address readers and in the narrative style of the sentimental and romantic novels. The reader was encouraged to feel that the author was speaking directly to him or her, to someone who shared the same values.

While Canby referred primarily to fiction in his discussion of reading in the late nineteenth century, prescriptive literature was important, especially in the antebellum period. Reading was part of the "civilizing process," as Norbert Elias has documented.[10] Like the middle-class home, reading was both a haven and a moral nursery. By the 1830s middle-class men and women thought of the public sphere, the world outside the home, as increasingly threatening; confidence men, gamblers, political demagogues might divert the honest young man or woman from the path of virtue. In the etiquette books (especially popular during the 1830–1850 period), women's magazines (*Godey's Ladies Book*, America's leading fashion magazine, started publication in 1830), child-rearing guides, and other self-help literature, middle-class moralists advised their readers on how to dress, entertain guests, raise children, and distinguish themselves from others.

Godey's Ladies Book spoke to middle-class fears but also articulated new ideals.[11] While the public sphere, which was becoming increasingly commercial and urban, might require some necessary deceit or "theatricality," the private sphere represented by the genteel lady was to counterbalance this deceit with perfect transparency. This ideal was expressed in part through genteel manners, the symbol of middle-class status. While genteel manners were a marker of social class, they were thought of as much more than this. Moralists, influenced by the American republican as well as Protestant traditions, made a distinction between democratic and aristocratic manners.[12] Democratic manners reflected inner virtue. They were a sincere expression of inner character, while aristocratic manners were only superficial symbols of inherited status. Etiquette books and magazines such as *Godey's* informed their readers on how to be sincere. Sincere conduct was to reveal one's true character, the fixed moral core of the individual. There were instructions on the proper way to introduce oneself to an acquaintance, on the use of a calling card, on entertaining guests, on how to tactfully exclude undesirables as well as prohibitions on excessive familiarity and offensive odors. Such behavior was to separate the true gentleman and lady, regardless of birth, from others. After the Civil War, when the middle class began to separate themselves into distinct neighborhoods, many of these rules of etiquette disappeared. Nevertheless, gentility continued to be the standard of behavior.[13]

Catherine Beecher's prescriptive writings for young women on domestic economy and the moral education of children were perhaps the most popular and significant expressions of the "cult of domesticity"—the view of woman's sphere as compensating for and counterbalancing the male pursuit of success. Beecher's *Treatise on Domestic Economy,* published in 1840, provided women with practical domestic advice about cooking, gardening, cleaning, decorating as well as raising children. According to Sklar in her biography of Beecher, "Many cultural indicators point to the heightened concern over the quality of domestic life in the 1840's—a concern that grew more emphatic when increasing geographic mobility removed many families from traditional sources of domestic knowledge." [14] The popularity of domestic advice reflected the growing importance placed on family life combined with the loss of traditional knowledge of how to manage it. The reader of Beecher's *Treatise* was an anxious reader, not the confident one that Canby remembered.

"Family house magazines" sought to continue the reading habits that had begun earlier in the century. The editor of *Harper's Monthly* in 1894 explained: "Our rule is that the Magazine must contain nothing which could not be read aloud in any circle." [15] Magazine publishing experienced rapid growth during the two decades after the Civil War and again during the mid-1880s with the rise of the mass-circulation magazines like *Ladies' Home Journal* and *Youth's Companion.* Within a decade after the Civil War, the family house magazines—*Harper's Monthly, Century, Scribner's,* and *Atlantic Monthly*—developed a large readership; *Harper's Monthly* had a circulation of 150,000 by 1870, and *Century* achieved a circulation of 250,000 by 1885.[16] More importantly, they were the main outlet for American and English fiction and became increasingly influential through their publication of historical essays, biographies, political commentary, and editorials. A new generation of middle- to upper-middle-class magazine readers became acquainted not only with the standard sentimental and "local color" stories but also with some of the well-known English Victorian authors and with American writers like Mark Twain, Henry James, Bret Harte, and W. D. Howells, among others.

But the Victorian reader of books and magazines, of imaginative and prescriptive literature, was also becoming a newspaper reader. During the 1870s "quality" magazines were fond of criticizing the "partisan press." These were papers that were often directly subsidized by political parties and represented what mugwump editors thought were the worst of the partisan party system.[17] Most newspapers during this period were not large or professional operations. The local party organization could provide valuable advertising or reward editors with federal patronage positions as well as use their influence with senators or congressmen to provide printing contracts. Curtis, in his "Easy Chair," did not approve. Why, he asked, "can't the daily press show the cool moderation and freedom from excess shown by Hawthorne, Thackeray and Bryant?" [18] F. B Sanborn applauded the trend toward more literate and educated newspaper editors "and yet . . . the number of really able editors is small." He observed a welcome trend toward "pecuniary independence," and overoptimistically (for him) declared that "the Presidential Campaign of 1872 . . . marks the end of partisan journalism in its old form." [19] James Parton, while defending the integrity of many newspapers, observed that "the number of newspapers upon the payroll of the [Tweed] Ring was eighty-nine, of which twenty-seven were so dependent upon this plunder for subsistence that when the ring was broken they gasped and died." [20]

During the 1880s and the 1890s, Gilder and E. L. Godkin were two of the leading critics of the press. E. L Godkin of the *Nation* was fond of attacking the sensational New York papers and the "irresponsibility" of the press.[21] Gilder devoted more than a few editorials to the same topic. In an 1885 editorial Gilder argued that "the newspaper, which has grown to be a daily necessity to half the American people, must be divorced from the low work of partisan politics." [22] In one commentary called, "Journalists and Newsmongers," Gilder compared the personal journalism of a previous age, where "the soul of the newspaper was its editorial page," with "newsmongers" of contemporary journalism. Newsmongers "make mere merchandise of the news" and measure "the value of news of the affairs of the public or of obscure persons by the surprise it will cause to the many or to the few." Public men stand in awe of the newsmonger because "in one issue of his newspaper, he can give a hundred thousand blows to their one." [23] Here Gilder was attacking the growing commercialization and power of the metropolitan press.

By the late nineteenth century, many of the editors and contributors to *Harper's Monthly, North American Review, Century, Scribner's,* and a small number of other upper-middle-class publications began to react to the spread of a nationally oriented print culture. Mail-order publications, story papers, the famous Sears catalog, mass-circulation newspapers, and by the early 1890s the new magazines that adopted the newspaper as a model—all expressed an alarming trend according to the older family house publications. The decline of the Victorian reader was a central theme in many of these articles as well as a nostalgia for the role of literature as a haven and as a disseminator of genteel values.

In an *Atlantic Monthly* article published in 1900, Samuel McChord Crothers, a former minister, contrasted the "gentle reader" of "a generation or two ago" with "the Intelligent Modern Public." He began by discussing the narrative devices of the "books of the good old days" filled with narrative intrusions (the novels of Henry Fielding and Samuel Richardson were mentioned specifically), which addressed the reader in a personal, conversational tone. He remembered, nostalgically, that during an earlier period, books were something to be read leisurely in contrast to the contemporary "literary quick lunch."

Crothers was contrasting the leisurely, genteel Victorian reading style, in which a commonality of values was assumed between author and reader, with the modern newspaper, mass-circulation magazine, and realist fiction that had become the dominant mode of expression over the two decades of the 1880s and 1890s. For the "gentle reader," the

> book becomes a person, and reading comes to be a kind of conversation. The reader is not passive as if he were listening to a lecture. . . . He is sitting by his fireside and old friends drop in on him. He knows their habits and whims, and is glad to see them and to interchange thought. They are perfectly at their ease and there is all the time in the world, and if he yawns now and then nobody is offended.

In contrast, the modern reader "goes to a book just as he goes to a department store. Knowledge is a commodity done up in a neat parcel. So that the article is well made he doesn't care wither for the manufacturer or the dealer." In addition, it appeared that the gentle reader was bored by academic treatises. Crothers devoted much of his essay to a critique of the academic and ostensibly objective historical discourse that was much in vogue during this period.[24] In Crothers view, the "Gentle Reader" wanted not an analysis or information, "divested of all human passions," but an account of an historical event that would connect the reader to a shared cultural tradition.[25]

This critique of literary commercialization and specialization was echoed two years later in the same publication by the editor, Bliss Perry, who bemoaned the decline of the "cheerful reader." He complained in a lead article that too many readers of the *Atlantic Monthly* were "cheerless"—too quick to write angry letters complaining when an author took a position in contrast to their own. He attributed this problem to the fact that "people insist on regarding themselves primarily, not as human beings, but as members of some organization ending with *ist* or *er* or *an*." To have no ulterior aim should be the goal of both reader and editor, he maintained. "The ideal reading mood—is it not?—is that of well-bred people listening to the after-dinner conversation in public which has happily succeeded after-dinner oratory." The editor is compared to the toast-master at such an event, and Perry assured his readers that it would be a pleasure to add more leaves to the dining table, "yet it would do no harm to sit closer too with an amiable disposition to be pleased, if possible, with one's fellow guests, and to make all needful allowance for the most fallible Toastmaster."[26] In the same issue of the *Atlantic Monthly*, Charles Eliot Norton worried about the spiritual consequences of scientific and journalistic writing.

> To-day the writing about material things and of the daily affairs of men, of politics and of society, history, biography, voyages and travels, encyclopedias,

> and scientific treatises, far outweighs, in quality no less than quantity, the literature of sentiment and the imagination. The whole spiritual nature of man is finding but little, and for the most part only feeble and unsatisfactory expression.[27]

A number of articles in *Atlantic Monthly*'s "Contributors' Club" published between 1900 and 1906 placed the blame for this change in the reader to the "invasion of newspapers" and to the "magazines, reviews and the multitude of new books of to-day." Arthur Reed Kimball, one of the contributors, blamed the "habits of business" as well as the direct language of journalism for the decline of oratory (the lecture circuit was one of the chief avenues for the dissemination of genteel culture). "Thus it has come that we have seen the last of the eloquent lawyer of tradition and almost the last of his once twin brother, the eloquent preacher."[28] After pointing out how the invasion of journalism had influenced even the "popular high-class magazine" like *Harper's Monthly* and *Scribner's* and fearing that opposing it would be "fighting against the future," he concluded by associating timeliness and journalism with a decline in standards. In "A Retrospective View," the author proposed "a monthly or a weekly magazine devoted entirely to the literature, art, and history of past times." Another contributor railed against "the tyranny of timeliness." It is interesting that one of the examples of magazine "timeliness" provided by the author was the appearance on magazine covers during the month of July of illustrations of Fourth of July fireworks. "Now there is no intelligent man who does not dread the most unspeakable of all holidays. . . . It is a hideous day at best, a day of noise and heat preceded by a night of sleeplessness and profanity." While not explicitly mentioned by the author, there were running battles in many American cities during the late nineteenth century over Fourth of July celebrations, often pitting immigrants against the Protestant upper and middle classes.[29] The author's concern about loud holiday celebrations may have spoken to the widespread anxiety of the educated middle class over what was perceived as a threat to their own cultural tradition, posed not only by an emerging mass culture but by immigration.[30]

Two articles that appeared in *Atlantic Monthly* during 1905 expressed concerns with the "commercialization of publishing" and the rise of a "reading mob." In "The Mob Spirit in Literature," Henry Dwight Sedgwick applied some of the concepts in vogue in studies of the "irrational" characteristics of urban crowds to changes in the reading public. Just as the "street mob" was characterized by suggestibility, "animal magnetism," "contagion," and other qualities suggesting a "rudimentary intellectual life," there existed a "reading mob" that was equally suggestible and unintellectual. Sedgwick's "reading mob" was in effect the mass market that certain publishing companies, newspapers, and popular magazines were trying to appeal to. Publishers who appealed to this group, Sedgwick asserted, relied heavily on advertising in order to convince the reader that "everyone is talking about it" or "everyone is reading it." Interestingly enough, Sedgwick argued for the central role of the critic as a "disciplinary and coordinating force." Mobs were incapable of thinking for themselves, but the true critic (not the easy to please "mob critic") could interpret true art for the public so that their standards would be raised, allowing them to distinguish art from commonplace literature. In contrast to the unreasoning "reading mob" and those that catered to it was the special genius of the artist and the "authority and judgment" of the critic. The job of a critic was to transform the reading mob into "an educated body of readers."[31]

In "The Commercialization of Literature" Henry Holt, a leading publisher, expressed alarm at the changing role of the publisher from literary patron and gatekeeper of literary standards to purveyor of commodities. The proper role of the publisher, Holt asserted, was to "recognize literature" and cultivate talent through suggestions to authors on how to improve their work and also through careful development of audiences who might be interested in an author's work. Holt characterized the publisher as a "professional," as an individual bound by collective standards "approved by a body of experts." Unfortunately, "anyone who has enough cash or credit to start the business can be a publisher." Holt analyzed the relationship of publisher to author, publishers with one another, and publisher to the market and discovered a pervasive and, for him, unwelcome trend toward commercialization. One of the chief culprits was the literary agent who interfered with the personal relationship that the professional publisher worked hard to cultivate with their authors and often sought to create bidding wars between publishers for the services of successful authors. In the long run, Holt argued, this worked against the interests of both publisher and author and only the agent benefited. In terms of relations between publishers, "the old traditions of courtesy" that had worked well for so many years had been replaced by cut-throat methods of competition, sowing the seeds of mistrust and creating demands for new laws to regulate commercial relations. In terms of the relation between publisher and the market, Holt asserted that publishers spent too much on advertising. The best books don't need advertising while the worst cannot benefit from it. Moreover, the readers of books, an intelligent and highly discriminating subgroup of the larger population, were not likely to be influenced by the same kind of advertising used to sell "patent medicines, tobaccos, food stuffs, clothes, real estate."[32]

A gentle reader presupposed a genteel editor whose ideal was that of the "educated man, the philosopher, who is at home not merely in his own land and his own age, but in all lands and ages; from whose point of perspective the Babylonian seal-workers are as interesting as the Pittsburgh steelworkers."[33] In contrast was the "intelligent" reader who was part of a market, a public, an interest group. This new reader sought information or entertainment, not necessarily companionship combined with self-cultivation. The gentle reader and genteel editor were imbued with that nineteenth-century ideal—"character," a quality that allowed the reading experience to steer between excessive emotionalism and immorality on the one hand and contextless information unrelated to larger moral and public ends on the other.

It is clear that editors in the late nineteenth and early twentieth centuries believed there were new demands for timeliness from readers. Did the perceptions of the genteel editors conform to any objective change in the magazine reading public? Were there changes in content of the magazines that can be considered concessions to the timely reader? There is no question that magazine and newspaper circulations went up during the two decades after the Civil War, and beginning with the mid-1870s there were some significant changes in content, both fiction and nonfiction. In fiction, "local color" and realist fiction began to compete with the sentimental stories that had been a staple since the 1850s. Local color stories had a regional flavor, often using dialect.[34] Sarah Orne Jewett's stories of New England towns or Kate Chopin's vignettes of Louisiana Creoles or Hamlin Garland's stories of Midwestern farmers paved the way for the more daring realism a few decades later.[35] These stories often had a retrospective flavor to them as if they were trying to capture in memory a way of life that would soon fade away. Nevertheless, the use of idiom and the realistic development of character marked an important change in fiction. Also in the 1870s, *Harper's Monthly* and other publications began to print editorial features that documented the latest scientific discoveries. In *Harper's Monthly* historical and biographical articles appeared in greater numbers throughout the 1880s and 1890s than previously, and the *Century* acquired a reputation for its public affairs emphasis and its biographies. In summary, magazine content was already changing in the direction of timeliness well before the new popular magazines came on the scene.[36]

Harper's Monthly had a monthly "Editor's Scientific Record" department that reported on developments in astronomy, physics, meteorology, zoology, engineering, and so on. It was also common to find one or two articles each issue that reported on new discoveries in the fields of archaeology, geology, or economics or explained how economic institutions operated or how new technology worked. While not always written by academics or experts, all the articles relied on scientific research and technical information. Some examples are "The Stone Age of Europe," a four-part series appearing in 1875 that explained recent archaeological discoveries; "Living Glaciers of California" (November 1875); "Some Talks of an Astronomer" (October 1874); "The New South' (September 1874); "The American Railroad" (August 1874); "The Brain of Man; Its Architecture and Requirements" (March 1885); and "A Pair of Shoes" (1885), which explained in detail the technology of shoe manufacturing and how this differed from preindustrial methods. These summaries of scientific research and explanations of the workings of technology and social institutions were exactly the kind of concession to journalism and timeliness that many of these editors would decry in other publications. Their tone was decidedly scholarly and not journalistic, but they appealed to their readers' curiosity about developments in science and technology and sought to demystify the rapid process of economic and political development occurring in the country. A comparison of four issues in *Harper's Monthly* in 1854 with four issues in 1874 shows a negligible percentage of pages devoted to topical and descriptive themes (less than 4 percent) in 1854 compared to 20 percent on the average in 1874.[37] It should also be kept in mind that *Scribner's* had begun publication in 1870 and had acquired a reputation for its "Topic of the Times" editorial commentaries and, according to Arthur John, devoted more space (between 1871 and 1880) to problems of religion, education, women, and "similar sociological themes" than *Harper's Monthly*.[38]

Travel articles in *Harper's Monthly* and *Scribner's* began to focus on the American West rather than only foreign and exotic places.[39] *Scribner's* and later the *Century* focused on American fiction while *Harper's Monthly* began to print a higher quality of American short fiction (while sticking to its emphasis on English reprints in serialized fiction), and by the 1880s the former had published the work of leading American realists (Henry James and W. D. Howells, to name a few). The *Century* in the 1880s emphasized Southern fiction and in their Civil War series claimed to be making a contribution to national unity and overcoming the divisions of the Civil War and Reconstruction. What is significant here is that the quality family house magazines did change with the country. The image that they acquired decades later of being stodgy, conservative, elitist, and resistant to change is not justified. Genteel editors shared and helped to propagate many modern values—religious toleration and a basically secular outlook, national unity, reform and professionalism in politics, and an optimistic faith in economic development and scientific advances.[40]

There were no market surveys of readers until the twentieth century, but there were many comments about the female readership of *Harper's Monthly, Scribner's,* and the *Century. Harper's Monthly* publisher (until 1877) Fletcher Harper claimed to be putting out a magazine for the "plain people" (in other words, the middle class) and not for philosophers and poets.[41] But in its devotion to "the family circle" it had a decidedly feminine emphasis. It was a commonplace observation since the 1850s that women dominated the market for literature. Josiah Gilbert Holland of *Scribner's* explicitly identified his readership as predominately female, and the predominance of sentimental fiction in this publication reflected Holland's belief. The frequent periodical contributor H. H. Boyesen complained that the American girl was the "Iron Madonna who strangles in her fond embrace the American novelist."[42] But the "Iron Madonna" (which implied prudery and a taste for the sentimental in fiction) was changing. More women were attending college, although most of these were women's colleges in the East.[43] Women were working, by the 1870s and 1880s, as clerical workers, secretaries, and "shop girls" in the department stores. By the early 1890s, magazines began to refer to the "new woman," who flirted with men, rode bicycles, and could combine career and marriage.[44]

Before the development of the popular magazine that depended on advertising for its revenues, subscription-based periodicals like the *Century* were expanding their circulation and, it seems, tapping into new segments of the reading public, The post–Civil War period up until the late 1890s was a time of rapid growth in magazine and newspaper reading. There were seven hundred periodicals in 1865 and nearly 3,300 in 1885. According to Mott, there were 8,000 to 9,000 periodicals, not including newspapers, published between 1865 and 1885. There were thirty periodicals with a circulation of 100,000 or more within this twenty-year period. Between 1880 and 1900 the number of new books increased by 300 percent and within the 1870–1900 period newspaper circulation increased by 700 percent. Not only were the family house magazines experiencing a growth in circulation (*Harper's Monthly* had the unprecedented circulation of 200,000 by the Civil War), but by 1885 new mass-circulation magazines (i.e., *Ladies' Home Journal* and *Youth's Companion*) began to reach an even larger market.[45]

It is also well known that this "communications revolution" paralleled the growth of the middle class and the rise of professional occupations requiring college training, specialized knowledge, and membership in professional associations. By 1870, for example, more American universities were offering undergraduate degrees, and there were more law and medical schools than in all of Europe.[46] "New middle-class" occupations grew rapidly as well. Clerical occupations rose from .6 percent of the labor force in 1870 to 2.5 percent in 1900, and the professional class increased from 2.6 percent in 1870 to 4.1 percent in 1900. From 1870 to 1910 the population increased two and a third times while the "new middle class" of clerical workers, salespeople, salaried professionals, and public service workers increased almost eight times—from 756,000 to 5,609,000. The new middle class grew faster than the working class or the old middle class of small businessmen, entrepreneurs, and independent professionals.[47]

In a country without a landed or titled aristocracy or even an aristocratic tradition, middle-class status was something that had to be earned and justified. An appeal to specialized knowledge became an important part of this effort to earn and justify middle-class status, whether it was the specialized knowledge of the professional or the "domestic science" of the middle-class housewife or the specialized vocabulary of leisure subcultures like cycling, sports, and gardening. Knowledge, expressed in the wide variety of printed materials of the period (professional and academic journals, leisure-oriented magazines like the *Cyclist,* women's magazines as well as books), was not a connecting link to the past or a haven from uncertainty but a tool to achieve mastery over some segment of the world. The belief of the family house editors that readers were demanding facts and information rather than a leisurely conversation was probably connected to the rapid spread of universities and professionalization. A commentary published in the *Dial* on "American periodicals" in 1900 observed,

> When we reflect that there now come about as many graduates each year from these institutions [universities and colleges] as there used to be undergraduates in all four classes thirty years ago, we ought readily to understand why so many periodicals are seeing and realizing the advantage of endeavoring to attract the friendship and support of minds that do not need spice to arouse them into action. There is now an encouraging recognition of the public's demand for intelligent presentation of the important facts and questions of the world's current history.[48]

The Political Economy of Magazine and Book Publishing

This section explores the technological and organizational developments that led to the publication of the family house magazines of the mid- to late nineteenth century. I have focused on both book and magazine publishing because they were inseparable. *Harper's Monthly*, *Scribner's*, *Atlantic Monthly*, and the *Century* were appendages to major publishing houses and their raison d'être was to publicize and sell books. Moreover, their editors came from a literary background and thought of their role as, primarily, cultural gatekeepers. The development of modern magazine publishing coincided with other significant changes in American print culture, most notably the development of the modern newspaper, the beginning of a distinctive American literary tradition in the 1850s, the growth of the "dime novel" in the 1860s, and the proliferation of mass-circulation magazines in the mid-1880s. With the "magazine revolution" of the late nineteenth century, a nationally oriented mass print culture had appeared, reaching an audience of millions on a regular basis.

Technological innovations—the steam-driven flatbed press, stereotyping, and electrotyping—influenced the growth of the reading public during the early nineteenth century. Stereotyping (1811) and electrotyping (1841) allowed an impressment to be made of set type, resulting in the making of a permanent metal plate that could be used for second and third editions. The steam-driven press, developed by Isaac Adams in 1836, reduced much of the backbreaking labor of operating printing presses and speeded up the printing process. New papermaking machines allowed paper to be produced for the first time on a continuous roll rather than sheet by sheet and helped to reduce the cost of production. These technological developments had the effect of supporting the successful publishing houses by increasing the costs of capital and thereby making it more difficult for authors to buy their own plates. Also, with the older technology, second editions were often prohibitively expensive since compositors would routinely redistribute the type they used and would have to recompose the type for each new edition. Stereotyping and electrotyping allowed for long-term advertising campaigns and for flexible production of books to accommodate demand.[49]

In addition, developments in transportation allowed for the distribution of reading material to a wider market. Railroads had extended markets to the nation's interior, although they left the South and most rural areas out of the literary distribution system. In 1830 there were twenty-three miles of railroad while in 1840 there were three thousand. By the Civil War there would be thirty thousand miles of railroad lines. The extension of democratic rights and political participation during the early nineteenth century (the "Age of Jackson") may have encouraged an increase in literacy as well as the purchase of new reading materials by those already literate. It is not likely that the growth of the reading public for newspapers and books was a simple effect of the technological developments in printing. It is more likely that the development of market relations and the extension of democratic rights gave more citizens a reason to read—either the new penny press that provided the "news" or diversionary reading that often popularized democratic and nationalistic themes.[50]

Harper's and Mathew Carey's, while successful, were representatives of the older model of book publishing, one that sought markets for artistic literary productions to rather specialized audiences. A contrasting model of book publishing was emerging in Boston. The Beadle Brothers pioneered in the development of the mass-market paperback (Boston publishers such as Gleason sold similar stories for twenty-five cents in the 1840s). *Malaeska, the Indian Wife of the White Hunter,* published in the summer of 1860, netted the firm over $13 million.[51] These inexpensive books were filled with action and adventure but, at least initially, adhered to strict moral standards. Many authors of dime novels turned out stories in a workmanlike fashion. Colonel Prentiss Ingraham, the most prolific of all dime novelists, wrote more than six hundred stories (one was written in twenty-four hours). While acknowledging that dime novels were not created by "plain people," one historian called these novels a "'true proletarian culture'—that is, written for the great masses of people and actually read by them."[52]

The Beadles and other publishers of dime novels were pioneers in formula publishing—seeking out a large market, finding what worked, and giving their readers the same product repeatedly. This approach to publishing required some way to maintain contact with the reading public in order to be sure that old formulas were still popular.[53] In the absence of marketing research, publishers had to experiment with new story themes and plots or hope that markets would not be saturated when another Wild West story or tale about the American Revolution appeared. The few national magazines were not an adequate means for mass-market publishers to survey public tastes because their readership was limited to an Eastern-educated readership.

Theophilus Peterson of Philadelphia became known as one of the firms specializing in the middlebrow "sentimental fiction" that appealed to a largely female audience. Women were to play an important role as readers and producers of the "sentimental school" of fiction. While eighteenth-century moralists had viewed novels as a potentially corrupting influence on middle-class youth, especially women (giving them "false notions of life"), much of this fear had dissipated by the mid-nineteenth century.[54] Still, women writers would typically begin their work with a reassurance to the reader that novel-writing did not take away from their domestic responsibilities as well as a disavowal of any personal ambition. The sentimental novels that were among the first American bestsellers dramatized the themes of feminine self-sacrifice for God and family that would redeem the male quest for success. In this fiction (the height of the sale of sentimental fiction was the 1845–1875 period), the world outside the home was presented as a danger to the young man and woman—filled with demagogues, gamblers, confidence men, and seducers of women. Feminine heroines, with their selfless and compassionate stance toward the world, were to compensate for the individualism and acquisitiveness in society. Authors endowed their sentimental heroines with religious fervor, sincerity, and purity. Through their feminine influence women would refine, spiritualize, and ennoble the rough world of man.

It is well known that *Uncle Tom's Cabin* was a bestseller, but a few years before the publication of that book, in 1850, Susan Warner's *Wide, Wide World* sold 500,000 copies in the United States. It had originally been rejected by Harper's and most of the New York publishing companies. By 1852 it was already in its thirteenth printing. A few years later, in 1854, Maria Cummins's *The Lamp Lighter* sold 40,000 copies in eight weeks. Fanny Fern's (Sarah Payson Willis) first novel *Ruth Hall,* published by Harper's, sold 50,000 copies in eight months in 1855. All this was occurring during the height of what twentieth-century critics would call "the American Renaissance"—the publication of the best-known work of Emerson, Thoreau, Melville, Whitman, and Hawthorne.[55]

By 1855, not only women's magazines and the sentimental novel but also the forerunners of the dime novel (intended for a lower-class audience) had appeared. In addition, the historical romance and the reform novel (antislavery and temperance) had achieved respectability. All the masterpieces of the "American Renaissance" (Thoreau's *Walden,* Emerson's essays, Melville's *Moby-Dick,* Whitman's *Leaves of Grass*) had been published, but few of these works could compete with sentimental fiction. In addition, the penny papers marked an important development in American journalism in the 1830s, relying on advertising and large circulation rather than subscription fees, and emphasizing political neutrality and the "news."[56]

Taken as a whole, we can say that a mass print culture had emerged in America. A large group of readers had begun to purchase novels, newspapers, and other materials on a regular basis. Publishing became a more professional enterprise as well as a more commercial one from the relations between publishers and authors to those of managers and the employees in the print shop. But it was not yet a national mass print culture. Newspapers were oriented to local markets while books, whether reprints of English fiction or written by American authors, had a distinctly regional appeal as well as one limited by their price and often specialized language. Despite the development of a reading public and the industrialization of printing by the 1850s, this did not result in a "literary democracy." Most books were still too expensive for working people to purchase (the price of hardcover books ranged from seventy-five cents to $1.25 while skilled male workers earned approximately one dollar a day). Most paperbacks sold in fifty-cent editions (rather expensive for the working-class reader). Books and magazines were still highbrow or middlebrow literature outside the reach of working people. Because of the dependence upon the railroad, some areas of the country received more printed material than others since they were closer to rail lines.[57]

The era of the family house magazines began with the first issue of *Harper's Monthly* in 1850; *Atlantic Monthly* (1857), the earlier *Scribner's* (1870), and the later *Scribner's* (1887) followed. These publications were owned by the major publishing houses, which were operating as profitable business enterprises by the mid-1850s. Nevertheless, magazine publishing was not the highly specialized, professional, market-oriented and advertising-dependent enterprise it was to become. Editors took for granted a core readership as well as a steady stream of contributors. Publishers too, in this early period, acted more like literary patrons in relation to their authors than businessmen interested in the bottom line. Many publishers of magazines were themselves editors or authors. For example, James T. Fields, an early editor of the *Atlantic Monthly* and publisher of many of New England's great writers, was at the center of Boston's literary culture, conversing with authors at his bookstore and at the dinners he sponsored. Establishing personal contact with him was important for the aspiring Boston author. The entry of William Dean Howells into the Olympian heights of the literary establishment was through Fields. Fresh from his hometown of Columbus, Ohio, Howells had first met Fields in 1860. The editor of the *Atlantic*, James Russell Lowell, admired some of the work Howells had submitted and invited him to dinner along with Fields at the Parker House in Boston. A few years later, this personal contact was renewed in a dinner at the home of

Bayard Taylor, well-known writer and editor. Shortly after, Fields wrote Howells a letter inviting him to become assistant editor of the *Atlantic Monthly*, then considered America's leading literary periodical.[58] In the world of 1860s Boston literary culture, personal relationships still counted for a lot. According to Tomsich, the major publishers before the 1900s were more interested in finding a quality literary product than selling it.[59] In large part, this concern for discovering a quality literary product was linked to the need for publishing houses to attract prominent authors. Magazine content, which ranged from travel and exploration articles to history and biography and family-oriented literature, all corresponded to the books that the major publishing houses had in their catalogs.

Standards of payment for contributors were informal and noncompetitive. The "courtesy of the trade" made it difficult for an editor to offer higher prices for manuscripts to an author committed to another magazine. This informal publishing norm not only limited competition for manuscripts but established a gentleman's agreement that an American publisher who printed a foreign author's work was entitled to the writer's subsequent works. Moreover, the absence of the International Copyright law made it advantageous for periodicals like *Harper's Monthly* to rely on cheap reprints of English fiction rather than pay American authors considerably more.[60]

There were significant changes under way by the mid-1870s in the world of family periodicals. Magazine publishing became increasingly profitable, while a small but influential group of magazine writers ("magazinists," they were called) were able to make a living by selling their articles and fiction to the leading American magazines. In 1877 a magazine asserted that "writing for magazines has become a profession, employing a considerable number of trained experts."[61] Many of these people had begun their careers on newspapers. A kind of career path had been established that started with work on a newspaper and often led to regular contributions to magazines and, for a few, magazine editing or the successful sale of a novel to one of the major publishing houses. Eventually, the trend toward professionalization led to the top writers hiring literary agents as intermediaries. Payments to authors went up, perhaps explaining the dramatic increase in manuscripts submitted. The *Century* received 1,700 manuscripts in 1873, 2,000 in 1874, 2,400 in 1875, and 3,200 in 1876.[62]

The establishment of *Scribner's Monthly* in 1871 in New York in offices located just off Union Square marked the emergence of that city as a cultural center. During the 1870s and 1880s, New York was becoming a center not only for industrial and finance capital but was taking over from New England as the source of new literary talent as well as a center for European influences in the arts. *Scribner's,* and later *Century,* provided an opportunity for these American writers to publish their work—many of them in the emerging local color school and many others in the genre of historical fiction.

With the establishment of the American News Company in 1864, distribution became more rationalized and, as a result, more efficient. The American News Company organized a large segment of the nation's newsdealers, removing from publishers many of the risks of doing business with so many small firms. The passage of the Postal Act of 1885 also facilitated magazine distribution by reducing rates for all second-class mail from three cents to one cent. The major technological change was the development of the rotary press, replacing the much slower flatbed press. In 1886 the *Century*'s rotary press did ten times the work of their older flatbed press. Mass-production methods were introduced into the printing trades, including conveyer systems and assembly lines.[63]

By the 1880s *Century, Scribner's,* and *Harper's Monthly* carried extensive advertising. Periodical advertising more than tripled between 1880 and 1890 (although patent medicines, newspapers, books, and magazine advertisements provided the main source of revenue). *Harper's Monthly* was the last to accept advertising other than its own (even though it was during most of this period the circulation leader), but even the Harper brothers gave in and offered advertising space to other companies in 1882.[64] Nevertheless, most advertising was paid for by local retailers and other publishers who were more likely to use newspapers as an advertising medium. This had only begun to change in the mid-1880s with the development of advertising paid for by manufacturers and intended for a national audience. With *Scribner's, Harper's Monthly,* and *Century* all doing well in circulation and appealing to the same readers, the editors of the "big three" competed with one another for the best writers and illustrators.

Illustration, Photography, and the "Halftone Effect"

The last quarter of the nineteenth century marked a revolution in book and periodical illustration. There was also a variety of technical advances, including the "halftone method" of illustration and photographic reproduction. The vast majority of commentators was enthusiastic about this "golden age" of periodical illustration.[65] Many illustrators by the 1890s had acquired national reputations and high salaries (Howard Pyle, Edwin Austin Abbey, Edward Pennel, Charles Dana Gibson, and Frost, to name a few). An article in *Munsey's* proclaimed that

> In the past few years America has seen a great awakening in many fields of art, a growing realization that something more than commercial success and practical achievement is necessary to the growth of a people. . . . But if we would find where in the world of art the artist is most sure of winning and keeping the heart of the people,—and of the American people, perhaps most of all—must turn to illustration.[66]

There was, though, a minority of genteel critics of book and periodical illustration. According to a number of articles published in the *Nation, Harper's Monthly,* and the *Atlantic Monthly,* magazine content was distorted by a too liberal use of illustrations; they were dangerously suggestive and detracted from the printed word. The mania for illustrations represented the standardization and vulgarization of art. The *Nation* criticized a newspaper, the *Philadelphia Ledger,* for "joining the pictorial army." Illustrations, the article maintained, promoted "indifference to the truth and that jocular view of lying, perverting, and deceiving, which play so large a part of successful journalism."[67]

The problem, it seemed, for these genteel critics was that many illustrations were inaccurate representations of the text. This was one of E. L. Godkin's complaints about newspaper illustrations.[68] Closely related to this concern was the claim that illustrations would impede the reading process as a rational and deliberate experience. Illustration was thought by some to be a more primitive form of expression than the printed word and one that appealed to the emotions more than the mind.[69] An article in the *Bookman,* while focusing on the "artistic poster" and not periodical illustration, nevertheless expressed the same association of illustration with "lewdness."

> In thousands of the homes of the poor these posters are the only pictures they have to adorn their dwellings, and even in well to do households young men and women preserve what they call a pretty girl, and hang it up in their den or chamber . . . The question might be asked, What harm can come? A great deal of harm. A vulgar taste becomes very soon a depraved taste by feeding on suggestion, and quickly breeds lewdness.[70]

A much more serious concern throughout the 1890s was over the development of the new halftone photoengraving.[71] Photoengraving allowed for pictures to be made directly from photographs, drastically cutting down on expenses without sacrificing quality. The *Century* had paid up to $300 for a woodcut, but a halftone photograph could cost less than $20 (the *Century* routinely paid

$5,000 or more per month for woodcut illustrations). The *Century* had pioneered in halftone reproduction of drawings and in new methods of wood engraving. But something qualitatively new seemed to have happened with the ability to reproduce photographs inexpensively and with high quality. Even the finest halftone illustrations conveyed to readers a clear impression of artifice—they were drawn by someone and this fact was readily apparent. But the halftone photograph ("a photomechanical reproduction of a photochemical image") appeared to be a real image of something, not a product of human subjectivity.[72] Before the 1890s and the development of the halftone method of photographic reproduction, photographs could not be effectively reproduced; images were often distorted, with shadings and contrasts missing or indistinct.

Gilder resisted this development because it threatened his conception of the *Century* as a vehicle for good taste and high culture. "There is," said a *Century* editorial, "a distinct difference between picture-making and art."[73] Another editorial saw the use of photographs in magazines as symptomatic of a larger problem—the "recording tendency in American life, a religion of the commonplace."[74] This was one compromise Gilder was unwilling to make, even though he was told by his business manager in 1899 that he had to drastically cut expenditures.[75] Why was this such a principled matter for Gilder? After all, the development of photoengraving in 1885 held the potential of drastically reducing magazine costs, which could have helped the *Century* to compete with the new arrivals—*McClure's*, *Cosmopolitan*, and *Munsey's*.

Gilder's concern was that photography failed to live up to the aesthetic standards of true art. The question of whether photography was art was an important one since art held an exalted status for Victorian Americans. The objection some raised about photography was that it was a passive and objective recording of the world in contrast to an artist's active and interpretative expression. Photography recorded its subject and was believed incapable of idealizing it. Others responded by asserting that photography was a new art form and that the photographer could be as creative and interpretative as the sculptor or painter with the choice of lighting, lens, apertures, distance, and background. Portraits would pose the special artistic problem of capturing the individual's true character. According to one advocate of photography as art, a good photographic portrait "should not be merely a likeness of some fleeting expression; it should be typical, a summary of characteristics into one look."[76] Victorian photographic portraits sought to idealize the subject through manipulating the background as well as through posing. These were efforts to overcome what was thought of as the limitations of the medium in order to achieve the status of art. The camera, in other words, in order to be accepted, had to be assimilated into Victorian values.[77]

Behind this debate about the artistic status of photography was the concern about the loss of control over events. Gilder's worry and those expressed by other editors and writers was that photography would mark the rule of events over people, a loss of mastery over the world which might lead to moral decay. After all, moral principles were absolutes to be imposed by people on contingent events and situations. If these events and images were to be simply recorded, they might achieve the power to sweep people in a direction that could not be ordered and controlled. The "real" implied a world of tenements, labor unrest, immigrants with alien ways, political corruption, dangerous amusements, and the like. How could this be recorded without imposing some idealized standard on it? The photograph could not do all of this, but the hostile reaction it inspired supports the view that it became a symbol for much more, the dangers that a "mass society" posed to the Protestant middle and upper classes. What was real might, on some deeper level, refer to experience that eluded the containment of form, energy without direction or purpose. For Victorians who valued reason and sought to impose order on the world, an apparently unmediated view of reality was a threatening prospect. Moreover, by the 1890s millions of people could create their own record of events and homemade artworks as a result of the mass sale of cameras. As one cultural historian has said, "Each person could be his own artist."[78]

The development of the halftone method of reproducing photographs was not the first technological development in magazine illustration. As a result of an assortment of innovations in wood engraving in the 1870s, magazines were able to mass produce works of art so that they were accessible to a wider audience. This was one of Gilder's proudest achievements. In the late 1870s Alexander Drake, *Scribner's* art superintendent, developed a technique that allowed a woodblock to be sensitized like a photographic plate and a drawing or painting transferred to it with a camera. But highly skilled engravers had to re-create the original picture. The process was expensive, but the result was of such high quality that some of the best American artists contributed their work for woodcut reproduction. This was a compromise between the technologies of mass production and the ideal standards of art (the chromolithograph had been commonplace in the American home since the 1870s).[79]

The camera had the potential to be used to produce an image that seemed to represent the "real thing," or it could, through the artistic intervention of the photographer, express ideal and typical images more consistent with Victorian views of art. Francis Galton, the English scientist, had developed the technique of the composite photograph, which allowed the photographer to combine a number of prints in order to obtain a synthesis of the individual's character. The composite would be shown in the center of the page with the original prints along the edge around the composite. The composite was also used by Galton to reveal the typical representative of a category as with the composites of "twelve Boston physicians" or composites of Italians or Jews. In either version, whether of a number of prints of the same individual or a number of different individuals, the composite was an expression of the typical pattern. This typical pattern, an artificial construction by the photographer, was considered more truthful than the use of the camera to represent an actual event or person.

The problem for the Victorian middle class was that the camera could be used for improper purposes by journalists and others. Photographs as representations could pose the danger of capturing the transient and misleading appearance of a subject, mistaking it for character.[80] The journalistic photographer, no matter how heroic and daring, was, after all, at the mercy of events and could not manipulate the subject and setting in order to achieve the desired effect. John Gilmer Speed, in an article in the *North American Review,* argued that journalistic photographers were invading the privacy of public officials. "The illustrated journalism now prevalent finds its finest achievements in the publication of photographs surreptitiously taken. . . . Now, such practices are unquestionably invasions of privacy."[81]

Many of these issues were addressed in Walter Benjamin's widely discussed article, "The Work of Art in the Age of Mechanical Reproduction." The major consequence of mechanical reproduction, he argued, was to deprive a work of art of its "aura," to "detach the reproduced object from the domain of tradition."[82] Magazine illustration, beyond the reproduction of masterpieces, brought the artist closer to the public and reduced art to a nonartistic purpose—illustrating a story or a theme in an article or making a political point in a cartoon. Photoengraving threatened the status of the quality magazine by allowing competitors with little capital to present to the reader quality illustrations. The popular fiction in Sunday newspaper supplements also threatened to deprive literature of its aura as well, as a realm of tradition and permanence. Recording events through photography or journalistic reporting had the democratic implication of making events accessible to more people and inviting readers to use their own judgment in responding to what they were reading. Since the world seemed to be speaking directly to the reader, no special skill, knowledge, or sensitivity seemed to be needed to understand and react to a photograph or news story.

The *Century's* circulation went down from a high point of 250,000 to only 125,000 in the late 1890s. Gilder died in 1909, and the magazine continued publication until it was bought out by the *Forum* in 1930. *Harper's Monthly*, *Scribner's*, and *Atlantic Monthly* stayed in business but were no longer the preeminent magazines of the middle class and could not maintain their circulations at their nineteenth-century high marks. William Allen White in his autobiography provided a vivid account of the genteel magazines by the first decade of the twentieth century.

> Often he [William Dean Howells] put me up at the Century Club, and there I met many writing men of renown—men who lingered over from another day and time. The distance was short in time and space from the Century Club, with its ancients and honorables, to the Century Magazine office on Union Square where Richard Watson Gilder resided in a frowzy old office, book lined, paper strewn, charming, or to the office of Harper's Magazine far downtown, which seemed to be covered with the mold of Harper's antebellum antiquity, or to Scribner's . . . which in those fin de siècle days, was brighter, more alert, less covered with the hoarfrost of forgotten winters. But even so, those magazines—the staid old standbys of upper middle class America in the middle 1910's—were still printing reminiscences of the Civil War, articles on archeology, stories of the old western ranchers and Indians. . . . Each magazine was produced after its own formula, discovered sometime in the seventies, edited by men in their fifties and sixties, and some who had reached their fourscore years and ten.[83]

How do we account for the inability of these magazines to compete with their rivals? An editorial in the *Independent* (a weekly religious magazine that later advocated social and political reform) predicted the decline of the "higher-priced magazines" because the "revolution in the art of engraving, not to say its destruction, is threatening a change in the conduct of monthly magazines." In addition, the article predicted that the higher-priced magazines would not want to reduce their prices in order to compete because "they will wish to maintain that higher, purer literary standard which succeeds in securing the best but not the most numerous readers."[84] Accurate as this prediction turned out to be, it does not account for the positive attraction the new magazines had. That is the subject of the next installment in our story—the magazine revolution and the popular magazine editor.

2

THE MAGAZINE REVOLUTION

CHAPTER THREE

The Magazine Revolution of the 1890s

Was There a Magazine Revolution?

In May 1895 a new magazine named *McClure's* announced in its lead article that it had reached a circulation of 100,000. In April 1895, *Munsey's* announced that it had exceeded the 500,000 circulation mark, less than two years after lowering its price to ten cents.[1] In the *McClure's* article, special importance was attributed to the ability of the magazine to succeed "without capital," despite the "absolute axiom" in the magazine industry that $500,000 would be required to start an illustrated monthly. How was this possible?

For the new magazine publishers the Great Panic of 1893, a major depression that was to last for four more years, was a very good year. Prospective magazine publishers could purchase paper and printing facilities at a low cost. In addition, the development of halftone photoengraving drastically reduced the cost of reproducing illustrations and photographs, allowing for new competitors to challenge the established "quality" magazines. S. S. McClure observed that "the impregnability of the older magazines was due largely to the costliness of wood-engraving."[2] The combination of the depression and the development of national advertising created a business opportunity that Frank Munsey would soon exploit.[3] A reduction in the price of the magazine itself would, under conditions of economic distress, seem particularly attractive to customers. Publishers could make their profit directly from advertising revenue. Ironically, during a period of unprecedented business mergers and consolidations, magazine publishing became intensely competitive. *McClure's* began publication in June 1893 with a price of fifteen cents, and shortly after July 1893 *Cosmopolitan* lowered its price to twelve and a half cents.[4] Then in October *Munsey's* lowered its price to ten cents, which became the standard in the industry.

S. S. McClure, editor and publisher of *McClure's,* and to some extent John Brisben Walker, editor [5] and publisher of *Cosmopolitan,* modeled their new publications on the successful quality monthlies of the nineteenth century. The *Century* was still a successful magazine in the 1890s, highly regarded in terms of quality, and competitive in terms of circulation.[6] Of the three leading quality magazines, the *Century* made the greatest effort to adapt to new developments in journalism and to the new popular magazines. According to Mott, the "journalistic side" of the *Century* was emphasized in the 1890s—articles addressing "matters of contemporaneous human interest."[7] A content analysis published in *Atlantic Monthly* claimed that the three quality monthlies were printing 10 percent more "journalistic articles" than it had over the previous twenty-five years.[8]

But the influence of journalism was perhaps more significant as a model for the popular magazine, both the independent journalism that had become dominant in the major cities as well as the "yellow" or sensational journalism of Joseph Pulitzer and, by 1895, William Randolph Hearst.[9] The Sunday supplements that many newspapers were putting out were also an important influence.[10] This chapter examines the magazine revolution of the 1890s and the ways in which popular magazines departed from their genteel counterparts by conveying a sense of energy and vitality. Chapter 4 will explore the individuals responsible for the popular magazine's development and how they understood their new enterprise.

The development of the popular general interest magazine, driven by advertising revenue and reaching an audience significantly larger than the earlier quality publications, has been described as a "magazine revolution." This view, common among magazine historians, focuses on the growth of advertising, technological changes, new distributions systems, the increasing educational level among the middle class, and cultural developments like the Chatauqua movement, the interest in self-improvement, and social reform. The precipitating event that brought about this revolution was *Munsey's* price cut to ten cents.[11] As a result, it is argued, of a higher circulation and increased reliance on advertising for revenue, magazine content became more "popular" and topical.

But there is some reason to question how much of an abrupt change actually took place. We have already seen that many of the most significant technological and organizational changes had taken place a decade or more earlier—from the rotary press to innovations in reproducing illustrations and works of art. The quality magazines were beginning to carry extensive advertising by the 1880s, and there is evidence magazines were tapping into new markets of readers interested in information as well as diversion.

There were close affinities in content, at first, between the new "popular magazines" and their predecessors. In fact, Gilder of the *Century* regarded *McClure's* as a serious competitor. The content of *McClure's* was similar enough to the *Century* that Gilder could reasonably assume that this new magazine was attempting to appeal to the same "highbrow" market as his. Gilder complained in an issue of the *Century* that the "cheap magazines" carried much less reading matter and artwork than his own. This seemed to indicate some anxiety about the competition. In response to a question about *McClure's,* Gilder derisively characterized his rival by saying, "They got a girl to write a life of Lincoln" (the "girl" was Ida Tarbell). McClure responded editorially to these criticisms in a light-hearted way: "How exceedingly prone are we all to pronounce the new thing impossible! The literature of progress may be summed up in this simple dialogue: 'The old to the New. Thou art impossible! The New to the Old. The future is mine.' "[12]

McClure's started publication in 1893 and was in heavy debt with a circulation of only 30,000. McClure was using the *Century* as his model (although the *Century* was already becoming more "timely" and journalistic), so it is not surprising that *McClure's* had a similar content. In January 1894, McClure printed an account of the life and work of Jules Verne, an article on "Whittier's Faith and Character" from unpublished letters, an adventure story of "hunters, trappers and tradesmen," a short piece of romantic fiction, an interview with the inventor of the "air-ship," an account of a thousand-mile ride on the "fastest engine in the world," a biographical sketch of Francis Parkman (the famous historian who had recently died), a regular feature on scientific developments, and a series of photographs called "Human Documents." The March 1893 issue of the *Century* carried an illustrated article on the Chicago World's Fair (the World's Columbian Exposition), serialized fiction in the sentimental and historical romance traditions, a recollection of Lord Tennyson, more genteel poetry, an illustrated article on Nicaragua, a short story by Thomas

Bailey Aldrich, a firsthand account by Napoleon I's eldest brother Joseph Bonaparte, a short article on English royalty, a biography of John Muir, and an "inside view" of the pension bureau. It is clear that both publications emphasized literary figures, past and contemporary. *McClure's* would soon imitate the *Century* and other magazines with a series on Napoleon by Ida Tarbell beginning in the November 1894 issue (which raised its circulation to 100,000). Throughout the 1893–94 period *McClure's* articles on Lincoln, "The Christ-Child in Art" (December 1894), "John Ruskin at Home" (March 1894), and "Personal Traits of General Grant" (May 1894) all gave the magazine a *Century*-esque retrospective and artistic flavor (see appendix 4).

Historical pieces on the life of Lincoln, including the series by Tarbell (*McClure's* 7:1896), resembled the *Century*'s immensely successful Civil War series and reflected McClure's own interest in the Civil War as well as his belief that he could give this material a "human interest" slant. In the Civil War articles, McClure sought to "discover unknown aspects of popular battles and events." This was part of *McClure's* emphasis on "a realistic portrayal of living personalities." Ray Stannard Baker contributed a series on his father's experiences as a member of the Northern army's secret service, beginning with "Capture, Death and Burial of J. Wilkes Booth."[13] Ida Tarbell's series on Lincoln involved interviews with many of the people who knew him and was accompanied by a large quantity of illustrations and photographs. The "human interest" approach gave the *McClure's* Civil War articles a somewhat different tone than the earlier *Century* series.[14]

Despite these clear similarities in content, popular magazines had a different appearance and tone. There was a distinct difference in appearance caused in large part by the use of photography ("Human Documents"), which gave *McClure's* a contemporary and journalistic look. In addition, *McClure's* had an emphasis on scientific developments that went beyond short editorial commentaries. "The Story of Dr. Morton's Introduction of Ether," articles on trains[15] and airships,[16] the Paris municipal laboratory, and others gave *McClure's* a topical and lively tone. Descriptive accounts of hunters and trappers, "The Glamour of the Arctic," "Wild Beasts and Their Keepers," "The Poisonous Snakes of India" all provided a robust quality lacking in the genteel competitors. There were glowing biographical sketches of industrialists—Phillip Armour, for example (February 1894). In addition, the self-promotions in the table of contents alerted readers to "Articles, Stories and Pictures of Contemporary Human Interest," and "Personal Studies of Men of Achievement." The editorial voice had changed; McClure was not shy about self-

McClure's "Human Documents" series, one of the magazine's early attractions. It consisted of a series of photographs of famous people, providing a kind of photographic biography. These photographs are of William Dean Howells (*McClure's*, June 1893, p. 20).

promotion. He was a natural entrepreneur and in many ways the editorial voice anticipated advertising techniques that were used successfully in subsequent decades.

More than the other popular magazines, *McClure's* gave its readers a sense of immediacy, of being on the "inside" or behind the scenes, allowing them a glimpse under the surface.[17] In vivid fictional prose, the well-known magazinist Cleveland Moffett told *McClure's* readers "How the Circus Is Put Up and Taken Down"(December 1895). "It is a mountain side, silent and gloomy in the dawning day," began this factual essay on circuses, an essay that attempted to uncover the hidden circus world for readers. Readers could tag along with publisher-editor S. S. McClure as he took an Atlantic voyage on an ocean liner (March 1895). Hamlin Garland took his readers through "Homestead and Its Perilous Trades" (June 1894). This was not merely a factual description or essay but "impressions of a trip." In fact, like a good reporter, Garland managed to get inside the steel mill and talk to the workers only two years after the famous Homestead strike.[18] The article was a sharply worded indictment of working and living conditions for the steelworkers. In the July 1894 issue, *McClure's* printed an account of the conditions at Homestead written by "one of its workmen."[19]

In August of the same year Stephen Crane traveled "In the Depths of a Coal Mine." The January 1895 issue contained a "firsthand account" of an author's experience in writing a famous children's book—an explanation of "how the book was written." Even the literary pieces were often written as inside glimpses of a writer's personality and thoughts. *McClure's* carried a continuing series of "Real Conversations," dialogues between famous authors. Hamlin Garland interviewed James Whitcomb Riley. H. H. Boyesen interviewed W. D. Howells. Edward Evert Hale talked to Oliver Wendell Holmes.[20]

It is true that this emphasis was submerged and mixed with features that were quite similar to the *Century*'s genteel, retrospective, and leisurely tone. But it may have been the Tarbell series on Napoleon that made the difference in raising *McClure's* circulation enough so that people began to notice some of these different qualities.[21] Tarbell's multipart biography of Napoleon, promoted heavily and filled with illustrations, was *McClure's* contribution to the widespread fascination during the 1890s with Napoleon and anything connected with his life. Other popular magazines had a different mix of articles but all adopted the *McClure's* editorial voice and tone and, to varying degrees, *McClure's* sense of immediacy. These new arrivals to the magazine world may have lacked the solid character of the *Century* or *Harper's Monthly*, grounded as they were in tradition and literary values, but they certainly had personality.

Cosmopolitan, founded in 1886, was originally considered a "quality" publication, a smaller version of *Harper's Monthly* or *Century*, with expensive, woodcut illustrations and a subscription price of four dollars a year. The magazine could only achieve a circulation of 20,000, and by 1888 it had been sold to John Brisben Walker. In 1890, two years after Walker took over, *Cosmopolitan* was selling for twenty cents and was still considered one of the quality magazines.[22] By July 1893 Walker's *Cosmopolitan* cut its price to twelve and a half cents (a month after the first issue of *McClure's* hit the market at fifteen cents). By 1895 *Cosmopolitan* and *McClure's* lowered their prices to ten cents to keep up with *Munsey's*. One critic in 1897 credited Walker with introducing "the newspaper ideas of timeliness and dignified sensationalism into periodical literature."[23] A comparison of the May 1890 issue and the May 1897 issue shows significant continuity in terms of content. Yet Walker, as early as 1890, had begun to depart, in some ways, from the pattern of the quality magazines (see appendix 5).

The lead article in the May 1890 issue was an account of "Artists and Art Life in Munich" with a series of woodcut illustrations. Other articles in the May issue included an account of "The Thieves of New York," an essay on the pleasures of country strolls, the second part of a travel series by Elizabeth Bisland called "A Flying Trip Around the World" (modeled after a feature in Pulitzer's *New York World*), an essay on the growth of Denver by Walker, an essay on the rise of the "tall hat," the first part of a series on "Southern Problems," and the regular editorial feature by Murat Halstead. The next few issues included a continuing *Cosmopolitan* staple, "Some Glances at American Beauties" (June 1890), which consisted of a series of photographs of attractive, well-known actresses; continuing features on European artists and monarchs; articles on the American military;[24] as well as literary, travel, and topical pieces that were quite similar to the material appearing in *Harper's Monthly* and *Century*.[25] In this early period the *Cosmopolitan* carried little fiction. H. H. Boyesen's "A Candidate For Divorce" (March 1890), a short story that depicted the "new woman" in the realist tradition, was one notable work of fiction. A number of historical pieces were interspersed with contemporary articles on journalism, Wall Street, and education.[26] The 1890 issues of *Cosmopolitan* had already begun to reflect the journalistic emphasis on "timeliness" and "dignified sensationalism." The use of halftone illustrations and photographs was also extensive. On the other hand, the focus on world literature, European art, and travel pieces was quite consistent with the "big three" quality magazines, although there was more of a reliance on illustrations and the articles were shorter.

By 1897 *Cosmopolitan* was carrying a serialized novel by H. G. Wells ("The War of the Worlds"), a discussion of "The New Congressional Library" (May 1897), part of a series on "Great Business Enterprises" (the article in the May issue focused on "The Collection of the News"), a collection of Civil War photographs, and continuing series on "The Progress of Science" and "Modern Education." A serialized novel in the historical romance tradition, *The Turkish Messiah* by Israel Zangwill, contained a photograph of a Turkish man and a blonde woman in his arms with the caption, "He knew for the first time the touch of a woman's lips." Other articles in 1897 included a report by Julian Hawthorne on the "horrors of the plague in India" (July 1897), a descriptive essay on "poultry farming" by Walker (June 1897), a first-person travel essay on "Constantinople" (June 1897), and "Some Recent Examples of Art" (May 1897), which focused mainly on photographs of women. Between 1893 and 1896 approximately 15 percent of all *Cosmopolitan* articles were on politics and current events. Between 1897 and 1900 this percentage increased to 26 percent (see appendix 5). As with *McClure's, Cosmopolitan* began to emphasize biographies of famous businessmen ("Captains of Industry") and accounts of vigorous outdoor sports ("The America's Cup") and outdoor adventures. Sympathetic accounts of new amusements, from the roof-gardens in New York (May 1899) to "Music Halls and Popular Songs" (September 1897), also gave the 1897 *Cosmopolitan* an energetic and "vital" quality.[27]

The differences between the *Cosmopolitan* of 1890 and 1897 were one of degree, not a qualitative or revolutionary one. While *Cosmopolitan* under the direction of Walker was not a carbon copy of *Harper's Monthly* or *Century*, there were clear similarities throughout the 1890s. W. D. Howells's brief period as editor guaranteed a "highbrow" literary quality that characterized *Harper's Monthly* and *Century*. At the same time, the influence of independent and sensational journalism was evident before *Munsey's* October 1893 price change and before *Cosmopolitan* lowered its price to twelve and a half cents in 1893 and ten cents in 1895. In other words, *Cosmopolitan*'s content did not seem to change substantially because of the lowering of its price and increased reliance on advertising. In 1892, a year before the "revolutionary" price change of *Munsey's*, one critic singled out *Cosmopolitan* for its "supremacy" in halftone illustrations, its "journalistic dash," combined with "literary taste."[28]

An examination of some of the articles published by the popular magazines shows a continuing link with the mugwump reform tradition. While these articles were not plentiful and certainly not promoted, they do show that popular magazines retained a political perspective quite similar to the genteel magazines. *McClure's* in the 1890s printed a number of articles on liberal Republican reformers in the mugwump tradition. Carl Schurz wrote a laudatory biographical sketch of George William Curtis upon his death.[29] Curtis, as discussed earlier, was a leading advocate of civil service reform and a member of the Eastern "gentry." Like the quality magazines, *McClure's* published articles by Washington Gladden (August 1894) and others in the Social Gospel movement who were critical of the extreme economic individualism of Social Darwinism and classical political economic frameworks. Other articles in the liberal reform tradition included, "Dr. Charles H. Parkhurst: His Recent Work In Municipal Reform" (January 1895), and a series on the Tammany Hall "spoil system" (beginning in April 1895). *Munsey's* published an article on "Civil Service Reform" by Secretary of the Treasury Lyman J. Gage (May 1898). *Cosmopolitan* published a positive assessment of the liberal Republican newspaper editor Horace Greeley by Murat Halstead (February 1890) as well as a series of articles on urban reform during the 1890s.[30] Beyond articles that covered urban reform campaigns, a genteel discourse was quite common throughout the new popular magazines as reflected in numerous lead articles on art as well as the occasional concerns expressed by Walker and others about "overcivilization."

On the other hand, Brooks Adams, brother of the famous historian Henry Adams (and grandson of President John Quincy Adams), wrote an analysis of America's place in the world political order that broke from the mugwump anti-imperialist stance. Along with Henry Cabot Lodge and Theodore Roosevelt, he urged a strong role for the United States in the world political order in order to preserve the country's growing industrial potential. The problem of finding outlets for surplus industrial production was the foremost problem of the times, he argued, and an activist foreign policy would be needed to protect the country's economic interests.[31] Theodore Roosevelt, when he was police commissioner of New York City, wrote an account of his efforts to remove politics and graft from the city's police department.[32] While this was typical of mugwump efforts to reform city politics, Roosevelt as discussed earlier had already broken from the genteel tradition in espousing an expansionist foreign policy and in his "plea for masculinity in politics." Like a young man or woman making his or her way in the world, the popular magazines were striking out in new directions but still showed evidence of their parentage—the mugwump reform tradition and the genteel view of culture.

In a provocative article, Robert Stinson has questioned the existence of a "magazine revolution."[33] Stinson demonstrates that McClure, who had worked for a year at the *Century*, used the famous quality monthly as his model in editing the trade publication *The Wheelman* and in his first few years as editor of *McClure's*. Moreover, there is some evidence that he also used the English magazine the *Strand* as a model. While the *Strand*'s editor, George Newnes, claimed that he was inspired by reading the quality American monthlies, he also said that he wanted to make a magazine that was accessible to the masses. Newnes observed that there were two types of journalism—the "information" variety and the type that explicitly sought to entertain its readers.[34] The *Strand*, "though somewhat between the two, tended to waver toward the side of fun."

Stinson's point is that *McClure's* was a hybrid, modeled both after the quality monthlies and the more popular English monthly, the *Strand*. S. S. McClure's hope was to make the *Century*'s style accessible to the masses but also to add elements of entertainment that seemed to be working well in many of the urban newspapers of the period. Such a thesis undermines any naive notion that the popular magazine was a complete departure from its predecessors as well as any simple dichotomy between the genteel "high culture" of the quality magazines and the "mass" culture of the popular magazines. The valuable point in Stinson's essay is not so much that popular magazines were, at first, similar to their predecessors but that the magazine revolution did not occur abruptly and cannot be equated with price reductions and increased advertising. As we have seen, *Cosmopolitan* had moved in new directions in terms of the use of halftone illustrations and the adoption of sensational journalistic techniques before *Munsey's* price reduction and before its heavy reliance on advertising.

Moreover, the quality magazines had begun to change in content toward more topical articles, local color and realism in fiction, and editorial departments that catalogued the latest scientific advances. Over the two decades of the 1870s and 1880s, the supposedly conservative genteel publications were largely espousing the liberal reform program that was, at least partially, to transform journalism and politics. Many of the contributors and staff members of the popular magazines in the early period of the 1890s were also regular contributors to the quality magazines (see appendix 6). But rather than demonstrating that the a magazine revolution never took place, as Stinson argues, the continuity between old and new magazines may reflect the fact that elements of the magazine revolution had begun a decade earlier. The concept of "revolution" may be more appropriately used to refer to the "communications revolution" of the 1880s of which magazines were a part.

The Fin de Siècle Magazines

A review of "The Publisher's Desk," a regular feature in *Munsey's*, "Editorial Notes" in *McClure's*, self-promotions in Walker's *Cosmopolitan* and, after 1905 (under the ownership of Hearst), the "Shop Talk" department in *Cosmopolitan*, reveals how the new popular magazine editors presented themselves and their publications to their readers. We might dismiss some of the hyperbole as self-serving promotion, but all three publications went to great pains to outline a "mission" or project that is worthy of being taken seriously.

A number of themes stand out after an examination of these features. "Vitality," "human interest," "lively," "intellectual vigor," "blood-stirring," and "timely" were some of the more common adjectives used to construct a public image for the popular magazine. Frank Munsey during the early years of the magazine made the contrast between popular and genteel publications in the most vivid terms. More than the other editors, Munsey was influenced by the newspaper model. The quality magazines were associated with "the effete East," with being "dull, heavy and technical." They were "juiceless as a husk," in contrast to the "seasonable, palatable food" offered in *Munsey's*. The popular magazine dealt with "live subjects." In Munsey's words: "Dead subjects are good enough for dead people, but not for the wide awake American. Live subjects appeal to the man and the woman who live in the present."[35] Munsey railed against the fiction commonly published in the genteel quality magazines as "washed out studies of effete human nature" and "tales of sickly sentimentality." He was referring to the local color and "domestic realism" of fiction that was still the staple of the quality magazines. Instead, he urged writers to send "fiction in which there is a story, action, force—a tale that means something—in short, a story."[36] In the November 1893 issue, Munsey proclaimed that "We believe that the time has come to throw conservatism and conventionality to the winds, and to open our eyes and learn a thing or two from the great daily journals with their marvelous Sunday issues. They are the keenest observers and best typify public taste."

This was part of what Munsey called his conception of the "fin de siècle magazine." The new monthly magazines would imitate the newspaper's emphasis on current affairs and appeal to public taste. Unlike the daily newspapers, though, the monthly magazine could produce a higher quality of illustration since they were not hindered by the demands for rapid printing. Illustrations combined with the occasional literary feature and regular departments on literature, current events, the theater, art, and music gave *Munsey's* some legitimacy as a serious publication, but other features—including many short unsigned articles and an emphasis on short fiction ("storiettes") as opposed to serialized novels by big-name authors, and frequent photographs of artists' models—seemed to indicate that Munsey was seeking to expand the readership of monthly magazines to a lower-middle-class or white-collar working-class audience—an audience that had already begun to read the Sunday supplements put out by the leading newspapers.

McClure's proclaimed in an early issue that it was

> designed to reflect the moving spirit of the time; by portraying in close personal studies the character and achievements of the great men of the day; by reporting through the contributions of those who speak with authority the new discoveries, tendencies or principles in science and their application in new inventions; by setting forth, with text and picture, present day phases of the human struggle for existence and development; by describing great industrial enterprises and their effect upon contemporaneous life; and by giving to its readers the best imaginative literature by living writers—all presented with virile and artistic illustrations.[37]

As with Frank Munsey, McClure presented his magazine as "vital" and timely because of its illustrations and its focus on new discoveries in science and the publication of "living authors."[38] It is also of interest that this well-known statement of purpose highlights the "personal studies of great men of the day" and "those who speak with authority." The "human interest" focus and the magazine's attention to personality were in part efforts to capitalize on the popularity of the new journalism developed by Pulitzer and imitated by many others.

Cosmopolitan, under the reign of John Brisben Walker, did not have a monthly feature in which the publisher or editor promoted the magazine. There were editorial features, a "Review of Current Events," and "In the World of Art and Letters," and Walker was a regular contributor to the magazine. In an 1897 unsigned article, the magazine provided a clear account of "the aims, methods and progress of the magazine which claims the largest clientele of intelligent and thoughtful readers reached by any periodical—daily, weekly or monthly—in the world."[39] Unlike *Munsey's,* the authors of this article did not try to distinguish themselves from the quality monthlies, *Century, Harper's*

Monthly, and *Scribner's*. All were "superb publications" but at twenty-five to thirty-five cents an issue were "prohibitive to a large number of people." *Cosmopolitan*, unlike *Munsey's*, portrayed itself as a quality publication that made itself accessible to a wider audience. Yet an examination of its content, even during the early years of John Brisben Walker's reign, shows a combination of "Kipling and Kitsch,"[40] a hybrid of discourses, from the quality magazine's emphasis on cultural uplift to the independent newspaper tradition of political education to the sensational newspaper's focus on personality and human interest.

The success of *Cosmopolitan* (it had a circulation of 300,000 by 1897) was attributed not to a departure from the genteel publications but to the building of its own printing plant and the use of advertising as a primary source of revenue rather than to subscription price. This "radical departure in offering the public a magazine of the highest class for ten cents" was portrayed as an "educational movement of the greatest importance." Like *McClure's* and *Munsey's*, the editors of *Cosmopolitan* also promoted their quality illustrations and their aim to "give the best in thought, literature and art." While less vociferous than *Munsey's*, *Cosmopolitan* also portrayed itself as timely, engaged in the world of current affairs and "manly." The article reminded its readers that the editors were on the lookout "for what is new and interesting—ever on the alert lest something of great thought or charming literary quality may escape them."[41]

After the sale of *Cosmopolitan* to Hearst in 1905, there was a monthly "Shop Talk" editorial feature. In the February 1906 issue, the readers were told that *Cosmopolitan* had reached the 400,000 circulation mark. How, asked the editor rhetorically, has this been possible? It is because "of the character of the contributors—the men and women behind the pen—and their recognized ability to discuss vital things in a vital way. Vital things! Ah, how many subjects that have no vitality—no real human interest—are discussed in the magazines!"

Advertising was presented to popular magazine readers as a means to keep in touch with the "moving spirit of the times." Munsey devoted considerable attention in the "Publisher's Desk," as well as in special articles, to a discussion of the latest in modern advertising in an effort to counter some of the more common resistances to advertising. It was still necessary in 1894 to justify including a large number of pages of advertising in a magazine, even if they were included in a special section at the end. Advertising, argued Munsey, was an expression of his magazine's desire to "reflect the best of contemporary thought." Advertising provides "a photograph of contemporary and foreign

MUNSEY'S MAGAZINE.

VOL. X. MARCH, 1894. No. 6.

MODERN ARTISTS AND THEIR WORK.

Some of the famous pictures by Hans Makart and others, which were shown at the World's Fair, and other characteristic canvases by painters of the day, are given in a fine series of engravings.

By C. Stuart Johnson.

"To Arcadia!"

From the painting by Wilhelm Kray.

ONE of the signs of the popular development of the art education of the western world is conveyed in the fact that we of today view without offense pictures and statues that our ancestors would have regarded as of questionable propriety. No one seriously supposes that this change of taste is due to any lessening of morality or of modesty. It comes simply and solely from a widening of our knowledge, a greater familiarity with the world of art, and a better understanding of its canons.

It is almost difficult to realize, now, how sweeping was the old fashioned prejudice against anything that could be classed as "the nude in art," and into what recent times its sway extended. A little more than twenty years ago, when Hiram Powers' great work, the "Greek Slave," was brought to his native country for exhibition, as soon as it left the Atlantic coast cities it was among a people who, practically speaking, had never seen an undraped statue before. When it came to Cincinnati a delegation of clergymen was sent to make a preliminary inspection of it, and to report whether it "should be countenanced by religious people." It seems positively ludicrous,

enterprise . . . for the reader who rightly interprets it." Through advertising the reader may "keep abreast of the times." By 1895 Munsey was asserting "the dignity of advertising." The most significant development was that advertising was "designed for mediums of general circulation—not to local advertising." The advertiser is no longer, Munsey claimed, the patent medicine confidence man (though advertising abuses were still rampant during this period) but

Munsey's, "Modern Artists and Their Work." This was a popular feature in *Munsey's,* in part because it provided the publisher with an opportunity to show readers half-dressed models (*Munsey's,* March 1894, p. 562).

respectable businessmen and educators of the public. "It is through him [the advertiser] that the reader keeps in touch with progress, with the trend of prices, with inventions and improvements and these mean something to the man who would spend his money wisely."[42]

In a speech devoted to "Advertising in Some of Its Phases,"[43] Munsey hailed the advent of national advertising and the "tendency toward concentration" in

THE COSMOPOLITAN.

From every man according to his ability: to everyone according to his needs.

VOL. XIV. JANUARY, 1893. No. III.

THE MAKING OF AN ILLUSTRATED MAGAZINE.

THIS number of The Cosmopolitan, the first of the fifth year since the purchase of the magazine by Mr. John Brisben Walker, will be issued from its own printing-house. The edition of 150,000 copies has been prepared upon presses designed expressly for the finest work and manufactured throughout by the most improved machinery—folding-machines, stitching-machines, smashers, revolving gathering-table, cutters, and a covering-machine with a capacity of 20,000 magazines per diem, all being the most complete that are constructed for the making of an illustrated magazine of the highest class. They are designed especially for magazine work, and constitute one of the most perfect magazine plants in the world. Not only is the machinery of the best, but the workshop is of the brightest and healthiest, lighted by a hundred and forty-five windows, free to the sunshine. Most satisfactory of all, however, is this: there are no employés of The Cosmopolitan, from the highest to the lowest, working more than eight hours a day.

It may not be uninteresting to our read-

John Brisben Walker's *Cosmopolitan:* an early issue informing readers of how the magazine was produced (*Cosmopolitan,* January 1893, p. 259).

industry. The wave of business consolidations and mergers was, for Munsey, a progressive development since it eliminated the middleman and brought the producer and consumer closer together. Advertising, as Munsey acutely observed, would become a necessity as large firms, with high fixed costs, would need to reach out to national markets in order to maintain a high level of sales. After outlining some of the recent developments in advertising, he devoted most of his speech to an attack on abuses of advertising agencies and inflated circulation figures of many of his competitors. Despite the abuses, he argued that the magazine was an ideal medium of advertising since it reached a national audience and the costs of magazine advertising were comparatively less than running ads in a variety of daily newspapers.

In a 1902 article on "Beauty in Advertising Illustration," Walker commented on the "vast sums of money" spent on magazine advertising. He attributed this to the realization "years ago" by advertisers that magazines reached a "large class of busy people" during their leisure hours when their minds are "free from business cares" and "free to accept new impressions." The article was an enthusiastic description of the "genius employed in their [advertisements] preparation fully equal to that bestowed on the reading matter of the magazine." The focus of the article was "advertising illustration," and this provided Walker with the opportunity of showing off his magazine's halftone reproductions of a series of women modeling "summer parasols," hats, and so on. The only qualification in this enthusiastic treatment of advertising came near the end of the article where Walker reassured readers that "never a taint of commercialism appears in the text" of the leading magazines. Somewhat defensively, Walker pointed out that the public is not aware of the sacrifices made by magazine publishers when they reject thousands of dollars of advertising because of "unsound schemes and articles injurious to men and women."[44]

In short, advertising was promoted by editors such as Munsey and Walker as having artistic and educational merit. This was not entirely disingenuous, at least not during this early period in the development of advertising. Both editors thought of advertising as part of the progressive movement of society to a more organized and cooperative form. Advertising allowed the new national corporations to sell to large markets and kept the public informed of advances in new technology. Moreover, Munsey and Walker took pains to reassure readers that their editorial decisions could not be purchased and that they exercised judgment in deciding what advertisements to print.

For Munsey advertising was a central part of a publishing "revolution" that he started when he lowered the price of *Munsey's* to ten cents. This business decision was presented as a popular and democratic revolution in publishing (*McClure's* claimed the credit for being the first to lower its price below the twenty cents mark to fifteen cents). Munsey argued that this price reduction was made possible because of a bold decision to eliminate the "middleman," the distribution monopoly held by the American News Company. Moreover, Munsey boasted that his magazine carried more and higher-quality illustrations[45] than any other, claiming to demonstrate this fact with comparative charts showing the number of pages of illustrations of his main competitors.[46]

Despite being the circulation leader during the 1890s, Munsey complained about his problems in attracting advertising. He attributed this to the "wretched system of bribery" among publishers and advertising agents in which he refused to participate.[47] *Munsey's* problems in attracting advertising may have also been because advertisers thought of *Munsey's* as a "lowbrow" magazine and sought readers with higher incomes. *McClure's,* which never exceeded 400,000 in circulation, led in amount of advertising. According to business manager Albert Brady, *McClure's* carried the "largest amount of advertising of any magazine in the world."[48] Some of this success may have been a result of businesses that had advertised with the *Century* and other quality magazines turning to its nearest and more successful competitor—*McClure's.* In addition, *McClure's* advertising rates were considered a "good buy." Far more than *Munsey's, McClure's* contained a critical, antibusiness edge in large part because of the contributions of Hamlin Garland and Stephen Crane but also as a result of some of the fiction. Heavy reliance on advertising did not seem to interfere with this emphasis, at least during *McClure's* first decade.

A New Conception of Culture

A structural equivalence between Eastern, feminine, past, dull, and sickly on the one hand and virility, masculinity, Western, timely, and lively on the other was explicit throughout *Munsey's* "Publisher's Desk" commentaries as well as in the editorial features of the other magazines. American politics was intensely sectional and there were undoubtedly political connotations in any opposition between West and East. But the "West" also had a mythic dimension that carried with it images of the frontier and rugged individualism, the cutting edge for scientific exploration and economic development, and an escape from the restraints of civilization.[49] Moreover, the cultural center of the country had already begun to shift to the West. Many of the leading writers, including Hamlin Garland who wrote frequently for the leading popular magazines, were from Western areas of the country. Chicago became a center for some of the leading journalists and writers—Theodore Dreiser, Finley Peter Dunne,[50] and Henry Blake Fuller, to name a few.[51] One critic observed that *Cosmopolitan*'s "unconventional spirit" made the magazine "popular with our western folk. It has a true Western adaptability, fertility of resource and quickness in seizing a point, all of which tend to dismay the more staid eastern mind."[52]

Implicit in this series of contrasts was a conception of American culture that departed in some respects from the Victorian view discussed in the previous chapter. As Trachtenberg points out, culture for the Victorian gentry "filtered downward from a distant past, from overseas, from the sacred founts of wealth and private power."[53] The association of this conception of culture with femininity was well understood; the idea that middle-class women were a "civilizing" force was central to the creed of domesticity propagated by Catherine Beecher and others. In contrast, popular magazines were projecting themselves as fearless innovators throwing off the old conservatism by immersing themselves in contemporary developments in politics, literature, and society. "Culture," while not a term used often within the popular magazine, was implicitly redefined. It now seemed to stand for the combination of attributes that most worried the Victorian gentry—the dynamism and energy of urban life, popular amusements and entertainment, and scientific and technological progress. Rather than straining to maintain the boundary between genteel culture and the "masses," popular magazines were, rather unselfconsciously, blurring this boundary. The notion of culture as a civilizing force, a repository of learning and refinement, was not entirely absent in the popular magazines, but it was to play a secondary role. In their emphasis on "keeping in touch with the moving spirit of the times," popular magazines defined, implicitly, culture as a process, something in the making, rather than a heritage that reassured a select group of readers that they were connected to a stable past.[54]

Much has been said about the fin de siècle obsession with virility, forcefulness, and vitality. Ann Douglas observes near the conclusion of her much discussed work, *The Feminization of American Culture,* that by the last two decades of the nineteenth century there was a reaction against the secluded domestic world of sentimental literature as well as the domestic realism of Howells and others.[55] John Higham has argued that there was a "profound spiritual reaction" against the "restrictions of a highly industrial society" among the middle class.[56] In a broader sense, concerns were expressed throughout the quality magazines during the 1890s, with regard to "overcivilization." This is a complex issue, but certainly part of the meaning of "overcivilization" was the feeling of a loss of individual mastery ("willpower") in an increasingly rationalized and bureaucratized society. It is not surprising that the restraints of civilization would be associated with the East (the most economically developed region) and with the middle-class home and femininity (both of which were thought of as civilizing forces). *Munsey's* call for "real stories" that were plainly written was clearly an effort to appeal to this larger sense of "dis-ease" among the middle class.[57] Vigorous outdoor sports, Social Darwinism, the more vigorous Christianity of Billy Sunday, the mythologizing of Teddy Roosevelt's charge on San Juan Hill all attested to this emphasis in the larger stream of American culture. *Cosmopolitan,* especially, printed numerous articles on the American military and the Boer War, and of course all three magazines covered the Spanish-American War with intense interest. The upper-class "martial ethic" had made its way to a broader public through the pages of the popular magazine.[58] This will be the focus of chapter 5, but it can be observed for now that popular magazine editors and publishers were able to construct an image for their publications that tapped into this new sensibility.

During the 1890s, popular magazines conveyed to their readers a sense of energy and vitality in large part through a nonfictional form of "realism" that emphasized authenticity and experience. The first-person accounts of travels to Homestead or in "the depths" of a coal mine or on an ocean liner or on a trip around the world with Elizabeth Bisland suggested that readers wanted not only information but firsthand accounts of an event or a "problem," interspersed with "inside information." A number of these accounts also suggested that authenticity—the view that "truth" comes from one's own experience—was beginning to challenge the genteel view of the "truth" as an idealized expression of life. Hamlin Garland's effort to convey his reactions to the conditions at Homestead, and the subsequent article written by one of the workmen, clearly implied a standard of authenticity—that a firsthand account could be trusted more than an editorial diatribe or a moralistic exhortation.

Elements of the *McClure's* approach of giving the reader a behind-the-scenes look (often through interviews) into the private homes of famous literary figures or the way a circus actually works, or the way a children's book is written were borrowed from the newspaper "human interest story," a technique that dated back to the 1870s if not to the penny press of the 1830s.[59] The human interest story was intended to bring famous and "interesting personalities" closer to readers by giving them a glimpse of the public figure's private life. Gradually, magazines provided a new kind of human interest story.[60] In addition to the feature that encouraged an interest in the wealthy and powerful, *McClure's* began to look behind the scenes (through articles and fiction) at the urban poor.[61]

As discussed throughout this chapter, popular magazines were not complete departures from the genteel nineteenth-century magazine. Instead they were a hybrid, a collage of at least three elements borrowed from other media. The merging of these media texts was one important way in which the boundary between "high" culture and the "popular" culture was blurred. On the one hand, as we have seen, popular magazines retained the genteel focus on "high culture" through prominent articles on American and European artists as well as features on English and American poets and novelists of the past. This was the genteel discourse of "cultural uplift" (as discussed in chapters 1 and 2). The appeal of independent journalism to the "nonpartisan" educated reader was the second discourse that influenced the popular magazine. Developed during the 1870s and 1880s to counter the influence of the party-dominated press, the independent newspapers pioneered in distinguishing editorials and news, and emphasized the presentation of "decontextualized" information to an audience of educated readers.

On the other hand, the focus on "human interest," "great personalities," editorial stunts, and contests were expressions of the "sensational" newspaper discourse, developed first by Pulitzer and intended to appeal to a working-class and immigrant audience.[62] In various ways, by the mid-1880s, newspapers had encouraged a sense of reader participation, breaking down the "aura" that surrounded Victorian print culture. Headlines in the *New York World* appealed to its readers' fascination with the grisly details of crime and the shocking revelations of a sexual scandal. The liberal use of puns in headlines and articles showed a playful disregard for the "proper" use of language.[63] Overall, sensational journalism departed in important ways from the "culture of self control," order, and rationality that characterized Victorian print culture.[64] Popular magazines did not, by any stretch of the imagination, go as far as Pulitzer in shocking and scandalizing their readers but presented a "dignified" version of the "sensational newspaper" style.

The Popular Magazine Reader, Real and Implied

While there were many areas of continuity between the quality and the popular magazines, it is important to understand why these publications seemed to resonate with a new group of readers. After all, the quality magazines had hovered around the 200,000 circulation mark for decades. But *Munsey's* was able to increase its circulation to 500,000 in a few years. It is possible of course that the price change alone accounts for the increase in circulation, and that surely had a lot to do with it. But such an "explanation" is hardly adequate since it explains only that magazines were affordable, not what kept people reading them. Another attraction was the emphasis on halftone illustrations and photographs. Walker was a strong advocate of the halftone method of illustration over wood engraving[65] (the fact that it was a lot cheaper was rarely mentioned), and Munsey saw the popular magazine as a better-illustrated version of a Sunday newspaper supplement.

Who were these new readers? There were no surveys of readers until much later, but we can ask who the editors and contributors thought were reading their magazines. *Munsey's* seemed to be particularly oriented toward urban readers, or at least toward readers who were interested in such topics as "The Playground of the Metropolis,"[66] "New York's Riverside Park,"[67] "Ball Giving in New York."[68] The focus on wealthy urban families, theater, public buildings, and vacation resorts of the rich were also common features in the largest-circulation New York newspapers. It is quite likely that Munsey, who was a newspaper man himself, was aiming for the growing population of new urban residents. Many of these people were "shop girls," clerical workers, workers in sales, and others employed in the growing white-collar segment of the labor force (the number of white-collar workers expanded sixfold from 1870 to 1900).

All three magazines, especially *Cosmopolitan,* carried articles that seemed to assume an audience of educated readers; "Choosing a Profession," "Problems of Education," "Should Your Boy Go to College?" as well as an assortment of literary themes and analyses of political developments. It is quite likely that both middle-class professionals as well as white-collar workers (often called "middle class") were attracted to popular magazines for differing reasons. Before advertising agencies developed departments for market research and audit bureaus for determining magazine circulation, it is likely that magazines experimented with articles directed to a variety of audiences.[69]

Joseph Pulitzer had said that he was aiming his paper "for the masses and not for the classes."[70] By that he meant that anyone should be able to enjoy his newspaper. He also seemed to be rejecting narrow appeals to the "cultured" and the educated middle class. But magazines were clearly not aiming for the same immigrant, working-class audience that read the *New York World.* At the same time, it is likely that they were moving beyond the highly educated middle-class Eastern audiences that had read *Harper's Monthly* or *Century.* Some articles were clearly intended to placate highbrow critics[71] and confirmed the pattern set by the quality magazines, while others were genuine expressions of the editor's politics and desire to educate readers. The mass-circulation newspapers, especially Pulitzer's *New York World* and Hearst's *New York Journal,* showed what kind of articles and format could expand circulation to a largely urban audience. McClure, Walker, and Munsey developed their own "dignified" version of this sensationalism, which may have appealed to a less-educated group of white-collar workers, who aspired to live like the people described in *Munsey's* articles on seaport resorts.

Cyrus Hermann Curtis, publisher of *Ladies' Home Journal,* claimed in 1893 that a majority of *Journal* readers lived in the suburbs of large cities and that many of his small-town readers "belonged to the professional ranks."[72] We must be a bit suspicious of these claims since they were intended in part to attract advertising, but it is reasonable to conclude that readers were middle class or white-collar working class and likely to live in urban areas. William Allen White had no interest in boosting the circulation of *McClure's* when in his autobiography he observed of the *McClure's* staff, "They were making a magazine for our kind—the literate middle class."[73] Edward Bok, editor of the *Ladies' Home Journal,* did not want to place advertisements for his magazine in newspapers with a "high grade constituency," preferring to reach a "broad middle-class" audience.[74] In a conversation with his friend Ellery Sedgwick, then editor of the *Atlantic Monthly,* Bok disclosed that *Ladies' Home Journal* had some of the same Boston–Beacon Street subscribers as *Atlantic Monthly.* "But there is a difference," said Bok. "You see, Sedgwick, you go in at the front door, and I at the back. I know my place."[75]

Another way of understanding the popular magazine reader is to utilize the concept of the "implied reader" developed by reader reception theorists. According to the leading proponent of this view, every "text" anticipates, in various ways, particular reader responses and characteristics.[76] This does not have to be an intentional process. Instead, the very act of writing or producing a text presupposes a reader with a certain level of background knowledge and cultural competence. Even more than this, though, every text constructs a "subject position" for its readers.[77] The popular magazine can be thought of as constructing three main subject positions or social identities for its readers:

the reader as spectator and consumer, the reader as a client of professional expertise, and the reader as member of a "public."

According to the historian Richard Hofstadter, urban newspapers of the late nineteenth century appealed to the "rural mind's" fascination with the spectacle of urban life. It has also been argued that newspapers were a modern equivalent of village gossip, making an increasingly complex urban world more human and intelligible.[78] Joseph Pulitzer, publisher of the *New York World,* used headlines, stunts, and halftone photographs to "provide a window out into the larger world outside the narrow circle of the immigrant community."[79]

George Juergens has argued that many of the techniques developed by Joseph Pulitzer's *New York World* in the mid-1880s were adaptations not only to cultural competence and the rural background of immigrants but to the changing experience of city life.[80] During this period the trolley and other forms of urban transportation allowed the middle class to live in suburbs and commute to the city. Juergens suggests that newspapers adapted to the novel experience of viewing the city from these trolleys, a perspective that urban dwellers did not have a generation earlier. The large headlines, use of pictures, short articles, and simple language of the sensational New York newspapers were also an adaptation to reading on moving "omnibuses." Of course, magazines were not newspapers and could not easily be digested in a few minutes on a railway line traveling to and from work. But traveling to work every day and viewing from the window of a railway car the changes in the social and built environments of the city may have created a "way of seeing" the world (as a spectator) that popular magazines reflected and perhaps contributed to.

Popular magazines conveyed the kind of voyeuristic awe of a tourist or spectator or, more specifically, a tourist from a small town visiting a big city. *Cosmopolitan*'s breathless descriptions of the "Wonders of New York," or the descriptions of world's fairs and expositions, reflected an obvious awe and fascination with the symbols of "progress." *Cosmopolitan* carried a multipart, tongue-in-cheek tour of New York "from the deck of the Rubberneck coach." On the third trip, the spectators were taken to Wall Street.[81] *Munsey's* exhibited this quality more than the other two magazines. Pieces like "Behind the Scenes in the Big Stores" and "Broadway's Grenadiers," which appeared in *Munsey's* during 1899, seemed to reflect the awe-struck view of the small-town tourist. Moreover, the many travel articles on foreign and "exotic" places addressed readers explicitly as spectators in a foreign land. For the tourist and the spectator, sights and sensations are a continuous surprise. Their world is not a taken-for-granted one but a dazzling spectacle.

Readers were addressed not only as urban spectators but as consumers. As Theodore Dreiser described so vividly in *Sister Carrie,* city life was also experienced as a dazzling spectacle of consumer goods. Dreiser describes Carrie's first experience with a department store.

> Carrie passed along the busy aisles, much affected by the remarkable display of trinkets, dress goods, shoes, stationary, jewelry. Each separate counter was a show-place of dazzling interest and attraction. She could not help feeling the claim of each trinket upon her personally, and yet she could not stop. There was nothing there which she could not have used—nothing which she did not long to own. The dainty slippers and stockings, the delicately frilled skirts and petticoats, the laces, ribbons, hair-combs, purses, all touched her with individual desire, and she felt keenly the fact that not any of these things were within the range of her purchase.[82]

The city as a center of consumption could stimulate both desire and envy, an intense awareness of status distinctions. Moreover, everyday life in the modern city, as urban sociologists have observed, sensitizes the urbanite to differences in the outward appearance of other people and to the "world of artifacts" rather than nature.[83] The popular magazine readers' awe at the tall buildings of New York, the mansions of New York's millionaires, the latest in "clothes and fashion," and accounts of urban entertainments from vaudeville to popular music may not have approached the intensity of Carrie's experience, but it may have reminded readers of their own excitement, envy, and desire in viewing the urban spectacle of consumption.

The popular magazines took a variety of stances toward their readers, but one that was to assume an ever-greater importance was the expert or the therapist helping the bewildered reader cope with the problems of modern life.[84] *Cosmopolitan* helped readers to "Choose a Profession," purchase a house, stay healthy, and keep up with the rising cost of living. Many of these articles were clearly directed toward female readers ("The Art of Buying Food for a Family," "The Art of Delightful Cooking"). Articles by G. Stanley Hall ("What Is to Become of Your Baby?") and an assortment of doctors telling readers how to stay healthy reflected the growing importance of professionals and the reliance of middle-class men and women on them. Other articles described for readers new technology or told them about the way products were made and

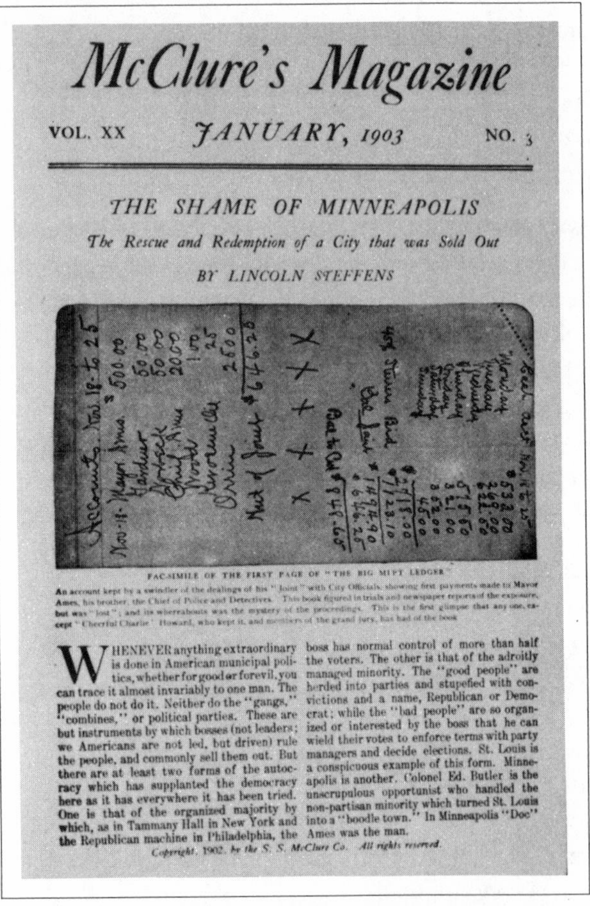

McClure's Magazine

VOL. XX JANUARY, 1903 NO. 3

THE SHAME OF MINNEAPOLIS

The Rescue and Redemption of a City that was Sold Out

BY LINCOLN STEFFENS

FAC-SIMILE OF THE FIRST PAGE OF "THE BIG MITT LEDGER"

An account kept by a swindler of the dealings of his "Joint" with City Officials, showing first payments made to Mayor Ames, his brother, the Chief of Police and Detectives. This book figured in trials and newspaper reports of the exposure, but was "lost"; and its whereabouts was the mystery of the proceedings. This is the first glimpse that any one, except "Cheerful Charlie" Howard, who kept it, and members of the grand jury, has had of the book

WHENEVER anything extraordinary is done in American municipal politics, whether for good or for evil, you can trace it almost invariably to one man. The people do not do it. Neither do the "gangs," "combines," or political parties. These are but instruments by which bosses (not leaders; we Americans are not led, but driven) rule the people, and commonly sell them out. But there are at least two forms of the autocracy which has supplanted the democracy here as it has everywhere it has been tried. One is that of the organized majority by which, as in Tammany Hall in New York and the Republican machine in Philadelphia, the boss has normal control of more than half the voters. The other is that of the adroitly managed minority. The "good people" are herded into parties and stupefied with convictions and a name, Republican or Democrat; while the "bad people" are so organized or interested by the boss that he can wield their votes to enforce terms with party managers and decide elections. St. Louis is a conspicuous example of this form. Minneapolis is another. Colonel Ed. Butler is the unscrupulous opportunist who handled the non-partisan minority which turned St. Louis into a "boodle town." In Minneapolis "Doc" Ames was the man.

Copyright, 1902, by the S. S. McClure Co. All rights reserved.

S. S. McClure's most famous issue. Appearing here were three of the magazine's most talked-about muckraking series, including Lincoln Steffens's "Shame of the Cities" (*McClure's*, January 1903).

distributed. The purpose of this advice was in part to demystify for readers the new urban world of production and consumption, but it also spoke to growing concerns about psychological and physical health.

Alvin Gouldner has argued that "the emergence of the mass media and of the 'public' are mutually constructive developments."Members of "traditional groups" interact with one another, fostering "common understandings and shared interests." A public "refers to a number of people exposed to the same social stimuli, and having something in common even without being in persisting personal interaction with one another." The development of the mass media, according to Gouldner, marked the beginning of cultural communities linked not by shared interaction but by "shared information." Information is "decontextualized" communication, presented so that it is intelligible to diverse groups of people.[85]

Popular magazines addressed their readers not as party loyalists and certainly not in the language of class solidarity (a discourse found primarily in the labor press). Moreover, they began to depart from the genteel magazines which, as we have seen, addressed readers as members of a common subcultural community. Instead, popular magazines readers were addressed as citizens of a nation and called upon to redress a series of national problems—from the conditions of working women to business bribery and fraud, political corruption, public health issues, crime, and so on. An S. S. McClure editorial (one of the few he wrote), introducing three articles on "lawlessness" among workers, capitalists, and political bosses, ended by proclaiming, "There is no one left; none but all of us. . . . We forget that we all are the people."[86] Lincoln Steffens maintained that the "good people" who are "herded into parties" are as responsible for political corruption as the "bad people" who do the work of the political boss.[87] Even before muckraking, many popular magazine articles had a political but "nonpartisan" tone in that they appealed to readers' concerns about particular issues and problems, educating them about these issues and, at times, arousing their indignation. The assumption was that learning the "facts" about a problem would lead to some kind of political action—either voting, participating in voluntary associations of various kinds, or demanding legislation and other forms of government intervention.

What was this category of "the people" used so often by popular magazine editors and contributors? The meaning of this category had little connection to the populist conception of "the people" as the powerless and excluded majority arrayed the privileged few. Instead "the people" were the educated citizenry, at times slumbering and apathetic, at other times mobilized for action. They were open to rational persuasion and to the marshaling of facts and evidence, much of which came from the new academic disciplines of social science. Popular magazines assumed that "the people" had a cosmopolitan rather than localistic view of politics, an assumption that followed from the focus on social problems that were national and not merely local in scope.

Our story now takes us into the offices of the popular magazine editors and publishers, the "cultural entrepreneurs" who fashioned a new medium of information and entertainment for a national audience. But we will not be able to find them sitting in their offices reading manuscripts. So grab your hat and coat, as we explore the popular editors' venture into the "whirlpool of real life."

CHAPTER FOUR

"The Whirlpool of Real Life": The Popular Magazine Project

This chapter explores the popular magazine project from the vantage point of the cultural entrepreneurs who created it. The focus is on John Brisben Walker, a man strangely neglected by scholars interested in popular magazines. The chapter will also focus on S. S. McClure, the energetic force behind *McClure's*, and Frank Munsey, the publishing tycoon who turned his magazine, in large part, into a celebration of success and the spectacle of urban life. In their roles as publishers and editors, these men were cultural entrepreneurs, mobilizing cultural and economic resources, seeking out timely stories, new authors, and new ideas.

While the thrust of this chapter is to treat the three magazines and their editors as a composite, there were significant differences. Frank Munsey and his magazine were never a part of the mainstream of "Progressive" social reform thought. While supporting the Progressive party financially in 1912 and believing that organization in industry was the wave of the future, his magazine said little about the social and political questions and reform movements that were on the minds of so many Americans after 1902. For Munsey the popular magazine was primarily a vehicle for the energy of economic expansion and the opportunities it afforded readers as consumers and producers. On the other hand, Walker and McClure as editors, and in part through the pages of their magazines, gave expression to a growing "civic consciousness," a desire to heal the wounds afflicting American society during the 1890s and the turn of the century.

Of particular interest in this chapter is Walker's view of the popular magazine as an "educator" and its relationship to what he thought of as a new "political economic order." Education as an institution and through the medium of magazines could serve a central role in this new order in educating voters and citizens, preparing young men and women for careers, introducing them to the rapidly changing world of science and technology, and helping them live their everyday lives. For Walker the state, schools, and modern "mass communications" would help citizens to make the transition to this social order. While outsiders to Eastern literary culture, popular magazine editors were enthusiastic advocates of "progress" who identified themselves and their magazines in a variety of ways with national rather than regional developments. In their promotion of science and technology, activist government and social efficiency, popular magazine editors expressed a perspective often identified with an emerging professional-managerial elite. But this perspective had an appeal that cut across class and other social divisions.

All three publishers sought to take their readers into the "whirlpool of real life." Walker's colorful phrase had its positive and negative connotations. The "whirlpool" could connote energy, engagement with life, a willingness to dive head first into the many mysteries of the city, the romance of industrial enterprise, the underside of politics. Another positive connotation of "whirlpool" was energy in contrast to rigid formalism. All through the country, after the depression of 1893, there was a questioning and a rethinking of American institutions. While this will be discussed in greater depth in chapters 6 and 7, for now it can be noted that economists were challenging the principles of classical political economy, journalists and sociologists were investigating the conditions of the urban poor and calling into question the association of poverty with moral depravity, advocates of the Social Gospel movement began to challenge the traditional Protestant emphasis on saving souls and proposed instead to change society, and educational reformers were questioning the reliance on rote memorization and the classics in American schools and began to reach out to the working class and urban poor. Moreover, Americans were flocking to university extension courses, women's clubs, and other voluntary associations to learn about these developments. Old dogmas could perhaps be shaken by this "real life" whirlpool of energy. But the whirlpool, or what some called the "vortex,"[1] could also connote annihilation rather than constructive change. How could middle-class readers cope with the disintegration of the coherent society and culture with which they had been brought up? Swirling in this whirlpool or "vortex" were the forces tearing American society apart, from the instability of a largely unregulated economic system to the often violent class conflict disrupting industrial life. By the end of the 1890s there were the "trusts," which seemed to be acquiring an amount of wealth and power that could present a danger to the "Republic." As S. S. McClure put it in his famous article, America was disintegrating into "lawlessness."

The emphasis on "real life" expressed, in part, a desire to overcome the class divisions that had been central to the genteel tradition. The lower orders or the urban, immigrant poor were thought of, largely by the mugwumps, as a political threat to good government or as an object of moral reform to be civilized and uplifted. As we have seen, the mugwumps also mistrusted the enormous wealth of the "captains of industry." But in various ways, popular magazines broke from this tradition in their project of presenting to their readers glimpses of the worlds of scientific and technological wonders, urban abundance, poverty and the lives of immigrants. The popular magazines' focus on "real life" (in the form of vigorous historical romances or human interest stories of Homestead steelworkers or accounts of captains of industry) was an expression of the growing discontent with the bloodless aestheticism and moralism of the genteel tradition.

John Brisben Walker and the "Whirlpool of Real Life"

John Brisben Walker attended Georgetown College and the U.S. Military Academy. He resigned his cadetship in order to serve as a military adviser in China from 1868 to 1870. He made and lost a fortune in iron manufacturing (Kanawha Valley, West Virginia) and later became successful in Denver real estate. Walker ran for the U.S. Congress in 1872. He wrote a number of articles for Murat Halstead's *Cincinnati Commercial,* which led to a position as managing editor of the *Pittsburgh Telegraph* in 1876. From 1876 to 1879 he was managing editor of the *Washington Chronicle.* He organized the Mobile Company of America in 1899 and built an automobile factory at Philipse Manor, New York. Walker was the first president of the Automobile Manufacturers'

Association and an organizer of a national highway commission. He also was the first president of the American Periodical Publishers' Association.[2]

Unlike the genteel editor, John Brisben Walker was active in looking for new features, in bidding for popular authors, in promoting his magazine, and in promoting personal ideas and projects. In 1891, in order to promote his newly bought publication, he hired a railroad coach filled with canvassers. He offered college scholarships to successful *Cosmopolitan* salespeople. In 1892 he sent editorial staff member Elizabeth Bisland on a trip around the world. She reported back in a series of articles. "The idea crystallized in Mr. Walker's brain between Jersey City and Cortlandt street on the morning that Miss Nellie Bly, of the *New York World* fame, began her 'globe-trotting' experience."[3] In a more spectacular vein he sent former Spanish consul Hobart C. Chatfield to Spain to offer $100 million for the liberation of Cuba. Needless to say, the Spanish government refused the offer, but Walker received valuable publicity. Walker offered a $3,000 prize in 1896 for the best "horseless carriage." The contest took place on May 30, 1896, and at the event were a host of dignitaries who acted as "*Cosmopolitan* judges." In the March 1902 issue he informed his readers that "under the direction of the *Cosmopolitan,* the preliminary work has begun in Europe and America looking to the assemblage of 'A World's Congress,' " which would consist of one hundred representatives of the world's nations. The *Cosmopolitan* would organize this congress and send out "nominations, representing the highest thought and most practical statesmanship of all nations." While this can be thought of as a wildly impractical idea, or perhaps a publicity stunt, Walker's extensive military and diplomatic contacts and his sincere internationalist perspective made this at least a partially serious proposal. Like the New York editors of the "sensational" newspapers—Pulitzer and Hearst—Walker was not content to report the news but also sought on occasion to make it. Like Pulitzer,[4] Walker defended some of his more sensational journalistic devices as necessary in order to create a large circulation so that readers would benefit from some of the more serious, educational features.[5] While this may appear to be a rationalization, designed to appease his more highbrow critics, there is no reason to believe that Walker was not sincere in his view of *Cosmopolitan*'s mission.

Both William Randolph Hearst (who succeeded Walker as publisher of the *Cosmopolitan*) and Walker were quite similar politically, at least for this period. In 1896 both supported William Jennings Bryan against William McKinley, a very unusual position for upper-class Easterners who were generally protariff and opposed to the Democratic party's "free silver" plank. Hearst's New York office was Bryan's unofficial Eastern campaign headquarters while Bryan stayed at Walker's house during a campaign visit to New York.[6] By 1901 Walker was an enthusiastic supporter of Republican Theodore Roosevelt.[7] Like other upper-class reformers, Walker was not wedded to one political party. In other articles Walker made clear his support for the nonpartisan political style that the mugwumps had helped to popularize.[8]

Walker's imprint on *Cosmopolitan* was unmistakable. Ellery Sedgwick remembered the first time he met Walker when he was the young editor of *Leslie's.*

> If there were giants in those days, John Brisben Walker was an admirable specimen. He was eccentric but he was impressive. He it was who had first cut the magazine quarter in two and offered the Cosmopolitan at twelve and a half cents a copy, a revolutionary though singularly inconvenient price, squeezed down to ten when Munsey's took the final inevitable step. His extensive printing plant stood at the gates of his mansion house at Irvington-on-the-Hudson. His Cosmopolitan sold and deserved to sell four copies to Leslie's one. He was rich. He was feared. It was rumored that he was the stiffest man in New York to work for, and he certainly looked the part. Six feet odd inches tall, straight as an athlete, he would not have lacked for backers in any prize ring. All sorts of picturesque legends surrounded him. On each birthday past his prime he would jump a four-barred gate and remark that he was good for another year.[9]

While S. S. McClure was the manic force behind the scenes, Walker's name was everywhere to be found within the pages of the magazine. Some of these pieces were quite similar to features commonly found in other publications while others were unique to Walker's *Cosmopolitan.* An 1892 piece, "The Homestead Object Lesson,"[10] advocated a national income tax, government control of the railroads and telegraph lines, and criticized the vast "inequalities of wealth." His criticism of Henry Clay Frick's use of force in breaking the Homestead strike didn't pull any punches.

> Raised up under the system which declares that any man has a right to control without limit the earth's surface and its productions, or the labor of his fellow men, Mr. Frick doubtless feels that he is performing a sacred duty in protecting his property at Homestead by any means that the law permits. Thousands of good men held the same thought regarding their slaves during the war.[11]

Later in the article Walker spoke of Terrance Powderly, leader of the Knights of Labor, the largest labor organization in the country, as a "statesman of the highest order." Upon the death of John Altgeld, the Democratic governor of Illinois who pardoned the Haymarket prisoners, he wrote a very sympathetic short eulogy, even though he realized that Altgeld "was without doubt the most unpopular man who was ever in American public life" and "even if it meant that a certain number of my readers would stop their subscriptions or loose confidence in the judgment of the editor."[12] Walker's unusually prolabor views were, nevertheless, from an upper-class perspective. He made it clear the labor vote had been "purchased" by the big city machines and that the success of labor depended on intelligent, independent voting. The magazine managed to retain a nonpartisan (independent of any political party) but not nonpolitical tone, despite Walker's frequent editorial comment.

Walker's most interesting project, promoted over many months, was his idea for a "*Cosmopolitan* University." In the April 1897 issue Walker started a series on "Modern College Education: Does It Educate in the Broadest Liberal Sense of the Term?" He wrote the first paper in the series. In this opening article Walker criticized colleges for not preparing students for adult life. "Young men are not prepared to do two things most important to them after college: choose a profession and choose a wife. . . . Plutarch's Lives are not enough." Instead Walker argued that students need "knowledge that can be used, as a guiding oar, when in the whirlpool of real life, the frail boat on which we are embroiled is roughly tossed over foaming waters." More specifically, he recommended courses to help students "choose a profession," more of an emphasis on physical education and, quoting Spencer approvingly, an education not for the gentleman but "one which would aid the young man in life." Following this introductory article were essays by some of the leading college and university presidents on various aspects of higher education reform. In the May issue President Daniel Coit Gilman of Johns Hopkins urged an upgrading of scientific facilities and, like Walker's article, proposed that universities emphasize the development of the body as well as the mind. In subsequent issues President Henry Morton of Stevens Institute of Technology and President Elisha Benjamin Andrews of Brown, among others, presented their proposals and analyses.

The August 1897 issue contained an announcement of a "*Cosmopolitan* University." Walker began by comparing the establishment of a low-priced *Cosmopolitan* five years earlier "with an educational movement of the most far-reaching importance, designed to bring literature and art of the highest character within the reach of every household." Now, proclaimed Walker, *Cosmopolitan* had reached "a new stage in its evolution." *Cosmopolitan* would take on the responsibility to bring a university education to the millions who "desire for broader education . . . yet have not the means for entrance at the universities." His idea was to provide the funds for a correspondence school with a distinguished advisory board and an assortment of the top university faculty. In the September issue Walker announced that Elisha Benjamin Andrews of Brown had agreed to be president of *Cosmopolitan* University. Students would be allowed to attend free of charge. By October 1897, 5,856 students had applied (the eventual number was close to 21,000 by December 1899). Walker claimed that the students "were drawn from every class, ranging from minister of the gospel to hard working mechanics, and covering every profession and division of workers." In a November announcement, Walker presented a breakdown of the occupations of a sample of the students who had enrolled. The majority were professionals but approximately 40 percent were described as "mechanics, clerks, laborers and wives and daughters at home."[13]

Eventually, Walker had to abandon the idea but not because of lack of students or lack of interest from at least some segments of the academic community. On the contrary, there were so many applicants that Walker's financial resources were not adequate for the constantly expanding project. Moreover, President Andrews of Brown University requested and received a release from his contract with *Cosmopolitan,* and this put Walker's plans on hold. By January it had become clear that the popular response was so great (12,000 students by January 1898) that the original amount of money allocated to the project would not be sufficient. He asked each student to contribute five dollars. By the end of 1898 it was clear that without national legislation (a bill for a National Correspondence University was before Congress) the *Cosmopolitan* University could not be started.[14]

The *Cosmopolitan* University is an interesting example of the continuities as well as departures of the new editors from the "quality" magazines. The idea was one with which many of the mugwumps and genteel editors would have been comfortable. After all, they too wanted to use books, newspapers, and other print media to educate the public, to "forge the educated into an organized class." Only an educated middle class, they believed, could counteract the power of the immigrant poor and the corrupt political machines.[15] Walker too wanted to improve the educational level of a largely middle-class readership in order to elevate the quality of a democratic citizenry.[16] Like the mugwumps he assumed that a more educated public would demand better political leaders.[17]

But Walker's tone was decidedly different from the quality magazines. The patronizing quality of the genteel publications was missing in Walker's series on education. Higher education was to be made accessible to the masses, from minister to mechanic. Walker, unlike the mugwumps, did not see the educational mission of his magazine as part of an admittedly upper-class program to make politics less partisan and therefore less accessible to non-upper-class groups. Walker also made it clear that social reforms would have to go far beyond the efforts of the mugwumps for civil service reform, secret ballots in elections, and municipal reform. In style as well, the "correspondence university" owed more to the sensational newspaper style of making news (rather than simply reporting it) and shaking up readers with new schemes and stunts that seemed lively and timely.

Beyond specific projects like the *Cosmopolitan* University, Walker saw his magazine as part of a project of bringing a scientific worldview to the public. Just as "the trust" would replace competitive economic enterprises as a more rational and efficient form of economic organization and just as government would play a role in redistributing wealth and in economic regulation, citizens would need the help of scientists and experts on a range of personal issues. Articles devoted to running a household on a scientific basis, or the series in which well-known representatives from various professions told readers "how to choose a profession," suggest that Walker thought of the popular magazine as part of this new social order. The new social order that Walker believed America was entering would depend on economic specialization and scientific expertise. Americans could no longer rely on older community traditions or educational institutions that refused to prepare young people for the "whirlpool of real life."

In a short essay, Walker urged, with a fair amount of passion, that universities end their reliance on an "out of date" curriculum that emphasized the teaching of Latin and Greek.[18] The ideal reform in higher education, Walker suggested (with some tongue in cheek), would involve professors "laboriously trained to teach Latin and Greek," publicly proclaiming, "Yes we will step down and out, and yield our places to new men who can teach science; giving the new studies the most important place in our university." "The modern man," Walker asserted, "believes that the great body of scientists are the world's truth-seekers." The rest of the essay Walker devoted to demonstrating the importance of a scientific education for a variety of professions including engineering, manufacturing, law, the clergy, and even literature.[19]

A three-page editorial appeared in *Cosmopolitan* (shortly before its sale to William Randolph Hearst) that illustrates Walker's optimistic view that America stood at a crucial juncture in history.[20] We stand, Walker argued, at the point where "machinery and scientific method" hold the promise of eliminating human want and poverty. Formerly, this dream of "a new system of political economy" that would relieve mankind of the struggle for survival was thought of as a mere utopian fantasy, but it is, Walker maintained, now possible. Walker referred to debates about "overproduction" and maintained that such a thing is impossible "until every man, woman and child the world over is comfortably clad, living in a comfortable home . . . and provided with sufficient food to nourish the body properly."

He proposed a "scientifically regulated" system of production to eliminate waste from the production and distribution of goods. Walker indicated that the route to a more scientific method of production and distribution lay in the corporate form of economic organization—"the great trusts."

> The great trusts are rapidly teaching us what can be done by concentration of interests in the hands of intelligent men. The financial powers which control these institutions seek the best brains. No one is allowed to have unlimited sway. The consulting boards bring to bear upon the manager's conduct the criticism of their united wisdom, while the execution, in order to secure greater virility, is left in his hands. Plants in unfavorable locations are abandoned, old machinery is thrown on the scrap heap. Every effort is concentrated upon producing the maximum of product, both quality and quantity, at a minimum price.[21]

Walker shared the view of many that a regulated corporate capitalist system held the utopian promise of eliminating the waste and inequities of the more competitive and unregulated economic system of the "Gilded Age." In an 1899 series, "Great Problems in Organization," Walker commented upon an article by J. P. Morgan. Walker argued that Morgan paid too much attention to "problems of production" and not enough on "how to distribute the results of well organized production."[22] By 1900 Walker openly proclaimed that the trusts should be publicly owned.[23]

A central part of this project of creating a new political and economic order was education. True education, not "along the lines handed down to us from past ages but in that knowledge which is necessary to right thinking and right living," can increase citizens' knowledge of and concern for the "public welfare." While not explicitly developed by Walker in this essay, it seems clear why Walker believed that education was related to an emerging corporate economy. Opportunity for the middle class increasingly required training for a profession in order to be employed by a corporation or in the public sector. While the development of corporations closed off many opportunities for self-employment, it opened up opportunities as salaried employees. The development of professional associations with uniform standards required formal education and certified credentials. Moreover, continuous scientific and technological innovation would require educated consumers who could keep up with new developments and educated "household managers" as well.

A central part of this new order was the elimination of partisan party politics. Like the mugwumps, Walker believed that the intelligent voter considered the candidates' qualifications and integrity and studied proposed legislation rather than voting the party line. The era of partisan party politics was part of a decentralized political system centered in local communities, where parties served to unite diverse constituencies and allocated economic resources and privileges. The new political order would be a centralized one in which political responsibilities would be concentrated in the federal government. Clearly, for Walker, the modern citizen must shift his loyalties from the local community to the nation and from allegiance to the party to a general allegiance to "good government" and the public welfare. Compassion must be expressed not simply in local charities, but in working for good government.

Certainly Walker's series on "Captains of Industry," a glowingly sympathetic series of biographical sketches of industrialists and financiers, was a departure from the Victorian gentry's concerns about the lack of gentility of the new industrialists. Yet Walker shared with the mugwumps the view that the elite, or as Walker quite honestly put it, "members of my class,"[24] must demonstrate the qualities of social responsibility and public service. In his biography of Theodore Roosevelt, Walker praised the new President for exemplifying "the ideal which was in the minds of the founders of our form of government—the man born with all the advantages of comfortable position and excellent family tradition who, after being carefully educated, gives himself in all sincerity to the best interests of the Republic."[25] Walker shared Roosevelt's desire for a reinvigorated "masculine culture," through involvement in the world of science and technology, numerous articles on military issues and wars, and features on vigorous sporting activities. Walker advocated an interventionist government that would redistribute wealth, arbitrate strikes, control the money supply,[26] and regulate industry in various ways. Such a perspective, which saw government and the trusts as partners in a more rational political-economic order, went beyond the regional and laissez-faire perspective of the mugwumps.

S. S. McClure: "Making Chaos Out of Order"

S. S. McClure attended Knox College (Galesburg, Illinois), where he obtained his degree in 1882. Knox College had been a hotbed of support for abolitionism and moral reform, inspired by the Great Protestant Revival of the 1830s. McClure assimilated this culture (he came from a Protestant background) and acquired a lifelong fascination with Lincoln. Like many of his generation, he saw a parallel between the battle against the "oligarchy" of the trusts and the evils of industrialization—from child labor to the exploitation of women, and the earlier abolitionist battle against the evils of slavery.[27] While at Knox college, during the summer break of his freshman year, he traveled around the country selling a new type of coffee pot that someone in town had invented. He later said that his education as an editor began during that summer of traveling and learning firsthand about American society. After graduating from college, McClure worked for the Pope Manufacturing Company in Boston—the famous manufacturer of bicycles. Eventually, he was asked to edit *The Wheelman,* a company publication devoted to publicizing this new product. While he had been an editor of his college newspaper, he had not been an avid magazine reader until his position as editor of the *Wheelman.*

> When I was in college I had never read magazines. They were too expensive to buy. It had always seemed remarkable to me that a man could ever feel rich enough to pay thirty-five cents for a magazine. . . . I remember one night taking up a copy of the Century Magazine and beginning the new serial, which happened to be 'A Modern Instance,' by Mr. Howells. In doing so I became acquainted with the Century Magazine.[28]

McClure used the *Century* as his model and claimed that the first issue of the *Wheelman* "looked like a thinner *Century.*" Eventually he obtained a position with the *Century* where he got the idea of a literary syndicate, an idea that the editors of *Century* rejected. He left the *Century* and for nine years before the first issue of *McClure's* hit the newsstands, S. S McClure developed one of the first literary syndicates. He purchased literary material from leading authors and then sold them to newspapers, usually for publication in Sunday supplements.[29] In his autobiography he described the syndicate (launched in November 1884): "My plan, briefly, was this: I could get a short story from any of the best story-writers then for $150. I figured that I ought to be able to sell that story to 100 newspapers throughout the country, at $5 each. News was syndicated in this way, and I did not see why fiction should not be."[30]

S. S. McClure's conception of the popular magazine editor clearly differed from his predecessors at the *Century, Harper's Monthly,* or *Atlantic Monthly.* With experience at the leading genteel magazine (the *Century*) and as editor of a magazine devoted to publicizing one of the fastest-selling products in the country (the *Wheelman* at Pope's), McClure was ideally suited to put together a new publication that combined both cultural styles. His years as proprietor of a literary syndicate prepared him for the aggressive entrepreneurial style of looking for new stories and new contributors that the competitive popular magazine environment demanded.[31]

The evidence is that McClure relied on his own "instincts" in editing the magazine during its first decade. While claiming in one issue that he edited *McClure's* for his readers, he said to his staff, "I do the thing that's really in me, precisely as a painter does."[32] Perhaps George Juergens's observation about popular journalism also applies to the popular magazine editor: "This is the genius of popular journalism, to combine a point of view that is common with an altogether uncommon ability to project that point of view."[33]

Most of the ideas for articles in the early issues of *McClure's* came from McClure himself.[34] He would seek out a free-lance writer to produce the article he wanted. By 1895, though, McClure began to assemble a permanent staff of nonfiction writers.[35] This was one of S. S. McClure's innovations, to be adopted on a grander scale by George Horace Lorimer at the *Saturday Evening Post.*[36] Previously, writers of articles were hired on a free-lance basis. McClure, on one of his many travels abroad, had met Ida Tarbell in Paris. She was working on a book, and he eventually hired her to write a series on the life of Napoleon and to join the editorial staff of the magazine.[37] Three of the best-known staff members hired after Tarbell were Ray Stannard Baker, who had previously worked on the *Chicago Record* newspaper; William Allen White, who had been a reporter and the publisher of the *Emporia Gazette*; and Lincoln Steffens, who had worked for the *New York Post* and as city editor on the *Commercial Advertiser.* By 1897 McClure had assembled a "staff of reporters."

McClure could not rest comfortably in an editor's "easy chair."[38] In fact, according to those who knew him, he could hardly sit still. Lincoln Steffens, who became known as a great muckraker for his work on *McClure's* and

American magazines, presented his impressions of the great magazine editor S. S. McClure in his autobiography.

> Blond, smiling, enthusiastic, unreliable, he was the receiver of the ideas of his day. He was a flower that did not sit and wait for the bees to come and take his honey and leave their seeds. He flew forth to find and rob the bees. He was rarely in the office. "I can't sit still," he shouted. "That's your job. I don't see how you can do it." . . . To Africa, he traveled, to Europe often, to the west, south, east, and the north of the United States to see things and men, to listen and to talk. Field work was his work. Ideas were his meat, and he never knew where he got them. . . . It was always so when S.S. went away; there was always some act of enthusiasm for us to counteract. And it was always so when he came back from a trip. He would come straight from the ship to the office, call us together, and tell us what he had seen and heard, said and done. With his valise full of clippings, papers, books and letters, to prove it, he showed us that he had the greatest features any publisher had ever had, the most marvelous, really world stunning ideas or stories. Sometimes he had good things. . . . And we accepted calmly, but appreciatively also, some of his suggestions. But we had to unite and fight against, say, five out of seven of his new, world-thrilling, history making schemes.[39]

Of course, McClure provided a somewhat different slant on his organizational abilities and his relationship to his staff, but the undisputed truth in all the accounts of S. S. McClure was his boyish enthusiasm, energy, and entrepreneurial zest for new material. William Allen White remembered that "Sam had three hundred ideas a minute."[40] Ellery Sedgwick, who was a *McClure's* editor for a year before becoming editor of *Atlantic Monthly,* said,

> A week in the McClure office was the precise reversal of the six busy days described in the first chapter of Genesis. It seemed to end in a world without form and void. From order came forth chaos. . . . Yet with all his pokings and proddings the fires he kindled were brighter than any flames his staff could produce without him.[41]

S. S. McClure's chief editorial method consisted of keeping up with new developments in politics, literature, science, and technology through daily reading of major newspapers as well as the quality magazines. His New York and London offices collected clippings from daily papers. McClure would select from this information, as well as from his own reading, ideas that he thought "would work." His years running a literary syndicate established a network of contacts with authors and reporters around the world that could be called upon to develop projects that McClure proposed. For example, Elisha Jay Edwards, who had written about politics for the syndicate, continued to write about New York City machine politics for *McClure's* magazine. Permanent staff members were able to respond even more quickly to at least some of S. S. McClure's suggestions. McClure's one guiding principle in choosing whether to publish an article was whether it contained "a realistic portrayal of the human personalities involved." The emphasis was on "human interest" and on the personality behind a political development, invention, or work of literature.

McClure identified with the Protestant reform tradition and the Republican party that had dominated Knox College (Knox College had been a center for moral reform causes such as abolitionism), and saw his magazine as a vehicle for bringing to the public the "great personalities" behind new developments of his time.[42] While writing little for his magazine during the first decade, he developed a perspective that would become *McClure's* major theme by 1903.

In the January 1903 issue of *McClure's,* three muckraking pieces appeared; Ray Stannard Baker's "The Right to Work: The Story of the Nonstriking Miners," Ida Tarbell's "History of Standard Oil," and Lincoln Steffens's "The Shame of Minneapolis." McClure observed in his editorial that all three muckraking features had documented a growing lawlessness in American society. They showed "capitalists, workingmen, politicians, citizens—all breaking the law." Ultimately, citizens were responsible for tolerating "vice and a contempt for order," and only they could ensure that corporations, unions, and big-city machines live up to legal and moral standards of conduct. By "lawlessness" McClure meant something more than crime. His concern was with the "disintegration of society" that stemmed from the social and economic forces of urbanization, industrialism, and economic concentration. How could America's republican traditions cope with these changes?[43] As Theodore Greene has pointed out, by the first decade of the twentieth century many popular magazines had defined a large part of their role as "judges of contemporary American institutions."[44] They defined for the public the qualities of good citizenship in the emerging age of national "nonpartisan politics."

It is important to mention that neither Walker, McClure, or Munsey used their magazines as simply an expression of their own personal philosophies or political views. All three editors were quite aware of the need to separate personal politics from editorial decisions about magazine content. While Walker's editorials expressed a clear political perspective, this was not always represented in the pages of the magazine. The "Captains of Industry" series sung the praises of some of the industrialists that Walker criticized in his editorials. *McClure's* was more complex. Articles by Hamlin Garland on "Homestead and Its Perilous Trades," as well as Stephen Crane's "In the Depths of a Coal Mine" (published shortly after the Pullman strike), were published along with laudatory biographical sketches of Philip D. Armour and the Pinkerton overthrow of the Molly Maguires (December 1894). But perhaps even this inconsistency contributed to *McClure's* popularity, for most Americans had the same ambivalent mixture of admiration and resentment for the power and wealth of industrialists and financiers.

Frank Munsey: "Do and Dare"

Frank Munsey, the son of a poor farmer-carpenter, started his journey from rags to riches as a manager at Western Union Telegraph in Augusta, Maine. Along with cotton and lumber mills, Augusta was a center for the production of pulp fiction, "Nice Nelly tabloids" that served primarily as advertising vehicles. The nation's two leading mail-order magazines were both located in Augusta. The leading publisher of these fiction magazines was Edward Charles Allen, who published the *Peoples' Literary Companion.* Munsey, as a boy, thought of Augusta's publishing enterprises as "the great business of the city, completely overshadowing everything else." Moreover, Munsey remembered, "It had about it an element of romance and picturesqueness that was startlingly and abnormally interesting because of the smallness of the town."[45] Eventually, with a small loan, he decided to move to New York to start a magazine of his own. The *Golden Argosy* (modeled after Allen's successful publications) was an adolescent version of what would later become *Munsey's,* with features on the glamour of city life, inspirational stories of small-town boys who struck it rich, and an assortment of serialized fiction. Perhaps the most famous feature of the *Golden Argosy* was a series of stories by Horatio Alger.[46] The very first issue (December 2 1882) contained the first installment of a serial by Horatio Alger called, "Do and Dare, or a Brave Boy's Fight for a Fortune."[47] In 1887 the *Golden Argosy* published a serial by the famous showman P. T. Barnum. *Munsey's Weekly,* which was to become *Munsey's Magazine,* was founded in 1886.

During the mugwump split with the regular Republicans in 1884, Munsey was in the middle of the action. Augusta was Maine's capital, and Munsey had met the powerful politician James Blaine while working for Western Union. Munsey became a supporter of Blaine after he had been nominated by the Republicans for president. With Blaine's support, Munsey began publication of *Munsey's Illustrated Weekly,* primarily to counter the highly influential *Harper's Weekly,* whose editor, George William Curtis, was a vehement Blaine detractor (and a prominent mugwump). *Munsey's Weekly,* endorsed by the Republican National Committee, became the publishing arm of the Blaine campaign—ironically imitating its competitor *Harper's Weekly* in some respects while also trying to reach a mass audience with its staple of serialized, sentimental fiction, adventure stories, and accounts of Arctic explorations. While *Munsey's Weekly* did not last much past Blaine's defeat in the election, it was significant because both candidates in the 1884 presidential election used the print media as a key component of a national election campaign. This emphasis on campaign documents, educational literature, polls, and the independent press has been called the "educational style of politics" in contrast to earlier campaigns that were dominated by the mass mobilizations and other spectacles of the nineteenth-century party system. Even Blaine, who was identified with corrupt party politics, began to use this new style of political campaigning.[48] Three decades later, Munsey was Theodore Roosevelt's leading fund-raiser in Roosevelt's unsuccessful third-party presidential campaign in 1912. Munsey was also a member of the influential National Civic Federation, a national commission of business leaders, academics, representatives of labor, and the press which played a central role in crafting procorporate economic policy.

Frank Munsey purchased his first newspaper, the *New York Star,* in 1891. While there were many failures in Munsey's emerging newspaper empire, he was to become one of the major newspaper publishers in the country. Munsey eventually dominated the chaotic and competitive world of New York newspapers, helping through consolidations to drastically reduce the number of papers competing with one another. During the 1901 to 1924 period he was an owner of seven New York dailies. At one time he owned a total of eighteen newspapers.[49] But the early years were a struggle. By the panic of 1893, his publishing ventures were in trouble. *Munsey's,* which had switched from being a weekly to a monthly in 1891, was in serious financial trouble, and his decision to slash the price to ten cents was a desperate effort to save his fledgling publishing empire. Eventually, as is well known, *Munsey's* became the circulation leader in the nation, and Munsey acquired a number of newspapers and a grocery store chain as well.

Following the lead of Edward Bok of the *Ladies' Home Journal,* Munsey adopted a personal style of interacting with his readers in "The Publisher's Desk." Edward Bok may have been the first to adopt this style with his "Side Talks with Girls" feature (the feature was signed "Ruth Ashmore"). This feature had the tone of a confidential chat with young women who could not speak as frankly with their own mothers.[50] By 1897 the "Publisher's Desk" department in *Munsey's* had the subheading, "A Personal Chat with Our Readers." Like features in other magazines, including the Hearst *Cosmopolitan's* "Shop Talk," these features presented the editor as the "personality" of the magazine. Readers were encouraged to think that they were being provided with access to inside, behind-the-scenes knowledge of the magazine business—how stories were chosen, what other readers thought of leading features, what the publisher or editor had planned for future issues. Unlike Edward Livermore Burlingame of *Scribner's,* "who believed strongly that editors should keep themselves very much in the background and that the reading public should be content with knowing them through their magazines,"[51] Munsey and other popular magazine editors made themselves well known to their readers. The popular editor's persona as the reader's friend, if not confidante, anticipated the advertiser's desire to present the company and its product as the friendly adviser to the anxious and insecure consumer.[52]

McClure's promoted itself extensively, highlighting features that S. S. McClure thought would attract readers. Walker's use of contests was symptomatic of the sales techniques used by many popular magazine editors to encourage in readers a sense of participation with the magazine. The lack of consistency, ideologically or thematically, was also a departure from the nineteenth-century genteel magazine and perhaps part of the popular magazines' attraction. One commentator remarked that *Cosmopolitan* had "the quality of unexpectedness which is imparted by its unhampered management."[53] A more heterogeneous group of readers (compared to the quality magazines) could find some feature in the popular magazine that resonated with their own interests.[54] The popular magazine "text," in other words, was somewhat open and "undisciplined."[55]

While some have characterized Munsey as a crude businessman concerned only with profits,[56] he had a "visionary" sense of his mission as a publisher. His *Golden Argosy* was one of the first to publish success stories that challenged the Victorian emphasis on success as the consequence of good character. The Horatio Alger stories published by Munsey had a strong "wish fulfillment," melodramatic, even "fantastic" quality that many middle-class moralists found troublesome.[57] *Munsey's* later developed this theme for an adult audience, presenting an image of the life of luxury and power as one that the readers could someday obtain. Art for Munsey was clearly not the replacement for religion as a unifying and transcendent ideal as it was for the mugwumps.

Instead, the ideal of "success" through bold, energetic, willful action seemed to serve the same function. For Munsey popular magazines were business vehicles to be sure, but they were also vehicles for the spread of a view of success no longer constrained by earlier notions of gentility and character.

Outsiders to the Eastern Cultural Establishment

It has been suggested that the content of the popular magazine reflected the immigrant or "outsider" background of many of the popular editors.[58] Most, it is argued, were outsiders to the Eastern literary establishment and to the literary and academic subcultures of Boston's and New York's cultural elite. S. S. McClure and Edward Bok of the Curtis-owned *Ladies' Home Journal* were first-generation immigrants who did not, it is claimed, carry with them the weight of American cultural traditions.[59] George Horace Lorimer of the *Saturday Evening Post* was second-generation Scotch-Irish. As Christopher Wilson has pointed out, the outsider status of these new members of the cultural establishment may have contributed to their sense of estrangement from the genteel values of the "Boston Brahmins" and to their attack against a feminized genteel culture.[60] The fact that the pioneers in the movie industry, including the early nickelodeon houses, were immigrants (many from eastern Europe) seems to lend support for this position. Joseph Pulitzer, who was responsible for the sensational journalistic style that William Randolph Hearst was to imitate later, was an Austrian-German immigrant. The popular magazine, like the early movies, had a voyeuristic quality rather than the view of a cultural insider.

It is important, though, to exercise some caution in making a simple correlation between immigrant, outsider status and the perspective embodied in new cultural forms like the popular magazine, amusement parks, and movies. Munsey and Walker were not recent immigrants. Many of the members of Walker's staff, during the height of *Cosmopolitan*'s circulation, were former contributors to the quality magazines. While immigrating to the United States from Ireland (the McClure family was from County Antrim, Ulster, Ireland), McClure quickly assimilated. As mentioned earlier, McClure was very much influenced by the moral reform culture of Knox College where he acquired a lifelong fascination with Lincoln. *McClure's* syndicate was solidly involved in disseminating the best of late nineteenth-century "Victorian literature," and McClure worked with W. D. Howells in planning the first few issues of his magazine. This is hardly a picture of a cultural outsider. Munsey, on the other hand, was an outsider to the Eastern literary establishment, though this had nothing to do with being a recent immigrant.

Moreover, estrangement from nineteenth-century Protestant culture was expressed in many ways, including by members of the elite themselves. Henry Adams, historian and editor of the *North American Review,* and Theodore Roosevelt are examples. Many of the younger generation of middle-class writers and reformers, who reached adulthood in the 1880s and 1890s—like Lincoln Steffens, Jane Addams (one of the leaders of the settlement house movement and a leading Progressive reformer), Stephen Crane, Harold Frederic (journalist and author of the best-selling *Damnation of Theron Ware*)—wrote about how it felt to be detached from vigorous experience and engagement with life.[61] This middle-class anomie, which often took the form of a yearning for "real life,"[62] made many educated Americans feel like outsiders in their own culture. Lincoln Steffens, in his *Autobiography,* reflected on his fascination with immigrant ghettos when he worked as a reporter, especially the Jewish ghetto in New York.

> I had become infatuated with the Ghetto as eastern boys were with the wild west, and nailed a mazuza on my office door; I went to the synagogue on all the great holy days. . . . The music moved me most, but I knew and could follow with the awful feelings of a Jew the beautiful old ceremonies of the ancient orthodox services.[63]

This almost mystical identification, not only with an urban immigrant community but with one that had lived as outsiders in other cultures for two millennia, indicates (among other things) a fascination with marginality as well as an estrangement from the dominant culture.[64] The raw energy and vitality of the city provided a kind of antidote to the overcivilization of genteel Protestant culture.[65] Unlike the overly intellectual and "repressed" Victorian middle class, immigrants seemed somehow more "primal" and closer to "life." In the city, said Lincoln Steffens, you can find "human nature posing nude."[66]

There does seem to be some merit to the view that popular magazine editors and publishers were not as a group as tied to the Eastern cultural establishment—the Eastern universities, publishing houses, and New England literary culture as the genteel editors. Moreover, as we might expect, popular magazine editors came from a different generation than the quality magazine editors. William Allen White observed that the McClure staff "were at heart midwestern. They talked the Mississippi vernacular."[67] Walker's *Cosmopolitan,* as we have seen, was thought to have a "Western" flavor, and Walker, while born in the East, made his home in Mount Morrison, Colorado. In generational terms, the publishers and editors of the six highest-circulation magazines (as well as the two leading women's magazines) for this period, had a median birth year of 1861, while among the genteel editors Richard Watson Gilder, born in 1844, was the youngest. More than half of the eighteen most prominent popular magazine editors and publishers were born outside the East, and two were immigrants—Edward Bok and S. S. McClure. Six did not have any college education while six were educated in Midwestern or Western colleges or universities. Twelve of the eighteen had journalistic experience on New York, San Francisco, Boston, St. Louis, or Philadelphia newspapers before obtaining their positions as editors or publishers. Only S. S. McClure and Edward Bok had positions with any of the leading Eastern publishing houses before beginning their magazine careers. Bok was advertising manager for *Scribner's,* and McClure had a position for a short period of time with the *Century.*[68]

The Popular Magazine "Cultural Diamond"

The popular magazine emerged in a social environment characterized by industrial conflict, economic crisis and, later, an unprecedented merger movement. The economic crisis provided a business opportunity for the new editors, and they took advantage of it by lowering prices, reaching out to new markets, and making advertising their chief source of revenue. The movement among the upper class for an expansionist foreign policy and for revitalizing the nation's military was also an important part of the larger political context within which the popular magazine emerged and will be discussed in the next chapter. In addition, the urban reform movements of the 1890s (sparked, in part, by the depression of 1893) made many readers eager for topical information that the new magazines began to supply.

The popular magazine can be understood as a hybrid of elements of metropolitan journalism, including the independent, nonpartisan journalism represented in part by George Curtis's *Harpers Weekly* and the "sensational" New York press dominated by the Hearst and Pulitzer chains. The emergence of the "story papers" during the 1880s, which mass-produced pulp fiction, as well as the mail-order magazines influenced *Munsey's* more than *Cosmopolitan* or *McClure's.* By the mid-1880s the family house magazines were already giving more space to native fiction rather than English reprints and moving away from sentimental fiction toward local color realism. The popular magazines, most notably *McClure's,* continued this movement, publishing the work of some of the best-known realist authors (as well as helping to make many authors well known to the public). But this trend was far from unambiguous as swashbuckling adventure stories in the historical realist tradition were also quite common (as well as historical biographies), especially during the 1890s. We have also seen that in the 1890s popular magazines still showed a close resemblance to their genteel predecessors in their articles on high culture, mugwump reform, and in their nonpartisan tone.

In contrast to genteel magazines, *Munsey's, McClure's,* and *Cosmopolitan* sought to assemble their stories and articles in a coherent and digestible package, no longer assuming an audience of cultural insiders who had the leisure and patience to read long articles in small print. The editor now presented himself to his readers as a friendly confidante and took a more active role in looking for more timely material to reach new markets of readers and attract advertising. The new halftone photographs assumed an important place in these magazines as a way of presenting to readers an image of timeliness and authenticity. Firsthand accounts of events from circuses to train trips to visits to coal mines also provided a contrast to the idealizing and moralistic tone of the genteel magazines.

The new publishers and editors differed from Curtis, Gilder, Howells, and others in the genteel tradition in their unambiguous praise for the emerging political-economic order of corporate capitalism, in their positive assessment of the wonders of new technology and consumer goods, and in their view that the mass media could play a major role in helping readers to make the transition to this new social order. They were more likely than the genteel editors to be outsiders to the Eastern literary establishment, to come from business and journalistic backgrounds, and to present in their magazines a national rather than a local or regional perspective. In the case of Walker, there is a clear break from the earlier mugwump fear of working-class unrest and uncritical support for business. It is tempting to equate the ascendancy of the popular magazine with larger class developments like the growing wealth and power of industrial capital and the growth of a new middle class of professionals and managers. An emerging national market and the need for national advertising, the curiosity of readers about methods of mass production and distribution and the lifestyles and leisure patterns of the new millionaires, provide part of the context for the popular magazine's emergence. Walker and McClure were particularly enamored with the expertise of college-educated scientists, engineers, and other experts on topics that ranged from child care to exercise to nutrition. But genteel magazines, as we have seen, were also moving in this direction, and during the 1890s the differences between popular and genteel magazines were not so clear-cut or well defined.

Readers of popular magazines were most likely to have come from major cities and to contain both middle-class professionals as well as working-class readers—especially the growing white-collar segment of the working class. These increasingly literate readers were hungry for information on new scientific and technological developments, new consumer goods, how an increasingly national economic system worked, and how to cope with the consequences of "progress." Finally, popular magazines helped to construct three new social identities for their readers—as consumers, as clients of professional expertise, and as educated, nationally oriented citizens.

What was the popular magazine project? For Walker the popular magazine was an educator, helping to prepare readers for a new social order. To a great extent this project also characterized *McClure's,* particularly in the magazine's steady stream of articles on new scientific and technological developments and insider accounts of important events. For Munsey the popular magazine transmitted a vision of material abundance within reach of the average reader and no longer limited by moral imperatives associated with character and self-control. For all three publishers magazines were to take their reader into the "whirlpool of real life," beyond what was perceived as the moralism and elitism of the genteel tradition.

The next three chapters will discuss the emerging culture that popular magazines presented to their readers, a culture that revolved around three utopian projects or "cultural dreams"—the dream of material abundance; the dream of a society governed by rational, scientific principles, eliminating the waste and irrationalities of unregulated capitalism; and the dream of an industrial society balancing economic growth with social justice. Taken together, these three cultural dreams presented a clear contrast to the emphasis on cultural preservation within the genteel tradition.

3

DREAMS OF ABUNDANCE, SOCIAL CONTROL, AND SOCIAL JUSTICE

CHAPTER FIVE

The New Secular Religion of Health

The 1890s and first decade of the twentieth century saw the emergence of what Theodore Roosevelt called the ideal of the "strenuous life." Colleges developed competitive sports programs, the upper class pursued an interest in sports and vigorous physical activity in their exclusive country clubs, urbanites sought health through bicycling, new professionals and experts in physical culture, nutrition, athletic training, and sports sought to master and understand the human body as well as to instill an appreciation for its dynamism and regenerative powers. Men and women were camping, exploring, bird watching, and communing with nature, and environmentalists were taking an interest in preserving nature through the creation of new state and national parks.

John Higham, in his much discussed essay, argued that these and other developments can be understood as part of a "profound spiritual reaction" against industrial society. Americans, according to Higham, began to react against the growing "mechanization of social life," what Max Weber called "formal rationality." Implicitly, Higham also argued that Americans began to react against elements of Victorian culture, against "rooms cluttered with brica-brac," the "masking of aggressions behind a thickening facade of gentility," and a "faith in automatic material progress."[1] The reaction against the formal rationality of industrialism took a variety of forms, according to Higham, from the athleticism of the "new woman" to the energy of new forms of popular entertainment, to willful vigor of war making and empire building.[2]

The return to nature and the search for healthy bodies, minds, and spirits seemed to be related in complex ways to larger social and cultural developments, which this chapter will explore. In what ways did the quest for good health support efforts to revitalize America's military and build a national community? How did the new therapeutic culture articulate with an emerging consumer-oriented economy? In what ways did the "new women" who were active in a variety of reform movements contribute to the turn-of-the-century quest for abundant energy? How did the Social Gospel movement and various spiritualist developments contribute to this new culture? It is perhaps of more than passing interest to explore this phenomenon for the turn-of-the-century quest for good health was a forerunner of our own.

Neurasthenia and Its Cure

Concerns about "neurasthenia" (exhaustion of nervous energy) were widespread since the 1870s and were well represented in the family house magazines.[3] The classic statement had been popularized years earlier by George M. Beard, a graduate of the College of Physicians and Surgeons of New York. Beard argued in *American Nervousness: Its Causes and Consequences* (1866) that "nervousness," or what was called neurasthenia, was a product of five features of modern civilized societies: steam power, the periodical press, the telegraph, the sciences, and the "mental activity of women." Beard made it clear that nervousness was a problem primarily of the small percentage of "brain workers" among the middle and upper classes. Despite their small numbers, Beard maintained that a civilization would lapse into "degeneracy" without this small educated middle class.

Beard argued that specialization in industry, caused by "steam power," reduced the health of the artisan as well as the "professions." The perfection of clocks and watches "compel us to be on time." The telegraph increases the flow of business as well as the ability to communicate about business activities, thus adding to stimulation and anxiety. Cities increase the amount of noise, not the noises of nature "which are the occasions not of pain but of pleasure" but the "unrhythmical, unmelodious" noises of urban industrial life.[4] Newspapers "increase a hundred-fold the distresses of humanity." In addition, because of the "extension and complexity of the populations of the globe . . . local sorrows and local horrors become daily occasions of nervous disorders."[5]

In an article that appeared in an early issue of *McClure's,* "Nervousness: The National Disease of America," Edward Wakefield reported on the research and career of S. Weir Mitchell, president of the Medical Society of Pennsylvania.[6] Mitchell claimed that the number of "nerve deaths" had "multiplied more than forty times in the past twenty years" and attributed this to overwork. According to Wakefield, Mitchell believed that the "Anglo-Saxon" Americans were far more susceptible to nerve disorders than other races, especially "those in the higher walks of life." Females and town dwellers were more likely to be afflicted than males and country folk. The two specific causes of this "national disease," mentioned near the end of the article, were the "Dollar Devil and the School Fiend." The first cause afflicted the male more than the female and concerned the tendency of the young male to go into business too early and assume prematurely too much responsibility. As a result, the author of the article reported that Mitchell (with perhaps a bit of exaggeration) thought that "America is the country of young invalids, young wrecks, young drug victims, young inebriates, young maniacs, young suicides!" As for women,

> The flower of American womanhood is wilted by over-culture before it comes into bloom. The long hours, the multiplicity of studies, the number of teachers . . . the craving rivalry to be well graded, that all devouring ambition to command a means of living . . . the want of exercise—it is these, and these alone that condemn tens of thousands of American women to a life of misery and uselessness.[7]

Neurasthenia was a metaphor for concerns about the psychological and spiritual consequences of a half century of progress. The proposed solutions to the various symptoms of neurasthenia and to their underlying causes in the conditions of modern life were diverse and often contradictory. Many physicians claimed that isolation and rest were the cures for nervous exhaustion. On the other hand reformers, especially during the height of the "new woman" movement of the 1890s, asserted that active engagement in life, particularly in useful humanitarian pursuits, was the best cure for loss of willpower. Some constructed the problem of neurasthenia in gender terms—as stemming from an overly feminized culture and a lack of masculine willfulness and risk taking while others saw the issue of neurasthenia in class and ethnic terms. Many members of the upper class saw the nerve diseases of their class as an expression of the weakening of upper-class Protestant culture caused by the infusion of non-Protestant immigrants. Both George Beard and S. Weir Mitchell asserted that those with sensitive dispositions, primarily professionals and "brain workers," were more apt to contract this disease than members of the working class. Numerous articles appeared in *Century, Atlantic, Scribner's,* and other genteel magazines on the "degeneracy" (based on the work of Max Nordau) of the upper class, although others used this term to characterize immigrants or working-class agitators. Another common diagnostic category was "overcivilization." This referred in part to concerns that the middle class was mired in "narrow materialism" and "morbid self consciousness" and as a result was cut off from real life. One might be "overcivilized" because of a sedentary life, a worldview dominated by materialism, a bookish delight in intellectual fads rather than in simple moral virtues, or a "morbid self consciousness" resulting from a glut of self-absorbed intellectualizing rather than willful action. Cures for overcivilization were as diverse as the prescriptions for neurasthenia. They might range from escaping the city for the more healthful environment of the countryside to escaping from the stultifying life of the small town into the new energies of the city. Others urged an infusion of transcendent purpose to counteract the narrow materialism of a commercial society.[8]

The turn-of-the-century language of health was heavily influenced by scientific developments over the course of the nineteenth century—in physiology, psychology, and especially physics. In part, as a result of the discoveries during the 1840s and 1850s of the laws of thermodynamics (energy conservation and entropy) and the associated interest in the physiological capacities and limitations of the human body, scientists and intellectuals increasingly used the term *energy* to refer to fundamental forces in nature as well as in the human body and personality.[9] The idea that the body and mind contained untapped energies that could be used more efficiently to enhance either human creativity, personal health, or social efficiency was a departure from an earlier discourse in which work and idleness were moralistic categories and in which the body and its needs were distinctly secondary compared to the immortal soul.[10]

Economic metaphors were often used in describing neurasthenia, as when Anna Bracket in "The Technique of Rest" asked, "What shall people do who are conscious that they are overdrawing their deposits in the bank of nervous supply, and yet must go on working and continuously?"[11] The problem here was that the limited human energy supply (like a bank account) could not continue to absorb the constant withdrawals of energy required for modern life. But even within the genteel tradition, some were questioning the assumption of a limited or scarce supply of human energy. In a famous article William James relied not on metaphors of economic scarcity but on metaphors of abundance. James counseled his readers to escape the "inhibiting influence of egoism" by taking hold of "vaster and more permanent realities." For James energy was abundant, not in short supply, a perspective that became increasingly common in popular magazines. Within the genteel tradition, the remedies for neurasthenia were more often than not "antimodern": simplifying one's life, returning to a more natural state of small-town or rural life, or trying to recapture a preindustrial community that left little room for diversity. In contrast, for the bulk of popular magazine articles the route to good health was through therapeutically encountering new sources of abundant energy.

A review of the pages of *Cosmopolitan* shows a continuing concern with how to stay healthy—mentally and physically. Frederic W. Burry in a contribution to *Cosmopolitan*'s "Men, Women and Events," worried that the majority of Americans just want to "get along" and lack "that generous share of that stuff—Will power—that makes the man." Americans, he maintained, were afflicted with a "suspicious, fearful habit of mind." The solution, he maintained, was for Americans to "take time to train their Will, to cultivate their character." After all, "there are stores of force . . . contained in him, lying latent, waiting for personal control and direction."[12] Frank Morgan, in a *Cosmopolitan* article, wondered whether, "In our day and generation we have gained much in material things; in spiritual things have we not lost much?" We are too preoccupied, Morgan maintained, with "getting and spending." "We moderns are machines for making money, automatons adjusted to that purpose . . . wound up and started afresh each morning to perform this function." In the pursuit of material success Americans give little thought to "the purpose of our lives. . . . With feverish pulse and straining nerves and eyes we look in but one direction for the solution of the great problem of domestic economy—the direction of getting more; while the simpler solution lies in the opposite direction of spending less."[13]

Upton Sinclair spoke directly to a fear of loss of purpose and willpower in his contribution to a *Cosmopolitan* series called "What Life Means to Me." Describing a psychological crisis in his life he confessed, "I had tried to the full power of the individual will and had found its impotence; I had watched the beginning and the swift progress of degeneration—in body and soul."[14] Sinclair regained his health after achieving literary success and after finding renewed purpose in the Socialist movement.[15] In another article Upton Sinclair wrote about his own illnesses and his homemade cure—a series of fasts. This was part of a series of articles on "Osteopathy, Christian Science, Hydrotherapy, Fletcherism, and the like, each contribution giving the personal experiences of a distinguished adherent."[16]

The fiction of neurasthenia was a popular magazine staple. One short story appearing in *Cosmopolitan* during the 1890s concerned a young man, Allison, who "had come down from the country with the intention of learning to be a banker and a broker." He falls in love with the daughter of the business's owner. Unfortunately, Allison meets Hector, who is the cousin of the owner (a French immigrant). Hector begins to hypnotize Allison with the use of a "mirror-like contraption." Having gotten control over Allison's will, he introduces Allison to "lower Broadway" and "pleasures as you never dreamed of before." Eventually Hector is caught and provides a convenient ending by shooting himself. Allison fully regains his will and his middle-class respectability but learns a valuable lesson about the dangers of degeneracy stemming from the loss of purpose and self-control. In this case the loss of willpower and self-control is associated with hypnotism and the amusements of the lower classes.[17]

In a tale involving a number of flashbacks we are told of a high-society woman who marries an aristocratic man. After the man's death she is charged with murder. Eventually she is acquitted and falls in love with her lawyer (the narrator). But the lawyer finds out that she is really guilty! She becomes suicidal. She is described as "a woman composed half of hysteria, half of passion and insatiable of pleasure." Shortly after we are told that she "died of suicide," we discover that whole story is a delusion. The lawyer is suffering from a nervous disorder.[18] Adele Marie Shaw told the story of a wealthy businessman in danger of losing his wife and his business. The central character, John Farjeon, is close to suffering a nervous breakdown; "With each effort to work there came now the knowledge of grim bodily distress. The buzzing of the fly sounded loud as the dropping of iron nails upon stones." His problems begin when his wife falls in love with his cousin Alfred, "a man shallow of emotions and dilettante fashion." It turns out that Alfred has sapped her of her will through the art of mesmerism.[19]

Bret Harte, in "Zut-ski, the Problem of a Wicked Feme Sole," contrasted the hustle and bustle of Western civilization with the "great traditions of Egypt's past." We are told that "old English gentlemen and women" would often retire to Egypt in their declining years. The story's main characters are Midas Pyle, a retired editor of a "vulgar London newspaper," a Frenchman (Chevalier), a

Scotsman, and the Scotsman's friend, a "noted physician." The plot involves a number of European visitors staying at an Egyptian hotel and a mysterious and beautiful Egyptian princess. After a rivalry for the Princess's affections and a warning from the doctor that she is "beautiful on the outside but empty on the inside—without a soul," we discover that the whole thing is a charade. It turns out that every character is a patient of the noted physician who is a "well-known nerve specialist." "He believed in humoring his disturbed patients and letting them follow their fantasies under his management." The Princess turns out to be a music hall singer suffering from delusions.[20] Doctors and sick people seemed to be everywhere.

Sports, Leisure, and Physical Culture

For many, vigorous outdoor activity was the cure to nervous exhaustion. The *Review of Reviews* featured a piece on "The World's Sporting Impulse."[21] The author noted that Americans were struck by an impulse for the "open air, swift movement and muscular activity." Moreover, he observed, it was not just the upper class with leisure but ordinary people in the "great cities."

> The whole world seems to be feeling some such impulse now. There is an open air movement almost revolutionary in its degree and which cannot by any means be accounted for by theories of a more numerous leisure class. People are bicycling, yachting, running, jumping, hunting, playing baseball, tennis and golf, to an extent which is new in this generation. Nor is any considerable fraction of these people of the class whose wealth makes such a diversion inevitable; they are the workers in stores and offices of the great cities; typewriters, elevator boys, barbers, physicians, lawyers and clergy-men—in short, 'the people.' If it be true that the times are too 'strenuous,' that Americans are a nation of dyspeptics because they work too hard and take too little physical exercise, the signs of 1896 are very promising of better things.

Here was a cure for a "nation of dyspeptics" that was no longer limited to the "leisured class." Ordinary Americans could now emulate the rich in their ability to divert themselves in their leisure time with sports and recreational activities. A major source of the turn-of-the-century interest in the "strenuous life" came from the leisure activities of the new elite of industrial capitalists in their exclusive country clubs. One of the three discourses[22] on sports, leisure, and physical culture to be discussed in this section presented upper-class sports and leisure activities as part of a lifestyle unconnected to larger social purposes. Just as the American upper class sought to emulate the artistic taste and lifestyle of European royalty, this popular magazine discourse presented a positive image of upper-class sport as conspicuous consumption and not so subtly encouraged their middle-class readers to emulate or at least envy the upper-class lifestyle.

In "Diversions of Some Millionaires," Walter Germain Robinson provided a history of the sporting activities of upper-class Americans (primarily New Yorkers) since the mid-nineteenth century. Much of the article was devoted to yachting, a favorite sport since it limited participants to those with money, and the more recent sport of automobile racing. Other upper-class sports like polo, hunting, and falconing were also discussed. Robinson ended the article with the hope that the spirit of exclusiveness in upper-class sport would be replaced by a more democratic spirit, but this seemed more of an afterthought.[23] An article that also appeared in the 1899 *Cosmopolitan* was an account of "The America's Cup" race, an event organized by the exclusive New York Yacht Club. A number of years later Cleveland Moffett aroused the curiosity of readers with an account of "Luxurious Newport," which described activities from sports to gambling in this new upper-class resort.[24] This article appeared during the height of the Hearst *Cosmopolitan*'s muckraking assaults against the "greedy plutocrats."

Articles on upper-class lifestyles filled *Munsey's,* especially during the turn of the century. In 1899 *Munsey's* reported on "Ball Giving in New York." The year 1893 was when the Waldorf Hotel in New York opened with an elegant and extravagant decor and a hotel dining room "surpassing anything of the kind yet seen in this city." The Waldorf became a social center for the city's wealthy citizens, the center of fashionable nightlife. In "Ball Giving in New York" Clinton Van Horne described the "ultra fashionable set of rich people" who competed with one another in holding "restaurant balls." The article described the extravagance of these balls and expressed some regret that entertainment among the fashionable had become a public affair in contrast to the "delightful entertainments in the fine old homes," which had the "charm of simplicity."[25] There wasn't a hint of disapproval in *Munsey's* illustrated account of "The Hotels of New York," an article that gave readers a tour of the new upper-class palaces from the Murray Hill Hotel to the Waldorf-Astoria.[26]

The author of "The Sporting Impulse" referred to urbanites other than the upper class who were enjoying their own sports during the turn of the century.

The most talked-about recreational activity was bicycling. By 1900 ten million bicycles had been sold, and according to one author bicycling associations had become a political force. With perhaps a bit of exaggeration, *Review of Reviews* claimed that "the League of American Wheelmen is an institution which any Presidential candidate would be loath to offend." The bicycle industry was not only one of the first to mass-produce consumer goods, but bicycling was one of the first sports in which both men and women participated. In fact, many of the articles about bicycling written for popular magazines were written by women and featured illustrations of women bicyclers.[27] In contrast to the exclusiveness of upper-class sports, here was an activity that not only demanded energy and activity but seemed to bridge the social distinctions of class and gender, uniting a range of groups in a community of exercise.

The second discourse concerning sports came from the genteel tradition, or at least one strand of it. In contrast to articles that explored the conspicuous consumption and exclusiveness of upper-class sports and amusements, the genteel discourse saw sports as a means of character building and nation building. Theodore Roosevelt was the leading advocate of this view, and *Cosmopolitan*'s John Brisben Walker was an enthusiastic supporter of "the strenuous life" as a cure for overcivilization and self-indulgence among the middle and upper classes. The *Century*'s Richard Watson Gilder saw college athletics as contributing to a "manlier, healthy tone" and a "gain in studious qualities." He disagreed with some critics who believed that college athletics could not coexist with "self-control, steadiness and temperance."[28] Roosevelt explicitly associated sport not only with the cultivation of self-discipline and the subordination of the individual to the group but also with the mental and physical toughness needed among the citizenry of a modern state. Roosevelt, as will be discussed later in the chapter, was one of a number of upper-class advocates of a revitalized military and an expansionist foreign policy. The team sports that were becoming an increasingly important part of college life as well as personal exercise programs were part of that effort to create a citizenry that could rise above "mere materialism" and sacrifice for higher values.[29]

Walker was a strong advocate of sports and physical education programs in colleges although he criticized college sports, especially football, for carrying competitiveness to the extreme and encouraging a single-minded concern for winning. In an article published in the special edition on the St. Louis World's Fair, Walker stated that physical culture was of value not only to the individual but also to the larger society. Walker was especially impressed with the German section of the "Department of Physical Culture" at the fair. He quoted approv-

BICYCLING FOR WOMEN.

BY MRS. REGINALD DE KOVEN.

THE development of the exercise of bicycle-riding has assumed proportions of universality which recall the Egyptian plague of flies; by day and night, in town and country, forked black creatures, with semi-transparent means of locomotion, fly past with bewildering velocity; the human animal has become an air-propelling, exulting creature, with mysterious prehistoric attributes, half beast, half bird.

Invention, the angel of the nineteenth century, has abolished space, shattered time, and now with this wonderful machine, the bicycle, is making a determined onslaught upon sickness and old age, despondency, idleness with its resulting crime, and all the ills which mortal flesh is heir to.

To men, rich and poor, the bicycle is an unmixed blessing, but to women it is deliverance, revolution, salvation. It is well nigh impossible to overestimate the potentialities of this exercise in the curing of the common and characteristic ills of womankind, both physical and mental, or to calculate the far-reaching effects of its influence in the matters of dress and social reform.

As to dress-reform, the possibilities would, indeed, seem limitless. Since woman has taken up the bicycle it has become more and more apparent every day that its use demands a more or less radical change in their costume. Moderate women have met the demand with gaiters and a three-quarter skirt—one reaching perhaps to the ankles, but even

Cosmopolitan covers the newest fad and appeals to female readers. Similar features also appeared in *Munsey's* and other popular magazines (*Cosmopolitan,* August 1893, p. 386).

ingly from a German government publication that proclaimed, "The maintenance of the health of the individual is the chief requirement of the healthy growth of the state. . . . All progress in the direction of health is synonymous with economic gain. On the other hand, health is the chief source of the nation's ability to defend itself."[30]

This interesting connection between healthy individuals and the "healthy growth of the state" and its ability "to defend itself" was expressed in a contribution to *Cosmopolitan*'s "Men, Women and Events." The short contribution was titled "The Brotherhood of Strenuosity," and it compared President Roosevelt's espousal of the strenuous life with William of Germany who "lo these fourteen years has personified the 'strenuous life' in Europe." Roosevelt was described as having "rectilinear qualities carried in a body of model robustness." The author surmised that Roosevelt's "meteoric rise" from the "estate of simple country gentleman" to "Assistant Naval Secretary, Rough Rider Colonel, Governor . . . and to his present high office while excelling as rifleman, fencer, rider, hunter, boxer, walker and sprinter, with records in football and baseball" must have impressed the Kaiser.[31] If nervousness was the national disease, perhaps here was the cure.[32]

Football and boxing were two sports that grew rapidly during the 1890s, primarily on college campuses.[33] While Walker and regular contributor Elbert Hubbard were vigorous supporters of athletics as part of a balanced school curriculum, they feared an excess of competition would turn sports into an end rather than a means to build character and an ethic of service and sacrifice. Hubbard worried about the effects of "a sport more brutal [football] than ever Claudius countenanced." While in 1902 Hubbard reported two men had been killed in prize fights, "in a season of three months just past, twenty-one men have been killed playing football."[34] Even advocates of physical culture like John Brisben Walker thought that the mania for competitive college sports had gone too far. In an article published in 1904, Walker referred to the "hysterical movement in college physical competition," which was at its height during the 1890s. The methods of college athletics, Walker argued, "could not be explained upon any reasonable ground, and even very able and otherwise honest college presidents lent themselves to the fraud of advertising their colleges through athletic games."[35] Elbert Hubbard was especially critical of colleges for allowing the sport of football to flourish, arguing that "the game will have to go, and its passing will not be regretted by those who love books and ideas."[36]

"Physical culture" referred to exercise programs devoted to building up the body or maintaining physical health and were often associated with educational programs in colleges and public schools. Ironically, while camping, bird-watching, and nature-exploring were often associated with an escape from the formal rationality of modern society, the cultivation of "physical culture" led to a further development of this very phenomenon (formal rationality) as an array of experts developed programs for schools and supervised the physical activity of children.[37] Implicit in the view that the human body could be improved and made more energetic, efficient, and healthy was the assumption that various attributes and capacities associated with the body were open to modification.[38]

The perspective of the new health professionals was part of the project of using scientific knowledge to create a more ordered, regulated, rational life for the individual and for society. New professions associated with physical education, nutrition,[39] athletic management and training, and children's recreation sought to apply scientific knowledge to physical activity, sports, and play and helped to popularize the view that the human body did not have a fixed energy supply but could be restored and regenerated. In addition, as we have seen, a significant strand of upper-class genteel thought associated "physical culture" with the reinvigoration of the nation through service to the state and through a martial spirit. Systematic exercise, particularly through team sports, could provide a useful antidote to lives of luxury and "narrow materialism," teaching middle-class and upper-class youth the value of work, sacrifice, and cooperation. But what separated the middle-class professional discourse from the genteel discourse on sport and exercise was that the new health professionals were not as interested in "character" as the chief benefit of exercise, and the genteel advocates of sport were not convinced that good health and athletic ability required the aid of scientific expertise.[40]

Articles advising readers on how to improve their health were common throughout popular magazines.[41] *Cosmopolitan* contributor Elbert Hubbard wrote about "How To Keep Well," in which he characteristically criticized the medical profession, claiming that most diseases were caused by the medications prescribed by doctors.[42] Julian Ralph reported on "Famous Cures and Humbugs of Europe," which featured a large photograph of "a typical cure fountain" in one resort.[43] Bernarr MacFadden (editor of *Physical Culture* magazine) addressed female readers in a series called "How to Administer a Household." His contribution was titled, "Health Made and Preserved by Daily Exercise."[44] MacFadden had, a few years earlier, acquired a national reputation with his popular book *The Power and Beauty of Superb Womanhood,* in which he advocated "vigorous exercise for women." Woods Hutchinson, M.D., wrote about the "Exercise That Rests," which counseled readers that "intelligent rest and recreation are the secret of successful work and high efficiency during the hours devoted to labor. Exercise, to be helpful, must be play."[45]

By the end of the first decade of the twentieth century, a number of sports had become professional, money-making enterprises, and sports stars were beginning to acquire national fame. For the first time, articles on professional sports appeared in popular magazines, and the earlier genteel discourse that valued sports primarily as a means to cultivate larger social and political objectives declined in importance.[46] The professional middle-class discourse that sought to apply scientific principles to the body in order to enhance its strength and regenerative capacities remained a staple in popular magazines.[47]

The Outdoors

The "sporting impulse" was part of a larger phenomenon, the intense interest in nature and the outdoors.[48] "Nature" has for every human culture signified some sphere existing prior to or outside of culture, yet any representation of nature is always bound up with a particular culture. So a focus on how magazines represented nature and the human stance toward it may tell us something about larger cultural changes.

By far the most dominant expression of the "outdoors" movement in popular magazines was the emphasis on "virility," adventure, and challenging oneself against the forces of nature. The hero, not only in adventure stories but also in the popular historical biographies of the 1890s and first few years of the twentieth century, was larger than life, a man who could utilize a seemingly endless supply of energy to tame his environment. Two other outdoor magazine themes, less important but still present, were an appreciation of the "outdoors" as an object of aesthetic pleasure and as an escape from the pressures of "civilization"—part of the tradition of "naturalism" and a depiction of the cataclysmic and unpredictable forces of nature.

An emphasis on "virility" and daring adventure can be seen in a number of articles that appeared in *Cosmopolitan.* Orrin E. Dunlap provided an account of "Niagara—The Scene of Perilous Feats." The article described various "daring feats" related to Niagara Falls, most of which ended in death. A series of dramatic photographs showed "Steve Peere Crossing Niagara Gorge [on a tightrope]," Harry and Sarah Allen standing alongside of a barrel "in which they went together through the rapids," and a somewhat comical portrait of "Charles D. Graham Dressed to Swim the Rapids."[49] Mrs. Aubrey Le Blond discussed the "Perils of the High Peaks," an account of some "terrible mountaineering tragedies" as well as advice on how to survive this dangerous sport. "Mountaineering," Mrs. Le Blond counseled, "is always dangerous." "It calls for exceptional qualities—strong bodies, iron nerves, a power to act on the instant. Only years of learning can give the knowledge that makes a competent mountaineer."[50]

In "Wonderful Whale-Hunting by Steam," the author described the growth of the steamboat whaling industry where "a kill of one thousand annually will be achieved." "No marine enterprise," the author continued, "has attracted such world-wide attention, or has been accompanied with such dramatic and hazardous incidents as whale hunting in its various forms." Evidently the sportsman could now have his cake and eat it too, since "the chase of the rorquals of Newfoundland" offered "exciting enthusiasm" and adventure but "without involving the hazards attending the old-time pursuits." A number of photographs showed the whaling ships in action with shots of "Whale Carcasses Stripped of Their Blubber," "The Markings on a Whale's Body as They Appear After the Operation of Flensing" and "A Newfoundland Whaler with Three Prizes in Tow."[51] An opening *Cosmopolitan* piece described the pleasures and dangers of "Winter Sports," highlighting the "dangers and skills in ice-yachting, skiing, ice-hockey, tobogganing, sleighing." A variety of unusual and challenging winter sports were depicted in photographs, including shots of "Skating with the Aid of Sails," "An Ice-Yacht Under Full Sail," "Skiing—in Mid-Air," and "Racing with Sleighs."[52]

Magazine fiction contained more than a few adventure stories involving dramatic and daring confrontations with nature or that highlighted some vigorous physical activity. The stories of Jack London, Rudyard Kipling, and Owen Wister's best-selling novel *The Virginian* seemed to provide a clear contrast to the sentimental fiction of the mid- to late nineteenth century. A *Cosmopolitan* article on London's upcoming trip around the world on a forty-five-foot boat was accompanied by a half-page photograph of the young adventurer as well as a dramatic illustration of a small sailing boat on stormy waters.[53] *Cosmopolitan* published a serial by Frederic Remington, "The Way of an Indian," which told of "White Otter, a Cis-chis-chas boy" who "grows to manhood and wins the eagle plume of the warrior."[54] The "Indian" was widely thought of as "primitive" and therefore close to nature. Here the lead character was also a warrior who, unlike his civilized counterparts, seemed to have no problem with lacking a purpose in life. In "East of Eden: The Story of a Man's Fight with Death in the Snow," Leo Crane told of two agents for a mining company who were sent to explore a mine that required a perilous journey through a riverbed and a canyon. The story also included references to "mind control," hypnotism, and

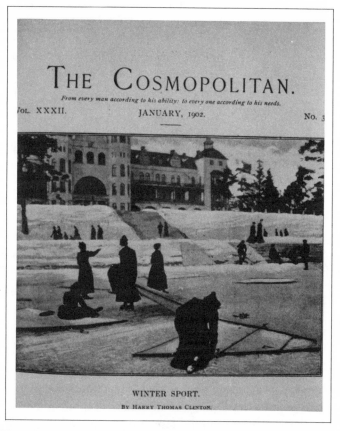

"Winter Sports," one of many popular magazine features on vigorous outdoor activities (*Cosmopolitan*, January 1902, p. 235).

mediums. One of the characters had been an assistant to a hypnotist and medium. Eventually both went crazy and "rushed down a slope fading into the leaden mists." Here we have a combination of themes—a dangerous and adventurous confrontation with nature as well as a loss of purpose and will associated with hypnotism and spiritualism, ending with death.[55]

The aesthetic appreciation of nature was reflected in the growing interest in bird-watching and in "naturalism."[56] This theme was dominant in Gilder's

Century in part because of the editor's environmentalist concerns but also because of the opportunity such articles afforded for quality woodcuts. Camping and more active forms of nature exploration were often discussed in terms of their healthy effects in providing a reinvigorating and restful escape from the artificial and pressured world of "civilization." The outdoors could provide a place to test one's will, to experience the pleasure of overcoming an obstacle, or on the other hand, the pleasure associated with the outdoors might be more akin to that of "losing oneself" in one's surroundings, what Freud called the "oceanic feeling." Losing oneself in nature could provide a release from one's own ego, from the "morbid self consciousness" that many believed had become a national affliction.[57]

In "A Glacier Excursion in Norway," Hjalmar Hjorth Boyesen described his adventure on the fjords of Norway.[58] He described the "magic suspense that seems to pervade the air," and the silence that "is so intense that it vibrates upon a spiritual sense, subtler than hearing. . . . There is such a surfeit of the sublime that it becomes, after awhile, a weight upon your shoulders." Later he described the sense of the traveler in Norway "of his own vanishing insignificance in the presence of the titanic landscape." Boyesen described a conversation with his guide, a young Norwegian woman who had spent time in America but decided to return to her native land. Why, he asked, did you leave the United States? She replied,

> They [Americans] have no time for anything except making money; and what is the money good for, if you give yourself no time for spending it? Somehow, I don't know how to put it; but there isn't the right joy in living in America. They don't know what it is to be gay and happy; and nothing will ever teach them.

Later in the adventure Boyesen confessed he fantasized that he was part of a glacier, "embedded in a huge gigantic block." Here was an outdoor adventure that provided an account not of nature as an obstacle to be conquered through willful, vigorous engagement but as an opportunity to lose oneself, to feel the sublime majesty in nature, to escape the joyless money-making of American civilization.

In "The Music of Nature," Helen Lukens Jones celebrated nature "in her most entrancing moods." The "music of nature . . . gives man a new lease on life." This appreciation of nature's beauty and majesty was combined at the end of the article with a contrast between nature and civilization.

> But the culminating victory of Nature-music floods the heart of man when, after toilsome climbing, he stands on the crest of some high mountain. Far below, with coverlet of erst mist, is the titanic cradle of the world. Strife and wretchedness and corruption, and all other cankerous discordances of earth are shrouded by distance.[59]

Photographs of foggy mountain peaks, tranquil country ponds, and waves crashing onto rocks were accompanied by captions that compared "nature's moods" to music.[60]

But nature was not always characterized as so benign and accommodating to human needs. There were numerous articles in popular magazines that described cataclysmic natural events like volcanoes, floods, and cyclones. These articles conveyed an image of nature as untamed, chaotic, and powerful, defying human will. For example, in "Wonderful New Island Sea," the author reported on an irrigation project that attempted to tap the Colorado River for use in a long canal. But this effort to control nature didn't succeed. "The river ran forth with a vengeance cutting a deeper and wider channel than the irrigators had dreamed of. . . . Now instead of a great desert there is an inland sea. The sea is expanding in spite of all efforts to check the flood. The towns, railroads, and ranches are being inundated."[61]

The lead article in the July 1902 issue was a firsthand account of "The Eruption of Mont Pelee."[62] The science fiction story, "Omega," which was serialized throughout the 1893 *Cosmopolitan,* told of a collision between the earth and a comet. H. G. Wells's *In the Days of the Comet* was carried as a serialized novel in 1906. The April 1902 issue led with "Vesuvius, Destroyer of Cities," which described the adventures of B. F. Fisher and his party in climbing Vesuvius and provided a short history of the volcano which "like the beast, can never be tamed or chained." The large photograph on the opening page of the issue showed Vesuvius erupting in a fiery explosion. A full-page photograph showed the homes of Naples with "Vesuvius Smoking in the Distance." Other shots were of the ruins of Pompeii and "The Interior of the Crater During a Period of Inactivity."[63] The May 1903 issue of *McClure's* saw the beginning of a science fiction serial by astronomy professor Simon Newcomb called, "The End of the World."

In "Frozen Mountains of the Sea," Mary Elizabeth Jennings told of her trip to the northeast coast of Newfoundland to view some icebergs. She informed her readers that "the object of the trip were rest for tired brains and over-

THE COSMOPOLITAN.

From every man according to his ability: to every one according to his needs.

VOL. XXXII. APRIL, 1902. No. 6.

VESUVIUS, DESTROYER OF CITIES.

BY B. F. FISHER.

THE feeling of him who for the first time sees looming in the distance Vesuvius, destroyer of cities, is one of awe not unmixed with admiration. As one approaches nearer the dark, somber wastes and looks up at the smoke-wreathed brow of the "burning mountain," one cannot help thinking of the history of devastation and ruin which surrounds it. The fate of Pompeii, through whose ruins we are to pass in our ascent to the flaming crater, comes to our minds. The stately streets and pillared houses, the men and women pursuing their usual vocations without a thought of danger, life going busily on as in many other Roman cities—then the sudden destruction which this monster volcano had been brewing for centuries.

More than eighteen centuries ago—and yet the story of that dreadful day is as plain now as it was to the younger Pliny as he wrote the only good account which survives of the destruction of the splendid city. The number of lives blotted out can only be guessed at, but the mode of death can be seen in the moulds of bodies

"Vesuvius, Destroyer of Cities," part of the popular magazine depiction of nature out of control. This article described the adventures of B. F. Fisher and his party in climbing Vesuvius (*Cosmopolitan*, April 1902, p. 573).

strained nerves." But rather than experiencing pleasure at the sight of the "dashing waves" caused by the icebergs, she felt "as if the whole world swayed to and fro." Her final comment was that

> there was no longer any pleasure in the sight. . . . [The icebergs] seemed to our excited fancy like huge monsters waiting for their prey. Even the waves

> laughed sullenly as they pounded them, and that night our desire for an intimate acquaintance with icebergs was quenched forever.[64]

The author's two motives for her excursion into nature, an escape from civilization and "an intimate acquaintance with icebergs," ended with a fearful escape from an environment now perceived as threatening and unpredictable. Prominent photographs on each page showed a number of large icebergs of varying shapes and sizes. One shot demonstrated the size of an iceberg by showing a small rowboat nearby.

What should we make of this theme (rarely found in the *Century*) of nature out of control, a malevolent rather than a benign influence? While many readings are possible, the interest in the awesome powers of nature can be understood as a symbol of the economic and social crisis facing American society during the 1890s and the turn of the twentieth century. The experience of humility in coping with the forces of nature must have resonated with readers trying to understand the massive social forces transforming American society, from economic concentration and rapid urbanization to the unprecedented impact of science and technology on industry and the daily life of citizens. Just like a volcano, these massive social forces must have seemed to many Americans as mysterious, unintelligible, and even frightening. In addition, human nature (as well as "external" nature) seemed to be erupting with energy. The "new psychology,"[65] the mind cure movement, and various spiritualist developments[66] began to depict the human psyche as containing a store of energy of which the "will" or ego was only one part.

Perhaps we can also understand the depiction of nature as malevolent and unpredictable in terms of what some have called the national ideology of American exceptionalism. Part of this constellation of beliefs, deeply embedded in American history, is the notion that America, whether because of its frontier and abundant resources, successful revolution (in contrast to the French Revolution), stable republican institutions and other factors, would somehow escape the conflicts that faced the industrializing nations of Europe. America was a "new Adam," a great experiment in democracy that would be a departure from the past. Such a view located the nation not in terms of its place in history but as a refuge from history—a utopian experiment in a perpetual state of nature rather than a nation subject to evolutionary and qualitative change. But with growing class conflict and economic crisis, America seemed to be turning into a version of Europe, to be reentering history. Nature, a symbol of the uncorrupted American Republic, no longer seemed so benign.

New Women and Restless Women

While magazines were commenting in various ways on sports, the outdoors, and the forces of nature, they were also exploring through articles and fiction the activities of a new generation of women in college, athletics, and social reform.[67] As we have seen, nervous disorders were thought to be particularly common among women, especially educated women. The diagnosis differed depending on the gender and political persuasion of the diagnostician. Some male doctors thought the problem could be traced to "overeducation" and the pressures and strains of career.[68] Dimest S. Denison of *Woman's Home Companion* traced women's health problems to the "enlarged opportunities and sense of new duties" of the modern woman. But rather than urging women to refrain from these activities, she urged more rest, leisure, and recreation. Rest and recreation were to complement rather than replace women's new duties.[69] Many women reformers and writers in the late nineteenth century attributed the poor health of the late Victorian woman to a lack of vigorous engagement with life. Increasingly, college-educated women were chafing at the restrictions of Victorian respectability. Jane Addams spoke for many other women of her class and generation when she looked back nostalgically on the "useful contributions" women made during an earlier generation when women were contributors to the rural household and longed for a chance to be part of "life."[70] Neurasthenia was, for many of this generation of middle-class women, a result not of too much study at college or the pressure of earning a living, but a consequence of being trapped in a claustrophobic world of Victorian gentility.

Ella Wheeler Wilcox expressed this view in "The Restlessness of Modern Women." Wilcox believed, in contrast to the medical profession, that "the happiest women are the hard-working ones. Not the overtaxed drudges, but wives and mothers, whose hands and minds are busy . . . or the women who hold responsible positions requiring all their waking hours and thoughts." It is the wealthy and the idle woman who feels "restless and aimless," plagued by "purposeless discontent." "Beneath jeweled corsages beat restless hearts; from under the flower-laden brims of modish hats look unhappy eyes, gazing into the world with longing for an indefinable something—a happiness imagined but unattained." Wilcox reported that a woman wrote to her complaining, "I drag through the days, glad when night comes and I can go to sleep. Can you tell me how to find an object, an aim, which shall give me an interest in existence?" The restless woman was a burden not only to herself but, according to Wilcox, they also drive their husbands to strain every nerve "to accumulate great fortunes." Evidently, restless wives created nervous husbands. The answer was for the restless woman to "look and try to see what is the nearest avenue of usefulness open to you."[71]

The emphasis on usefulness and athletic vigor as an antidote to restlessness and lack of purpose could also be found in the world of fiction. Sentimental fiction written largely by women writers for a female audience had its stock set of female invalids, illnesses, fragile heroines. The death-bed scene in which a woman or a young girl lay dying, surrounded by loved ones, was so common that it became the object of parody. Mark Twain parodied the sentimental obsession with death and illness in his famous passage from *Huckleberry Finn* on the Gangerfords.[72] William Dean Howells characterized Victorian middle-class society as "a hospital for invalid females."[73] Catherine Beecher in *Letters to the People on Health and Happiness,* published in 1854, claimed that "female invalidism" was rampant. In a sample of American communities she came to the remarkable conclusion that sick women outnumbered the healthy by a ratio of three to one.[74] The fiction of vigorous adventure and realism provided, for many readers, a refreshing contrast to the sentimentality that dominated women's fiction in the nineteenth century. The adventure story and the historical romance, many with female protagonists or at least secondary characters (often exotic, foreign females), allowed the female reader to vicariously experience the adventure of the wide world. Realism appealed to the urge to be useful, to see life as it is. Rather than viewing life through sentimental blinders, the new "domestic" realism presented the realities of marriage and motherhood—with all the conflicts, ambiguities, and doubts.[75]

Female contributors to popular magazines began to depart from the Victorian image of women in their articles on social reform, college life, athletics, marriage, and motherhood. In certain respects, many of the women writers who contributed articles for *Cosmopolitan* and other popular magazines were a product of a generation of women who were working outside the home and attending college in larger numbers. In 1900 a third of all women between sixteen and twenty were employed in paid labor, the majority of whom were single women. Many worked in the rapidly growing clerical sector of the business world. Back in 1870 most women wage earners were domestic servants, farm workers, factory hands, or seamstresses.[76] Among middle-class women, there was a growing number attending women's colleges. There were 85,000 women enrolled in college in 1900 and 250,000 by 1920. In 1900, 17 percent of all college alumni were women, and by 1920 the figure was 40 percent.[77] Clearly the older concern that college was harmful to the health of women had been largely refuted.[78]

Eleanor Gates, in "The Woman Who Travels Alone," a much talked-about series on the problems of the "lone girl traveler," expressed some of the anxieties associated with changes in Victorian conceptions of womanhood.[79] Gates, "a young woman of the West who has spent several years in New York," was a passionate supporter of women's rights and urged that women "not accept insults without resistance" in order to "keep herself womanly." "I admire the woman," Gates proclaimed, "who knows her rights and . . . claims them."[80] In the introduction to the series, the editor asked, "Is Chivalry as pervasive and dominant a characteristic of our national life as it was a few decades ago?"[81] The conclusion of the series focused on "The Brave Young Woman Who Faces the Problem of Earning Her Own Living."[82]

The phrase "new woman" applied primarily to the women who were educated in the new women's colleges.[83] While small in number, their cultural influence was significant as many were active as reformers, journalists, professionals, and writers. Following shortly after a series on American universities, Harold Bolce in 1910 wrote a number of articles for *Cosmopolitan* on the higher education of women. According to the "Shop Talk" introduction to this series, the "friends of the higher education of women . . . believe that it means a new and revolutionary era, in which creeds and many conventions and institutions will go down."[84] In "Away From Ancient Alters," Bolce described "the newer womanhood" of college women. The new women, according to Bolce, reject a life "of either resignation or ease." She is intent to live life joyfully, hearing the age-old "call to service . . . to wage war on the powers of evil." The new woman was an advocate of the methods and approaches of social science (Bolce considered this to be part of the "new religion") and an opponent of the "laissez-faire policy." On the same page in which Bolce discussed the new woman's "ethic of service" was a photograph of a crew of Wellesley women rowing in an athletic competition.[85]

Approximately a decade before the Bolce articles, Lavinia Hart wrote approvingly about the new women's colleges in the pages of *Cosmopolitan*. Hart described the rituals and traditions of Vassar, Bryn Mawr, Smith, and Wellesley. The female students "are mostly drawn from those medium walks of life wherein ambition is given impetus by necessity." Unlike male colleges "the spirit of restlessness" is noticeably absent. There were vigorous athletics but also, Hart observed, a spirit of camaraderie and fair play. "The winners argue it is sweet enough to win; crowing over the defeated ones will add nothing to their glory. . . . It is this consideration for the feelings of others that gives to the girls' colleges their distinctive feminine tone." Hart devoted a large portion of her article to female athletics, describing basketball as the "universal favorite sport" as well as tennis, golf, lacrosse, swimming, cycling, high-jumping, and running events.[86] Photographs showed college women engaged in fencing, playing basketball, "Marching to the Athletic Field," and doing gymnastics "On the Flying Ring." Hart's distinction between men's sports and women's sports was an important one, for even female advocates of physical education made this distinction. Like Hart, many women believed that athletic activity among women did not have to suffer from the overly competitive, overly specialized, and often violent character of male sports. Sports for women should reflect not only perceived gender differences but also should focus on the mental and physical development of the student or athlete—a perspective that reflected the growing number of women in physical education and other health professions.[87]

The vigorous and athletic image of the "new woman" was presented in a wide range of articles in *Cosmopolitan* and *Munsey's* as well as the *Woman's Home Companion.* In "The New Woman and Golf Playing," Mrs. Reginald de Koven asserted that "what the bicycle has left undone toward the transformation of life of the American woman, the game of golf bids fair to complete."[88] During the same year, Anna Wentworth Sears observed, "If our respected great- grandmothers could be recalled to this time and generation with what amazement they would behold the attitude of the present race of young womankind to all things athletic."[89] Gertrude Lynch wrote about the "Yachtswomen of America."[90] While Cleopatra may have been the first yachtswoman, living an "inactive, sensuous life on the flower-decked barge," the modern woman is "tense in muscle as in purpose, with a clear eye fixed on a far horizon or studying the quadrant at her side."[91] Many of these articles expressed the discourse that focused on the exclusivity and separation of upper-class sports from the larger society (rather than an ethic of social service and usefulness).

Woman's Home Companion printed a short article titled "Sixteen *Woman's Home Companion* Readers Explain to Us How They Enjoyed Themselves Last Summer." One woman, who described herself and her husband as both "office-workers," "put up a tent and camped on their land." She and her husband built a tree house together. Three women—a stenographer, a bookkeeper, and a cashier—went canoeing and camping together. Another woman "like Molly of Owen Wister's story" settled down with her "Virginian" in a "sleepy little

Oregon town." On their honeymoon they went horseback riding and "also spent days with friends fishing, crabbing, gathering clams and starfish and odd shells." Still another couple went "Camping Out in a Farm House."[92] Alongside articles on "How to Pay Off Church Debts" and "Fads and Frill of Fashion," *Woman's Home Companion* printed articles on "Home Health Exercise for the Busy Woman," "Winter Sports at Home and Abroad," "For the Woman Who Travels Alone," and "The College Girl at Play" as well as articles that were appearing in general interest magazines such as "The Wonders of Modern Warfare," "My Recollections of Abraham Lincoln," and "General View of the St.Louis Exposition—Most Wonderful of the World's Fairs."[93]

A series of articles and stories portrayed a new ideal of marriage—based on companionship. By "companionship" many contributors seemed to be referring to breaking through the formalities of Victorian gender roles. They also expressed the growing concern among the middle class with the rising divorce rate. Julius Henri Browne asked, "Are Women Companionable to Men? Does idealization mean companionship? Many a man is ready to die for a woman who would not and could not live with her." Companionship, he argued, is "very rare between men and women." The evolutionary trend, Browne maintained, is for "sex differences to narrow" so that men and women may eventually achieve what is now only an ideal.[94] Elizabeth Cady Stanton contributed a short critique of the institution of marriage, stating that men do not consider what it is like for the married woman "who loses her individual sovereignty, her personal independence and her civil rights."[95]

Rafford Pyke asked, "Why do so many women marry the wrong man?" Most young women, he argued, have not thought seriously about marriage. They confuse love for being admired and never get to know the man they are to marry. "The actualities of marriage find her totally unprepared. The biggest revelation is one of character; the character of the man to whose life her own is linked; and what is often more startling, she knows her husband as he really is. The veil is drawn aside." Pyke recommended that women should cultivate more friendships with men. "By falling in and out of love, by testing and comparing, she will at last become an expert who makes no mistakes."[96] Lavinia Hart asked, "Has love a time limit? Are ideals impossible of attainment?" She counseled "extreme candor and broadest intercourse" as "absolute essentials in the conduct of a happy married life." Unfortunately, the "way of young lovers" is to "hide their true selves."[97]

A number of short and serialized stories illustrate the interest in the new ideal of companionship in marriage and changing conceptions of gender among the middle class. *Munsey's* serialized a novel by English author Anthony Hope, *Double Harness.* The focus was on "the greatest problem of modern life—the marriage question." The protagonists are Grantley Imason, a rich banker, and his wife Sybilla. During the first episode Sybilla considers what she means to her husband, "a great acquisition perhaps expressed it, a cherished treasure. She was outside his innermost thoughts." For Grant, the problem of marriage, from the vantage point of men, is that "if he's not emotional, he's not interesting, if he's emotional, he's not manly. Take it as you will, the woman is bound to win." Sybilla complains that Grant is distant from herself and their child. Grant feels that his wife has had overly high expectations of marriage.[98]

Other stories in *Munsey's* dramatized various features of the "new woman." In "A Man of Success" a daughter of a wealthy self- made man refuses to marry her father's choice—a young executive. Instead, she falls in love with a "Church organist whose church was known for its work among the poor of the city." When told by her father that the organist cannot support her "in her position" she replies, "I care nothing about my position as you call it. . . . I want to live in earnest, with people who work and do things."[99] In "The Burton House Beautiful," the new woman shows up as a friend of the wife of the protagonist. Eugenia Burton is described as a "very unconventional woman." Along with her unmarried sisters, "they drink, smoke, engage in opinionated conversation, discuss sex—all the things that Curtis believed were unfeminine."[100] Quite often a "new woman" was contrasted with a more conventional one as in "Bertha's Mr. Wentworth." Bertha is described as a "plain looking, only mildly interesting young woman." Her sister Caroline is an "attractive, unconventional new woman." Bertha's suitor is a "stuffy priggish" lawyer, Mr. Wentworth. On a double date, Bertha becomes upset because she thinks that Wentworth is more attracted to the charismatic Caroline. It turns out that Wentworth "prefers the seriousness and domestic virtues of her sister Bertha."[101] In "A Symphony in Two Flats," two college-educated women, Penelope and her sister Alice, who both attend Smith, have a romantic adventure. Penelope is described as "energetic, assertive . . . somewhat scatterbrained and thoroughly unconventional."[102]

Popular magazines also helped to spread the professional ethos into the family sphere, urging a redefinition of women's roles within the family. Ella Wheeler Wilcox wrote about the "profession of parentage," arguing that both motherhood as well as fatherhood were professions and that American parents were failing to prepare themselves for this task.[103] Lavinia Hart echoed this theme in urging that the young mother resolve "to give her girls a more thorough education for motherhood than her foolish or ignorant mother gave her. . . . What course of training are our girls receiving for motherhood? Every college lacks the curriculum which will directly influence their standards and status as wives and mothers."[104]

John Brisben Walker, as part of the series "On the Choice of a Profession," also wrote about motherhood. "Should motherhood be a profession?" he asked. His response was that a profession is "an occupation which undertakes to direct intelligently the lives and affairs of others." Therefore, women must "adapt themselves by a study of the scientific principles affecting the requirements of their life work."[105] Women could be useful by applying modern scientific principles to the management of a home and by successfully raising children.[106]

Abundant Energy and Widening Horizons

The way out of restlessness for Ella Wilcox was to "do something useful." But Wilcox, Lavinia Hart, and many others believed that this was only part of the solution. After all, how do you summon up the energy to do something useful? Increasingly, middle-class women and men spoke of a source of abundant energy located within the self. Many writers were influenced by the mind cure movement as well as other spiritualist developments.[107] Here was a way out of depression, lack of energy, and purposelessness. The cure was to tap the inner reaches of one's being, and there one would find the answer. In "To Love or to Be Loved," Lavinia Hart spoke of "The Great Source of human life which is the power to breathe, is the Great Source of the higher life which is the power to love."[108] For a woman *to be* loved, Hart argued, was not enough. She must learn *to* love and thus connect herself to this "divine source" of energy and purpose. Wilcox in her short autobiographical essay confessed that she persisted in her literary career despite early rejections because she relied on her own inner resources rather than seeking advice. "I am glad I did not [seek advice] for the moment we lean on anyone but the Divine Power and the divinity within us, we lessen our chances for success."[109]

In an article published in *Arena*,[110] Wilcox commented on the "large number of intellectual and reliable people" who had "given their testimony . . . to investigation into the occult, and proofs of the existence of forces not yet explained by science or reason." The article sought to explain "Theosophy" and relate it to other spiritualist movements. There is a knowledge of a higher reality, available to everyone, "a knowledge which reveals to every man the

Christ within himself." This knowledge is "the marriage tie between Science and Religion, and an armor of strength to every soul who seeks and finds it." Clearly, the Christian concept of sin and alienation from God were not central to the spiritualism that Wilcox advocated. One only had to remove psychological blockages to become rejuvenated by sources of abundant energy.[111] Spiritualism often inspired fear among defenders of the genteel tradition because of its association with the loss of willpower, the merging of the ego into some larger sphere or "plane of energy." But a temporary release from or regrounding of the ego could be therapeutic and serve to reinvigorate the self for another day's worth of striving.

In her contribution to the series, "What Life Means to Me," Wilcox used the terms "exhilaration, anticipation, realization, usefulness and growth" to characterize her sense of life's meaning. The article was filled with images of abundance. Despite facing economic need as a child, "I always expected sudden opulence." "While hungry in heart and brain, I believed that splendid banquets were in preparation for me." As a result of her outlook on life, "unusual things did happen." "The commonplace meadows blossomed with flowers of beauty; and buttercups and daisies looked to me like rare orchids and hothouse roses." With each new opportunity her "world widened," and the "earth palpitated with new experiences as the years passed. Always I expected more and more of life, and always it came in some guise." She confessed that "the taste of city life and its pleasures intoxicated me." She reported that she had taken up athletics and physical culture and had become "intimate with the sea and knew the intoxication . . . found in and on the ocean waves." This sense of being in touch with a source of abundant energy also led to her conviction that one must live a useful life, to have a sense of social obligation. "Instead of being merely a helper in the home, I realized that I must be a helper in the universe . . . and from that hour humanity became my family."[112] Wilcox's sense of expansiveness was connected not only to the spiritualist movements of the period, but like many other reformers she was influenced by the Social Gospel movement, which taught that the message of Christ required a commitment to improve the social conditions of the poor as well as to save individual souls. Wilcox's deep conviction that within the self was a source of abundant energy led her to another personal insight, a feeling of connection to the wider universe as well as a deep feeling for her fellow human beings, a feeling that was quite consistent with others of her generation (even those who did not have her interest in spiritualism). Clearly, Wilcox was not worried about exhausting her supply of energy.

The pages of *Cosmopolitan* contained numerous articles on Christian Science, and references to mind-cure and other spiritual movements were common. Mark Twain caused a minor sensation when he parodied Christian Science in "Christian Science and the Book of Mrs. Eddy."[113] A few years later two articles defended Christian Science vehemently.[114] In a series of articles on American colleges, Harold Bolce tried his best to arouse the interest of *Cosmopolitan* readers with a discussion of the non-Christian forms of spirituality among university professors. "The schoolmen," Bolce asserted, "have replaced Christianity." But "they are not atheists. They assert that we need not less of God but more of God."[115] Bolce claimed that "evangelical emotionalism" was not in favor among university faculty, but Christian Science, New Thought, and the Emmanuel movement, which study spiritual phenomena "in a cold scientific manner" were highly regarded.[116] "God is a spirit, not a potentate, the professors insist." Bolce asserted that the professors "have allied themselves with the forces of spiritual health and healing." Associated with these forces of spiritual health and healing was "the new psychology," which Bolce claimed "teaches that the spirit of man is the highest conscious expression of the Infinite and that by invoking the powers—the divine forces—resident in the human, all that humanity desires may be accomplished."[117]

The Christian social gospel rather than mind cure or spiritualism was the source of inspiration to many who were looking for an alternative to growing secularization. But there were some close affinities between these movements. Whether it took the form of mind-cure, spiritualism, or, more commonly, the new Social Gospel movement, God was becoming more immanent, a force *in* the world, as well as more impersonal.[118] The new Social Gospel movement was still part of the Protestant tradition and so retained the concept of sin and human fallibility. Nevertheless, both the new Social Gospel movement and spiritualist groups challenged the orthodox Protestant view of man as radically alienated and detached from God.

Popular magazines, by the mid-1890s, in a variety ways were expressing as well as contributing to the new culture's emphasis on *energy*, *action*, and *desire*. These were the key words that appeared over and over again in articles on a variety of topics. In a 1905 lead article ("The Philosophy of Staying in Harness"), James H. Canfield articulated his philosophy of human nature.

> That which seems to be the impelling force in man is his desire. To satisfy desire he puts forth energy—from the feeblest and crudest manifestations by which he hopes to prolong mere animal existence, to the most exalted efforts

> of the human soul to understand the illimitable and to master the eternal plans of the Infinite.[119]

The conclusion of the science fiction serial "Omega" informed readers of the vastness of the universe of which the earth is a part. While planets may come and go, "infinite space" remains. "There is an incommensurable Power, which we are obliged to recognize as limitless in space and without beginning or end in time."[120] In a caption to a one-page illustration of muscular workmen that opened the February 1911 issue of the Hearst *Cosmopolitan,* readers were told, "To be healthy and sane and well you must work with your hands as well as your head. The cure for grief is motion. The recipe for strength is action."[121]

The Martial Ethic and Other "Manly Virtues"

Central ingredients in this popular magazine recipe for strength and action were the masculine heroes of magazine biographies and the articles on the military and war. State building and war-making were central themes in Ida Tarbell's biography of Napoleon, a series that was a major contribution to a national cult of Napoleon. Accounts of Napoleon's life and anyone remotely related to him appeared frequently in popular and genteel magazines during the 1890s. In addition to these magazine articles, there were twenty-eight books about Napoleon published between 1894 and 1896.[122]

The Tarbell series on Napoleon ran throughout 1894 and 1895 in *McClure's.* Tarbell traced the career of Napoleon from his childhood in which he "domineered over his brothers and fearing no one, ran wild on the beach with the sailors or over the mountains with the herdsmen, listening to their tales of the Corsican rebellion and of fights on sea and land." In discussing Napoleon's stint in a government military school, his promotions to the military school at Paris, and eventually to the command of an army, Tarbell quoted classmates, teachers, and generals who were struck by Napoleon's strength of will and character and "clairvoyant eyes that knew how to compel obedience." While Tarbell devoted many pages to Napoleon's military campaigns and successes, she also devoted over one-third of the series to "Napoleon as Statesman and Lawgiver," "Founding of Bank of Finance," "Codification of Laws," and his founding of the "Legion of Honor." The fact that so many political leaders and industrial empire builders (first and foremost, Theodore Roosevelt) were compared to Napoleon would seem to indicate that Tarbell's emphasis on Napoleon as warrior as well as nation builder struck a responsive chord.

But in addition to Napoleon, many other biographies appeared in both popular and genteel magazines. The multipart historical biography was a popular genre in virtually every magazine during the 1890s. *Cosmopolitan*'s contribution to this phenomenon, in addition to Napoleon, was its "Great Passions of History" series. Biographies included Anthony and Cleopatra, Marie Antoinette, Christ, and Napoleon.[123] Consistent with the emphasis in *McClure's* (like all magazines it also carried biographies of Christ and Napoleon), these features seemed intent on demonstrating that "the individual can still make a difference."[124]

Theodore Roosevelt, in the many articles he contributed to magazines during the 1890s, articulated this combination of martial and "masculine" values along with nationalistic themes. Roosevelt and others from genteel, upper-class backgrounds saw the building up of a strong military, capable of leading an active and interventionist foreign policy, as part of a larger project of cultural revitalization. Sports and athleticism were part of this project because they taught an ethic of duty and sacrifice to the state and prepared the citizen for other forms of commitment and sacrifice. It is not surprising that during this period the armed forces for the first time began to use sports as part of their training for new recruits.[125] In "Military Preparedness and Unpreparedness," Roosevelt attributed the successful military campaign against Spain (in Cuba and the Philippines) to the "far-sighted" naval buildup and the training of seamen and naval officers, starting in 1883 under President Chester Arthur. He went on to make an appeal for a better-equipped and prepared army.[126]

A few years earlier, Roosevelt had attempted to define a unifying national ideal beyond that of material success and "Yankee ingenuity." The country suffered, he argued, from an absence of idealism, vision, and patriotic sense of duty. Most dangerous were the "professional labor agitators" and "the dangerous criminals of the wealthy classes." Roosevelt claimed that "demagogues" like Gov. John Altgeld of Illinois catered to the "mob," while those "bent only on amassing a fortune" were "insensible to every duty, regardless of every principle." A theme in both essays was that the upper class and political leadership of the country had to develop a long-range view of the nation's future and that narrow "materialism" would not suffice. "The mere materialist is, above all, shortsighted." As evidence for this Roosevelt mentioned an article by Edward Atkinson arguing that the country did not need to spend money on building up its military. Roosevelt derided such a view by pointing to the role the army played in saving "Chicago from the fate of Paris in 1870" (the use of federal troops to put down the Pullman strike) and in preventing "a terrible social war in the West." "To men of a certain kind, trade and property are far more sacred than life or honor, of far more consequence than the great thoughts and lofty emotions, which alone make a nation mighty." Perhaps we can see the connection here between "overcivilization" (in this case the narrow pursuit of wealth) and a short-sighted inability to put the nation's interest first. Revealingly, Roosevelt characterized the "mere materialist" as "utterly incapable of feeling one thrill of generous emotion, or the slightest throb of that pulse which gives to the world statesmen, patriots, warriors and poets, and which makes a nation other than a cumberer of the world's surface." No wonder "mere materialists" suffered from exhaustion and lack of willpower—they had no transcendent ideal for which they were ready to sacrifice, no purpose that would cause a "throb of pulse" or a "thrill of generous emotion." What America needed was a new sense of national purpose, a revitalization of the nation's store of energy through service to the "higher and nobler" ideals of patriotism and empire building.[127]

Roosevelt was certainly not alone in articulating these themes. Former mugwump Francis Parkman, historian, also espoused a "cult of masculinity and toughness" that corresponded to his own experiences of overcoming physical difficulties.[128] Henry Cabot Lodge, [129] who was in the U.S. Senate, and Alfred Mahan, who headed the Newport Naval War College, were among those who argued for investment in the military—especially the navy—as early the 1880s.[130] A large part of their argument for a revitalized military was that industrialism produced large surpluses that required foreign as well as domestic markets. A powerful navy would be essential to protect these distant markets and thereby the wealth of a growing industrial nation. Brooks Adams was a late convert to this view that had already gathered considerable adherents among the upper class and among national politicians. Adams expressed this view in his *McClure's* article, "The New Struggle for Life Among Nations."[131] But Roosevelt and Lodge were not entirely comfortable with narrow economic justifications for a military buildup and developed a broader moral and even psychological perspective connecting national military power with personal health, public service, and patriotism—an "ideology of empire."[132]

John Brisben Walker, while far more sympathetic to labor than Roosevelt, had a similar perspective on military preparedness, on associating political reform with "manly courage," and in his emphasis on personal health and physical culture.[133] Walker believed (perhaps influenced by Herbert Spencer) that the new phase of social evolution would be a pacific one and that various forms of international arbitration of conflict would eventually do away with war. Nevertheless, the pages of *Cosmopolitan* were filled with articles on "Recent Developments in Gun-Making," "The Militia," "The Fighting Forces of Germany," "National Guard Camps of Instruction, and Their Faults," "The Swedish Military Forces," "The Army of Japan," "Detention and the Military Prison," "War: Some Generals Who Would Command in Case of War," "The Meloban and the Pentheroy; An Episode of Modern Warfare," among others. This international perspective, which compared and found wanting aspects of the American military, provided support to the view that advocated a military buildup. It may also have served the "agenda setting" function of bringing military and international issues to the attention of a national audience. *McClure's* and *Munsey's* as well, popularized the martial and "manly virtues" that were becoming a national creed. While Walker was not as stridently pro-imperialist as Munsey, he was an ardent internationalist and believer in the importance of preserving and extending American economic and political interests throughout the world. As is well known, William Randolph Hearst, who bought *Cosmopolitan* from Walker in 1905, played a major role in arousing popular opinion against the Spanish rule in Cuba.[134]

Cosmopolitan readers were kept informed every month on developments in the Boer War with a "firsthand account of Mr. Kruger," who "just returned from the battle line when I saw him in Pretoria" (articles on the Boer War included"The Youngest Soldiers in the World" and "General De Wet and His Campaign"). While opposing England's effort to hang on to its territorial possessions in South Africa, John Brisben Walker asserted,

> The Boers have demonstrated what a people not deprived of virility by luxury may do. In their forces merit has commanded position. . . . Incidentally attention may be called to the strength of that commonwealth where every republican possesses a gun, becomes familiar with its use as a part of the republic.[135]

Shortly after the intervention of foreign troops (including U.S. marines) to crush the Boxer Rebellion in China, Walker wrote about "China and the Powers." While criticizing this intervention, Walker expressed the dominant position among U.S. policymakers that Chinese territorial integrity had to be preserved in order to counter Russian expansionism. The many photographs in Walker's article appealed to his readers' interest in the foreign and the exotic with shots of a Chinese "Court of Justice," "Well Born Chinese at Their Favorite Game," "Mandarins Assembled at Peking," and "Entrance to the Palace Grounds, Peking."[136]

Of course, all the popular magazines devoted a large percentage of space to coverage of the Spanish-American War in Cuba and the Philippines. *Munsey's*[137] carried an eleven-part series on "Our War with Spain" by managing editor Richard H. Titherington, which depicted "the story of the struggle in which the United States won so remarkable a triumph, opening a new era of our national expansion."[138] Edwin Wildman, U.S. Vice Consul at Hong Kong, contributed to a series on "The Filipinos," which told the story of "the eight million orientals who have come under the American flag—what they are today and what education and good government may help them to become."[139] Walstein Root, a *New York Sun* correspondent who was stationed at Havana, wrote about "the critical period of change through which Cuba is passing today—what our government has done for the island, and why it is not satisfied with American control."[140] John Barrett, formerly U.S. minister to Siam, discussed "The Value of the Philippines." While assuring *Munsey's* readers that American occupation was good for the Filipinos, he was primarily interested in demonstrating "that they are a good financial investment on the part of the United States and capable of extended trade and business development. . . . The Philippines afford the most valuable field of development, exploitation and investment yet untouched beyond the borders of the Untied States."[141]

Among the many *Cosmopolitan* articles on the wars with Spain was an account of "A Dangerous Mission to Spain," written "by the only person of American nationality who rendered secret service in Spain during the war."[142] Other articles included "After the Capture of Manilla," "Philippines—Shall They Be Annexed?"[143] and "In Southern Spain During the War."[144] Stephen Crane's short story, "The Woof of Thin Red Threads," captured the drama of the Spanish-American War with graphic descriptions of battles and soldiers' wounds. But unlike *The Red Badge of Courage,* there was no subtext about the contrast between heroic sentimentality and the realities of war in this work. As the protagonist's friend lies dying on the battlefield, Crane tells us that "he had loved the regiment, the army, because the regiment, the army was his life." The story ends with the soldier and his dying friend singing "The Star-Spangled Banner."[145]

Conclusion

This chapter has suggested that popular magazines gave expression to and helped to popularize a new therapeutic culture or what some have called a "secular religion of health." If anything the new religion of athleticism, health, and abundant energy has intensified today as Americans join health clubs, jog and work out, diet, show off their physiques in various ways, and visit therapists, among other things.[146] In contrast to the Victorian emphasis on self-control and conservation of a limited energy supply, the new therapeutic culture sought to tap into new energies that were thought to be inexhaustible.

The discussion in this chapter of the turn-of-the-century interest in health shows a close connection between the genteel and popular magazines. Certainly many of the concerns about neurasthenia and overcivilization expressed in *Atlantic Monthly*, the *Century*, and *Scribner's* found their way to *Cosmopolitan*, *McClure's*, and *Munsey's*. We have seen how the genteel discourse on sports and athleticism as a vehicle for character building and nation building was part of popular magazines during the 1890s. This is not surprising since contributors to the two sets of magazines were quite similar in the 1890s. The point here is that the genteel tradition and the perspective of the mugwumps should not be equated in a mechanical way with the family house magazines. The genteel discourse could be found throughout popular magazines during the 1890s and in other cultural forms as well. Nevertheless, the trend over the entire period is that popular magazines began to depart from the genteel discourse in many important ways. Modern life was no longer the problem—causing a range of physical and psychological disorders—but was in fact part of the solution. While George M. Beard thought that the noise of cities contributed to nervousness, popular magazines began to highlight the noises of popular music and urban nightlife. While S. Weir Mitchell worried about the nervousness of career women, Ella Wilcox counseled female readers to "do something useful" and found new purpose and energy in reform activities, athleticism, and the excitement of urban life. While Gilder's *Century* continued the tradition of sedate pieces on nature appreciation, popular magazines emphasized the willful confrontation with the forces of nature as well as characterizations of nature as out of control. Popular magazines gave expression to the professional discourse on health and the body, a discourse that emphasized scientific expertise, in marked contrast to genteel concerns about narrow specialization. Moreover, the professional discourse, in contrast to the genteel tradition, saw self-development and self-fulfillment as an ideal rather than self-control and sacrifice for larger social goals and purposes. Finally, popular magazine articles on upper-class sports and leisure activities presented to readers an ideal of luxury and freedom from want that contained an implicit utopian ideal—a society in which the majority of citizens would be freed from dependence upon work. Such an ideal, part of the dream of abundance to be discussed in the next chapter, was a far cry from genteel concerns with excessive materialism and luxury. The abundant energy that many popular magazine contributors located within the self presented another alternative to the cultural ideal of self-control and "character" espoused by genteel writers since the early nineteenth century.

A question that remains is how do we assess the impact of this culture, this search for health and vitality? One school of thought argues that therapeutic culture served to reinforce the hegemony of a new elite. Bodies and minds could be regenerated in order to better be able to pursue the gospel of work and success. Moreover, the concern for physical, mental, and spiritual health served to displace a host of potentially politically disruptive dissatisfactions with alienated labor, bureaucratization, and what was later called the "spiritual wasteland" of modern society onto the private sphere. The personal quest for health, which has intensified in recent years, encouraged consumers to assume responsibility for their ill health (or more broadly their dissatisfactions) and for their cure. In directing the attention of consumers away from the social sources of their dissatisfactions and the need for collective action, therapeutic culture can be thought of as an ideology, preparing the way for a modern consumer-oriented economy.

Nevertheless, it would be misleading to see these developments only as an ideology associated with the rise of consumerism and a modern state. Instead, they had deeper roots. They were part of a new national sensibility, or as Raymond Williams has put it, "structures of feeling."[147] Moreover, concerns about neurasthenia cannot be neatly explained away as "antimodern" or as a "reaction against industrialism." The language of illness and health went well beyond the genteel tradition's revolt against aspects of modern life. This language was also a staple of the popular magazine project to engage readers in the "whirlpool of real life," and to connect them to the very modern developments associated with urban life, social reform, and consumerism. In short, previously dormant energies were bursting through the pages of popular magazines, at times under control but at other times erupting like a volcano.

CHAPTER SIX

"New Worlds To Conquer": The Dreams of Progress

City of Dreams: The White City and Other Expositions

In the last chapter we saw how popular magazines, in a variety of ways, tapped into a national sensibility. Americans could feel revitalized through sports, physical culture and the outdoors, and regain a transcendent purpose through identification with the nation or involvement in social reform. There was, in other words, a desire to recapture something felt to be lost or missing—purpose or will, energy, a sense of fellowship with other human beings, a connection to the past, and a connection to nature. Within this context the popular and genteel magazines' fascination with historical biographies and historical fiction (in the 1890s) is understandable. On the one hand, these lively adventure stories and accounts of heroic deeds appealed to the growing taste for vigorous, willful action, and on the other hand it provided a sense of historical continuity in an era of rapid social and technological change. It is, in other words, not so much one stance or another toward industrial society that characterized American culture, but ambivalence. While retrospective and historical articles as well as concerns about "overcivilization" were certainly present, one cannot read these magazines without also being struck by their forward-looking and expansive celebration of progress, their sense that America was on the verge of taking the place of Europe as the center of technological, scientific, and industrial development.

In this chapter, three aspects of this celebration of progress will be explored. First, popular magazines reported on the technological drive to dominate and master the forces of nature. Accounts of explorations of the Arctic and Antarctic were especially popular as well as discussions of mammoth engineering projects and new transportation and manufacturing technology. The domination of nature was closely associated with the domination of non-Western societies, not only for economic resources but also as objects of curiosity for Western tourists. The fascination with non-Western and tribal societies, with the foreign and the exotic, was a particular focus of Walker's *Cosmopolitan,* although it was also a feature of the "family house" magazines. Central to the ideology of progress was an evolutionary view that placed Western societies, in terms of science and industry as well as art, in the vanguard of human development. Finally, progress was associated with the amassing of great wealth by financiers and industrialists who built industrial enterprises that spanned the entire country or used their wealth to build monumental public buildings—art galleries, museums, libraries, and other cultural centers. Closely associated with the production of wealth was its consumption, and the development of advertising was an important component of the turn-of-the-century dreams of progress.

An examination of the "White City," the great World's Columbian Exposition of 1893 in Chicago as well as the Pan-American Exposition of 1901 in Buffalo and the Louisiana Purchase Exposition of 1904 in St. Louis, provides a useful starting point in our examination of the meaning of progress in "late Victorian" America. *Cosmopolitan,* under the reign of John Brisben Walker, saw these urban, industrial expositions as especially important, as did as most of the leading family house magazines that provided extensive coverage of the 1893 Columbian Exposition. Perhaps more than any other world's fair, the Columbian Exposition in Chicago expressed a new urban ideal—a positive image of city life that sought to impose a sense of order and control on the chaotic energies of industrial cities.

Industrial fairs were a characteristic spectacle of industrial societies. The "Crystal Palace" in London (1851) was the first, with many expositions following throughout Europe. Paris was the location for three fairs preceding the Columbian Exposition in Chicago (in 1867, 1878, and 1889). Vienna, Dublin, and Glasgow also hosted industrial fairs. In America the first world's fair was the New York Crystal Palace in 1853, followed by the more grandiose 1876 exposition in Philadelphia—a celebration of the Declaration of Independence.

All these expositions differed in many respects, but there was a common pattern set by the original Crystal Palace in London. According to Cawelti, the theme of these fairs was "a linking of industry, science, agriculture and the arts under the aegis of progress."[1]

The Columbian Exposition in Chicago promised something more than any of the others. Articles in the *Century*,[2] *Atlantic Monthly*, *Harper's Monthly*,[3] and the *Nation*[4] praised the Chicago fair for its architectural harmony, the beauty of its giant fountains, boulevards, and statuary, and the planning of its director of works, Daniel H. Burnham. Most of all, writers for these magazines saw the fair as bringing civilization to the great bustling city of America's West. When the fair opened in May 1893, Henry Van Brunt of the *Atlantic Monthly* heralded the event as a "great moment in civilization." The Columbian Exposition was compared to four other turning points in the development of world civilization—the Age of Pericles, the Italian Cinquecento, the Protestant Reformation, and Elizabethan England. Van Brunt saw the Columbian Exposition as supplementing the cultural institutions of schools, universities, and museums "in the work of civilization." Most of the article was devoted to a description of the artistic merit of the fair, the "monumental harmony" of the architecture, the decoration of walls and vaulted ceilings, the statues and paintings.[5]

Cosmopolitan devoted all of the September 1893 issue, as well as numerous articles throughout 1892 and 1893, to the Columbian Exposition.[6] M. H. Young, a member of the Board of Control of the Columbian Exposition, provided *Cosmopolitan* readers with a preview of the upcoming fair in an 1892 issue. The prime object of the fair, he maintained, is "national glory," not any utilitarian purpose, which he equated with something "primitive." Young placed the Chicago fair in the context of the other industrial expositions since the Crystal Palace of 1851. The Philadelphia Exposition of 1876 marked a turning point, Young maintained, in its "broadening influence" on the American people. Americans in 1876 were narrow in their views, and the fair "opened our eyes to the fact that in many things we were mere infants." The trend in world's fairs from the Crystal Palace of 1851 to the great Paris Exposition of 1889 is that "each successive fair has tried to eclipse its predecessor in those points that are least utilitarian."[7]

The larger cultural division between the aesthetic and the practical (business culture and genteel culture) was reflected in the organization and architecture of the fair. As historian Neil Harris has observed, the buildings, most of which were temporary structures, had neoclassical, neo-baroque, or neo-Renaissance facades. In conformity to Victorian aesthetic standards, buildings were to reflect standards of beauty that came from the great civilizations of the past. Inside these buildings were the expositions, which conveyed an entirely different set of values. In Harris's words, "The exteriors emphasized tradition, order and control; the inside, physical progress, activity, newness." This division between art and commerce was also reflected in the department store and the museum. On the outside was a stately monument, an imitation of old-world European architecture conforming to dominant standards of beauty, while on the inside was an array of objects, a dazzling display of things, an expression of the new.[8]

John Brisben Walker's introduction to the issue of the Chicago World's Fair struck a somewhat different note in his discussion of the importance of the Columbian Exposition. For Walker and others, the White City was a model of urban planning and social harmony. After claiming that the exposition would advance American civilization by a quarter of a century and commenting on the expressions of "pleasure, satisfaction and joy" of the spectators, Walker commented on the large crowd that came for the Fourth of July. What amazed him most was that such a large and diverse group of people could peacefully assemble, "all feeling kindly toward each other, all taking part in the general joy and universal pride that this was the creation of their countrymen." Such a scene would not have been possible, Walker observed, before the 1860s and 1870s. Moreover, the great "palaces" built for the exposition represented a creation of government for the people, not for "the whim of one man." The success of planners in creating this minicity promised, Walker argued, a solution to

> problems of distribution—a consummation which will give to the common people the riches which they create, just as in this exhibition every bounty of nature, every magnificence of architecture, every creation of art, is brought together and opened for the benefit . . . of all, including the humblest citizen.

The fair was for Walker a great "college of democracy," teaching the political lesson of popular rule, the artistic lesson of "appreciation of the beautiful," the scientific lessons that should "serve the purposes not of the few but of the many," the lesson of equality between men and women, and the lesson that "transportation, from the movement of a letter or telegraph message up to the carriage of human bodies, is essentially a governmental function."[9] With each successive exposition Walker seemed to place greater emphasis on the need for urban organization and planning. By 1901 and Buffalo's Pan-American Exposition, Walker developed this new urban vision further. He remarked that it was a pity that the fair had to be dismantled. With a few more million dollars of

THE MIDWAY PLAISANCE LOOKING EAST FROM THE FERRIS WHEEL

Cosmopolitan shows readers a panoramic shot of the White City, focusing on the "Midway Plaisance" (*Cosmopolitan*, September 1893).

investment, Buffalo "could be converted into a model city . . . the Palace of Liberal Arts become a great factory; the Temple of Music stand as the theater hall; the Stadium remain the great amphitheater that it is." Walker maintained that the fair

> illustrates what men working in harmonious effort may accomplish for the delight of all. Who believes that the people of the second half of our new century will be content to live in those abominations of desolation which we call our great cities—brick and mortar piled higgledy-piggledy, glaringly vulgar, stupidly offensive, insolently trespassing on the right to sunshine and fresh air, conglomerate result of a competitive individualism which takes no regard for the rights of one's neighbors?

In contrast to the chaos of "competitive individualism," the city of the future would use "its best brains" and talent to choose sites for the building of cities. These experts and commissions would have "the highest good" of the community at heart in contrast to the "cornerers and peddlers of real estate."[10] With the St. Louis Exposition in 1904, Walker asserted that "the great fairs which the energies of Europe and America have held may be regarded as the tentative efforts which the civilization is making in the art of organization, grouping and harmony."[11]

The Columbian Exposition in Chicago represented, according to one historian, the first "urban dream" in the nation's history.[12] In other words, a series of positive virtues were associated with urban living in contrast to the traditional American celebration of the countryside. This new urban ideal was in part based on real developments in a nation that was rapidly developing large industrial urban centers, but it also pointed to the future. It is no coincidence that Chicago was ideally suited to represent the city of the future. It was a new city, located in the West, filled with immigrants and bustling with economic activity. The Columbian Exposition seemed to promise a future in which this cosmopolitan mix of peoples and cultures, this colossus of great wealth and poverty, could be made to work. Being made to work was largely a function of organization and planning. The White City, a huge financial undertaking, required coordination among Chicago's elite and professional classes. Architects, businessmen, artists, union leaders had to cooperate in a variety of ways to build the exposition and to manage it.

In Chicago and later, in Buffalo and St. Louis, the urban industrial elite in alliance with artistic and professional groups, dominated the organizing and planning of these fairs. Frederick Howe's article for *Cosmopolitan* on the St. Louis Exposition in 1904 asserted that the guiding forces financially and organizationally behind the St. Louis fair were also the "controlling spirits" behind the Chicago and Buffalo expositions as well as to the United States exhibits at the Paris fair of 1900.[13] But more importantly, the emulation of European cultural traditions superimposed onto a display of material abundance reflected the industrial elite's perspective. Their patronage of the arts was one way for them to expand their outlook beyond the sphere of production and to demonstrate a wider responsibility to "tradition" or to "culture." For all three turn-of-the-century expositions, the civic leadership that helped organize the projects continued after the exhibits and temporary buildings were taken down. This seemed, for many, to auger well for the city of the future.

William Dean Howells's "Letters of an Alturian Traveller," published in a series of installments during 1893, presented one version of the new urban dream, a version similar to the views expressed by John Brisben Walker.[14] Howells had his "Alturian traveller" write a series of letters back home about his visits to the White City and to New York. In contrast to the "physical and moral ugliness" of New York with its vast extremes of wealth and poverty, its disease-ridden slums and "plutocratic upper class," the White City was an "Alturian" vision of harmony and of the possibility of a new civic spirit.[15] Howells had his Alturian traveler exclaim that the White City "is like our own cities in being a design, the effect of a principle, and not the straggling and shapeless accretion of accident." The traveler from the future marveled not only at the aesthetic virtues of the fair but its practicality as well. This constructed city had its "own system of drainage, lighting and transportation, and its own government."[16] It required the cooperation of the commercial interests, usually at war with one another, and demonstrated one of Howells's favorite points, that ruthless competition in the economy had outlived its usefulness.[17] Howells's traveler marveled at the peaceful and gentle crowds, a point that was significant given the widespread concerns among the middle class with "overcrowding" and with social unrest in industrial cities.[18]

The White City seemed to represent a containment or control of the energies of urban life, without sacrificing its essential vitality and cosmopolitanism. The White City compartmentalized into identifiable, coherent, and ordered areas all the industrial, commercial, ethnic, recreational, and artistic features of industrial cities. The fairs were grandiose spectacles, and many commented on being enthralled, entranced, mesmerized by the great electric fountains, water terraces, monumental buildings, and the dazzling display of goods and technology at Machinery Hall or the Agriculture Building. But this abundance of material artifacts of industrial societies and grandiose sights and spectacles was above all ordered and controlled. Commentators, especially in the genteel magazines, praised the Chicago fair for its harmony of architectural design and the aesthetic sense of its planners. High and popular culture were represented, each in its own sphere. What is now the Science and Industry Museum was, during the Columbian Exposition, the Fine Arts Palace. There were halls for symphony orchestras and chamber music while the Midway Plaisance catered to the recreational desires of the ordinary folk.[19] Here were amusement park rides, animal acts, and exotic foreign exhibits like "Little Egypt." The Grand Court was the Chicago fair's civilized exterior, while Frederick Law Olmsted's Wooded Island provided visitors with a temporary respite from civilization in a carefully constructed bit of nature.

In *Cosmopolitan's* coverage of the turn-of-the-century fairs, we can continue to see the industrial exposition presented as a cosmopolitan assortment of ethnic groups and classes, a celebration of progress, tempered by the aesthetic sensibilities of artists and architects and the coordination of public officials and planners. Walter Bessant, an English visitor to Chicago, confessed that he "had no adjectives left" to describe the fair. "It is so big to begin with. . . . The bigness of the World's Fair first strikes and bewilders . . . the vastness of it!" Like many of the writers in this special *Cosmopolitan* issue, he described the fair as a "dream." After overcoming this feeling of awe, Bessant experienced the "poetry of the thing!" The fair was

> a miracle of beauty—thus designed so as to produce this marvelous effect. . . . English travelers who have written of Chicago dwell upon its vast wealth, its ceaseless activity, its enormous blocks of houses and offices, upon everything that is in Chicago except that side of it which is revealed in the World's Fair. Yes, it is a very busy place; its wealth is boundless, but it has been able to conceive somehow, and has carried into execution somehow, the greatest and most poetic dream that we have ever seen. Call it no more the White City on the Lake; it is Dreamland.[20]

Similar imagery was employed by Murat Halstead in his lyrically enthusiastic description of the Electric Building. Halstead described the White City as "that wonderful frozen dream." Halstead's description of the wonders of electricity expressed many of the themes discussed earlier, especially mastery over nature, only here it is combined with a quasi-religious sense of being in the presence of a divine force, of feeling connected to the wider universe.

> The potentialities and splendors of electricity were never before so exhibited as under this picturesque roof. It is not the building alone, stored as it is with wonders, that is the chief exhibition of the pervading and shining power that is marching from conquest to conquest, and ever finding amazing new worlds to conquer, for whether it is the crown of fire that glitters over the offices of administration; the basin, on whose blue waters the gondolas seem so at home, turned into a pool rich with colors as a sunset sky; the magnificent search-lights that sweep the horizon with shafts of flame that are revealing revelations; the lofty jets on either side of the MacMonnies fountains, converted to leaping rainbows, glowing, fantastical, mystical; the swift and silent launches, wafted without sail or oars or steam, burdened with people, through scenes of enchantment surpassing those by the waves of the Driatic when the doges were wedded to the sea; the intramural railway cars that fly over elevated roads without visible means of locomotion. . . . The same mighty, subtle, formidable, delicate, formidable agency and mastery perme-

ates the atmosphere that compasses the universe, and all this is but one breath of the all-embracing vital air, one sparkle of the surf that is the boundary of the ocean, the great deeps beyond, unfathomed, but one may believe not unsearchable, not past finding out, but holding their treasures for the swift unfolding of the slow centuries.[21]

In "A Farewell to the White City," Paul Bouget remembered the fair's "dazzling brilliancy" and its "dreamy vision of architecture." Bouget compared the unfinished state of Chicago with the perfection of the White City. Unlike European expositions, the one in Chicago was not a monument to an old civilization—"not an end but a commencement." The promise of the fair, for Bouget, was "the birth of a new art," the awakening of "the American passion for a superior civilization." But in addition to art, the exposition expressed the promise that the unruly forces of democracy and science could be forces for creativity and not destruction.[22]

Coverage of the Omaha Trans-Mississippi Exposition (1898),[23] the Paris Exposition (1900),[24] the Pan-American Exposition in Buffalo (1901), and the Louisiana Purchase Exposition in St. Louis (1904)[25] echoed many of these themes, although with somewhat more subdued language. In addition, both *Cosmopolitan* and *Munsey's* devoted some space to the Paris World's Fair of 1900. *Cosmopolitan* devoted considerable space to all these events, unlike its competitors *McClure's* and *Munsey's*. But *Munsey's* devoted many more articles explicitly focusing on some aspect of urban life, compared to *Cosmopolitan* and *McClure's*. While *Cosmopolitan* under the influence of Walker emphasized the need for urban planning and technocratic control, *Munsey's* was largely content to celebrate the expansive dream of urban abundance and consumption.

The Buffalo fair was in many respects modeled after the White City with a somewhat more internationalist theme, consisting in part of a "Spanish Renaissance" architectural style utilizing bright colors (the "Rainbow City"). According to one veteran magazinist, the Spanish Renaissance style "symbolizes our welcome to the genius of the Latins to mingle their strain with the genius of the Anglo-Saxon." The central idea of the Buffalo exposition, according to the same author, was "the idea of a united Western continent." While various exhibits of industrial, military, and scientific accomplishments (especially the Government Building) continued to take up a large portion of the turn-of-the-century fair, *Cosmopolitan* observers of the Pan-American Exposition focused more of their attention on "the nature-God electricity" and the Electric Tower, which was characterized as the "crowning and original feature of this exhibition." In addition, the Buffalo fair had its own Midway, the area originally designated in the Chicago fair for popular amusement. The athletic stadium seemed to represent, to a number of commentators, the growing American passion for spectator sports and recreation.

Unlike the Chicago fair, where the Midway was separated from the rest of the exhibits into a distinct region, in the Buffalo exposition it was well integrated into the fair—"accessible from a variety of points." The Buffalo Midway was described as an "alluring combination of circus, ethnographic bazaar and variety-show." Like Chicago, Buffalo had its "Little Egypt," called "Cairo Street," as well as other foreign exhibitions. The foreign and the exotic, especially from the Far East, were not only marginalized—placed away from the serious exhibits on material progress (particularly in the Chicago fair)—but made into an object of amusement for the spectator-tourists. Hawthorne described "the camels and the elephants and the dancing-girls . . . at least two charming Fatimas, more beautiful than ever; and the booths with their glittering and glowing display." Another commentator described

> the Street of Cairo with its glittering bazaar manned by olive-skinned attendants, who, in their whining, wheedling efforts to sell you many things, drop the price one hundred per cent, as they grasp your arm and whisper; "See here, beziness is bad, I'll let you have it for three dollars."

Grant also described the Indian Congress, which "contains one of the largest and most genuine looking bodies of warriors. . . . Many of the braves and squaws were large-featured, vigorous specimens of the race."[26] William Dean Howells in his article on the Chicago Midway used similar language. "The lascivious dances of the East are here, in the Persian and Turkish and Egyptian theaters as well as the exquisite archaic drama of the Javanese and the Chinese in their village and temple."[27]

Non-Western cultures could be appreciated but at a distance and only when they were safely contained in their own separate and subordinate sphere (the "Midway"). Other Midway amusements described were the "Trip to the Moon," based loosely on H. G. Wells's science fiction work. In this constructed science fiction fantasy, awe-struck spectators could enter a "moon cavern" and watch "Selenites" (moon people) do a moon-dance. Hawthorne described this kind of amusement as a new development that should be "indefinitely extended and improved."[28] Other amusements were the "House Upside Down" (imported from Paris), the "Infant Incubator" and a reproduction of a street in

The Electric Tower at the Buffalo World's Fair, 1901
(*Cosmopolitan*, September 1901).

Nuremberg. From the Electric Tower to the "Trip to the Moon" and the "Infant Incubator," we see the presentation of new technology and scientific fantasy as a source of popular amusement. Visitors to the fair could not completely escape the ideology of progress even when they sought a respite from the central exhibitions. Moreover, the context within which foreign cultures were introduced to visitors ensured that their sense of cultural hierarchy and superiority would be reinforced. While many of these amusements, especially the "ethnographic bazaar," were present at the Chicago fair, *Cosmopolitan*

THE BUILDING OF A SKYSCRAPER—OCTOBER 15, THE WALLS NEARLY COMPLETED.

Munsey's celebrates urban progress, the building of a skyscraper (*Munsey's*, October 1899), p. 54).

observers devoted more space and enthusiasm to the Buffalo Midway eight years later. It is tempting to suggest that the White City and the Midway were America's version of the City of God and the City of Man.

Cosmopolitan issues on the three major American industrial fairs (as well as the one in Paris) devoted space to articles explicitly introducing readers to the cities of Chicago, Buffalo, and St. Louis.[29] The city was the setting, the environment within which the dream of progress was to be realized. On the one hand, these turn-of-the-century industrial fairs were showcases for these growing industrial cities, and on the other hand they were "visions" or dreams of the future. The new urban dream was really a composite of all the positive virtues of progress—from the harnessing of new sources of power to the new palaces of consumption (department stores and luxury hotels) to that ultimate symbol of reaching upward and onward—the skyscraper.[30]

In addition, the urban dream was a vision of the harmonious city of the future, administered by professionals and planners, with an improved and revitalized public sphere, devoid of party patronage and corruption as well as ethnic and class conflict.[31] Despite Howells's generally unflattering depiction of New York, which he called the "plutocratic city," there was a clear impression conveyed in these articles that the city was the place where the promises of American society could someday be realized. Despite his biting criticisms of New York's aristocracy, the architectural chaos, the "leprous spots" of poverty, he could not avoid vivid and engaging descriptions of urban scenes of vitality. There were the "mothers from the tenement-houses . . . with babes in their arms," the assortment of social classes and ethnic groups strolling in Central Park, the fishermen "fishing along the sides of the dock," and overall "the spectacle of human drama."[32] Almost a decade later, John Brisben Walker attempted to forecast what New York would be like in 1909. He predicted an improvement in public facilities like parks, libraries, highways, and public transportation. While pessimistic about the prospects for good government, Walker hoped that New York would "be a commonwealth solely for the public good."[33]

Of all the popular magazines, Walker's *Cosmopolitan* came closest to being a printed version of an industrial exposition. Here was the aesthetic exterior and the practical interior. Here were the articles on technology and science, the catalog of the new, prefaced by opening travelogues, illustrated poetry, or accounts of European artists. Here one could find utopian speculations about cities of the future and trips to the moon from the work of William Dean Howells and H. G. Wells (Wells's *War of the Worlds* and *A Trip to the Moon* appeared in 1897 and 1900–1901) to lesser-known science fiction and utopian fantasies. Here too, one could go on a printed excursion to a "Midway Plaisance," where there were accounts of vaudeville and popular music, as well as various descriptions of exotic Far Eastern societies and tribal cultures.

Little Fairies in the Home

One word used by the host of enthusiastic observers of industrial expositions was "dream." On the one hand this seems to refer to a vision of a possible future, but at the same time the word also suggests an awe-struck fascination with technology and the display of abundance. Rosalind Williams characterized a common reaction to the exoticism and spectacle of the Paris industrial expositions as a childlike fantasy of a "return to the womb, which has become a womb of merchandise."[34] Spectators were enthralled by the "chaotic-exotic" aesthetic of material artifacts, machines, ornamentation, and exotic amusements that assaulted their senses and produced a "numbed fascination."

While the department store and the industrial exposition provided spectators with experiences of a new world of abundance, the growth of advertising during the late nineteenth and early twentieth centuries provided readers with a printed view of this world and one that entered their homes on a regular basis. Munsey, McClure, and Walker were enthusiastic about the wonders of science and technology in liberating the human spirit, improving the quality of human life, increasing the productive capacity of American industry, and in providing consumers with a world of abundance. Advertising, for Munsey, McClure, and Walker, would educate the consumer about this new world.

The late 1880s marked an important turning point in the history of advertising. Prior to this period advertising was a local matter paid for by retailers and intended for local markets. Newspapers were the preferred medium. By the late 1880s, with the rapid development of a mass-production economy, rising incomes, and new retail outlets, manufacturers began to directly advertise their products and sought to reach national rather than simply local markets. Magazines were the only medium to reach a national audience on a regular basis, and all magazines, including the family house journals, experienced an increase in advertising, in terms of number of pages as well as advertising revenue. Also contributing to the growth of advertising was the use by manufacturers of trademarks. Some of the most popular products advertised during the late 1880s were typewriters (Caligraph and Remington), "Waterman's Ideal Fountain Pen," Royal Baking Powder, Armour's Extract of Beef, and "Warner's Celebrated Coraline Corsets" as well as various makes of pianos, music boxes, and bathtubs. By the 1890s the bicycle and the camera became two of the leading products advertised in magazines along with breakfast cereals, canned foods, soaps, and by the late 1890s, the phonograph.

During its first full year of publication, *McClure's* carried roughly sixty to one hundred pages of advertising per issue, compared to *Century's* 150 pages, *Harper's* 177 pages, and *Scribner's* 136 pages (this data is for December 1891). *McClure's*, during 1894, carried numerous local ads for correspondence schools, physical culture programs of various kinds designed to build muscles, summer camps, periodical advertising, patent medicines, and for local New York firms (insurance, "ornamental brick," and so on). Railroads were also popular advertisers. But in addition there were small (less than a quarter of a page) advertisements for Quaker Oats, Ivory Soap, Armour and Company Beef ("Highest Award World's Fair, 1892"), Wilbur Cocoa, and various makes of typewriters. By 1905 *McClure's* carried an average of 165 pages of advertising per issue at $400 per page (*Munsey's* charged $500 per page). Companies were buying larger ads and occasionally using color. Some companies imitated the popular poster art while others utilized the work of comic-strip artists and illustrators.[35]

Overall American companies increased their expenditures for advertising from $360 million in 1890 to $821 million in 1904. In addition, by the 1890s advertising agencies had become more than space merchants, buying blocks of space from publishers and then selling it to clients. Instead, they involved their clients in the composing of ads and sought to develop a systematic approach for determining what kind of advertising worked. Some attention was also paid to the use of psychological theory in the development of effective advertising.[36]

An examination of the May 1914 issue of *McClure's* shows the importance of magazines as part of the marketing system of national corporations. Manufacturers' ads were prominent. A one-page Ivory Soap advertisement consisted of a large illustration of happy baseball players getting ready to shower in the locker room. The copy told the story of the hero who was inspired to drive in the winning run in the tenth inning by the thought of an "Ivory Soap shower." Large ads for Campbell Soup boasted of its "natural color." Phonograph advertisements were also common with a two-page advertisement proclaiming that "Dancing is Delightful to the Music of the Victrola." Many of the advertisements were for various products for homeowners, including "Dutch Boy White Lead Paint," "Old English Floor Wax," "Fenestra Solid Steel Windows," "Mitray Sanitary Refrigerators," and "Barrett Specification Roofs." Other advertisements were for bicycles, motorcycles, automobiles, and a variety of products designed to enhance personal appearance—from soap to face cream to clothing. Instead of appearing only at the end of the magazines, these ads

An early *Cosmopolitan* advertisement (*Cosmopolitan*, June 1895).

were in a variety of places. In addition, a number of advertisements anticipated a development that became common in the 1920s—the presentation of the commodity as the savior of the consumer facing a host of anxieties connected to popularity, success, growing old, and so on. A one-page add for BVD underwear contained a large illustration of a businessman in an office sweating profusely in front of his peers and his boss who looks at him as with a mixture of amusement and contempt. The copy informs readers of the meaning of the illustration, "A typical summer day—a typical office scene—a round of smiles at the mingled discomfort and discomforture of the man who hasn't found out that B.V.D. is the first aid to coolness." An Eastman Kodak ad associated the camera with family memories, asking readers with a kindly paternalistic tone, "When was your baby's picture taken last?" The N. K. Fairbanks Company's famous ad for "Fairy Soap" also appeared, asking readers, "Have you a little fairy in your home?"

Advertising by 1914 became not only a central part of magazine publishing but also became an important vehicle for informing readers of the wonders of a host of new products. These products were increasingly depicted as having a kind of magical effect on the consumer, giving them speed, popularity, memories, status, physical attractiveness. Moreover, advertising performed the dual function of introducing readers to new products as well as to new values ("dancing to the music of the Victrola") while providing reassurance for consumers anxious about their health, popularity, status, or their abilities as parents. In other words, as Roland Marchland has suggested, advertisers were apostles of progress while addressing consumers' anxieties about progress.[37] Overall, the purchase of a commodity was more than the fulfillment of a need. It was, at least as depicted in the new advertising, the "little fairy in the home," a route into the world of fantasy and desire.

Subduing the Forces of Nature

The fascination with electric power as a source of abundant energy was discussed earlier in the context of the turn-of-the-century expositions. Other articles explicitly focused on the growing mastery over this force in terms of scientific knowledge and in terms of harnessing the power of electricity for human purposes. One short article summarized the great advances in the understanding and practical uses of electricity between the Philadelphia Exposition of 1876 and the Columbian Exposition of 1893.[38] Among other things mentioned were the development of new dynamos, the incandescent lamp, electric motors (run by galvanic cells used for running printing presses, looms, and machine shops), electric welding, and the new understanding of light as an electromagnetic wave (within a decade or so this was to change). John Brisben Walker in one of his many articles on the 1904 St. Louis Exposition listed some of the major scientific advances in the understanding and use of electricity from the 1893 Chicago fair to the 1904 St. Louis fair. He informed his readers of the new scientific understanding of the atomic nucleus and the mass and charge of the electron, developments in the "wireless telegraph," the storage battery, the electric locomotive, the "trackless trolley," and improvements in electric lighting, generators, and transformers. He was enthusiastic about further advances because of the developments in basic scientific understanding of matter.[39]

The building of new power plants, especially on the Niagara River, was the subject of numerous articles. In "The Diversion of the Niagara," Curtis Brown compared the poet's view of the Niagara Falls with the engineer's. The poets, Brown asserted, inevitably fail to capture the majesty and "sublime spectacle of the Falls." The engineer who is attempting to "put a harness" on that power might provide a better inspiration for the poet. Brown outlined the plans to develop enough power from the Falls "to equal one sixth of the entire amount in use in 1880," and in distributing this electric power around the country.[40] During the same year, A. E. Dolbear, in the "Progress of Science" department, described "The Electric Utilization of the Niagara," with a discussion of the Niagara Falls Power Company's construction of a tunnel running under the town of Niagara.[41] In the same year, *McClure's* discussed "The Capture of Niagara," which asserted that the near-completed power plant showed that "capital is not always timid." The article concluded by claiming that the power plant presented a more sublime and "finer epic" in "subduing the forces of nature to serve mankind" than the Falls themselves.[42]

In addition to the specific case of electric power plants, other engineering projects were described for readers in celebratory tones. Walter C. Hamm, in "Great Engineering Projects," spoke openly of the "victories over nature" in the early twentieth century that would eclipse "the two great material conquests of the nineteenth century—the building of the Pacific railroads and the Suez canal." The article described a number of future projects including the Siberian railroad and a "Cape to Cairo" railroad in Africa that would "open the dark continent to civilization and trade."[43] In the same year, *McClure's* described how "the ocean has become as minutely surveyed, and in its elements as closely tabulated, as the land." The article discussed the "nothing less than marvelous" efforts of the Hydrographic Office of the Navy Department to chart and observe ocean winds, currents, weather patterns, rocks, and icebergs. While the article catalogued the rather mundane work of this office, the illustrations depicted the dramatic and dangerous consequences of the loss of control over nature. There were photographs of "A Wreck of the Storm of November 26," "Clawing Off a Lee Shore," "A Typical Iceberg," and "A Typical Waterspout."[44] Shortly after the St. Louis World's Fair issue of *Cosmopolitan,* Alexander O. Brodie, governor of Arizona, discussed the "Reclaiming of the Arid West." Brodie began his piece by proclaiming that "The Maker of the universe left some portions undone. In the great West an empire lies slumbering." The article described the irrigation of arid lands in Arizona under the Hansbrough-Newlands reclamation law.[45] Henry Muir in the pages of *McClure's* provided a description of "The Making and Laying of an Atlantic Cable," an article that detailed the way cable was produced in the factory and the ships that lay the cable.[46] In the opening article of the issue, veteran magazinist Cleveland Moffett reported on "Marconi's Wireless Telegraph," a development covered in all three popular magazines.[47] The mastery over nature through engineering continued to be a focus of magazines as illustrated by the 1913 article in *Munsey's,* "The Great Catskill Aqueduct, New York's New Water Supply—A Tremendous Engineering Work Nearing Completion."[48]

Throughout the late 1890s, popular magazines covered the explorations of the Arctic and Antarctic. *McClure's,* with its editor's interests in science and adventure, highlighted these expeditions more than *Munsey's* or *Cosmopolitan.* While accounts of dangerous and adventurous expeditions were, in effect, adventure stories that appealed to some of the sensibilities discussed in the last chapter, clearly here was one final frontier to conquer. In the lead article for the November 1899 issue, *McClure's* published an account of an Antarctic expedition by Dr. Frederick A. Cook—the doctor for the expedition. Less than a year later, Walter Wellman wrote about "The Race for the North Pole." Wellman told *McClure's* readers of his "two thousand mile journey across mountains, tundras, steppes and rivers."[49] *Cosmopolitan* was not entirely left out, with an illustrated account of "Adventure and Death in the Far North."[50]

The human power over nature and the exhilaration of escaping corporeal limitations were themes in the many articles on transportation technology, from railroads to balloons to "air-ships" and especially the automobile. In one of the earlier issues of *McClure's,* Otto Lilienthal's efforts to construct a "flying machine" were detailed with illustrations that now appear a bit comical.[51] *Cosmopolitan* also reported on the balloon and the "air-ship." Jacques Boyer told *Cosmopolitan* readers, in the opening article of the issue, about "The Modern Aeronaut," an article that focused on ballooning and described the new sport of ballooning in Paris.[52] Another opening and heavily illustrated article by Walker described "The Final Conquest of the Air."[53] By 1910, *Cosmopolitan,* in yet another opening article, could report that most Americans "have taken the dirigible balloon, the monoplane, the biplane, and the rest of those interesting

MARCONI

THE SENDING OF AN EPOCH-MAKING MESSAGE

January 17, 1903, marks the beginning of a new era in telegraphic communication, the significance of which is as yet scarcely realized or even conceived. On that day there was sent, by Marconi himself, from the wireless station at South Wellfleet, Cape Cod, Mass., to the station at Poldhu, Cornwall, England, a distance of 3,000 miles, the messag—destined soon to be historic—from the President of the United States to the King of England. This photograph was taken by A. B. Phelan exclusively for McCLURE'S MAGAZINE *immediately after the sending of the message. It is the only photograph yet made inside of the Cape Cod station.*

McClure's covers Marconi's invention of the "wireless telegraph" (*McClure's*, March 1903).

types of uplifting apparatus as a sheer matter of course in the every-day evolution of civilization." The author of the article reported on his meeting with Orville Wright and on going out on a flight.[54] In the following year T. R. MacMechen and Carl Dienstbach heralded the "New Wonderful Feats of the Wizards of the Air."[55]

Cosmopolitan and *McClure's* during the 1890s were well known for their articles and fiction on railroads. In an opening article W. D. Kelley provided

THE CITY OF THE AUTOMOBILE.

BY EDWIN WILDMAN.

THE REIGN OF THE HORSELESS VEHICLE IN PARIS, WHERE IT HAS GAINED A SUDDEN AND REMARKABLE VOGUE AS A FASHIONABLE FAD, AS A MEANS OF SPORT, AND AS A PRACTICAL FACTOR IN TRADE AND TRANSPORTATION.

IT is most appropriate that Paris, with its matchless boulevards, its extensive parks, and its fine tributary highways, should be the city of the automobile. Then, too, Paris is the epitome of cosmopolitanism. Nowhere in the world, her citizens will tell you, is there such unrestricted freedom of action and speech. Her streets, her parks, and her newspapers are living voices of her republicanism.

The automobile solves the problem of a portable power adapted to the needs of personal and commercial transportation without the supplementary inconvenience and expense of oats thrice daily, or the limitations of steel tracks and prescribed routes of travel. Potentially, at least, its utility is unlimited. In Paris, it has long since passed the experimental stage, and has taken its place in every department of transportation. It rivals the horse and makes the steam engine look to

A MOTOR QUADRICYCLE IN THE BOIS DE BOULOGNE.

Munsey's, along with other popular magazines, informed readers of the uses and pleasures of the new automobiles (*Munsey's*, February 1900, p. 704).

an historical sketch of "The Intercontinental Railway."[56] Between 1892 and 1894 in *Cosmopolitan*, a series of articles by railway men celebrated the "Great American Railways." In 1899 Sidney H. Short prophesied "The Coming Electric Railway." Short was an engineer and inventor who Walker claimed "probably built more trolley lines than any other engineer in the world."[57] In the characteristic *McClure's* first-person style, readers were taken on "A Thousand Mile Ride on the Engine of the Swiftest Train in the World."[58] *Munsey's*

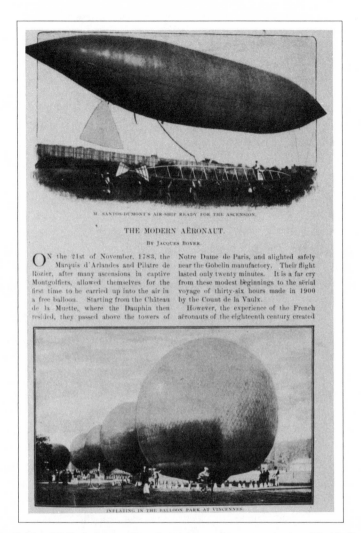

M. SANTOS-DUMONT'S AIR-SHIP READY FOR THE ASCENSION.

THE MODERN AËRONAUT.

BY JACQUES BOYER.

ON the 21st of November, 1783, the Marquis d'Arlandes and Pilatre de Rozier, after many ascensions in captive Montgolfiers, allowed themselves for the first time to be carried up into the air in a free balloon. Starting from the Château de la Muette, where the Dauphin then resided, they passed above the towers of Notre Dame de Paris, and alighted safely near the Gobelin manufactory. Their flight lasted only twenty minutes. It is a far cry from these modest beginnings to the aërial voyage of thirty-six hours made in 1900 by the Count de la Vaulx.

However, the experience of the French aëronauts of the eighteenth century created

INFLATING IN THE BALLOON PARK AT VINCENNES.

John Brisben Walker's *Cosmopolitan* devoted many features to the new "airships" and other forms of transportation technology (*Cosmopolitan*, November 1901, p. 13).

carried a two-part series written by the editor of the *Railroad Gazette* on "The Fastest Trains."[59] In 1902 William J. Lampton provided a composite sketch of America's "fascination with fast motion." The article discussed bicycles, cars, horses, trains ("a mile a minute"), steeplechases, and sailboat racing, among other things.[60]

All three popular magazines made the development of the automobile between 1897 and 1900 a major issue. In 1897 John Brisben Walker announced that "the horseless carriage has arrived." Less than a year after his contest for the best "motor vehicle," Walker reported that horseless carriages were being used as cabs on the streets of New York although they were still too expensive for the public.[61] A few years later, in "The Modern Chariot," John Gilmer Speed (believe it or not) boasted that ten years earlier the sight of an automobile would have caused spectators to stare but "now automobiles are so common that a passing carriage is only glanced at." While Speed pointed out that the automobile "is the newest favorite of the very fashionable" and not widely available, he asserted that it was "a serious factor in the work of progress" primarily by encouraging the building of new roads and the improving of old ones.[62] In *Munsey's,* Edwin Wildman described the widespread use of "the horseless vehicle in Paris, where it has gained a sudden and remarkable vogue as a fashionable fad, as a means of sport, and as a practical factor in trade and transportation."[63] In 1899, *McClure's* carried a detailed account of the rapid development of the automobile from "a year ago" when there were only thirty automobiles in America to May 1899 when "at least eighty establishments are now actually engaged in building carriages, coaches, tricycles, delivery wagons and trucks, representing no fewer than 200 different types of vehicles, with nearly as many methods of propulsion." *McClure's* staff member Ray Stannard Baker demystified this new product for his readers, explaining the use of the automobile throughout Europe, the cost of purchase and maintenance, the advantages and disadvantages of electric and gas-propelled vehicles, how the electric and gas vehicles worked, the need for new laws and regulations, and a variety of other practical questions. The article was, in effect, an introduction of the automobile to a large group of possible consumers (it was the opening article in the July issue). While most Americans were accustomed to thinking of machines as central to the industrial development of the nation, the idea of purchasing one for themselves was still a somewhat alien notion.[64] Baker's piece was, in effect, an article-advertisement that sought to proclaim the virtues of this new product and demonstrate how it worked and how it could be operated.[65]

In other ways, popular magazines introduced their readers to mechanized consumer goods. Women's magazines increasingly called their readers attention to the new technology of a "well-equipped kitchen" and portrayed the modern housewife as the "household engineer." *Cosmopolitan*'s series on "How to Administer a Household," equip a modern kitchen, and select a home expressed much the same view of a technologically modern household managed by an efficient and scientifically knowledgeable housewife.[66] The wonders of the motion picture camera were introduced to readers in a well-illustrated lead article, "Out with a Moving-Picture Camera," which described the shooting of a prison escape scene.[67] The camera was another machine that turned into a mass-consumer product, and popular magazines carried numerous articles that explained to readers various photographic techniques or simply showed, through the reproduction of photographs, what the camera could accomplish.[68]

The Civilized, the Exotic, and the "Primitive"

In a variety of genres (travel articles, quasi-documentary realism, fiction, and ethnographic accounts), *Cosmopolitan* informed its readers of Far Eastern and Middle Eastern, tribal and, on occasion, African-American cultures. While all popular and genteel magazines devoted some space to this type of article, *Cosmopolitan* seemed to specialize in it, perhaps because of the international perspective of Walker, whose military service in China had led to a number of contacts with American diplomats and military officers. This is worth exploring in some detail because accounts of non-Western cultures were related in various ways to the "aggressive nationalism" discussed in the previous chapter as well as to the efforts to break away from Victorian middle-class moral codes. For the purposes of this chapter, what is most important is an implicit cultural hierarchy that informed nearly all writing on this topic. Highest on the evolutionary scale of countries and "races" were the "civilized" Western industrialized societies, primarily America, Germany, France, and England. Within America, of course, not all people were part of the magazine's implicit and taken-for-granted vantage point. Certain groups, particularly African-Americans and Native Americans, were thought of as primitive and uncivilized. Second, there were the "exotic" Far Eastern and Middle Eastern cultures, especially Egypt, China, and Japan. Finally, there were the "primitive" cultures, thought of as a collective "other," representing the opposite of those attributes thought to characterize "civilized" societies. These attributes might have a positive or negative inflection depending on the author's characterization of "civilized" life, but the "primitive" was almost always thought of as a subspecies of the "natural."

Europe's "civilization" was an object of fascination as well as an example of what Americans should try to avoid. On the one hand, during the 1890s, *Munsey's* and to a lesser extent *McClure's* and *Cosmopolitan* were fond of carrying long, illustrated articles on European monarchs and how they lived, as well as numerous articles on European artists and writers.[69] Moreover, as we have seen, the German monarch, Kaiser William, was thought to exemplify the same vigorous and athletic qualities that were associated with President Roosevelt (after 1901).[70] On the other hand, American democratic institutions were contrasted with the monarchies of Europe and Russia.[71] American democracy represented the evolutionary trend while monarchy was a remnant of the past. As many have documented, American culture was heavily influenced by Germany. German universities were a model for higher education reform in the United States (particularly their emphasis on scientific training), and German industrial development was a model for American industry. In addition, German state bureaucracy was seen as a model for a more enlightened and efficient municipal government in America. But by 1906 there were indications of some anxiety about Germany's power. Charles Edward Russell could write for the Hearst *Cosmopolitan* that Germany might be in a position to dominate the world, economically and militarily.[72]

France (primarily Paris), which pioneered in the development of modern retailing and advertising, was generally viewed as the center of civilized or "enlightened" consumption.[73] Henry James in *The Ambassadors* located the ideal of civilized pleasure, of enjoying life rather delaying one's happiness for some future goal, with the life of the Parisian intellectual and artist. The Paris Exposition of 1900 provided *Munsey's* and *Cosmopolitan* with the opportunity to comment on the civilization and culture of France (the many articles on Napoleon had already introduced readers to a popular version of French history and nation building). William Stead (reformer and editor of the English *Review of Reviews*) characterized France as "the expert showman of the world" because of its fondness for the great spectacle of industrial expositions and catalogued France's industrial, technological, and cultural accomplishments.[74] Charles A Towne, in an article on "Plans for the Paris World's Fair," placed the upcoming world's fair in Paris in the context of other French industrial expositions. The new fair of 1900 would "indeed be a centennial exposition, not in the sense in which that of 1889 commemorated the birth of a new order of things in France a hundred years before, but in the sense of forming a compendium of the world's progress during the whole of the nineteenth century."[75]

Middle Eastern and Far Eastern cultures were characterized in very different terms. They were not like the "civilized West," yet magazines conferred upon the civilizations of China, Japan, and especially Egypt a degree of respect that did not exist for Native Americans and African-Americans. The exotic was neither natural nor civilized, but a strange, anomalous category overflowing with meaning. While often discussed from the vantage point of the Western tourist or colonialist, the exotic East and Middle East also represented the mystery, sensuality, and hidden sources of wisdom that might be of therapeutic value to overcivilized Westerners. Moreover, for middle-class men and women trying to break from Victorian moral codes but not quite ready to confront them directly, Far Eastern and Middle Eastern sensuality could provide a safe way of thinking about the allure of the sensual since it could be presented as a feature of a foreign culture.

In the opening article of the August 1899 issue, Alexander Harvey took *Cosmopolitan* readers on a trolley ride to the Sphinx. The article was more of an opportunity to show numerous photographs of Egyptian pyramids and to provide advice for tourists.[76] Saunders Norvell told the story of "A Nineteenth Century Daughter of Pharaoh." In this short story the narrator is a celebrated psychologist and expert on "diseases of the mind." A patient of his complains of vivid dreams and images of a past life as an Egyptian princess. But this princess has no nervous disorder. The end of the story suggests that the woman had really been an Egyptian princess and had been reincarnated. In "Some Types of Egyptian Women," Alexander Harvey asserted that "In Egypt things feminine go by contraries. Young women of sixteen are employed as hodcarriers, mason's attendants and builders. . . . Meanwhile there's hardly to be found in Cairo a woman who 'looks after the house' as we understand it here."[77] The article went on to provide a quasi-ethnographic account of Egyptian women's marriage customs, child-rearing practices and dress.[78]

Two other "exotic" cultures that appeared in the popular magazine were the Japanese and the Chinese. Alice Nielsen provided readers with a peek at Japanese "Geisha Girls." The author in this travel article bribed her tour guide to get an interview with a "troupe of geisha girls." She described their dances and songs as they entertained for her and explained that "a great majority of these girls are daughters of samari [*sic*]," and "the majority of them marry well."[79] In "Fan-Fan," George Francis Bird told an adventure story about the daughter of a famous Japanese juggler and acrobat. The story includes a passionate romantic affair, culminating in a double suicide by drowning.[80] A travel article on "The Wistaria Shrine of Kameido" described in romantic and sensual imagery the temple garden of the famous Shinto shrine in Japan: "Time has blended my memories of Kameido into one dreamy symphony of sunshine, gracefully gliding dancing girls and soft masses of purple flowers." As with all travel articles there were numerous illustrations. One showed a young, traditionally dressed Japanese woman seated in front of a pond with the caption, "Joy for To-Day and No Thought for To- Morrow."[81]

In "Through Oriental Doorways," Laura B. Starr discussed the interiors of Chinese palaces and wealthy Chinese homes.[82] Many other articles on China were political commentaries by Walker and members of the U.S. military who had been stationed there. General Edward Forester wrote a series of articles called "Personal Recollections of the Tai-Ping Rebellion."[83] In "The Cross and the Dragon," Ednah Aiken tells a story containing every imaginable stereotype of the Chinese. Ah San is the daughter of an American woman who lives in China and who has married a Chinese man. Ah San's mother, Nora, detests the patriarchal Chinese traditions and secretly calls her daughter "Victoria." "Her child was white; she must not be allowed to grow up to womanhood, which was a degraded state at best, among these people of a degraded race." With the help of a trusty Chinese servant, Nora plans her escape. But her Chinese husband discovers their plan and kills Nora. Somehow, Ah San is rescued and spends her childhood in a convent under the care of a group of "gentle sisters." "There was a cross, too, over the building where she was to live, a cross which had gained yet another victory; but the old bronze-dragon in the forsaken joss-house smiled on with his imperturbable smile—as though he alone knew of that denied yellow blood—and waited."[84]

The exoticism of the Middle East was a theme in "An Arab Fete in the Desert." Gertrude Bailey Tredick, the author, wrote about her trip "to an oasis in the great Sahara," Biskra, Algeria. Quoting from a book on Islamic culture, she informed her readers that "Our civilization seems a frivolous thing of yesterday when one meets these deep-set Arab eyes that look at you as Lazarus did at Karshish as if nothing temporal was of moment to those who learn in the desert to see life differently." She described meeting Arab women who had been to the Chicago fair. "We were pleased to see some of the performers of the Midway Plaisance in their own homes and wondered what these African damsels thought of Chicago." Eventually, she described a cafe.

> A group of sleepy, sensual looking Arabs were seated around the tables, while in the center of the room three or four Almee girls, painted and glistening with jewelry, were dancing, or rather making the slow, sensuous, evolutions of the abdomen, which compose their dance. With dreamy eyes, as if entranced, they swayed backwards and forwards.

The article concluded on a somewhat different note by asserting,

> The French have done a great deal for Biskra. . . . Their engineers have made the country fertile and generally healthful. . . . The irrigation ditches have done wonders in reclaiming desert land. . . . The surrounding country now yields, plentifully, the very best quality of dates, and naturally there is a large trade in exporting them.[85]

John Brisben Walker's multipart series on the Islamic empire began with an account of the prophet Muhammad's life and those who succeeded him. Walker praised Islam for having established a political system based on its religion and asserted that the twentieth-century project for Western nations would be to do the same for Christianity (in the sense of having a government based on Christian moral principles and not simply national self-interest). Muhammad and his followers were favorably compared in Walker's article to Napoleon.[86]

By 1905 the Hearst *Cosmopolitan* printed a number of articles that were critical of the European powers' efforts to dominate world markets and extend colonial rule. One such article discussed the rivalry between Germany, France, and England over Morocco. Morocco was described as "a land of white cloaks and veiled women, of galloping horses and grisly heads stuck on pikes, a land of mystery and yellow loot and impossible romance. There for centuries life went very well. Nothing much happened; few things changed."[87] A few years later, Morocco's "strange customs and mysterious people" were described by an English "author-artist-explorer" who discussed "this North-African wonderland with respect to its possible commercialization."[88]

Articles and fiction on Native Americans were common in *Cosmopolitan*. Frederic Remington's *The Way of the Indian* was a well-promoted feature of Hearst's *Cosmopolitan* in 1906 and, of course, the Western adventure story had come into its own with Owen Wister's *Virginian*. In addition, ethnographic or historically oriented articles provided readers with glimpses into various Native

American tribes. The tendency to characterize Native Americans in terms of racial characteristics was one of many indicators that they were thought of as "primitive" and therefore close to nature. William R. Draper worried that the "Indian Race" might be disappearing because of intermarriage. His article described "Indian" life on reservations and concluded by asserting that the old "warrior instinct" had disappeared among the Indians and that "absorption or amalgamation" was inevitable and "a good thing for the Indian."[89] An account of an Arctic Eskimo walrus-hunt provided an opportunity for Lewis Lindsay Dyche, in a lead article, to provide readers with a vicarious adventure and to describe the Eskimo's hunting practices.

> As I close this article, I am living over the whole experience again, while my heart beats with the excitement of the hunt, and I find myself trembling and perspiring and gritting my teeth. If the reader has never felt such a sensation, let him get into my boat, and come with me on my next walrus hunt.[90]

The Eskimos played a role here of helping the civilized readers of *Cosmopolitan* break free of civilized restraints, to feel the thrill of adventure and the challenge of danger. A more academic article discussed "The Curious Race of Arctic Highlanders." The author described the "strange customs and beliefs" of these people who live "isolated from the rest of the world . . . struggling against a harsh and difficult environment." In contrast to the depiction of the Native American as savage and warlike, in this article they were examples of a kind of primitive socialism.

> As they have no money nor means of accumulating wealth, their plan of existence, is a combination of socialism and individual liberty. . . . We may call them savages because they do not possess the arts and refinements of modern life, but in the conduct of life itself they can teach us by mere force of example some useful lessons.[91]

In "A Legend of the Navajos," William Crocker Duxbury provided an account of how the Navajos, "the bravest and most intelligent of the red men of the century were lured into loyalty by a trick." According to Duxbury's account, the Navajos had a legend that they could not be conquered until the "dancing man" appeared. Major Backus heard about this legend and proceeded to trick one of the Navajo prisoners, with the aid of an "automaton" and some wires, into believing that the dancing man had arrived. The trick worked and the Navajos surrendered to the U.S. Army. We discover at the end of the article why the author regarded the Navajos as the "most intelligent of the redmen."

He attributed this to the "welsh miners who had married into the Navajo tribe, and exerted a strong civilizing influence."[92] Major Edmond G. Fechet provided an official army account of the death of Sitting Bull. The article was a largely military discussion of how the "Indian police" and army finally arrested Sitting Bull and his followers and the fight that ensued when he "resisted arrest." The ghost dance was described as the "Messiah craze," a "tide of fanaticism," and as a "disease."[93]

Mrs. D. B. Dyer's travel piece on "Some Types in Dixieland," was a good example not only of the stock racist stereotypes of African-Americans but also a quasi-documentary style, filled with illustrations, that served to give pieces of this kind a pseudoauthenticity. The article was a description of the black farmers she encountered in Augusta, Georgia. There were, though, no interviews with the farmers or effort to discover their point of view. Instead, they were treated as part of the landscape. "It is an almost inspiring sight," she observed, "to watch the darkies who are a happy, jolly throng of people." She lamented "the passing away of the old-fashioned negroes . . . a black mammy with ample proportions and ornate architecture." Finally, we were told that "superstition still holds unchallenged sway among all the negroes. Occasionally a modern, up-to-the-times darkey will pretend to scoff at the potent charms of a rabbit's foot caught in a graveyard at night, but in his innermost heart he firmly believes in its efficacy."[94]

Captains of Industry

As others have pointed out, social developments are often brought into the spotlight of public discourse precisely when they have begun to recede in importance. This was certainly the case with the fascination in popular magazines with "captains of industry." The great industrial and financial tycoons who presided over the competitive mass-production enterprises of the late nineteenth century became culture heroes in large part through the pages of popular magazines. Ironically, the "proprietary" form of capitalism was already changing by the mid-1890s and developing into the corporate, state-regulated form of capitalism in which individuals and families would no longer have a central role in the management of firms.

Theodore Greene in his excellent study of popular magazine biographies demonstrated that *Cosmopolitan* printed more biographies than any of the other general interest popular magazines during the 1893–1903 period.[95] More than half of all these biographies were either of Napoleon (*Cosmopolitan* also out-

Napoleoned its rivals) or of "Captains of Industry."[96] The series "Captains of Industry" consisted of short biographical sketches (running one to five pages per individual) of "the leading Captains of Industry now before the public in connection with the larger interests of production, transportation and finance."[97] The series began in May 1902 and ended in 1904. A review of the biographical sketches between 1902 and 1904 reveals some patterns in the descriptions of their personal qualities and the factors that led to their success.[98]

One question every biographical sketch addressed (often explicitly) was, "How do we explain the great success of this person?" The answers, despite the large number of individuals discussed and the differences in their occupations, were almost identical. The other question each sketch tried to answer is best illustrated by the Alexander Graham Bell biography. "Precisely upon what," the author asked, "does Alexander Graham Bell's claim to be regarded as one of the captains of industry rest?"[99] The answer usually involved a list of various accomplishments, either in the building of great industrial, transportation, financial, or retail enterprises or in new discoveries and inventions, usually supplemented with discussions of philanthropic and religious work and, in a few cases, social activism. What is interesting about this question is that, clearly, the author is not claiming that Alexander Graham Bell ever asked to be admitted into some kind of Captains of Industry club. Instead, the real the question is, "Are we justified in including Bell in this series?" This select group was clearly a cultural category developed by the *Cosmopolitan* authors and others in the newspaper and magazine world. Given the amazing similarity in the personal characteristics attributed to these titans of industry, finance, and invention, it is safe to say that we are seeing here the construction of a mythology—a composite of a culture hero with many faces but with the same set of attributes, and with almost superhuman capacities (can superman be far behind?).

What were these attributes? Like many mythological heroes, parental upbringing did not seem to explain very much about their future success. Particular attributes of parents—their values, child-rearing methods, and personalities—did not play, in these biographies, a significant role in the success of their children. In a four-page biography, the attributes of John Rockefeller's parents took up a few short paragraphs. Rockefeller attributed his success in part to his "early training" but primarily to his "perseverance." In fact, he regarded (according to the author) a rural upbringing as providing a better chance for future success than an urban one because there were more obstacles to overcome.[100] Occasionally, as with Alexander Graham Bell or James Gordon Bennett, the captain of industry came from a family of famous and successful people. In Alexander Graham Bell's case, the possibility of "heredity in mental tendency" was raised but little was said about environmental influences from childhood. In William Randolph Hearst's case, "He has succeeded in spite of wealth." Hearst's successful effort to mold a "newspaper of the people" required that he overcome his privileged background.[101] In other cases as well, being born of wealth was described as an obstacle to success. John Pierpont Morgan, who was "born to the purple" could have been "a rich loafer." "He could have been a pigmy, but he choose to be a giant."[102] The point was that he had to overcome a childhood that offered few challenges. The temptation would be to enjoy one's inherited wealth rather than create something new with it. The key words were *building* (or creating) and *contributing*, rather than being content with the status quo. Marcus Alonzo Hanna was not born into poverty but "is nevertheless self-made, for he has carved out his own career in paths his father never trod."[103] It seems that quite a bit of ingenuity was used to make sure that even with a wealthy upbringing one could be a "self-made" man.

Rather than heredity (although this was occasionally mentioned) or family environment, success was attributed to luck or "circumstances" combined with willpower, hard work, and persistence. The combination of fortuitous circumstances and personal attributes made it possible for the budding captain of industry to take advantage of opportunities. The shipbuilder John William Mackay took advantage of "certain chances and possibilities" and "after many years of hard work found himself one of the largest owners of Nevada mines."[104] William Ellis Core, president of the Carnegie Steel Company, attributed his success to "bull-dog tenacity and the spirit of not being satisfied with doing perfunctory work."[105] But persistence, pride, hard work had been stock features of the cult of success since the early nineteenth century.[106] What was new was the emphasis on willpower. Words like "forceful," "decisive," "great physical power," "genius," "prophetic," "masterful," "unhesitating," "dominating," and "commanding figure" connote somewhat of a different image than "diligence" and "persistence." It may well be the case that the small-producer virtues of a previous era did not seem to be plausible explanations for the enormous wealth and power of these captains of industry. Instead, they had to be endowed with attributes that were out of the ordinary although, paradoxically, they were to be models of success for ordinary people. This is only one of a number of paradoxes. Another paradox was that many of these individuals commanded large, impersonal organizations while their biographies emphasized their uniquely personal characteristics. The sketch of newspaper baron James Gordon Bennett (son of the founder of the *New York Herald*) characterized him as being the brain behind the *Herald*'s success and as "daring" and "aggressive." "His most striking successes" were "gained in the face of adverse advice." At the same time, his main accomplishment was in turning the *Herald* into "an impersonal organization."[107]

In a short commentary in the "Men, Women and Events" section of *Cosmopolitan,* Walker asserted that successful businessmen are dreamers. They are able to conceive of some great plan and then put it into practice. The dreamer, he asserted, is superior to the practical man. Yet the practical man is needed to implement the dream. "For the benefit of the very young man perhaps it should be added that the power to dream, to look far ahead, to prophesy even is not sufficient. To the power to foresee are occasionally joined judgment to organize and nerve to attempt." Here Walker touched on one of the ironies of the expansive individualism of this period. Great dreamers and forceful men produced great organizations that limited competition and consequently the opportunities for other men to realize their dreams. But Walker was still optimistic, if not entirely lucid. "The average business field is daily narrowed with increasing competition; but the greater world of business to which access is had only with the open sesame of an idea will ever remain open and continue rewards that must satisfy any ambition."[108]

One of the clearest paradoxes, and one that illustrates the mythic nature of the captain of industry, was the way Thomas Edison was characterized in popular culture. One of his chief accomplishments was to rationalize invention through the establishment of a well-funded (partially by J. P. Morgan) laboratory and a permanent staff. Nevertheless, he was portrayed as largely responsible for a wide range of inventions as a result of a variety of personal qualities.[109]

It is important to understand the "captain of industry" in context. While the "captains of Industry" popularized an expansive ideal of individualism, there were other cultural currents as well in the popular magazine. In *Cosmopolitan* the "Choosing a Profession" series, which started in 1897, provided advice to middle-class young people on the advantages and disadvantages of a variety of occupations (medicine, law, engineering, journalism, and so on) that required college education. While it was certainly true that the large industrial enterprises closed off entrepreneurial opportunities for many people, there were new opportunities as professionals in the corporate world and in the public sector. In other words, the cultural ideal of the small producer who, as a result of perseverance and hard work, could achieve economic independence, may have been superseded by the expansive individualism of the captain of industry. But at roughly the same time, the ideal of professionalism also emerged.

One other series of articles provides a useful context for understanding the captain of industry. In 1898 *Cosmopolitan* began a series of articles called "Great Problems in Organization." Among the articles in the November 1898 to April 1898 volume (volume 26), were discussions of "Recent Developments in Industrial Organization" by F. W. Morgan, "Flour and Flour Milling" by B. C. Church, "Wheat and Its Distribution" by Joseph Leiter, and "The Street-Cleaning Work of Colonel Waring" by Walker. The impression given by these articles was clearly one of admiration for industrial organization combined with a desire to explain the increasingly complex systems of production and distribution of industrial products to readers.

One of the more interesting articles of this series was by Theodore Dreiser, "The Chicago Packing Industry." The article followed the hapless animal through various stages of the production process as well as the storage, distribution, and inspection of the finished product. Dreiser proclaimed that readers would "grasp the meaning and value of the system" as they followed him through the "immense yards of today." The Union Stockyards were described as a "city in itself—a city of pens and factories, immense and noisy . . . and yet so systematically is everything organized, no interest is left unprovided for, and no item of expenditure escapes its proper assignment." Here was another city that worked because of organization and planning. Moreover, the owner was not mentioned once in the article. The organization was not personified, but instead its efficiency and rationality were positively valued. The illustrations allowed the reader to follow each stage in the process (except slaughtering). Some of the captions read, "Drawing In New Animals," "United States Inspectors Marking Pork," "Wool-Pulling Room," and "Beef-Cooler."[110] It is hard to imagine, from our vantage point, why readers would be interested in such an article until we realize that the American of 1898 had not yet learned to take for granted the existence of national corporations and could obtain some pleasure from learning how these mysterious organizations worked. Industrialization had created a gap between the spheres of production and consumption, making the world of "things" somewhat mysterious. These articles may have appealed to readers' desires to understand the connection between the things they used and consumed and how these things were produced and distributed.

Progress in the Genteel Tradition

How did the *Century*, the most popular family house magazine of the 1890s, respond to and represent these dreams of progress? The *Century*'s retrospective flavor can be seen in the high number of historical biographies—Abraham Lincoln, Oliver Cromwell, Ben Franklin, Joan of Arc, Napoleon, Stonewall Jackson, Daniel Webster, John Muir, Otto von Bismarck, George Washington, Alexander the Great, and Ulysses S. Grant, among others (some 15 to 20 percent of all *Century* articles, including fiction, in the 1890s were historical biographies). When combined with historical pieces on great artists and literary figures and with historical fiction, we can see that the bulk of the *Century*'s articles during the 1890s were historical and retrospective in character. While it is true that the popular magazines also carried historical biographies and historical fiction, there was a clear difference in emphasis. While *Cosmopolitan*, *Munsey's*, and *McClure's* balanced features on the Civil War and biographies of Napoleon with articles on scientific and technological wonders, a minuscule percentage of articles in the *Century* focused on scientific and technological developments (approximately 3 percent between 1893 and 1900). All three popular magazines carried features on captains of industry, but biographies of industrialists were noticeably absent in the *Century* (see appendix 4).

Richard Watson Gilder's *Century* expressed in halting and contradictory ways elements of the "new civic consciousness" beginning to take hold in America's cities.[111] The *Century* continued to advocate civil service reform in editorials and in featured articles. A series of articles and editorials in volume 47 (November 1893 to April 1894) focused on political reform with editorial diatribes against "Buying and Selling Votes" and suggestions on "How Bribery at Elections May Be Prevented," as well as a number of articles making various suggestions concerning "municipal reform." This was clearly in the mugwump reform tradition. But in addition, articles during the 1890s explored the kindergarten movement,[112] "The Duty of the Nation in Guarding Public Health," and presented the work of "the sociological group," a group of fifteen Social Gospel ministers, economists, university presidents, and social scientists. The members included clergyman and Social Gospel advocate Washington Gladden, economist and critic of economic orthodoxy Richard Ely, and Charles W. Shields, a professor at Princeton, as well as Charles Dudley Warner. The group's objective was "so far as may be, to bring scientific methods, with a Christian purpose and spirit, to the study of the questions to be considered." The questions considered ranged from "Problems of the Family" (January 1890) to labor reform (April 1890) to "The Problem of Poverty" (December 1892).[113]

The *Century* published an inspirational piece by Jacob Riis (author of *How the Other Half Lives* and a good friend of Gilder) on life in the New York tenements[114] and an essay by William Dean Howells, who advocated an ethic of human brotherhood and solidarity as the true application of Christian principles and as the project for the new age.[115] In addition, Gilder published the early premuckraking work of Josiah Flynt (to be discussed in the next chapter), who had already accumulated experiences throughout Europe and the United States in various hobo communities. Flynt's work appeared in a five-part series during October and November of 1893 and February, March, and October of 1894. "Tramp Life Among the German" and "Tramping with Tramps" appeared in 1893, followed by "The Tramp at Home" and "The City Tramp" in 1894. The next year (1895) saw two more Flynt articles, "Two Tramps in England" and "How Men Become Tramps." Flynt's work was a departure from the genteel tradition in his somewhat sympathetic depiction of tramp life and in his environmentalist view of poverty.

But the trend toward a "new civic consciousness," toward environmental explanations for poverty and sympathy for society's "other half," was not clear or unambiguous. Along with a growing awareness of the environmental causes of poverty and other social problems expressed in the work of social scientists and reformers, the *Century* continued to express the typical mugwump fears of immigration, the declining birth rate among educated women, and labor radicalism. Gilder was no more sympathetic to the labor movement in the 1890s than he was after the Great Upheaval in 1886. In "Plain Words to Working Men by One of Them," Fred Woodrow urged his fellow workers to refrain from boycotts, strikes, and other "injudicious methods" and behave as "responsible citizens." He advocated workers' cooperatives and profit sharing rather than "anarchy and revolution."[116] Two articles by eyewitnesses to the Paris Commune painted a near hysterical picture of anarchy and lawlessness, clearly intending to connect the Commune to the dangers of labor unrest in America.[117] Gilder supported President Cleveland's use of federal troops against the Pullman strikers and blasted John Altgeld, governor of Illinois, for refusing to request federal troops to break the strike (October 1894). These positions presented a striking contrast to the commentaries by Walker appearing in *Cosmopolitan* and *McClure's* inside view of the Homestead steel mill from the point of view of the workers (see chapter 4). Henry Cabot Lodge provided statistical evidence purporting to show the connection between immigration and crime and recommended immigration restriction, while Gilder in an editorial took a more moderate position in urging the passage of a law delaying the right to vote for immigrants until one year after naturalization (August 1894).[118] Gilder did make an important stride in the direction of greater tolerance toward Catholic immigrants with the publication of Washington Gladden's "The Anti-Catholic Crusade," which expressed concern for "a discouraging outbreak of religious rancor" and urged greater tolerance.[119]

Throughout this decade the *Century* carried a beautifully illustrated series (with expensive woodcuts) of "Pictures by American Artists" as well as numerous biographies of painters, musicians, opera composers and singers, authors, and actors, along with news of artistic developments in other countries. This was part of Gilder's project of encouraging an appreciation for the visual arts and especially for the development of an American artistic tradition. The civilizing project of encouraging an appreciation for high culture was more than window dressing for Gilder. It was the staple of his magazine. Even articles on industrial expositions retained Gilder's emphasis on high culture as an antidote to materialism. It should be noted here that the popular magazines were also carrying features on American and European artists, but not nearly as many, and they were certainly not paying for expensive woodcut illustrations. A reader primarily interested in a finely illustrated account of classical and contemporary artists would not have purchased *McClure's*, *Cosmopolitan*, or *Munsey's*.

Century's coverage of the Columbian Exposition also showed its interest in art and high culture. Gilder's October 1892 editorial on the Chicago fair highlighted the promise that the fair would propel America to artistic heights, inspire America's artists, and demonstrate that a democratic society is capable of high cultural achievements. Walker's *Cosmopolitan* was also impressed with the fair's aesthetic achievements but discussed this in the larger context of America's rise to industrial and scientific prominence and the possibility of constructing well-planned and well-managed cities.

Reflecting Gilder's (and other mugwump) opposition to American military expansion, the *Century* devoted some space to a debate over the issue of annexing the Philippines and the other former Spanish territories. Carl Schurz opposed military expansion while Whitelaw Reid supported it (September 1898). While Gilder opposed going to war, he believed it was his patriotic and perhaps journalistic duty to support it once it had started. As a magazine the *Century* was caught up in war fever—perhaps not as much as *Munsey's*, but nevertheless there was extensive coverage. Volume 58 (May 1899 to October

1899) contained no less than seventeen well-illustrated articles written by military officers ("The Story of the Captains"). Illustrations included portraits of leading military figures as well as "photographs taken on the day of the battle of the 'Iowa,' 'Indiana.'" Gilder's editorial on the series referred to the magazine's famous Civil War series, arguing that the new war deserved commentary that was "equally commanding and notable."[120]

Gilder's *Century* contained numerous features on exotic people and places, usually in the context of travel articles. In this area *Century* was quite similar to Walker's *Cosmopolitan*, which also emphasized the foreign and the exotic. Unlike *Cosmopolitan* though, there were few military articles other than the series on the war with Spain and few topical articles on world affairs. *Century* devoted space to articles espousing one of Gilder's favorite projects, environmental preservation, with articles by naturalist John Muir[121] and on such topics as "The Song of American Birds" and an August 1898 piece called "How India Saved Her Forests—A Lesson for the U.S." While a few articles on engineering projects, new scientific discoveries, and exploration could also be found, these were few and far between.[122]

Dreams of Progress

One way of thinking about the cluster of beliefs associated with "progress" is to consider it an ideology. An ideology "naturalizes" some set of social arrangements or practices so that these arrangements cannot be critically questioned. Moreover, ideologies work to support or legitimize some system of power relations. The view of progress discussed throughout this chapter can certainly be understood as an ideology supporting new property relations in industry, an expansionist foreign policy, technological mastery over the forces of nature, and domination of non-Protestant groups within the country. But it is also important to note how this ideology was expressed. The discussion of progress in popular magazines had a utopian, almost messianic quality. The word *dream* reappears again and again, especially in discussions of world's fairs.[123] Electricity was a force of nature to be understood but, at the same time, it was held in awe as a "new god" to be worshipped. Industrialists were endowed with the magical capacity of transforming the world through force of will. Thomas Edison was widely called "the Wizard," as were the "wizards of the air." Scientific advances were hailed as "miraculous" while *Cosmopolitan* could, in all seriousness, print an account of how vanilla and a variety of other products are made from coal ("The Magic of a Piece of Coal").[124]

A late twentieth-century sensibility finds the association of science with dreams and wizardry as strange. But around the turn of the twentieth century, Americans had not yet taken progress for granted, nor had science and technology achieved the degree of routinization and specialization it now has. Both the social and the natural sciences were not entirely disenchanted and secularized as they are today. The Protestant social gospel that sought a new social ethic rooted in the teachings of Christ, and the "new economics" that criticized the principles of classical political economy, were closely connected. Exponents of the emerging discipline of sociology did not see any contradiction between science and passionate involvement in social reform. Sociologists like Brown University's Lester Ward argued not only that men and women were social creatures whose patterns of behavior could be empirically studied but also that human beings had the capacity and obligation to shape and improve their social environment. "Is" and "ought" had not yet become separate principles. Objectivity in social science did not yet mean isolation from social activism.[125]

One of the dreams of progress was the expansive dream of a world of material abundance. Anne O'Hagan's enthusiastic description of the department store for *Munsey's* was one example. The opening of the article compared a village general store with a modern department store. Department stores were characterized as "gigantic organizations" with a "vast machinery behind it all," expending "gigantic energy and millions of dollars." The stores were filled with "gorgeous colors and rich fabrics." There were, O'Hagan explained, enough commodities to allow one to furnish one's home, to purchase paper for letters, to be manicured, or to have one's picture taken on a bicycle "with every device known to the order of the wheel." Overall the department store "creates appetites and caprices in order that it may wax great in satisfying them."[126] The dream of abundance was also a dream of abundant energy from electricity and the ability to harness and distribute it, or the dream of an abundance of commodities. The cultural dream of abundance was perhaps best symbolized in the turn-of-the-century fair, which provided urbanites and visitors to these cities with spectacles the likes of which they had never seen. The dream of abundance could also take the form of the larger-than-life captains of industry, bending the world to their abundant will.

The other cultural dream was one of order or social control, an updated version of the older "dream of reason." The dream of control was part of the middle-class utopian project in the early 1890s of creating an efficient, rational, and above all organized social order. Howells, Walker, and many others dreamed of an end to the waste of "competitive individualism" and the replacement of political bosses ruled by graft and allegiance to private interests with the objective, scientific perspective of experts. This dream of a society governed by enlightened experts concerned with the public good can be seen as an outgrowth of the genteel perspective, or at least one strand of it. Only now, by the early 1890s, the working class was no longer the enemy for many of these left-leaning academics, writers, publishers, and businessmen. They saw the need to unite various social classes and interest groups in order to overcome the divisions of a rapidly industrializing society. As early as 1888, Henry Demarest Lloyd expressed sentiments just as prolabor as Howells and Walker. In a speech delivered to the Chicago Ethical Society, Lloyd attacked economic individualism and "wage-slavery" and argued that the labor movement had become the leading expression of the suffering of humanity.[127] Urban reform movements, sparked in part by the 1893 depression, had also kindled a good deal of interest in some of these new ideas. The commentary of Walker and Howells in the early issues of *Cosmopolitan* was one expression of a perspective that became a dominant one only a decade later, in what historians call the "Progressive era."

Many of the utopian novels published between 1888 and 1896 were influenced by Edward Bellamy's *Looking Backward* (1888), which presented a utopian society where all industry had been nationalized (Bellamy had his utopian tour guide explain that this was an inevitable consequence of industrial concentration). Technology was put to the service of mankind, and all citizens served in a national army, which performed most of the necessary labor. The dream of control also led to efforts to build planned communities from the town constructed by Pullman for his workers to the "city beautiful" and "new town" movements of the early twentieth century.[128] If the captain of industry was the culture hero for the dream of abundance, the engineer and the manager were the culture heroes for the dream of control. Closely related to the dream of a society run by enlightened experts was the dream of social justice, inspired by a new generation of journalists and reformers—better known as "muckrakers."

CHAPTER SEVEN

Muckraking, Realism, and the Dream of Social Justice

Fraternity in Action

Whether true or not, a story was told frequently by the magazine journalists who Theodore Roosevelt immortalized with the name *muckraker*.[1] It seems a miner from Alaska comes to a newspaper editor with an idea he has for a "political crusade." He provides the editor with a wealth of information which so impresses the newspaperman that he comments, "Well! You certainly are a progressive, aren't you?" "Progressive!" the miner exclaims. "Progressive! I tell you I'm a full-fledged insurgent. Why, man, I subscribe to thirteen magazines!"[2] The great era of magazine exposés of corrupt urban politics, big-business domination of the U.S. Senate, the conditions of child laborers, the illegal activities of the "trusts," food poisoning and patent medicine fraud, insurance company scandals, the mistreatment of blacks in the "New South," and a host of other social, economic, and political issues coincided with a wave of reform throughout the country that roughly lasted from 1903 to 1910.

Local reform movements sought to unseat "political bosses," establish transportation and utility regulatory commissions and new structures of urban government, win the direct primary for candidates to the U.S. Senate and reform election laws to allow for a more direct democracy, pass legislation on the state and national level to eliminate child labor, regulate patent medicines and the food industry, win the right to vote for women and improve conditions for women workers, and to limit the activities of corporate lobbyists and campaign contributions, among many other things. Several of these reform campaigns eventually led to efforts to pass legislation or establish new governmental agencies on the national level. Local newspapers as well as the national magazines played a central role in these movements, especially in the crusade against the corruption of the political process by businesses and political bosses. In fact, it is impossible to separate many of these reform movements from the two leading forms of mass communications—urban newspapers and magazine muckraking—for reform movements and the new agencies of mass communications influenced each other in ways that will be discussed throughout the chapter. For the first time, a *national* medium of mass communications, the popular magazine, became a major political force, making news as well as reporting it. While Lincoln Steffens, whose "Shame of the Cities" series became a national sensation, admitted that major urban newspapers had been reporting on political corruption and urban reform movements for years, he realized that the national magazines turned these local movements into a national phenomenon, intensifying and nationalizing local developments.[3] Magazines, Steffens realized, could uncover patterns in local developments and provide readers with a deeper understanding of how corruption in their own city fit into this larger pattern. It was not a coincidence that the first truly national social movement had such a close relationship with the first national medium of mass communications—the popular magazine. Through this relationship, reformers all over the country (who after 1910 began to call themselves "Progressives") learned to develop a common critique of political and economic institutions.[4]

This chapter will focus on muckraking in *McClure's* and *Cosmopolitan* during the 1903 to 1910 period. *Munsey's* did not participate in the muckraking movement but nevertheless maintained itself as a circulation leader.[5] While the focus of this chapter is on the first decade of the twentieth century, the social reform thrust of magazine journalism was not entirely new. We can locate elements of what has been called the new "civic consciousness" during the years after the depression of 1893. Both *McClure's* and *Cosmopolitan* printed accounts of conditions of working women and among the Homestead steelworkers, efforts to reform city government, conditions among the urban poor, efforts to revamp the nation's educational system, and visions of urban harmony and planning.

But despite the local reform movements that were challenging American institutions in their efforts to develop alternatives to "competitive individualism," and the utopian visions of Howells and others, in the popular magazine this new consciousness did not become dominant until the early years of the twentieth century.[6]

This chapter is not intended to be a comprehensive study of muckraking, but instead focuses on two magazines that were central to this movement—*McClure's,* because staff members Lincoln Steffens, Ida Tarbell, Ray Stannard Baker, and William Allen White originated and dominated muckraking journalism during its early years; and the Hearst *Cosmopolitan,* because of the importance of William Randolph Hearst in the development of American journalism and the much talked-about "Treason of the Senate" series. Moreover, *McClure's* and *Cosmopolitan* represented two different strands of the muckraking tradition. *McClure's,* under its editor's moderate leadership, was "middle of the road." It refrained from direct assaults against big business, and McClure made sure that all articles were well documented and supported by "the facts." Labor unions were exposed as well as the "trusts" (e.g., Ray Stannard Baker's exposé of labor racketeering),[7] and there was little speculation about socialism.[8] Hearst's *Cosmopolitan* was not only more "sensational" in its muckraking exposés but also became a center for many of the turn-of-the-century socialist intelligentsia. Jack London and Upton Sinclair were popular novelists but also committed social activists and socialists who wrote extensively for *Cosmopolitan.* Charles Edward Russell, a regular contributor to the Hearst *Cosmopolitan*[9] as well as copublisher of the Hearst newspaper, the *Chicago American,* became a passionate reform journalist, biographer, and novelist. He joined the Socialist party in 1908 and became the party's candidate for governor of New York in 1910 and 1912. Eventually, he helped found the National Association for the Advancement of Colored People. Russell began his journalistic career on Pulitzer's *New York World* where he rose quickly to become city editor (as a reporter he was in Chicago when the Haymarket riot occurred).[10]

Cosmopolitan carried a series of "round-table discussions" in which leading writers and intellectuals debated the major issues of the day. A number of the debates centered around the ideas of socialist writers. The opening installment in the series was a debate between W. J. Gent, "author of 'Benevolent Feudalism' and a leading scientific socialist" and two regular Hearst contributors—David Graham Phillips, who was sympathetic to socialism, and Alfred Henry Lewis, who was described as a "strenuous individualist."[11] The next month's round-table featured Robert Hunter, author of the much-discussed book *Pov-*

erty;[12] Morris Hillquit, author of *The History of Socialism in America* as well as a leading lawyer in the New York branch of the Socialist party; and Hearst journalist Ambrose Bierce.[13] They debated "the question of social unrest in this country and the chances for and against its cure." Hillquit forcefully made the case "that we have rapidly reached a point . . . where society is well able to take care of itself, and does not any more require the benevolent protection of capitalists." Hunter, sympathetic to socialism, evidently let Hillquit present the socialist case and focused instead on the corruption of republican institutions. He argued that "our republican institutions are being debauched. . . . There is domination of our legislatures by a growing industrial and economic power; that this power is crushing the people into poverty and taking away their liberties." Bierce was the cynic who was skeptical about the perfectibility of human nature, arguing that there will always be poor people as long as there are inborn differences in ability. Hillquit, the socialist, had the better of this debate. In fact, half the discussion focused on the desirability of socialism with Bierce conceding many points to his ideological opponent. It is hard to imagine such a piece appearing in *McClure's*.[14]

It should be noted here that not all popular magazines were known for their muckraking. Moreover, even magazines known for muckraking carried a majority of articles and fiction devoted to other topics. Not only *Munsey's* but the *Saturday Evening Post* achieved high circulations without devoting themselves primarily to the exposure of corrupt institutions and practices.[15] Nevertheless, muckraking was not a minor development. Not only were the muckraking magazines central organs for what has been called a "great movement for social democracy," but a number of older magazines were revitalized when they turned to muckraking. *Collier's* had a circulation of 300,000 when Norman Hapgood was made editor in 1902. Hapgood had been a colleague of Lincoln Steffens on the *Commercial Advertiser* where Hapgood served as a drama critic. As editor of *Collier's*, Hapgood turned the publication into one of the leading muckraking magazines in the country. Its circulation rose from 321,000 in 1902 to 400,000 in 1903 to 568,000 in the 1905–1907 years when it was number three in circulation in the country (see appendix 1).[16] *Everybody's*, owned by Philadelphia department store owner John Wanamaker, turned toward topical and muckraking exposés under the editorship of Ernan J. Ridway, a former colleague of Frank Munsey. *Leslie's*, under Ellery Sedgwick's editorship, was also known for its muckraking articles. By 1905 the leading muckraking journalists on *McClure's* left the publication to take over *American* magazine. After the arrival of the *McClure's* group, *American* achieved a respectable circulation of

300,000.[17] If we look at 1905, during the height of this movement, we find that five of the top seven circulation leaders among general interest monthly magazines were involved in and known for their muckraking pieces—*Everybody's, Collier's, McClure's, Cosmopolitan,* and *American. Hampton's,* formerly *Broadway* magazine, increased its circulation from 12,000 in 1907, when it was purchased by Ben Hampton, to a circulation of 480,000 in 1910.[18] During these three years *Hampton's* was known primarily for its muckraking exposés. For a number of years prior to the Hearst takeover, *Cosmopolitan*'s circulation had been stagnating at 300,000–350,000 (Walker became distracted by his automobile business). With the turn to muckraking in 1906, circulation rose to 450,000. Even the *Ladies' Home Journal* printed a series of exposés on the "patent-medicine evil" in 1903.[19]

Muckraking magazines expressed, during the early years of the twentieth century, a growing awareness of the social character of human nature and a belief that public morality had to take precedence over "private selfishness." After the depression of 1893 there was widespread dissatisfaction with American institutions and with the dominant systems of thought from classical political economy to orthodox Protestantism. This was reflected in the Social Gospel religious movement, the reform movements launched by the "new women," as well as the interest in the social sciences, particularly the new economics, political science, and sociology. It was reflected not only in the sermons of Social Gospel preachers and the academic articles of economists and sociologists but also in the early "realistic" journalism of Jacob Riis, who sought to convey to his readers *How the Other Half Lives,* in Stephen Crane's early realist novel *Maggie: A Girl of the Streets,* as well as in the premuckraking work of Josiah Flynt, whose *True Stories from the Underworld* were based on years as a participant-observer among the urban homeless and underclass. These fictional and nonfictional accounts of poverty and other urban problems expressed a sympathy for the plight of the poor and the underclass largely missing in the work of the charity workers and moral reformers of a previous era. The new economics challenged the assumption that the business cycle was self-correcting and urged various forms of government regulation of the economy. But popular magazines during the 1890s were only partially influenced by these developments. The realist tradition in literature and journalism did not become a central feature of these national publications until the early twentieth century, with the rise of reform movements inspired in part by the unprecedented wave of business mergers during the turn of the century.

By the first few years of the twentieth century, it was impossible not to take notice of the increasingly socialized character of production as well as the advances in transportation and communication that were bringing areas of the country closer together. Moreover, the accelerating pace of urbanization also highlighted the reality of interdependence among diverse interests, occupations, and ethnic groups. This awareness of economic and technological interdependence as well as the sympathetic depiction of the lives of immigrants and the urban poor contributed to a new national sensibility. The belief that at the core of human nature was altruism, not selfishness, and that human beings were related to one another through complex bonds of interdependence, provided an ideal, a critical standard that could be used to attack the "selfishness" of individuals and institutions. Jane Addams, in her famous work *Democracy and Social Ethics,* criticized the factory system for "over-specialization," which did not permit the social side of the worker's nature to develop. Despite the socialized character of production, industry was privately owned so that capitalists had not fully developed a sense of "social ethics." "A large and highly developed factory," Addams maintained, "presents a sharp contrast between its socialized form and individualistic aim." Education, Addams argued, could compensate for this deficiency in the industrial system by unleashing people's potential and connecting them to "the rest of life."[20]

The social muckraking of the child labor exposés (to be discussed later in the chapter) made a similar point in referring to the need to "conserve" the nation's human resources by ensuring that selfish private interests—whether families, political bosses, or industrialists—did not abuse the rights of the nation's children.[21] Political muckrakers like Lincoln Steffens hoped through their articles to appeal to the public's shame as well as their pride as citizens in discovering that the public sphere had been corrupted by private interests. The rapid concentration of wealth in the hands of major corporations made it seem even more urgent for the magazine muckrakers to work for the building of a new social order based on solidarity—nationwide bonds of cooperation that would put "the people" ahead of the "selfish" private concerns of "the interests," whether they be political bosses, trusts, or labor unions. The reformers believed that social bonds rooted in community, local party organization, family and kinship were no longer adequate to address the problems of big business's corruption of the political process, or the abuse of children by unscrupulous employers and parents, or threats to the health and safety of consumers posed by industries willing to sacrifice the public interest in order to make a profit. Instead, new organizations (like regulatory commissions), laws, and institutions (schools were considered especially important) would be needed to put into practice this deeply felt sense of social responsibility and interdependence. Social reformers were searching for a new basis for an industrial order, one that would be consistent with the democratic traditions of the country but also one that could cope with the growth of modern corporations and increased social interdependence. As discussed in chapter 6, Howells and Walker in their *Cosmopolitan* articles during the 1890s expressed clearly their view that new forms of social cooperation (in term of economic organization, state planning and regulation, and social welfare agencies as well as new educational institutions) would represent an evolutionary advance over the wasteful competition and selfishness of the earlier era. By the early 1900s many magazines would take up this theme and develop it in new directions.

Reading the pages of *McClure's,* starting in 1903, and *Cosmopolitan* in 1906 (when *Cosmopolitan*'s muckraking period began in earnest), one is struck with the contrast in tone between these years and earlier years. The contrast is most vivid in *Cosmopolitan* where from 1902 to 1904 the "Captains of Industry" series had portrayed men like Rockefeller and Morgan as larger-than-life heroes. By 1906 they stood for everything that was wrong with the country. They were no longer dominating and masterful but were instead filled with animalistic greed and selfishness. The reason for this seemingly abrupt shift was probably because of a change of publishers, from the left-leaning but still probusiness Walker to the neopopulist Hearst. In addition, as a good newspaper and magazine publisher, Hearst knew that the widespread public interest in business corruption could be tapped into by his new magazine. Populist attacks directed at "captains of industry" may well have served Hearst's political ambitions during this period as well.

In the Hearst *Cosmopolitan,* businessmen were America's "plutocrats," "parasites," and "feudal lords." Bailey Millard, editor of Hearst's *San Francisco Examiner* as well as the Hearst *Cosmopolitan* between 1905 and 1907, expressed the new view with rhetorical zest in an article criticizing the "all-pervasive flunkeyism" of New Yorkers who idolize the rich.

> Our standard has been wealth. We must have a new standard—manhood; not a return to peak-hatted Puritanism, but simple manhood. We must have a state of society in which there will be no discrimination between the robber rich and the robber poor; that condition in which social flunkeyism shall mean social debasement, where to be caught in the company of one capable of instigating a Standard Oil inequity were no less a disgrace than to be seen walking down Broadway with a Jimmy Hope.[22]

It was neither the masterful and dominating captain of industry nor the qualities of a well-run industrial system like the Chicago Packing House industry that *Cosmopolitan* seemed to value most by 1906. Instead, the qualities of altruism, sacrifice, and solidarity rose to a prominent place. Following the San Francisco earthquake Millard wrote an editorial titled, "When Alturia Awoke." The lesson of the earthquake, Millard maintained, was the altruism it inspired.

> The higher altruism of the men and women of that hour loomed large in the eyes of one who gazed among the homeless. . . . While the city was still burning, and while out of the great heart of a great nation poured gifts impossible of adequate distribution, the free sharing from hand to hand among the homeless was as general as it was generous. . . . Here was a luminous lesson in Utopian economics—a lesson for the whole doubting, artificial, selfish world—a dropping off of all mean play at precedence and all the cunning trickery of gain.[23]

The earthquake, in other words, revealed the truth of human nature—it is unselfish altruism that "gave the world its noblest lesson in self-effacement."

A number of articles in the *Cosmopolitan* series, "What Life Means to Me," expressed similar sentiments in more personal terms. One of the more interesting in this series was the contribution by Edwin Markham, an assistant editor and regular contributor to the Hearst *Cosmopolitan* and author of the famous "Hoe-Man in the Making" series that exposed the plight of child labor in the factories. Markham's fame began with a poem originally published in Hearst's *San Francisco Examiner* in 1899. Markham had been a school principal in Oakland, California, before Millard discovered him at a poetry reading (shortly after he was made literary editor of the *Examiner*). The poem, "The Man with the Hoe," became a nationwide sensation, widely proclaimed as one of the great poems in world history and used in schools throughout the country, giving Markham instant fame.[24] The poem was a commentary on Jean François Millet's painting "The Man with a Hoe," and Markham used this image to comment in general on the plight of the oppressed everywhere and on the injustice of the human soul's being "distorted and soul-quenched" by a life of labor. The poem was such a sensation that Collis P. Huntington of the Southern Pacific Railroad (the company that was the object of Frank Norris's rage in *The Octopus*) asked, "Is America going to turn to socialism over one poem?"[25] It's safe to say that not often does a poem have this much immediate impact. It was in the same year reprinted in *McClure's* with a reproduction of the famous Millet painting.[26]

In "What Life Means to Me," Markham described the moment when, after searching "for the unifying principle of life," he discovered that "the Idea of Humanity is the core of religion, the core of the spiritual fact . . . that Fraternity in action is the holiest of all ideas—is the spirit of all gospels and the fulfillment of all revelations." Later in the article Markham asserted that

> the competitive struggle among men is simply a part of our brute inheritance. This struggle must give way to something nobler, or man's soul will never rise to the full measure of a man. Man's spirit needs a higher ground than the nature-ground. For his deeper and dormant nature is not wolfish: it is brotherly. The struggle for his own life must give way to a struggle for the lives of others. The survival of the fittest must give way to the fitting of all to survive. The Golden Rule must replace the rule of gold. Man was made for the adventure of love. All true morality must be based on unselfish love. . . . Man realizes himself only when he identifies his life with the common life. There is no rest for man but in fellowship—in beautiful concords, sympathies, and services of a Comrade Kingdom.[27]

Markham was enthusiastic about the "fire of social passion" spreading throughout the nation and the world and about the coming of a new millennium. In his language there was an expansive and utopian quality, a sense that the "secret power" of providence was at work in the world.

Other contributors to the "What Life Means to Me" series expressed a number of variations of this sense of solidarity and fraternity. Bailey Millard talked about his childhood and early adulthood as motivated by the ideal that "wealth was the lustrous mark at which mankind should aim his heart. When a wealthy man appeared in our village he was looked up to with awe and referred to with reverence." Later, during a crucial turning point in his life, when "I began to take particular notice of the lives of the men of affluence whom I had been emulating. I found that they were no nearer to a state of happiness than I was." Millard talked about this period of questioning in his life as "my revolt" and came to realize the extent of the corruption of politics by private interests and the immorality of the means by which many millionaires acquired their wealth. While explicitly rejecting "utopian dreamers of any school whatsoever" and doubting "if any vast system of fraternity would make us happy for long," Millard knew what he was against. "Methinks now I know the true meaning of life, and it is not in getting and hoarding, not in putting my heel upon my fellow-being's neck, not in that civilized pillage we call 'commerce,' nor yet in that strange malady which we call 'progress.' "[28]

Upton Sinclair in his contribution to this series described his participation in the socialist movement as the defining experience in his life, a kind of turning point. After discussing his unsuccessful attempts at a literary career and his struggle to keep his sanity, he confessed,

> My nightmare experience had to continue until I discovered the Socialist movement, until I learned to identify my own struggle for life with the struggle for life of humanity. I was no longer obliged to think of civilization as a place where wild beasts fought and tore one another without purpose and without end; I saw the anguish of the hour as the first pang of the great world-birth that is coming.[29]

Jack London as well described a kind of awakening in which he became aware of the suffering of others.[30] While being "born into the working class" his dream was to "climb higher," and he admired the "material goods of the rich but also the things of the spirit . . . the unselfishness of the spirit, clean and noble thinking, keen intellectual living." After becoming a successful merchant, he lost his business and "entered back into the working class, becoming exploited by one capitalist after another." Later, after becoming a "brain merchant" and being invited to associate with the "masters of society," he realized that "I did not like to live on the parlor of society. Intellectually I was bored. Morally and spiritually I was sickened." London described his introduction to the world of books, where he read, among other things, sociology and "discovered I was a socialist and a revolutionary." In the company of other socialists he found something he had searched for his whole life.

> Here I found, also, warm faith in the human glowing idealism, sweetness of unselfishness, renunciation and martyrdom—all the splendid, stinging things of the spirit. Here life was clear, noble and alive. Here life rehabilitated itself, became wondrous and glorious, and I was glad to be alive. . . . I believe that spiritual sweetness and unselfishness will conquer the gross gluttony of to-day. . . . My faith is in the working class.[31]

In these accounts a number of common threads can be detected. First, there was a realization of human solidarity and the obligation of one person toward another, and second this was not merely an intellectual process but a kind of religious awakening that marked a turning point in the person's life. Biographies written by magazines muckrakers described a similar process of awakening to the social nature of humanity and to an understanding of the corruption of the political process by business.[32] Of course, the majority of muckrakers were not socialists and did not identify themselves with the struggles of the working class as Upton Sinclair and Jack London did, but the deeply felt desire to overcome the divisions of industrial society and to build a new kind of community permeated the personal writing and social thought of this period.

McClure's and Muckraking

When Lincoln Steffens was interviewed for the position of managing editor for *McClure's* he was asked, "What will be your policy on the magazine?" In his autobiography, Steffens remembered his response.

> "Put the news into it," I answered. I had been 'thinking it over,' and it had occurred to me that there were some news stories which ran so long and meant so much that the newspaper readers lost track of them. A weekly might comment upon such stories, but a monthly could come along, tell the whole completed story all over again, and bring out the meaning of it all with comment.[33]

At this time (1901), Steffens was a well-known reporter whose work on Godkin's *New York Evening Post* and as city editor of the *Commercial Advertiser* had earned him a reputation as one of the nation's leading journalists. He had acquired a number of years of experience covering New York's Wall Street during the Great Panic of 1893 and the following depression years. He covered the crime beat and joined with the reform efforts of Rev. Charles H. Parkhurst, who was denouncing New York City police corruption. He became friends with journalist and author Jacob Riis as well as with police commissioner Theodore Roosevelt. He witnessed the clubbing of strikers and did interviews with J. P. Morgan and political boss Richard Croker.[34] He traveled throughout the immigrant ghettos and found time to write reviews of the new theatrical productions coming from New York's German community. He was a superb interviewer who had the uncanny ability to encourage his subjects to open up to him, perhaps because of his ability to suspend moral judgment and his boundless and engaging curiosity.[35]

But when Steffens accepted the position at *McClure's,* he had no specific idea of how to shift the magazine's focus to "news" and what deeper patterns to uncover in the local stories the newspapers were carrying. While he had experience covering the New York reform movement against police corruption, he knew little about developments in other cities. He had no plan to do a series on urban corruption. It all began when McClure realized that Steffens was not suited to be sitting in an office acting as a liaison with the magazines' contributors and editing other people's work. When McClure finally told Steffens that he didn't know how to edit a magazine, Steffens asked, "Where then can I learn?" McClure responded, "Anywhere . . . anywhere else. Get out of here, travel, go—somewhere. Go out in the advertising department. Ask them where they have transportation credit. Buy a railroad ticket, get on a train, and there, where it lands you, there you will learn to edit a magazine.[36]

It was good advice. Steffens wound up in Chicago with a list of "writers, editors and leading citizens" who might be able to provide him with material or ideas for material. From one of his contacts he learned of a St. Louis district attorney by the name of Joseph W. Folk, who "was raising the deuce of a row about bribery in the board of alderman."[37] Steffens's discussions with Folk (who admitted to Steffens that he needed help) led to the first of a series of articles on the corruption of city government by big business later called "The Shame of the Cities." The first article, "Tweed Days in St. Louis" (coauthored by Claude Wetmore, a St. Louis newspaper reporter), appeared in *McClure's* in October 1902. The reaction was so favorable to the article that Steffens and McClure decided on a series of articles, which began in 1903. Steffens was to go to Minneapolis, Pittsburgh, Philadelphia, Chicago, and New York to look for additional evidence of corruption that might demonstrate a national pattern in the "shameless facts" uncovered in St. Louis. The *McClure's* articles on corruption in St. Louis and the role of Joseph Folk in fearlessly battling the corrupt system of Boss Ed Butler made Folk a national hero (except in St. Louis) and was largely responsible for his election as governor of Missouri in 1904.

As many others have pointed out, Steffens did not discover the fact of corruption in urban politics. The corruption of the political process by business was a favorite topic of mugwump reformers after the scandals of the Grant administration, and similar concerns can be traced at least as far back as the Jacksonian period.[38] Reform movements in Chicago and St. Louis had the support of most of their city's newspapers in the 1890s, and Steffens himself had seen the corruption of New York City's municipal government firsthand as a reporter. But there was something new about Steffens's work for *McClure's.* He sketched for his readers a new kind of corruption and demonstrated a national pattern in the way an "invisible government" of corrupt political bosses, businesses (especially public service corporations), and the smaller businesses involved in "vice and crime" like saloon keepers, gambling houses, and prostitution ran the city for their own profit. This was the real government behind the legal one that Steffens uncovered, a "behind-the-scenes" exposé of the corruption of the democratic process.

Steffens managed to dispel a number of widely held beliefs that blamed corruption of elected officials on the ignorance of immigrant voters or the depravity of a few wicked political bosses. Mugwump reformers had faith that if local government could be run according to "sound business principles," corruption would disappear. Others blamed corruption on the overly rapid growth and lack of sophistication of Western cities.[39] But Steffens described political bosses like Ed Butler in St. Louis, Christopher Magee in Pittsburgh, and "Doc" Ames in Minneapolis as "good fellows" who were well liked, even loved by the people and, at least during the early stages of their careers, well intentioned. It wasn't just the Western cities like St. Louis that were corrupt but older Eastern cities like Philadelphia. Moreover, the immigrants were not to blame, at least not primarily. Chicago and New York, both "mongrel-bred," had successful reform movements, and Steffens described New York as "the best example of good government that I had seen."[40] It was the "better people," the businesses, who corrupted the political process through bribing public officials for franchises (the St. Louis Suburban Railway company) or for favorable legislation. While Steffens tended to blame "the people" for their apathy, for allowing themselves to be fooled by political bosses into voting straight party tickets and tolerating corruption because they might benefit personally through higher wages or tariff protection for their businesses, the real source of the corruption lay elsewhere. He made it clear that the older mugwump reformers had a naive view of the operation of government and the nature of the connections between business and government. In Pittsburgh and Philadelphia, Steffens described a highly organized and rationalized system of corruption that went far beyond the early Tweed system in New York. He described his shock in discovering the extent of corruption and how widely it had spread.

> When I set out to describe the corrupt systems of certain typical cities, I meant to show simply how the people were deceived and betrayed. But in the very first study—St. Louis—the startling truth lay bare that corruption was not merely political; it was financial, commercial, social; the ramifications of boodle were so complex, various, and far-reaching, that one mind could hardly grasp them, and not even Joseph W. Folk, the tireless prosecutor, could follow them.[41]

While Steffens never explicitly developed a theory of this new system of corruption, he seemed to be referring in a number of these articles to the growing dominance of large-scale industries combined with the fragmentation of political power in industrial cities. This was not the old haphazard "entrepreneurial system of corruption" but one that was highly organized and systematic, reflecting the need to protect the enormous profits of large corporations and the inability of municipal governments to cope with the new demands on them. Because corruption had become systematized, Steffens asserted that electing a "good man," getting rid of bad corrupt leaders, or running city government like an efficient business were not useful or effective reform strategies. Steffens, though, did not begin with these insights. They emerged as a result of his discussions with newspaper editors and reporters, reformers, and, especially, political bosses over the year in which the series appeared in *McClure's*.[42] Elements of a "theory of urban corruption" appeared in the last few articles and more clearly in the introduction to the book version (published in 1904).[43] His *Autobiography*, published many years later (1931), provided a useful "inside" account of his sources and methods of investigation as well as his relationship with S. S. McClure when "Shame of the Cities" was being written.

Each city represented a different variation on a common theme or a different phase in the corruption cycle. While Steffens acknowledged that all the forms of corruption he described as well as reform movements were present in each city, particular forms of corruption were more "highly developed" in particular cities and could be used to illustrate the larger pattern.[44] St. Louis was a good example of "boodle," the selling of "rights, privileges, franchises, and the real property of the city" to capitalists, through a sophisticated system organized by Boss Butler. Butler, who preferred to remain a private citizen, acted as a mediator between the businesses and unofficial committees of the Municipal Assembly. Members of this two-house legislative body had organized themselves into "combines," each of which elected a chairman (not necessarily the same men who were the chairmen of the official legislative committees), who in turn reported to Butler. In this way Butler controlled the Assembly and could deliver votes to the "business bosses." A price list was established for passing certain types of legislation favorable to various business interests, and there were accepted procedures for dividing the boodle money among the combines.[45]

Minneapolis offered a good example of police graft. Here Albert Alonzo Ames, a pioneer doctor whom Steffens described as a "genial, generous reprobate" ran, as mayor, a system of old-fashioned police graft. He put his brother in charge of the police and installed a "former gambler" as chief of detectives. Together they directed much of the criminal activity of the city, making sure to collect their cut from the gamblers, saloon-keepers, thieves, and prostitutes who operated with their permission and active supervision.[46] They established price lists for taverns, gambling establishments, and houses of prostitution to operate outside the confines of the law, and even thieves were organized by the police and required to pay a fee to the city for the privilege of operating there. Card games were fixed in gambling establishments set up by the city, with "streeters" getting the "suckers" from the hotels and railroad stations into the gambling houses, the "big-mitt men" running the fixed card games, and detectives standing outside the door to scare away the suckers if they realized they were being cheated by threatening to arrest them for illegal gambling. In many respects, this was similar to the New York police corruption, exposed by the Lexow investigations, which Steffens had covered during his days as a reporter.[47] This system of police graft was also similar, Steffens pointed out in his *Autobiography,* to the police graft in Seattle, Portland, San Francisco, Chicago, New Orleans, and "of most of the cities in-between."[48] Like St. Louis, the corruption in Minneapolis had been exposed by a combination of the local newspapers and the courage of one reformer, here a grand jury foreman, Hovey C. Clarke (in St. Louis it had been district attorney Folk). Adding a further sense of authenticity to the article on Minneapolis was a front-page photograph of the "big-mitt ledger," an account book kept by the big-mitt men of their financial transactions.

Steffens next studied corruption in Pittsburgh. In Minneapolis and St. Louis, Steffens had not uncovered anything that the local papers hadn't already reported. The scandals in both cities were big news in the local newspapers although the news had not reached the rest of the nation. Rather than doing any original "exposure," Steffens had extensive discussions with the reformers who were active in breaking up the corrupt "gangs" as well as reporters on local newspapers (in Minneapolis he also had one secret meeting with two "big-mitt" men). His articles in *McClure's* served to bring these local issues to the attention of a national audience and also hinted that these two cases were part of a national pattern. But in Pittsburgh, Steffens was on his own as an investigator, and this caused him more than a little anxiety. There were no ongoing newspaper investigations or district attorneys about to announce prosecutions of public officials. Instead, Steffens talked to local residents of Pittsburgh and discovered two inside sources of information on the Pittsburgh system of corruption—a "newspaper boss" that Steffens in his *Autobiography* described as part of the "Pittsburgh-Pennsylvania political business ring," and a much-maligned "merchant reformer" who had compiled a detailed record of the city's corrupt activities and was more than happy to share it with Steffens.

This account of Steffens's journalistic methods and sources appeared years later in his *Autobiography*.[49]

Pittsburgh, described as an "industrial machine," combined the worst of the Minneapolis-style police corruption and the St. Louis–style financial corruption. Commenting on H. L. Mencken's characterization of the physical aspects of Pittsburgh as "hell with the lid off," Steffens dubbed the politics of Pittsburgh as "hell with the lid on."[50] He described the corruption in Pittsburgh as integrally connected to the expansion of capital and the growth of corporations (at first the railroads). The system of corruption in Pittsburgh "was conceived in one mind," that of the great and much-loved boss of Pittsburgh, Christopher L. Magee. Steffens described the discussions he had with Pittsburgh residents who knew about and tolerated corruption but still defended Magee. Magee's method was "not to corrupt city government but to be it," to install his own men at every level and (in alliance with another boss) to control the rival party as well.

By the time Steffens got to Philadelphia, he was such a national celebrity (perhaps the first journalist-celebrity in the nation's history) that people were seeking him out not only to provide information but to ask *him* questions.[51] The editor of the city's leading reform newspaper, E. A. Van Valkenburg of the *North American*, supplied Steffens with useful information on the system of corruption of Philadelphia boss Israel ("Iz") Durham (Van Valkenburg had been threatened numerous times with assassination). But the editor also quizzed Steffens about what he knew about the success of reformers in St. Louis and Minneapolis. In addition, Steffens managed to get an interview with Durham himself, who frankly told Steffens (after a promise of no quotes) the details of his relationship to Mayor Ashbridge, who was widely known to accept bribes in return for granting franchises to Durham's clients. Durham was also intrigued by Steffens's knowledge of corruption in other cities and asked the reporter how Boss Butler in St. Louis was able to run the city with only a minority of supporters in each party (in Philadelphia the bosses had control of both parties). Durham was not satisfied with Steffens's rather vague response and wanted more details. Clearly, Durham was learning as much from the "Shame of the Cities" series as the reformers were. By the time the interview ended, Durham paid Steffens the highest compliment he could by saying that he thought Steffens was a "born crook that's gone straight" and that Steffens had all the instincts of a politician. As for himself, Durham said (as Steffens recounted it in the *Autobiography*) that he was a crook and wouldn't deny it. "What they charge me with is not so bad, not as I see it. I'm loyal to my ward and to my own." But Durham got Steffens to promise that as soon as he (Durham) retired, Steffens would meet with him to "tell me what I do that's so rotten wrong."[52]

The "Shame of the Cities" article on Philadelphia characterized the city as "corrupt and contented." The machine controlled both parties so completely, and the reformers and the public were so demoralized, that there seemed to be no hope for change. Moreover, Philadelphia, as an example of the most systematic corruption of all the cities, contradicted many of the myths about corruption held by the educated public. It was an old city, it had a "real aristocracy," it had a lower percentage of immigrants than the other cities, and it had a successful reform movement and a new charter (passed in 1887) that strengthened the power of the mayor. Reformers had hoped that a "good business administration" would clean up the city. Instead, Steffens described a machine that had learned from reform, even if the reformers hadn't. They used reform organizations to punish local bosses who had broken the "rules" and also learned how to eliminate the more noticeable and blatant forms of personal corruption that could attract attention to more important activities. The machine literally controlled the outcome of elections, making it unnecessary for most citizens to turn out at the polls. Unlike St. Louis, Philadelphia was part of a state and national system of corruption as the Republican party was dominant on the local, state, and national levels.[53]

Chicago offered a good example of reform and New York one of "good government."[54] Here Steffens began to systematically draw lessons from his investigations into urban corruption. Philadelphia was crucial in convincing Steffens that the bosses were not evil men and that reformers would have to be as rooted in the local community as the bosses were. Steffens at first expected to find in Chicago another example of systematic corruption, but instead he discovered a successful reform movement that he then used as an example of the right way to reform a corrupt regime, that seemed to confirm what he had learned from Boss Durham and others. Shortly after arriving in Chicago, Steffens discovered from James N. Keely, managing editor of the *Chicago Tribune*, and from the city editor of the *Chicago Daily News*, and from one of the bosses that Chicago had a reform organization that worked and that this organization—the Voters' League—controlled the city council. How did this happen?[55]

Steffens described in the *McClure's* piece on Chicago ("Half Free and Fighting On") how, in 1895, the Chicago Civic Federation, led by Lyman J. Gage, had "called together two hundred representative men" to do something about corruption in Chicago. Eventually, it was decided to find one man to organize a new reform organization, the Municipal Voters' League. The new nine-member group, led by Chicago businessman George E. Cole (and later Walter L. Fischer, a young independent lawyer who was the organization's secretary and later served in President Taft's cabinet), succeeded in unseating many of the machine alderman with the help of the Chicago newspapers (a favorite tactic of the League was to publicize a machine alderman's corrupt record in the newspaper).[56] Also, the League succeeded with hard work and organization in the local wards—mainly through hardball politics and political savvy (for example, by playing one party off against another, or being willing to run politicians rather than business-reformers for office, or even occasionally making compromises with the machine). In other words, they used the methods of the machine for the ends of reform.[57] This was a great accomplishment, as Steffens saw it, for it showed that a reform movement could go beyond the moralism and isolation of other urban reform movements, past and present, across the country. This was "political reform, politically conducted." The reformers succeeded in wrestling city council away from the control of street railway magnate Charles T. Yerkes. It was a high compliment, at this stage in Steffens's thinking, when Steffens referred to Fischer as a "reform boss."[58]

The importance of Steffens's work on urban corruption and reform was that, for the first time, it made a national medium of communications—the popular magazine—a major political force in national politics. It showed the potential for mass communications as a vehicle for reform movements, as an advocate for political causes, as an educator of the public in uncovering and exposing the "invisible government" of corrupt machines, and in delineating national patterns of corruption. David Nord has argued that urban newspapers were central in the development of the "new politics."[59] The new politics involved coalition building among interest groups around specific issues, in contrast to the partisan party politics rooted in the local community and in ethnic and cultural identities. In the new city politics of the early 1890s, various labor organizations, business groups, reform organizations, and professional associations formed alliances around local issues like election reform, utility regulation, the granting of franchises for urban utilities, and municipal ownership. The new agencies of mass communications were central in encouraging readers to identify themselves as citizen-consumers or citizen-taxpayers rather than in terms of community-based ethnic or job identities.[60]

Democracy, in the view of proponents of the new politics (like Lincoln Steffens), would require the dissemination of the "facts" to a wide constituency in order to build "publics" (independent of political parties) concerned with specific issues. The preceding discussion of Steffens's work shows that the urban reform movements in the cities Steffens studied depended on newspapers to publicize political positions, rally popular support, and educate the citizenry. But the new national magazines also played a role as the immediate reaction to Steffens's work suggests. Reformers used the Steffens series to learn about movements in other cities, about other successes and failures, while the entire issue of corruption of representative government by special interests achieved immediate national notoriety through Steffens's investigative work. As important as they were, newspapers with their local and regional circulation could not have played this kind of role.

Steffens's work is also important as an example of a style or rhetoric that, to a greater or lesser extent, characterized muckraking. Steffens was not quite sure how to characterize his work. He defensively responded to criticisms of his unabashed partisanship by saying that his work was not intended to be scientific.

> This is all very unscientific, but then, I am not a scientist. I am a journalist. I did not gather with indifference all the facts and arrange them patiently for permanent and laboratory analysis. I did not want to preserve, I wanted to destroy the facts. My purpose was not more scientific than the spirit of my investigation and reports; it was, as I said above, to see if the shameful facts, spread out in all their shame, would not burn through our civic shamelessness and set fire to American pride.[61]

Steffens was merely asserting here that he did not claim to be neutral in the war against corruption, that he wanted to arouse an apathetic public to action. But in many passages in *The Shame of the Cities*, as well as in his *Autobiography*, Steffens took great pride in his documentation (S. S. McClure also insisted on it), his inductive method of approaching a problem with an open mind and building toward generalizations through experience, and on his ability to expose the "invisible government" of cities. Moreover, he came around to the view that his special contribution was in pointing out the patterns in corruption scandals occurring throughout the country. Implicit in this view was a concern for facts and interconnections. Because public officials, businessmen, and even old-style reformers could not be trusted and because the real processes of public policy formulation were unofficial and hidden, investigative journalism was needed to discover or "expose" the facts. Moreover, he tried to discover the connection among the facts he exposed, to tell readers how society worked. In his *Autobiog-*

raphy Steffens commented on his new understanding that corruption was not to be explained as a product of a few bad individuals.

> If the graft and corruption of politics, which he [McClure] looked upon as exceptional, local, and criminal, occurred everywhere in the same form, then this universal evil must be, not an accidental consequence of the wickedness of bad men, but the impersonal effect of natural causes, which it might be possible to identify and deal with without hating or punishing anybody.[62]

In other words, corruption was an effect of social causes that were in turn rooted not in local circumstances or in the motives of individuals but in national social patterns. This view was quite consistent with the emphasis in the new social sciences which focused increasingly on "social interdependence" rather than on the actions of autonomous individuals. Individual actions were to be understood increasingly as products of social conditions rather than as springing from an individual's morality or character.[63]

Steffens's rhetoric included elements of a scientific appeal to "facts" and to building a theory inductively through identifying patterns in facts, but there was also a strong element of moralism in his work. After all, these were "shameful facts" that were to be exposed in order to be destroyed. Steffens's intention to provide a scientific analysis of corruption existed in an uneasy relationship with his essentially moralistic and religious appeal to the people's shame at allowing their republican institutions to be corrupted. He called the "Shame of the Cities" series a "disgraceful confession," suggesting clearly the Protestant language of confessing one's sins in order to expose and master one's selfish propensities. Despite the pessimistic tone of some of the articles, Steffens was ultimately an optimist because he could not entirely believe that people were the product of circumstances, constrained by factors outside their control. If the people could only be educated, if they could learn the facts, they would do what was right, and doing what was right would be enough. For Steffens, what was right meant primarily serving the larger public good and overcoming one's own narrow selfish concerns. When Boss Durham of Philadelphia asked Steffens, "Just what do I do that's so rotten wrong?" Steffens replied by saying that Durham was a "born leader of the common people," but that he had "taken his neighbor's faith and sovereignty and turned it into franchises and other grants of the common wealth." Steffens concluded by calling Durham a "traitor to his own."[64] But even the greed of bosses could be redeemed. "They [bosses] can be redeemed someday . . . ," Steffens maintained. "They may help us save society."[65] Steffens's rhetoric was a mixture of nineteenth-century evangelical Protestant moralism with emerging twentieth-century social science.[66]

The other early muckraking series that started at the same time as "Shame of the Cities" was Ida Tarbell's "History of Standard Oil." When the *McClure's* staff decided that Tarbell should do a series on Standard Oil in 1901, Tarbell was already well known for her biographies of Lincoln and Napoleon. In addition to being one of the most respected journalists in the country, Tarbell had a personal interest in the oil industry. She had grown up in the oil regions of northwestern Pennsylvania, in Erie County (she had graduated from Allegheny College), and her father had been an independent oil man until the Standard Oil trust destroyed his business and caused his partner to commit suicide. Her father eventually had to sell his business. Nevertheless, the original plan for the series (projected to be a three-part series) was to enlighten the public on this "Napoleon of industry," not to expose corrupt and illegal activities.[67] While the 1898–1902 period was a time of unprecedented business mergers and consolidations, S. S. McClure was not, during this period, anti-trust. He was at rock bottom an editor, and this was clearly a topic of interest to his readers. It was his idea (or at least he claimed it was in his autobiography) to provide a case study of one industry, to trace the development of one trust as an example of the larger phenomenon.[68] *McClure's* had already printed a number of laudatory articles on the great achievements of industrialists (similar to other popular magazines), and there was no reason to believe that the series on Standard Oil would not continue along the same lines.

The Tarbell "History of Standard Oil" series began in November 1902 and ended eighteen parts later in October 1904. When published in book form near the end of 1904, it was five hundred fifty pages long with over two hundred pages of documentation.[69] The work was richly detailed and documented with little of Steffens's rhetorical flourishes and with a much more scholarly tone. Henry Demarest Lloyd years earlier had written *Wealth Against Commonwealth*, a biting attack against the "mother of all trusts," and Tarbell had sent Lloyd a number of her early chapters for comment. But she was uncomfortable with Lloyd's openly partisan stance and with his socialist outlook.[70] The success and influence of Tarbell's work may well have been a result of the fact that she did not take a clearly ideological position. She was obviously not a propagandist for the trusts or a proponent of socialism. Instead she sought to present a well-documented academic history (although the writing was far superior to the typical academic work), making sure to give credit where it was due and to call

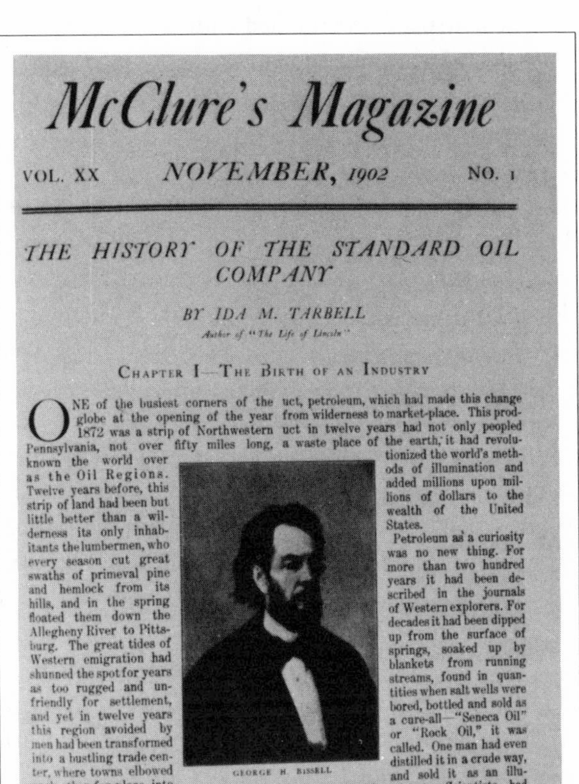

McClure's Magazine

VOL. XX — *NOVEMBER, 1902* — NO. 1

THE HISTORY OF THE STANDARD OIL COMPANY

BY IDA M. TARBELL

Author of "The Life of Lincoln"

CHAPTER I—THE BIRTH OF AN INDUSTRY

ONE of the busiest corners of the globe at the opening of the year 1872 was a strip of Northwestern Pennsylvania, not over fifty miles long, known the world over as the Oil Regions. Twelve years before, this strip of land had been but little better than a wilderness its only inhabitants the lumbermen, who every season cut great swaths of primeval pine and hemlock from its hills, and in the spring floated them down the Allegheny River to Pittsburg. The great tides of Western emigration had shunned the spot for years as too rugged and unfriendly for settlement, and yet in twelve years this region avoided by men had been transformed into a bustling trade center, where towns elbowed each other for place, into which the three great trunk railroads had built branches, and every foot of whose soil was fought for by capitalists. It was the discovery and development of a new raw product, petroleum, which had made this change from wilderness to market-place. This product in twelve years had not only peopled a waste place of the earth, it had revolutionized the world's methods of illumination and added millions upon millions of dollars to the wealth of the United States.

Petroleum as a curiosity was no new thing. For more than two hundred years it had been described in the journals of Western explorers. For decades it had been dipped up from the surface of springs, soaked up by blankets from running streams, found in quantities when salt wells were bored, bottled and sold as a cure-all—"Seneca Oil" or "Rock Oil," it was called. One man had even distilled it in a crude way, and sold it as an illuminant. Scientists had described it, and travelers from the West often carried bottles to their scientific friends in the East. It was such a bottleful, brought as a gift

GEORGE H. BISSELL

The man to whom more than any other is due the credit of what is called the "discovery" of oil; for it was he who first took steps to find its value and to organize a company to produce it. It was he, too, who suggested the means of getting oil which proved practical. After the oil company which he organized obtained oil in the Drake well, he aided in establishing the needed industries and institutions in the new country.

3

The cover page of *McClure's*; the opening article in Ida Tarbell's "History of Standard Oil" series (*McClure's*, November 1902).

to the attention of her readers the pattern of lawlessness in Standard Oil's behavior. The credibility of the work was, no doubt, enhanced for a middle-class audience by Tarbell's careful documentation and nonpartisan, academic tone. Here the facts really did seem to speak for themselves. These were also "shameful facts," but Tarbell did not have to point that out explicitly to her readers. Of course, it was also published at the right time, for the public was fascinated with the "trust" question, the merger movement was in full swing, and magazines and newspapers were filled with accounts, critical and sympathetic, of this new form of business organization.

Until the last paragraph of the opening article in the series, the reader could not have possibly guessed at what Tarbell's series would eventually say about Standard Oil. The first article presented a detailed overview of the development of the oil industry in northwestern Pennsylvania during the mid-nineteenth century. Tarbell described the geography of the region, the early use of petroleum as a medicine and as a lubricant for machinery, the first oil well near Titusville in 1859, and the discovery of underground oil supplies. The economics and technology of oil drilling, refining, building storage containers, constructing the first pipelines, and marketing were all discussed as were the increasingly complex and chaotic relationships between producers, refiners, teamsters, and the railroads during these early days in the oil industry. By the end of the article it appeared to be a happy story. Here was a "wilderness" developed by a new industry. Here were isolated towns turned prosperous, poor men taking advantage of numerous opportunities and being willing to take risks, relishing the challenge of competition. Here was an industry that had learned, or was in the process of learning, through trial and error of only twelve years, to overcome numerous technological problems, to increase refining capacity, and to handle the uncertainties of foreign markets, unscrupulous speculators, and "the unholy system of freight discrimination which the railroads were practicing." The future looked bright for, despite serious problems, "there was no discouragement or shrinking from them."[71]

But trouble was on the horizon, and here in the last paragraph we find a hint of what was to come in this remarkable work.

> But suddenly, at the very heyday of this confidence, a big hand reached out from nobody knew where, to steal their conquest and throttle their future. The suddenness and blackness of the assault on their business stirred to the bottom their manhood and their sense of fair play, and the whole region arose in a revolt which is scarcely paralleled in the commercial history of the United States.[72]

The next two articles (December 1902 and January 1903) detailed the beginning of John Rockefeller's career in the oil refining business starting in 1862 in Cleveland. Eventually, Rockefeller and his partners decided they had to eliminate the rival refineries in the "Oil Regions" of northwestern Pennsylvania. In order to do this "they conceived a great idea—the advantages of combination." A group of refiners and shippers, with Rockefeller in a lead position, formed a secret cartel (the Southern Improvement League) to take over the industry, primarily by securing for itself agreements with the leading railroads to give the cartel members rebates while charging others the standard rates (the railroads were violating their public charters by entering into such an agreement). When the producers and independent refiners found out, all hell broke loose and so began the "Oil War of 1872." This was one war Standard Oil and its associates lost, but there were others to come. Tarbell documented her account with court records, corporation records, congressional testimony, interviews with some of the principals involved, and local newspaper articles as well as pamphlets and other literature put out by various organizations like the Petroleum Producers League. There were reprints of court transcripts and the famous "Black List" of the Petroleum Producers Union.

Other articles documented Standard Oil's control over the transportation and marketing branches of the industry. Tarbell described how the company secured information from the railroads about its competitors' activities and how this information was used to undersell competitors, followed by the raising of prices once competition had been eliminated.[73] Rockefeller's influence in state and national politics was documented in the thirteenth article in the series, which explored, among other things, the company's role in the election of a favorable candidate to the U.S. Senate from Ohio, charges of company bribery to influence votes on various pieces of legislation, and Standard Oil's influence on the final version of the Interstate Commerce Bill.[74] All throughout, Tarbell provided accounts of the numerous charges against Standard Oil, accepting many but also rejecting quite a few and providing evidence for her assertions.

The two concluding chapters made it clear that Tarbell was neither a socialist critic of capitalism nor an advocate of competitive, proprietary capitalism. In "The Legitimate Greatness of the Standard Oil Company," Tarbell made crystal clear, without equivocation, her admiration for the organizational genius of Rockefeller and the system he had put together.[75] She also attributed a lot of the anger of the small producers and refiners who had been forced to sell out to Rockefeller to their disappointment at losing control over their own business, even though the end product was a gain in efficiency and economic stability. Her clear implication was that despite the company's "illegal and immoral methods," benefits did result from the Standard Oil trust. In contrast to the smaller producers and refiners in the Oil Regions of northwestern Pennsylvania, who stood for "recklessness," "extravagance," "little thought for the morrow" and "spendthrift generosity," Standard Oil the trust stood for "caution," "economy," "far-sightedness" and "closedfistedness." On the negative side, Standard Oil stood for selfish unscrupulousness, in contrast to the Oil Regions' "love of fair play."[76]

Tarbell was well aware of the waste and instability of a rapidly growing and overly competitive industry. Speculation, overproduction, unnecessary and duplicated expenses, and an inability to respond to changes in the market all made some form of cooperation necessary in the oil industry. She marveled at Rockefeller's ability to control every facet of oil production—refining, storage, transportation and marketing, his elimination of waste, his shrewd choice of managers, his use of competitive incentives within branches of Standard Oil to encourage productivity, his vast system of agents located all over the world supplying information to the central headquarters, and his understanding of the economies of scale.

Tarbell's assessment of Standard Oil was that it took the inevitable (and in Tarbell's view progressive) tendency toward combination in industry too far and with a callous disregard of the law and the rights of its competitors. After all, many of the central innovations of the oil industry came from the competitive sector, and the same qualities present in Rockefeller were surely present in other men who deserved their chance.

For Tarbell the central issue was the "transportation question." As long as one company could, in one way or another, become the exclusive carrier of a product, competition would be unfairly limited. Rockefeller was determined to eliminate his competitors not because of "business necessity" but the "greed of power and money . . . to build up and sustain a monopoly in the oil industry . . . using force and fraud to secure his ends."[77] One of the more dangerous consequences of this approach to business, according to Tarbell, was the degradation of ethics and public morality.

While Tarbell did not set down a political program for addressing the trust question, she strongly hinted at stronger government regulation, particularly of interstate commerce, as well as a renewed sense in the American public of the "standards of fair play" and public morality. Tarbell was hinting at what others would later call "positive government," not state ownership of industry and not a return to the competitive system, but a middle ground in which the corporation would assume the leading role in the economy, with its interests protected by law and with the government regulating them in the public interest. This was surely a reasonable position, hardly revolutionary in its implications, but nevertheless Standard Oil had a number of its spokesmen, official and unofficial, blast the book as sensationalism and misrepresentation, and Tarbell was called a "bitter, prejudiced and disappointed woman who wrote from her own point of view."[78]

Realism and Muckraking in the Hearst Cosmopolitan

William Randolph Hearst purchased the *Cosmopolitan* from John Brisben Walker in the spring of 1905 for $400,000. Hearst had entered the New York newspaper market in 1896 (after transforming the *San Francisco Examiner* into a circulation leader) and had successfully taken on the powerful Pulitzer-owned *New York World* (by luring away many of Pulitzer's top journalists and editors and playing a central role in galvanizing popular support for the war with Spain). Much has been written about this fascinating man and what motivated him. But there is no question about his central role in muckraking and, more broadly, in the politics of the period. He earned the friendship, loyalty, and even adoration of many of the leading journalists, including Lincoln Steffens and socialist Upton Sinclair (who believed that Hearst could have been the first "socialist" president in U.S. history). Steffens saw Hearst as a great genius and innovator who dared to upset established conventions in creating a people's journalism. At the same time, many others saw Hearst as an unscrupulous opportunist and demagogue who had taken journalism down the "yellow" path of sensation.[79] Perhaps both were right.

Hearst's team of editors and writers that he brought with him to the *Cosmopolitan* were among the best in the country (Charles Edward Russell, David Graham Phillips, Alfred Henry Lewis, Ambrose Bierce, Ernest Crosby, and Bruno Lessing, among others).[80] Also, unlike Walker, during the few years before the sale of the magazine Hearst had considerable financial resources to devote to increasing *Cosmopolitan*'s circulation. According to Louis Filler, during the 1890s and the muckraking period,

> there was hardly a reformer or revolutionist of note whose thoughts were not at one time or another woven into the stamp of Hearst's personality: Tarbell, A. H. Lewis, Henry George, [Ernest H.] Crosby, [Charles E.] Russell, Jack London, Upton Sinclair, Gustavus Myers—the list could be extended indefinitely.[81]

Hearst's newspapers, the *San Francisco Examiner* and the *New York Journal,* were raking muck a number of years before he purchased *Cosmopolitan,* with campaigns against franchise monopolies, the ice, sugar, and coal trusts, and for municipal ownership of public utilities. Before the ground-breaking work of Charles Edward Russell and Upton Sinclair on the "beef trust" and the Union Stockyards, Hearst's papers forced an investigation of the anticompetitive policies of the packers.[82] In 1905 Hearst ran for mayor of New York and narrowly lost, claiming (with justification it appears) that the Tammany machine had stolen the election from him. His unsuccessful campaign for governor of New York state in 1906 (losing by only 60,000 votes) is well known. If Hearst had won that election, Upton Sinclair's prediction would have been taken seriously—or at least half of it. Hearst would have been a serious candidate for president, but he was not committed to socialism or any other ideology.[83]

Cosmopolitan editor Bailey Millard decided that an exposé of the U.S. Senate, widely characterized as the "millionaires' club," would be just the feature to attract national attention for Hearst's new magazine. The idea of focusing on the Senate as the hotbed of plutocracy was not new. Reformer Robert M. La Follette had been elected from Wisconsin to the Senate and had attacked the body's reactionary stance on reform questions and urged direct popular election of senators. It seemed that the Senate stood in the way of a host of important reform legislation—from railroad regulation to pure-food and patent medicine reform. Steffens told a national audience of the corruption of state politics in his "Enemies of the Republic" series, pointing out the connection between various senators (who were then elected by state legislatures) and the dominant economic interests of the state.[84] It was widely known, for example, that Chauncey Depew of New York was the "railroad Senator" while Joseph Weldon Bailey from Texas represented the oil interests. But taking on the entire Senate was another matter and was filled with potential legal problems (lawsuits against muckrakers were quite common), not to mention the threat of possible financial retribution from corporations in the form of lost advertising revenue.[85]

But Hearst was not about to be intimidated by anyone, and Millard finally convinced (with some difficulty) the journalist and novelist David Graham Phillips to do the job. The nine-part series began in March 1906 and ended in November of the same year. In February 1906 an introductory article (written by Hearst) began with an account of a "plain, honest Californian . . . a good citizen, a man of family" and a member of the "Grand Army of the Republic," who upon hearing that a corrupt politician, "a tool of the trusts," had bought himself a Senate seat, decided to write a letter to Congress declaring himself and his family independent of the United States, a kind of personal declaration of independence. Hearst told his readers that the letter was the object of numerous jokes throughout Washington, but that this letter was an "object lesson" for other citizens. The lesson was that it was time for the people to fight back. In addition, the introductory article provided readers with a full-page photograph of the young and handsome Phillips, a vivid contrast to the photographs of the overweight, aging, and smug-looking senators that would appear

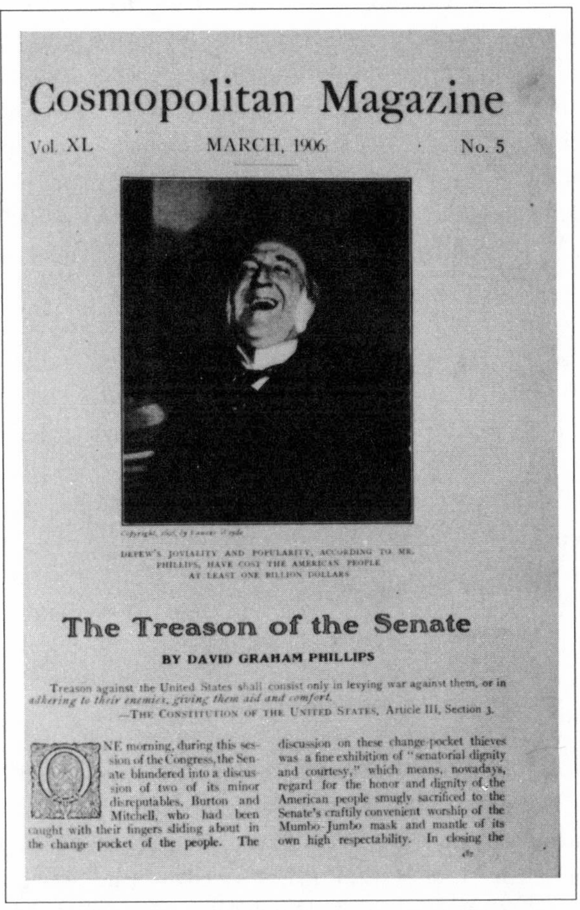

Cosmopolitan Magazine

Vol. XL MARCH, 1906 No. 5

DEPEW'S JOVIALITY AND POPULARITY, ACCORDING TO MR. PHILLIPS, HAVE COST THE AMERICAN PEOPLE AT LEAST ONE BILLION DOLLARS

The Treason of the Senate

BY DAVID GRAHAM PHILLIPS

Treason against the United States shall consist only in levying war against them, or in *adhering to their enemies, giving them aid and comfort.*

—THE CONSTITUTION OF THE UNITED STATES, Article III, Section 3.

ONE morning, during this session of the Congress, the Senate blundered into a discussion of two of its minor disreputables, Burton and Mitchell, who had been caught with their fingers sliding about in the change pocket of the people. The discussion on these change-pocket thieves was a fine exhibition of "senatorial dignity and courtesy," which means, nowadays, regard for the honor and dignity of the American people smugly sacrificed to the Senate's craftily convenient worship of the Mumbo-Jumbo mask and mantle of its own high respectability. In closing the

The first part of David Graham Phillips's "Treason of the Senate" series (*Cosmopolitan,* March 1906, p. 487).

in upcoming issues. Phillips had an expression of earnestness and intensity. He seemed to be just the sort of man to take on the "interests" on behalf of the people.[86]

As promised, the opening article in the "Treason of the Senate" series focused on New York Senator Chauncey Depew. Depew was described as a long-time servant of the "plutocracy" with close connections to the Vanderbilts and with Henry Hyde of the insurance industry that dated back to his days as a corporate lawyer. Phillips provided a sketch of Depew's early career, and like the other senators discussed in subsequent articles Depew was demonized as having a long, consistent history of serving the plutocracy. Unlike Steffens, who had expressed a certain sympathy for the corrupt political bosses, and Tarbell, who had maintained a neutral, academic stance, Phillips's piece was filled with ridicule and indignation. He described the wife of one of the younger Vanderbilts, who refused to have Depew "at her table," saying to her husband, "I do not let my butler sit down with me. . . . Why should I let yours?"[87] A photograph of Depew showed him laughing, with a look of smugness and arrogance. The caption read, "Depew's Joviality and Popularity, According to Mr. Phillips, Have Cost the American People at Least One Million Dollars." Another photograph showed Depew's Washington residence and home in New York City, both of which rivaled the estates of many a captain of industry.[88]

Nelson Aldrich, senator from Rhode Island, was characterized as "the chief of the money power in the Senate."[89] Phillips described Aldrich's links to the Rhode Island Securities Company, which ran the state's street, trolley, gas and electric franchises, and his relationship with John Rockefeller, "the chief exploiter of the American people." Even during his early days in the Senate, Aldrich was "a representative of local interests engaged in robbing by means of slyly worded tariff schedules that changed protection against the foreigner into plunder of the nation." The Senate was blamed by Phillips for the growing concentration of wealth.

> And yet, what has the Senate done—the Senate, with its high-flown pretenses for the Constitution? It has so legislated and so refrained from legislating that more than one half of all the wealth created by the American people belongs to less than one per cent of them: that the income of the average American family has sunk to less than six hundred dollars a year; that of our more than twenty-seven million children of school age, less than twelve millions go to school, and more than two millions work in mines, shops and factories. And the leader, the boss of the Senate for the past twenty years has been Aldrich![90]

Like Steffens in *The Shame of the Cities,* Phillips concluded the article on Aldrich with an appeal to the shame and pride of the American people.

Other articles in the series attacked Sen. Arthur Pue Gorman of Maryland, who had started his career as a Senate page in 1852, "when the slave oligarchy, then in the heyday of its haughtiness, was using the same methods and sophistries about alleged 'constitutional law' . . . that the industrial oligarchy is using in this heyday of its haughtiness." Gorman was a "railroad man" whose power in Maryland was based on the patronage jobs he controlled for the Chesapeake and Ohio Canal.[91] John C. Spooner of Wisconsin served the interests of the Omaha Railroad (he had earlier been a lawyer for the railroad). A full-page photograph, taken without his knowledge (he clearly wasn't posing), showed him at his plush Washington home.[92] Gorman's "chief lieutenant" was the senator from Texas, Joseph Weldon Bailey. As a Texas lawyer Bailey had helped Standard Oil get back into the state after being banned for antitrust violations, for which he received a very substantial fee. As a senator he opposed the pure-food bill as well as national legislation to protect consumers, claiming that these measures would violate states' rights.[93]

Phillips was somewhat short on documentation, although his fundamental point that senators served the most powerful economic interests in their states was well established by local reformers before the series appeared. But the impact of week after week of exposés of powerful senators and the power of Phillips's unrelenting tone of righteous indignation shook up the political world and captured the attention of the reading public. Circulation for *Cosmopolitan* shot up, reaching 450,000 by April 1906. According to Filler, "The newsstands were swept clean of the first issues and requests and subscriptions flooded the magazine's offices. . . . Even in Washington billboards were placarded with announcements in large type of forthcoming issues."[94] As noted earlier, Roosevelt's diatribe against the "muckrakers" was largely inspired by this series, which was also credited with helping reform candidates unseat a number of senators and with the strengthening of the progressive bloc in Congress. Finally, in 1911 an amendment to the Constitution was adopted which provided for the direct election of senators. This turned out, of course, to be no panacea, but Phillips never hinted that the evils he described could be so easily eliminated. Phillips and Hearst wanted to focus the attention of readers on corruption at the highest level of government, to demonstrate that the corruption of the public sphere by private interests was the issue of the day, and thereby to arouse the citizenry to action.

Cosmopolitan's "Shop Talk" department devoted considerable space to this series and to muckraking topics in general. The February 1906 "Shop Talk" advertised a number of features the new Hearst *Cosmopolitan* would carry for the upcoming year—the "Treason of the Senate" series, "the betrayal of the people by the trust-owned United States Senate"; Markham's series on child labor (to be discussed in the chapter); the "What Life Means to Me" series; and "*Cosmopolitan* Table-Talks," focusing on "the great social unrest of our people, their eager upward-looking, their feverish desire for economical and political reform."[95] The entire March "Shop Talk" was devoted to "Some Valued Opinions as to the Need for the 'Treason of the Senate' Articles." Five pages of congratulatory letters were printed. While realizing that the series would not please "Sir Knight of the Dollar Sign," the editors expressed their pleasure at the largely favorable "six hundred and seventy three letters, notes and post cards from the editors of small daily and weekly journals throughout the land." Overall, the letters "reveal the fact that the revolt against the dominance of dollars in this republic is stronger and more general than many of us had suspected."[96] A few months later the editors reported on the "Furor Created by the Tremendous 'Treason of the Senate' Series." "Never in its history," the editors asserted, "has the *Cosmopolitan* been so eagerly bought and read as in the instance of those historical March and April numbers." While a large edition of 430,000 was printed for March, the issue sold out after only five days of publication.[97] The August "Shop Talk" sought to respond to charges (encouraged by Roosevelt in his famous speech) that muckraking was "destructive." The editors replied that "the kind of journals that are attacking the *Cosmopolitan* are the very kind that we had hoped and shall always hope to antagonize." Destruction, the editors maintained, is sometimes needed before construction can begin.[98]

During the same year, *Cosmopolitan* ran a series that attracted almost as much attention, Edwin Markham's "The Hoe-Man in the Making" on child labor. The movement to protect children from the horrors of the factory and the mine, from the dangers of city streets, and from the inequities of the criminal justice system received a powerful rallying cry from this passionate and most biblical of all the muckraking series. Between 1902 and 1904, Judge Ben Lindsey of Denver, Colorado, had established his own Juvenile Court in order to protect children from being prosecuted as criminals, and organized the Kids Citizen's League and other reform groups. The settlement house movement, women's clubs, and the National Child Labor Committee were fighting for legislation on the state and national level on behalf of children and women's rights, and in the process the work of exposure was central to winning popular support. The many muckraking pieces throughout American magazines can be seen as the public expression of this movement.[99]

Cosmopolitan featured Markham's series on child labor with a number of "Shop Talk" segments. Readers were urged to join the Child Labor Federation, led by Gustavus Meyers, which was organized by the *Cosmopolitan* in order to push for favorable national legislation.[100] The December 1906 issue contained an editorial that discussed the Child Labor Federation in more detail. In "Child

Labor Must Be Swept Away; When Your Children Romp Around the Christmas Tree, Think of the Two Million Little Wage Slaves," the editors announced that the series "have acutely roused the indignation of millions of people" and that a "multitude of letters" were arriving denouncing child labor and applying for membership in the federation. The editorial clearly traced the ideal path of reform—from the communication of "facts to the American people" to a sense of national outrage, to the forming of "public opinion" that would "shape itself into political action." Eventually, "humane principles will supplant those of the commercial standard, and new systems and laws will evolve which will sweep away child labor and all the conditions that produce it." The editors were in full accord with the spirit of Markham's work when they urged that "Mammon must be fought and crushed."[101] The January "Shop Talk" devoted two pages to the Markham series, asserting that it would "put the facts in all their hideousness before the people." The magazine announced that President Roosevelt had appointed a special commissioner to investigate the problem and that Senator Albert J. Beveridge of Indiana (part of the reform bloc of the Senate) would introduce a bill "for the suppression of child labor."[102]

"The Hoe-Man in the Making" was a nine-part series that ran from September 1906 to June 1907. The rhetorical power of Markham's appeal to the nation's conscience, the vivid imagery of children locked in factories from early morning to late at night, of bloody hands and feet, of children blinded and going deaf as a result of dangerous workplace conditions and fatigue, bent bones, and diseased lungs, and overcrowded tenements turned into piece-work factories, can move even contemporary audiences. The muckraking mixture of facts and moral indignation reached, in Markham's work, a high point. The opening article in the series, "The Child at the Loom," began with a story about an "Indian chieftain" who was shown the wonders of New York. When asked what was the most surprising thing he had seen, he responded, "little children working." Many of Markham's articles began in a similar manner, reminding the reader of the barbarism that remained within a society claiming to be civilized, and in true muckraking style appealing to the sense of shame of his readers.

The early articles were illustrated with woodcuts by Warren Rockwell that presented silhouetted images of downcast children walking up to the factory gates at sunrise, the "Northern money- grubber who is grafting upon our civilization this new and more terrible white slavery," the little girl falling asleep at her work station, the coal-mining children "filing toward the colliers instead of toward the schoolhouses." Later articles were illustrated with drawings by Cory Kilvert and Harry B. Lachman. The February 1907 article, "The Smoke of Sacrifice," contained photographs of a "sweat shop worker on New York's east side" working in her home, "a ten year old boy who strips sixteen pounds of tobacco a day," and the "Enloe cigar-factory, Pittsburg [*sic*], in which inspectors found sixty people at work."

In the opening article Markham focused on the "weaving rooms of the cotton mills." Conditions in the Northern mills were no better than in the South and here were "children of old and pure colonial stock. Think of it!" Markham referred to some of the reports of Jane Addams, who had seen "a little girl of five, her teeth blackened with snuff." Markham reported that "the average child lives only four years after it enters the mills. Pneumonia stalks in the damp, lint-filled rooms. . . . Hundreds more are maimed by machinery, two or three for each of their elders." Markham used as sources the report of the labor commissioner of North Carolina, English visitors who inspected American textile factories, newspaper articles, and Mrs. John Van Vorst's famous book *The Woman Who Toils,* based on her own experiences as a worker, as well as firsthand accounts of the South Carolina mills by Elbert Hubbard. Hope to eliminate this evil lay in the "brave company of men and women both North and South" who were involved in the reform work of the New York City Child Labor Committee, Consumers' Leagues, labor unions, and women's clubs.[103]

The next installment exposed conditions for children in the glass factories, in which children were

> blinded by the intolerable glow of furnaces, working long hours, breathing powdered glass . . . in the summer, work in deadly heat from 10 to 16 hours a day. Think, comfortable reader, how would you feel? Does it not recall the damned children of Calvin's hell? . . . O Dollars, how diabolical are the crimes committed in thy name!

The evils of child labor, Markham asserted, rob children of their future and their potential and "adds to the ranks of the vagabonds at the saloon counter." Many others ended up in jails, orphan asylums, or reformatories. Markham urged that the proposal of the National Child Labor Committee that would prohibit glass factories from employing children under sixteen "be made into a universal law."[104]

The November installment examined the plight of the "Little Slaves of the Coal-Mines." The opening of the article painted a vivid picture of the life of a coal miner in the Appalachian regions. Markham, like the reformers he admired, had moved a far away from the moral condescension of his genteel predecessors. Rather than blaming the miner for sending his children into the mine, he urged the reader to "follow the coal miner to his home, and look there upon his poverties of mind and body, if one would know all the litany of his wrongs."

> Stand with me among the streets of a town of coal-miners. Everywhere is an air of dejection, a feeling of impermanence. Everywhere is the disheartening look that comes upon houses and lands in their last lapse toward discord and decay. The scene is as desolate as Dante's descending circles. Blasted tree-stumps start up grimly from the ground: yawning coal-pits blur and blacken the sides of hills once full of swaying trees, singing birds, and lowing cattle. High-piled dumps of culm, the gray refuse gutted from the mines by generations of miners, flank the pits and fill the hollows. . . . Streams once running silver white, splashing with fish . . . are now sucked under ground to imperil the mining-galleries below. . . . Hideous, unstable-looking 'breakers' loom beside the spuming pits. On the dreary levels of the gashed sides of the hills huddle the disheartening shanties and shacks which the miners call 'homes.' Here, too, are the huge, cavernous company stores. . . . In such an abomination of desolation, with a death-rate among children higher than the death-rate in the slums of cities, live the mass of miners of the anthracite and bituminous coal-fields.[105]

Markham wanted the reader to understand the entire context of the miner's life, including the seasonal nature of their work, the extreme overcrowding in their homes, and their failing health, in order to understand who should be blamed (and not blamed) for the plight of the child miner.

"The Grind Behind the Holidays" told the story of the children working in confectionery and box factories making the chocolate and boxes that others would use during the Christmas holiday. This was surely a topic designed to tug at the heart-strings of *Cosmopolitan* readers, and Markham was more than ready to meet this challenge. Near the end of the article, he told his readers that "I have chosen to speak 'not the pleasant but the true.' " The truth about these children was certainly not pleasant: chocolate dippers, making one half-cent a pound, getting their legs burned by the hot pot underneath them, working with little ventilation; "home-work in the tenements," a visit to a box factory where the illegally employed children were whisked away as Markham walked through the door. Markham described the East Side (of New York) box factories where the doors were locked, preventing the children from leaving

Cosmopolitan Magazine

Vol. XLI OCTOBER, 1906 No. 6

Illustrations by Warren Rockwell

The Hoe-Man in the Making

By EDWIN MARKHAM

Author of "The Man with the Hoe, and Other Poems"

II. Child-Wrecking in the Glass-Factories*

IN ancient Sparta every man felt himself responsible for the welfare of every child in the community. Had we in the United States such consideration for the good of the race as stern old Sparta cherished in her flinty constitution, we would tear out of our civilization the cruel and wasteful fungus of child-labor, a fungus that destroys the present and threatens the future.

Two and a half millions of children under fifteen years of age are now at long and exhausting work in the offices, shops, mills, and mines of our model republic. In Pennsylvania alone there are at least one hundred different kinds of work at which children are employed; and, unhappily, it is into the cheap and dangerous work that the children always swarm. They are doubled over the

* *We must not grind the seed corn.*—Jefferson Davis

Edwin Markham's "Hoe-Man in the Making" series, along with Warren Rockwell's woodcuts.

until late at night; the little girls with bleeding fingers who were worried about getting blood stains on the boxes; and a strike of child box workers (after a 10 percent wage cut), broken up by the police. Markham addressed his middle-class female readers, appealing to their sense of compassion as well as solidarity.

> Some of those fancy white boxes, my lady in which you sent out slices of your wedding cake, cake to carry good dreams—those white boxes came, perhaps, from this very factory, with its locked-up, hungry children. . . .

> Your glove-box madam, and your handkerchief, strewn with "pansies for thought" or "roses for the flush of youth" were shaped for you no doubt by little wizened girls with aching backs and heavy eyes.[106]

In a similar vein, one of the later articles in the series, published during the Easter holiday season, described the work of children making artificial flowers and men's neckties. In no uncertain terms Markham urged his readers not to purchase products that "are blighted by some drear mist from the gardens of death."[107]

"The Sweat-Shop Inferno" described the garment-making in tenement homes, which Markham and others called "home sweatshops." These were places where "the worker is at the mercy of middlemen, where his life-blood is sweated out by the pressure of the profit-sucking contractors piled up on top of him." Much of the article described the long hours of labor in overcrowded apartments for wages of one cent an hour or less. The tenements were described as "bacilli of consumption" in which "three out of five . . . who are making our clothes are led down to death by the White Plague." Markham described the "cockroach landlords" who raised rents whenever families took in more money from their labors, and the "dread of eviction haunting the minds of workers living on the crumbling verge of the abyss." The inadequate number of city inspectors (in New York) made it easy to evade licensing laws and to raise rents in response to new regulations. Markham appealed to the self-interest of his readers in the concluding pages of this article as he described, with testimony from doctors, union leaders, and settlement house workers, the spread of dangerous diseases in these home sweatshops and the strong possibility that these diseases were transmitted to the clothing purchased by middle-class consumers.[108]

All of Markham's articles relied extensively on evidence collected by settlement house workers, Social Gospel ministers, government commissions and supplemented by firsthand accounts of sympathetic journalists and other observers. In addition, Markham would visit one of the factories or "home sweatshops" and provide a firsthand report. In one case he brought his son with him to a tobacco factory in Pittsburgh employing children and reported that both of them were sickened by the smoke after only a few minutes in the building.[109] This reliance on the social science evidence collected by social reformers was supplemented by extensive biblical references and an appeal to the shame of his audience that such conditions could exist in a civilized nation. Another important element of Markham's work, which was also characteristic of the new reformers, was that he refused to reduce any of these problems to moral deficiencies in the immigrant groups. Instead, the work was strongly influenced by the belief that people are products of their social environment and that immigrants were capable of a decent existence if given the opportunity to do so by their society. Markham seemed to assume that if his readers could see the world of the immigrant poor without the filters of prejudice and condescension, they would eventually sympathize with their plight. Virtually all the articles included a passage in which Markham invited his readers to follow him into a coal-mining community, or into a tenement where an Italian family was busy making artificial flowers at home, in order to gain a glimpse of a hidden world. This was the "new realism," which sought to "speak not the pleasant but the true." But speaking the truth did not mean separating facts from advocacy of a position. Instead, facts were to be exposed precisely to open the public's mind to the need for reform, to imbue the public with a wider and more inclusive sense of social responsibility.

Two other series illustrate the range of *Cosmopolitan*'s muckraking. Alfred Henry Lewis did not regard himself as a muckraker (although others did), and in many ways his views departed from those of the other muckraking authors discussed in this chapter.[110] He was a well-known author of western adventure stories, most notably *Wolfville,* published in 1897. He had spent a number of years as a lawyer in Kansas City and later entered newspaper work with the *Kansas City Star.* Lewis eventually moved East to work as the Washington correspondent for the *Chicago Times.* In 1903 he published *The Boss* (*And How He Came to Rule New York*), about the career of New York political boss Richard Croker.[111] His series for *Cosmopolitan,* "Owners of America" was not filled with exposures of corruption, but it was nonetheless consistent with the muckraking sensibility. Lewis's series, which consisted of biographical essays of the people *Cosmopolitan* used to call "captains of industry," illustrates how far the magazine had come in only a few years in its characterization of big business.

The opening article focused on the career of Andrew Carnegie. Lewis's' style was more subtle than many of the other muckrakers and also more ironic. Carnegie was characterized as the "dominator of the Steel trust," and the opening of the article contained a paragraph of data on his personal wealth (estimated at over five hundred million). While Carnegie was not demonized and positive personal qualities were mentioned, the clear message was that he obtained his fortune through unfair protection from tariff laws that did not benefit the public, from rebates, and by crushing labor unrest (at Homestead), among other things. His early career was characterized as one of flattery of his superiors and a single-minded obsession with "gold-gathering." During the Civil War young Carnegie participated in the battle of Bull Run only to "have his health give way and he went back to Europe to recuperate." "I do not," Lewis asserted, "blame him; that first battle of Bull Run made a number of people sick." Carnegie's book, *The Gospel of Wealth,* which claimed that "he who dies rich dies disgraced" demonstrated for Lewis "the vast difference which subsists between saying a thing and doing a thing." In conclusion Lewis's asserted

> Every man and woman and child between the oceans is serf to Mr. Carnegie, and directly or indirectly must render him tribute. To what end? That he may drink deep and ever deeper of the money-goblet. Does it do him good? No. Does it do us harm? Yes. Is there no remedy, no power of cure? Remedy? There are half a dozen remedies. We pass laws against the man who carries a pistol. Yet far more deadly as a weapon of offense against the citizen is the concealed bank-book of a multimillionaire.[112]

Other articles in the series explored the careers of J. Pierpont Morgan, Thomas F. Ryan, the Vanderbilts, Charles Schwab, and John Rockefeller. Not all the articles were as uncomplimentary as the one on Carnegie. The article on J. Pierpont Morgan painted a generally flattering portrait of a banker who "never wrecked an enterprise . . . never fed his purse with rebates as did Mr. Rockefeller." Instead, Morgan's genius "was not made by tearing enterprises to pieces but by building them up."[113] Of course, John D. Rockefeller was the captain of industry that everyone loved to hate. Lewis was no exception, claiming that "no enterprise has been more merciless than Standard Oil, none more successful in killing off all rivalry. . . . There are no measures, no limits to its power, a power ever selfish, never generous, and having for its sole end its own aggrandizement." Lewis characterized Rockefeller, the man, as lonely, sick, and having no joy in anything except in inspecting his dividends.[114]

Josiah Flynt's "The Pool-Room Vampire and Its Money-Mad Victims" appeared in five installments in 1907. As discussed earlier, Flynt was the author of *True Stories from the Underworld*, published in 1901 and based on his own adventures in the underworld of urban crime. Flynt had had an interest in the world of the "hobo" ever since as a child he had run away from home, acquiring a fascination with the underside of life. These excursions would become the focal point of his life. His parents sent him to Europe to attend the University of Berlin, but he never finished his studies. Instead, he wandered throughout Europe, talking to notable journalists, intellectuals, and authors, and then running off to be in the company of the underclass of the slums of various European cities. He acquired a knowledge of tramp life based on personal experience that was unequaled, and he also knew firsthand about police corruption and published a series in *McClure's* called "The Powers That Prey" and later "Notes of an Itinerant Policeman" that told the story of the connections between the police and the "criminal class."[115]

The first article of "The Pool-Room Vampire and Its Money-Mad Victims" series explored the world of gambling at the racetrack and the poolroom.

Despite the title, this was no Victorian moralistic diatribe against the sins of the "lower orders." Flynt knew firsthand about the desire to strike it rich through gambling and told his readers of people he knew who had their lives ruined by gambling. This yearning for "something for nothing" through gambling, driving respectable people to take insane risks, Flynt called "Dopeland" after the street word for inside information on the horses—"dope." This article (and the other four in the series) established the connections between the "racing trust" (the four associations that controlled the nation's racetracks) as well as the illegal gambling rackets and the bookies, the horse-owners, the respectable corporations, and of course, the "poor suckers" who lost their money. Here was part of the three-sided system of urban corruption called "Vice and Crime" (charted by Steffens in his *Autobiography*) that existed alongside the corrupt systems of the political bosses and the business bosses.[116]

Closely related to muckraking were the fiction and autobiographical accounts called "the new realism." Jack London's, "My Life in the Underworld," was an eight-part series in which London discussed his experiences as a hobo wondering through the country, meeting a variety of characters and running up against the police and prison systems. The series began in May 1907 and ended in March 1908. Along with the short stories of Bruno Lessing, Israel Zangwill, and others, *Cosmopolitan* presented sympathetic accounts of the lives of the new urban immigrants and the poor that represented a significant departure from the genteel middle-class culture of the earlier generation of reformers and intellectuals.[117]

In "A Reminiscence and a Confession" London remembered his days as a hobo and panhandler, traveling through the West, "hanging out with the hobos," giving the porter on the train the "slip," going door to door begging for food. While knocking on doors looking for dinner, he met a man eating a meat pie who expressed the usual middle-class pieties like, "You don't want to work. The trouble with you is that you are idle and dissolute. . . . I have worked and been honest." He offered to employ London tossing bricks in return for dinner. London said he was too weak to do that, which is why he needed dinner—and anyway, "if we [the poor] became like you . . . allow me to point out that there'd be nobody to toss bricks for you." Eventually he deceived a kind-hearted widow into giving him food and money by telling a host of tall tales.[118]

The second article told of the fine art of "holding her down," holding onto a rapidly moving train despite the efforts of the crew to ditch the unwanted guest (the hobo).[119] The third and fourth installments exposed some of the inequities of the judicial and prison systems. London was arrested for vagrancy and without a lawyer or the chance to argue his case he was sentenced to thirty days, which was spent in a prison along with inmates convicted of far more serious offenses. He heard stories of police abuse from other prisoners, including accounts of "men who had died at the hands of the police and who therefore could not testify for themselves."[120] He described the heavy work in the prison yard, the rations of bread and water, the barter-system among inmates, and the inmate "hall-guards" (London was one of them) who acted as the agents of the guards in keeping order. In describing the small-scale system of graft of the inmates, London observed,

> Besides we but patterned ourselves after our betters outside the walls, who on a larger scale and under the respectable disguise of speculators, promoters and captains of industry, did precisely what we were doing, . . . Heaven knows we put bread into circulation in the Erie county Pen.[121]

In the next installment London began with the observation that the hobo's life allowed for the unexpected, for "perhaps the greatest charm in tramp life is the absence of monotony. . . . The hobo never knows what is going to happen the next moment; hence he lives only in the present moment." He described a "sit-down" (being invited into someone's house for a meal) with "two maiden ladies," swimming with a fellow hobo who had been a member of Coxey's army in the march to Washington, and finally a scene of horrible brutality among "a group of Gipsies." The impression a reader received in this most remarkable of the installments was the impossibility of capturing the wide range of human behavior in any simple intellectual or moral system, an acceptance of the rich variety of human life. As London put it, "In hoboland the face of life is phantasmagoria, where the impossible happens and the unexpected jumps out of the bushes at every turn of the road."[122]

Bruno Lessing's wonderful vignettes of Jewish ghetto life (occasionally Lessing explored the worlds of other immigrant groups as well) were popular features of the magazine. Lessing was one of many writers, Jewish and otherwise (including Norman Hapgood and David Graham Phillips), who had a fascination with Jewish ghetto life. Between October 1906 and November 1910, twenty-nine of Lessing's short stories appeared in the pages of *Cosmopolitan*, making him one of the magazine's more popular short story authors. Written in a realistic ghetto dialect with an obvious love for his subjects, Lessing's work—along with other authors like Israel Zangwill, a *Cosmopolitan* staple for many years—represented the turn toward realistic depiction of the lives of "the other half" in American fiction.[123]

Prophets of a New Social Order

Despite differences in rhetoric (the Hearst *Cosmopolitan* was far more sensationalistic and prone to demonize its enemies), both strands of the muckraking tradition were influenced by the Protestant social gospel and the new social science and were intimately connected to political and social reform movements. While *Cosmopolitan* explicitly attacked the "plutocrats" and "exploiters of the people" and gave space to leading socialists, in the final analysis the Hearst *Cosmopolitan* was not a socialist magazine. There was no consistent ideology or presentation of an alternative program, and no one could confuse this magazine with *Appeal to Reason*. Still, we shouldn't underestimate the importance of a mainstream, mass-circulation magazine engaging in a "dialogue with socialism," a dialogue that Martin Sklar argues extended into mainstream politics.[124] *McClure's* was far more restrained rhetorically and much of its muckraking revolved around the theme of "lawlessness" of political leaders and institutions. Implicit in this concept was the sense that new rules had to be developed to cope with changing economic realities. The rise of the corporation was, of course, the central issue. S. S. McClure was interested in bringing stability as well as social justice to this emerging political-economic order, not fundamentally changing it.

The muckrakers were part of a generation coming to adulthood during the 1890s—a period of immense social, political, economic, and cultural change. The autobiographies of Steffens, White, Tarbell, Baker, Howe, and others show that the depression of 1893 was central in causing these young journalists, writers, and reformers to reconsider many of the political beliefs with which they had been brought up. Almost to a person the muckrakers were shaped by experiences of big-city, "metropolitan" journalism, which gave them intimate experience with immigrant ghettos, police corruption, the hidden connections between economic and political power as well as the intellectual and reform cultures sprouting in America's industrial cities. In part this college-educated "nonacademic intelligentsia" can be traced to the expansion of higher education during the 1875–1900 period (during this period the number of college-educated people more than doubled) and in part to a growing publishing industry that required a core of writers and contributors to reach ever-expanding markets.[125] During the first decade of the twentieth century, a significant subgroup of this nonacademic intelligentsia turned even further to the left and became participants in the socialist movement.

In response to the attacks against muckrakers that were common by 1907, Ray Stannard Baker wrote in his diary, "When there arise men who cry woe: your politics are rotten, your legislatures are corrupt, your business is immoral, you turn on them . . . and call them pessimists. . . . You may discover that some of them are prophets."[126] Baker was only one of many of this generation of intellectuals, journalists, novelists, and social critics who regarded themselves as prophets, or in Harold Wilson's words, "spiritual midwives of a new social order."[127] Many readers of popular magazines were eager to learn from these modern prophets how to harness their newfound energies to build a better society.

CHAPTER EIGHT

The Dream of a New Social Order

Family House Magazines and the Muckraking Movement

During the era of muckraking both the *Century* and *Atlantic Monthly* generally supported many of the reforms advocated by the muckrakers but opposed what the editors and many of the contributors considered to be the extreme and unconstructive tone of muckraking exposés. Even in terms of substance, as we will see, the genteel magazines were not at all comfortable with the antibusiness rhetoric of *Cosmopolitan* and other muckraking magazines. Most importantly, neither magazine devoted much space to discussions of the issues raised by the muckrakers. In addition, *Atlantic Monthly* continued to see itself as the standard-bearer for high literary quality, viewing any direct appeal to the emotions of readers as an appeal to the mob.

Between 1905 and 1908 the *Century* continued to explore some of its favorite themes—art, literature, and opera (the "American Artists" series continued during these years), the Civil War, biographies of great historical figures, travel articles, and exhortations for good government and "civic improvement." But despite a few editorials and articles, one would not know from the pages of the *Century* that there was a national movement for social reform shaking up the country. According to Arthur John, the *Century* during the first decade of the twentieth century "remained a magazine of lavish, high-quality illustrations that were intended to inspire as well as to please."[1] This was surely not an accurate depiction of the popular magazines during this period, muckraking and otherwise.

Richard Gilder's editorials were generally sympathetic to the exposures of corruption shaking up the country but unwilling to see these events as symptomatic of any institutional problems. Instead, Gilder saw the problem as one of corrupt individuals and the solution as an improvement of the public's and business's moral standards. A March 1906 editorial praised the wave of exposures in insurance (especially in New York state), patent medicine, pure-food, railroad rebate, and election fraud as having the positive consequence of improving public standards of morality and leading to "a revival of the ethics of business as well as of the ethics of politics."[2] In September of the same year an editorial asked whether the exposures of the past year showed that the country was becoming ethically more sensitive or that "wrong-doing" had increased? Two commencement addresses were discussed, one taking the optimistic view and the other the pessimistic view. The editorial concluded with an affirmation of the value of the new and higher ethical standards emerging from the past year's exposures.[3]

In his January 1907 editorial Gilder seemed to breathe a public sigh of relief that William Randolph Hearst was defeated for governor (although he never referred to Hearst by name). He quoted a speech by New York's newly reelected Gov. Charles Evans Hughes in which the governor asserted that "The voice of the people is the voice of God when reason and conscience hold sway," and that "the man that would corrupt public opinion is the most dangerous enemy of the state." Gilder remarked that "one lasting result" of the previous gubernatorial campaign was a "deep sense of the crime of corrupting public opinion." It is safe to say that Hughes and Gilder had Hearst in mind, since the possible election of Hearst as governor had caused a near fit within the enclaves of both political parties and among the "respectable" opinion leaders. Gilder quoted Hughes as "pleading for that orderly and sober consideration of remedies necessary to true progress." Anyone reading the pages of *Cosmopolitan* during this period would not have used the words "orderly and sober."[4] The January and February editorials of 1908 returned to traditional *Century* themes—the need for civil service reform and the "merit system" in government appointments, and a passionate statement against the tariff on works of art brought into the country. The February editorial also returned to a favorite cause of Gilder's—environmentalism. Gilder called attention to a December 1904 editorial advocating that new areas be protected by the federal government, including the "upper altitudes of the Appalachian range." The growing distance of Gilder and the *Century* from a younger generation of readers was illustrated by a July 1908 editorial that introduced two articles on "Our Barbarous Fourth," decrying unruly and loud Fourth of July celebrations, an article that could have appeared twenty years earlier. Gilder also informed readers of an article detailing the "offenses to the eye" presented by advertising (signs that "disfigured" the environment).

Among the few articles that came close to the muckraking format was Alice Katherine Fallows's "Fair Play for Wayward Children," which discussed in favorable terms the new Children's Court in Chicago and in more general terms the juvenile court movement started by Denver judge Ben Lindsey.[5] Gilder printed a series of articles on the nation's railroads, but they were far from the kind of corruption-exposing exposés that were appearing in popular magazines. Andrew Carnegie explained in a short piece, "My Experience with Railway Rates and Rebates," in which he ended up supporting Roosevelt's stated policy of "supervising railway and other corporations strictly, as we do national banks." A revitalized Interstate Commerce Commission "is rapidly giving to corporate investments the security they possess in other lands by bringing them under supervision."[6] Ray Stannard Baker contributed a number of articles on railroads, but they were nothing like the work he was doing for *McClure's* during this period. Baker's railroad exposés in *McClure's* impressed President Roosevelt so much that Baker became an unofficial adviser to the President on railroad policy. Baker's short *Century* article, "Destiny and the Western Railroad," was a brief historical sketch of the importance of the railroad in the economy as well as the social and political development of the West without any effort to expose illegal activities or convey to readers a political position.[7]

Atlantic Monthly continued to represent reasoned and balanced discussion of political issues, a style of effortless erudition in its writing, and especially high literary standards. Articles on the railroad question (the degree of regulation that should be imposed by the federal government) and on some of the broader issues raised by the muckrakers also showed a clear gap between the genteel magazines and the popular ones in terms of both style and substance. Ray Morris reviewed congressional testimony on railroad regulation in order to demonstrate that much of the proposed national laws, especially the proposal to allow the Interstate Commerce Commission to regulate rates, would do more harm than good. He questioned the fairness of a regulatory commission acting as attorney, judge, and investigator and also questioned the practicality of proposed regulations that would benefit shippers but discourage railroads from taking risks needed for economic development.[8] In "President Roosevelt's Railway Policy," William Z. Ripley challenged the assertions of "railroad men" that new legislation wasn't necessary. Arguing that current laws were not adequate, Ripley urged the public to rally around the President's demand for new legislation.[9]

Three articles in *Atlantic Monthly* spoke directly to the general themes raised by the muckrakers. In "New Varieties of Sin," Edward Alsworth Ross (a sociologist, student of economist Richard Ely and disciple of sociologist Lester Ward) commented on the growing interdependence of American society (what Émile Durkheim had called organic solidarity), which "puts us, as it were, at one another's mercy. . . . Under the present manner of living, how many of my vital interests I must entrust to others!" One consequence was the emergence of "new varieties of sin." These new sins made possible by interdependence were the ones documented by the muckrakers—child labor in the factories, financial corruption, railway rebates, political bribery. The "old sins" were rapidly disappearing, Ross asserted. They were based on personal malice and aggression—more common in small towns rather than in the fast-paced urban communities at the core of "civilized life." The new sins were impersonal and often unaccompanied by guilt yet were just as dangerous as the older sins because they were so much more difficult to uncover. Moreover, Ross asserted, the public was still used to thinking of sin as personal—the child beater is "forever blasted in reputation" but not the exploiter of children. Like other progressives Ross urged the development of (in Jane Addams's words) a social ethic among the public as well as the business community.[10]

A quite different perspective appeared a few months later in the pages of the *Atlantic Monthly.* In "Large Fortunes" J. Laurence Loughlin directly responded to the widespread attacks against people of wealth. "The hostility to large fortunes does not diminish with time and events. The violent denunciations of the discontented classes, or of the more extreme socialists, find an echo in the ranks of more conservative groups." In response Loughlin used some standard arguments in defending the necessary role of capitalists as risk takers and of "the necessity of capital to the present output of wealth, and to the present welfare of all classes." The existence of inequality was a function of natural differences in ability combined with differences in "industrial efficiency." The accumulation of tens of millions of dollars of "great fortunes" was justifiable because the same "captains of industry" contributed far more to the wealth of the country than they received in compensation. While arguing against the condemnation of capitalism, Loughlin saw some validity to the attacks (he must have had Steffens in mind) against the corruption of local government. "The bribing morals of such members of the rich element among us are largely responsible for the corrupt municipal council and the venal legislature."[11]

In "The Literature of Exposure" George W. Alger took on the muckrakers directly in a way that anticipated Roosevelt's attack a year later. Alger argued that the new social reformers "with their methods and theories" were in fact a throwback to the old Protestant ministers who preached of man's sinful and depraved nature. Just as theology had progressed, Alger asserted, to a more optimistic view of human nature, recognizing the need to be constructive, so too must the social reformers adopt a more helpful and constructive tone. "From one branch of this cult," Alger explained,

> has come the modern literature of exposure. They show us our social sore spots, like the three cheerful friends of Job. They expose in countless pages of magazines and newspapers the sordid and depressing rottenness of our politics; the hopeless apathy of our good citizens; the remorseless corruption of our great financiers and business men, who are bribing our legislatures, swindling the public with fraudulent stock schemes, adulterating our food, speculating with trust funds, combining in great monopolies to oppress and destroy small competitors and raise prices, who are breaking laws and buying judges and juries.[12]

Alger said not a word disputing the truth of all these muckraking claims but only objected to a lack of balanced treatment which, he claimed, served to demoralize the public. Instead, "it is the good rather than the bad in us which needs encouragement and exposure." Despite the tacit acknowledgment that bad things were happening, Alger wanted good and uplifting news to be presented to the American public.

One study of the fiction of *Atlantic Monthly* during the period that followed muckraking (1909–1919) provides a useful account of the fate of the genteel tradition after the muckraking period (at least in *Atlantic Monthly*). During this period Ellery Sedgwick was the editor of *Atlantic Monthly* and it achieved a circulation of 100,000. Articles and fiction seemed to reflect what Santayana claimed was a split between a masculine business culture and the feminine genteel culture. Articles on political and economic issues, which were largely liberal and progressive, were written by men while articles on "literature, manners, morals and culture" were written by women. In an analysis of one hundred and twenty-seven articles and stories written by *Atlantic Monthly*'s seven leading female contributors, Sedgwick (the author of the article) discovered a growing alienation of the genteel tradition from the wider stream of American culture. These authors "looked to the past and not to the future for their models of utopias" and felt threatened by "the triumph of materialism," the triumph of science, and growing ethnic and cultural diversity.[13] It may also be said that genteel culture, while never attaining the honored place it had during the nineteenth century, established a niche in the years after World War I. Joan Rubin has documented many of these developments—from the establishment of Book of the Month Clubs to "great books" discussion groups, to the publication of classic literary texts for a mass market. University humanities departments have, until recently, continued to see themselves as defenders of a cultural canon of great literary, philosophical, or artistic works.[14]

Our examination of genteel and popular magazines in the mid- to late 1880s through the 1890s shows a growing diversity in genteel thought. On the one hand, one strand of thinking sought to recapture a preindustrial, homogeneous community through moral reforms like temperance, elimination of prostitution, and through immigration restrictions. Raising the artistic standards of middle-class readers was in part a response to the development of mass consumption, especially the reproduction of art. Gilder was especially interested in cultivating in his readers a more critical, discriminating, and enlightened taste in art, music, recreation, and household furnishings in contrast to the "lower" more sensual and undiscriminating consumption tastes of the masses. In addition, this strand of mugwump thought was uncomfortable with an increasingly polarized society divided, by the 1880s, into competing organizations and interests. Our examination of mugwump concerns about "overcivilization," overwork, urban noise, overeducated women, and mass consumption all reflect this somewhat conservative strand of thought.

But during the same period, another small but significant strand of mugwump thought moved more in the direction of accommodation with labor and with an emerging urban, industrial, and multiethnic society.[15] William Dean Howells represented this more progressive strand of mugwump thought that also was occasionally represented in the genteel magazines. A number of members of the *Century* "sociological group" were also moving in this direction, but by far the most important of these intellectuals were the economists, many of whom were trained in Germany in the "German historical school." It should be noted here that in the 1890s popular magazines had not completely broken with the mugwump tradition, so elements of both strands of mugwump thought can be found in the popular magazines as well.

In addition to Howells, who was sympathetic to a kind of utopian socialist ideal, a cooperative pastoral society governed by a class of enlightened experts—a generation of academics during the 1880s—were also influential in encouraging a break from the social thought of "Gilded Age" America. Many of these individuals have been discussed in other contexts throughout this study. Economist Richard Ely was one of the most important of these intellectuals. Like Howells, Ely was sympathetic with socialism. But the socialism that attracted many American academics during the 1880s was not the Marxian "scientific" kind, connected to proletarian struggle and state control of the economy. Instead, they were more influenced by the Protestant social gospel, the utopian experiments of Robert Owens and William Morris, the English Fabian socialists, as well the American religious utopian tradition which sought to establish millennial communities on earth. Ely, one of the founders of the American Economics Association in 1885 (Thorstein Veblen was a student of J. B. Clark who, along with Ely and Henry Carter Adams, founded the AEA) and an influential representative of the "new economics," thought of himself as a socialist. Even though his colleagues (Clark and Adams) were not as sympathetic to socialism, what characterized much of this strand of mugwump thought was that it took socialism seriously even if it didn't necessarily embrace it as an ideology.[16] According to one scholar, the word *socialism* was used in the 1880s as a rather general ideal referring to "the principle of association or cooperation in economic and political life."[17] While the term could refer to state direction of economic activity, it could also be used to refer to voluntary, nonstatist forms of association, as with producer or consumer cooperatives. But even Ely and novelist Edward Bellamy, who (for a time) characterized themselves as socialists, advocated peaceful evolutionary rather than revolutionary change.[18] In this sense, a strand of the mugwump tradition, sympathetic with socialist ideas, contributed to the thinking of a later generation of journalists and intellectuals who were influential in the Progressive movement and in the development of muckraking. In addition to William Dean Howells, *Cosmopolitan*'s John Brisben Walker, Elbert Hubbard, and reformer (as well as advocate of Edward Bellamy's Nationalist movement) Edward Evert Hale were three examples of this development among the American upper class and intelligentsia (see appendix 6).

The Decline of Popular Magazine Muckraking

Hearst's *Cosmopolitan* became well known for its "sensational" muckraking until 1911, maintaining a respectable circulation of 450,000 but not challenging the circulation leader, the *Saturday Evening Post.* As appendix 1 indicates, *Cosmopolitan* experienced a surge in circulation in 1911 from 440,000 to 750,000. While Charles Edward Russell's muckraking series, "What Are You Going to Do About It?" (another exposé of big business's corruption of city and state politics), was published during 1910, *Cosmopolitan* editors attributed the increase in circulation to another series. Robert W. Chambers's controversial novel *The Common Law,* which began to be serialized in November 1910 and ran throughout 1911, was the sensation of the magazine world.[19] The novel caused a good deal of controversy because it explored the romantic affairs of a young woman, an artist's model, who was part of the New York art scene, and because of the provocative illustrations by Charles Dana Gibson. The magazine *Everybody's* had refused publication of the novel, deeming it unfit for the American home. By 1912, a "Shop Talk" commentary called the serial novel the most significant factor in *Cosmopolitan*'s rise in circulation.[20] Perhaps as a result of this success as well as the decline of muckraking in the other magazines, Hearst decided to emphasize fiction. Despite this new emphasis, Russell and Alfred Henry Lewis were kept as regular contributors, Jack London continued to contribute fiction,[21] and the ever popular Ella Wilcox's poetry appeared throughout the magazine.[22]

McClure's continued its emphasis on muckraking even after the split that resulted in the defection of its leading staff members. In 1911, as a result of poor health and considerable debt (McClure was a great editor but a poor businessman), he sold the magazine to Frederick Lewis Collins (former secretary of the Crowell Publishing Company, one of the major chains) and Cameron Mackensie, a writer and editor who had married one of McClure's daughters. McClure stayed on as an editor for two years, but in 1913 he was replaced by Collins and later Charles Hanson Towne.[23] *Munsey's* experienced a decline in circulation after 1908 in part because Munsey (who McClure considered the most brilliant editor in the country because of his intuitive sense of popular taste) was distracted by many other business ventures, publishing and otherwise.[24]

There is no simple explanation for the shift away from magazine muckraking sometime between 1910 and 1912. In part muckraking, later called "investigative journalism," did not disappear. It became an accepted part of modern journalism, reappearing during various periods of reform throughout the twentieth century. The 1930s and the 1960s saw a reawakening of muckraking journalism. It has also been suggested that muckraking fiction, with its emphasis on the corruption of the "system," its effort to explore "behind the scenes," and its moralistic tone, provided the essential structure for the contemporary "blockbuster novel." Yet the recognition that muckraking has become a journalistic and perhaps novelistic genre does not explain why popular magazines like *Cosmopolitan* moved away from muckraking during the period when the Progressive movement achieved some of its greatest successes.[25]

Louis Filler argues that there was something close to a conspiracy of business leaders to crush the muckraking magazines by depriving them of advertising. Filler argues that "the trusts," concerned about the growth of the socialist movement, the activities of radical organizations like the IWW (International Workers of the World) as well as the successes of the Progressive wing of the Republican party (which formed its own party in 1912 and ran Theodore Roosevelt as its candidate against Taft, Wilson, and Debs), sought to destroy the leading popularizers of antibusiness ideology.

Filler suggests that bankers whom muckraking magazines relied on for loans ("the lifeblood of a magazine is credit")[26] began to insist on changes in editorial policy as a condition for providing capital. Crowell Publishing Company, controlled by J. P. Morgan among others, became affiliated with the *American* magazine (when Lincoln Steffens, Ida Tarbell, Finley Peter Dunne, and John Phillips were on the staff) and, according to Filler, shortly after there was a noticeable change in editorial policy away from muckraking. Filler cites muckraking publisher Ben Hampton (publisher of *Hampton's* magazine) as well as Charles Edward Russell, who claimed that the demise of *Hampton's* magazine was a result of a conspiracy of railroad interests. Russell and Hampton claimed that representatives of railroad interests, angered at a *Hampton's* exposé, contacted all of the magazine's shareholders with lies about misuse of funds and convinced bankers to refuse loans. But outside this anecdotal material, little evidence exists of a business conspiracy in terms of either an "advertising boycott" or an effort to cut off loans. But it seems reasonably clear that among the muckrakers there was at least a widespread perception that financiers and business interests played a leading role in the demise of muckraking.[27]

Popular magazines would never again play such a leading role in influencing American culture as it did during the 1893 to 1910 period. In part this was a result of the rise of new cultural forms, including film and later radio, but as Greene persuasively argued, popular magazines were influenced by the same economic forces they had described so well in the larger society. Perhaps here is a somewhat more plausible explanation for the demise of muckraking. Magazines like *McClure's* and some of the other smaller muckraking magazines were bought out by larger publishing interests. It became increasingly the case that only the publishing conglomerates—Curtis, Crowell, Hearst, and a few others—had the organization and capital to reach the mass market needed to attract advertisers. Advertising became increasingly important as the industry developed new methods to determine magazine circulation size and focus on specific markets. According to Greene, advertisers became more selective in their choice of magazines and tended to choose the ones with proven mass appeal, making it more difficult for smaller ones to survive.[28] Mass-circulation magazines became more specialized in appealing to specific markets in order to attract advertisers and more conservative in terms of their content. Moreover, the budding film industry could now appeal far more adroitly to the public's desire for visual images. The era of the publisher-entrepreneur experimenting with a variety of ideas and formats and using his magazine to express his own political and cultural visions was over.[29]

The changing nature of magazine publishing may in part account for the shift from political reform to what Filler called "escapism and romance" after the first decade of the twentieth century. But in addition, the six years leading to America's entry into World War I (after the panic of 1907) marked the beginning of the end of the intense politicization of the "trust" or corporation question in American politics. The muckrakers had contributed to a widespread consensus in public opinion that something had to be done about the growing power and wealth of the big corporations as well as the social and political problems of industrialization. In fact, *McClure's* concerns about "lawlessness" during the first decade of the twentieth century may have been in part an expression of the widespread concerns with bringing the legal (especially antitrust) and institutional orders in accord with changes in the economy.

But with the passage of the Federal Reserve Act of 1913 and the Interstate Trade Commission and Clayton Acts of 1914, the shape of a new social order had been, temporarily at least, resolved.[30] Moreover, it had been resolved in such a way as to depoliticize this issue by establishing an independent regulatory commission to review corporate activities. This regulatory commission (Interstate Commerce Commission) lacked the strong powers that Roosevelt originally wanted—which would have included federal licensing of companies engaged in interstate commerce, control over corporate capitalization, stock issue and investment policy (among other things)—but it did recognize the principle of "reasonable" corporate restraint of trade as legal (in accordance with the Supreme Court's "Rule of Reason" decisions in 1911), along with oversight of corporations by a body of experts. In doing so it removed the need for continuous court resolution of this debate on a case-by-case basis as well as direct, intrusive governmental regulation of the corporate-administered market (Roosevelt wanted in effect to treat all corporations as if they were public utilities, while Taft and Wilson opposed this "statist" solution). Both options would have put the question of the power and accountability of the large corporation continuously in the public spotlight. Instead, as Sklar has pointed out, the supremacy of society over the state was maintained within the context of a regulated corporate-capitalist system. This was not necessarily what muckrakers had in mind in considering the contours of a "new social order," but dependent as they were on reform movements and centers of power in the federal government, the resolution of the central debates of this era had to have an effect on their work.[31]

Within a few years America's entry into World War I, as well as the reaction against the Russian Revolution and labor radicalism, created a climate of reaction that permeated popular culture. The former muckrakers were also divided on these issues, with many joining Wilson's crusade and becoming participants in government prowar propaganda efforts while others like Steffens opposed the war. Well-known former muckrakers Samuel Hopkins Adams, Ray Stannard Baker, Harvey O'Higgins, and Ida Tarbell were appointed by Wilson to the Committee on Public Information, where they developed some of the first forms of state propaganda to galvanize popular support for the war.[32] By the 1920s *McClure's* was filled with diatribes against the "red menace" and immigration, a far cry from the bold experiment S. S. McClure established in 1893.

Revisiting the Mass Culture Debate

This study suggests that this first form of national mass communications cannot be reduced to an effect of economic causes, to a simple expression of "mass consumption," to some piece of corporate capitalist ideology intended to legitimate a new system of power relations. The editors and publishers, contributors and participants, who developed this new cultural form thought of themselves as contributing to a new social order. "Corporate capitalism" and consumer culture were not "things" they adapted to or legitimated. They were phenomena the popular magazines helped, directly or indirectly, to create. These magazines were not superstructural reflections of economic changes that somehow operated "behind their backs." Instead, we need to see the development of a national mass culture during the turn of the century as part and parcel of the process of creating this new social order, not simply adapting to or legitimating it. The economy should not be understood as existing in some separate and autonomous sphere which in turn acts as an independent variable influencing "culture," for beliefs about the state, corporations, captains of industry, social ethics, municipal reform, cities, and the working out of these beliefs were part of the process of political and economic transformation during the turn of the century.

As Martin Sklar has said, "corporate capitalism" should be understood as a new type of society, not simply in narrow economic terms, and it didn't just happen.[33] It was the product of the creative actions of business leaders, politicians, middle-class professionals and reformers, journalists and writers, elements of the labor movement, and others who were often quite conscious of themselves as historical actors at a crucial turning point in American history. As we have seen, a central element of the consciousness of this period was historical-evolutionary consciousness. All three popular magazines expressed the emerging pragmatic view of social evolution that saw the active and conscious mastery of society, and new forms of "social cooperation" (Frank Munsey saw the trust as a progressive development, while after 1903 McClure and Hearst saw the need for state regulation to supplement the development of corporations) as progressive evolutionary developments. Walker, Howells, McClure, Munsey, Steffens, Wilcox, Phillips (David Graham), Baker, Markham, and others in the cast of characters spoke repeatedly of their participation in making history and used evolutionary language in discussing the changes they were witnessing and in which they were participating. History was not for them a nightmare from which they were trying to awake, or the "dead weight of the past" but a series of utopian projects.

Popular culture during the Progressive era was a crucial arena in which mugwumps, a new generation of journalists, middle-class professionals and academics, politicians, businessmen, novelists, and, on occasion, radical reformers and socialists presented their visions of the future. The problem with the focus on ideology, hegemony, or "reproduction" in previous work on the popular magazine is not that a case cannot be made for this position, but that its theoretical framework is too limited to capture important complexities. Like the earlier generation of mass culture critics discussed in the introduction, the characterization of popular magazines as a vehicle of "ideological hegemony" treats a complex and contested process as an already accomplished fact. "Hegemony" becomes a synonym for consensus and a substitute for empirical research.

Unlike the older "family house magazines" that were a vehicle for the civilizing mission of the Northern upper class and for whom the concept of "cultural hegemony" makes a good deal of sense, popular magazines cannot so easily be made to fit into this framework. Even with the mugwumps' "gospel of culture," there was a tension between the efforts of some mugwump intellectuals to construct boundaries that separated the "civilized" middle and upper classes from the uncultured "rabble" and the more democratic project of those that sought to disseminate high culture to the working class in order to alleviate class conflict and "class envy."

Popular magazine publishers and editors had a coherent worldview that celebrated the dreams of progress, particularly in the form of the emerging social order of corporate capitalism, but unlike their genteel predecessors they had the problem of selling magazines to a mass audience in order to increase their major source of revenue—advertising. The need to be popular required an engagement with contemporary popular interests, from concerns about health to popular fears of concentrated corporate wealth and corruption to new conceptions of women's roles. Clearly, the producers of popular magazines had a clear ideological bias in the direction of supporting the emerging social order of corporate capitalism, but it would be more accurate to characterize these magazines as the site of a struggle for cultural hegemony, a struggle made necessary by the relative openness of the popular magazine form to a range of views. As one sociologist has argued, "Hegemony isn't just imposed on society from the top, it is struggled for from below, and no terrain is a more important part of that struggle than popular culture."[34]

Conclusions of the Study

We have seen that "culture" became redefined through the pages of *Munsey's*, *Cosmopolitan*, and *McClure's*. Instead of a link to the past, a source of reassurance, a repository of timeless and permanent virtues, "culture" was associated with a series of future projects or "dreams." The new culture sought not permanence but possibility, not character but desire. The word *desire* may be an apt one, for dreams, as Freud argued in a work published during this period, are intimately connected to human desires, to "wish-fulfillments."[35] Desire is a yearning for something one does not have, and there is perhaps no better word to characterize modern culture—a restless yearning to escape the limitations of scarcity, nature, and the divisions of industrial society. In all these ways popular magazines expressed an expansive sense of possibility, a pulsating energy that sought fulfillment sometime in the hopeful future.

The dreams of abundance, social control, and social justice became the cornerstones of a post-Victorian mass culture and through the pages of popular magazines attained a legitimacy and a national audience. Underlying all three dreams was an emphasis on activity, motion, and energy. Energy was to be found in electric power (e.g., Henry Adams's dynamo, a "new symbol of infinity");[36] in the body—now understood as capable of regeneration; in the department stores, skyscrapers, and immigrant ghettos of industrial cities; in the fast motion of trains, planes, and automobiles; and in the depths of the psyche. This study has also suggested that there were a number of contributors to this new culture. First, there was the middle-class desire to imitate the conspicuous consumption of the rich, expressed in articles that glamorized upper-class lifestyles and the world of mass consumption. While journalists and others from middle-class backgrounds wrote these articles, their source of inspiration was the life of luxury and consumption of the new urban industrial elite. Second, there was the middle-class professional discourse that sought to impose rationality and order on social and natural processes (from engineers to urban planners to experts on recreation and physical culture). Through the application of scientific principles, the abundant energy of nature, the body, the self, or society could be utilized. Third was the more progressive strand of mugwump or genteel thought represented by the socialism of William Dean Howells as well as the nationalism and "corporate liberalism" of Theodore Roosevelt. Finally, a segment of the middle class in coalition with other classes used popular magazines to articulate a vision of "cooperation" and a new national community in which the state would play an expanding role in protecting the interests of the citizenry in an economy dominated by large corporations. Here was the foundation of the core beliefs of twentieth-century American society—consumerism, therapeutic culture, and the social welfare state.

The dream of abundance promised for the first time a world of commodities and the leisure to enjoy them. Professional and white-collar working-class urbanites (and others) could dream of a version of the Newport lifestyle. They might have to settle for a bicycle rather than a yacht, or "Little Egypt" at the fair rather than a visit to the real Pyramids, but the dream of an escape from scarcity seemed within reach. Department stores, advertising, and industrial fairs celebrated the spectacle of things, illuminated by the miraculous energy of electricity, complemented by the foreign "exoticism" of amusement areas and the wondrous fantasies made possible by new technology. Science and technology seemed to point to a future of wonders, a Promethean dream of extending the reach of man's powers perhaps without limit. New religious sensibilities were central to this culture as middle-class writers spoke of unleashing a source of abundant energy. Mind cure, spiritualism, and the sense of a new "religious awakening" made many Americans feel connected to the wider universe, giving them a sense that one could overcome internal limitations by experiencing the energy of an abundant Self. Popular magazines were especially important in presenting an imaginative alternative to the increasingly rationalized sphere of work and public life. Through vicarious adventures in the outdoors, depictions of sports, and vigorous physical activities, magazines could therapeutically help readers cope with modern life and feel reinvigorated. Ironically, a new post-Victorian culture made use of widespread feelings of discontent with industrial society.

Dreams of control and social justice tapped into the same sense of possibility. The new civic consciousness of the 1890s received its first national exposure in the pages of popular magazines, allowing readers to "widen their horizons," explore the worlds of the urban poor, and feel sympathetically connected to groups who had previously been defined as outside the boundary of American society. This was part of the "whirlpool of real life" that so frightened mugwump reformers and intellectuals but tantalized a younger generation of middle-class writers, journalists, and intellectuals. We have seen how many contributors to popular magazines were quite sure that they were seeing the birth of a new social order, one based not on "selfishness" but cooperation, not on narrow materialism or individualism but on interdependence and solidarity.

Dreams of creating a reinvigorated public sphere of well-ordered and well-managed cities, of new state agencies to regulate industry in the public interest, were given important expression through the new agencies of mass communications—popular magazines and newspapers. Here readers were addressed as national citizens—not in terms of party loyalties rooted in community, ethnicity, or occupation. This was the new politics, which sought to unite various groups of citizens around specific issues and which also relied increasingly on activist government to protect the public interest. Here we see the foundation of the nonpartisan issue-oriented politics of the modern American social welfare state. While never fully realizing the dreams of many of the muckrakers of creating a just and fair social order, the underpinnings of popular support for the state as the ultimate guarantor of social welfare was established.

The dream of control was expressed in the collective vision of William Dean Howells, John Brisben Walker, and others who saw in the abundance of late nineteenth-century capitalism the danger of social disintegration through economic depressions, class conflict, and urban decay. This dream tried to balance the "selfish individualism" of middle-class consumers and capitalists with a new social ethic, a "civic consciousness." They believed that the unplanned economic growth of the competitive system of "Gilded Age" America was both irrational and dangerous. Proponents of this utopian project during the late nineteenth century proposed a new society in which social life could be rationally ordered and planned in large part on the expertise of professionals who would be guided by neutral and objective scientific principles. In fact, like the French sociologist Auguste Comte, they believed that this was the inevitable course of social evolution.

But the dream of control was too elitist for a new generation of journalists and intellectuals who became the leading contributors to popular magazines in the early twentieth century. A cooperative social order was not to be imposed on people but created through voluntary action, inspired by bonds of fellowship. For them, it was the social nature of men and women, a deeply felt sense of solidarity, that inspired them to expose a range of social evils. The dream of an industrial society in which every individual would feel responsible for each other and acknowledge one another's mutual dependence was not entirely consistent with the dream of overcoming all limitations through science, technology, and mass consumption. Implicit in this social vision was the claim that morality depended on the existence of a good and just society, the larger social environment within which science, technology, and consumption operated. Social justice, the muckrakers asserted, necessitated a balancing of interests that at times required people to sacrifice for the larger public good. The requirements of a new "social ethics" might interfere with the perceived right of unlimited economic growth or personal consumption.

While all three dreams were expressed and partially put into practice in the social order of modern twentieth-century societies, they existed in a dialectical tension with one another, one theme often inspiring an opposing one. The dream of abundance was in large part a new version of the quest for success, only now it seemed accessible to all, not only as a reward for the Protestant virtues of hard work, thrift, and character. But the depression of 1893 proved for many that there had to be some limit on the acquisition of wealth, some check on unrestrained "competitive individualism." Magazines portrayed the captains of industry as larger-than-life heroes filled with superhuman charisma that enabled them to shape their environment, but by the early twentieth century *McClure's* and *Cosmopolitan* mistrusted their unrestrained power and conspicuous consumption. Magazines sought to demonstrate that the individual could still make a difference but also that individuals were connected to and depended upon one another in complex ways. Magazines in some respects sought to blur the cultural boundaries that divided men and women, middle class and working class, native-born and immigrant, while in other ways they reinforced the prejudices and sense of cultural hierarchy of their readers. In other words, popular magazines were "multivocal," expressing a range of cultural themes and patterns.

Of the three popular magazines, *Munsey's* articulated an unambiguous version of the new dream of abundance, with its glowing depictions of urban luxury and new opportunities for success and achievement. Walker's *Cosmopolitan* developed this theme primarily in its presentation of new scientific and technological developments as well as in its coverage of industrial expositions. But Walker balanced his magazine's enthusiasm with these dreams of progress with a critical subtext that questioned the "selfishness" of an overly competitive and unplanned social order. Walker saw his magazine as a vehicle for the new cooperative social order he believed was on the horizon, one based on material abundance but also on rational social planning. Hearst's upper-class populism provided *Cosmopolitan*'s readers with a mass forum for the ideas of the left wing of the muckraking movement while *McClure's* in its second decade developed a more rhetorically restrained and ideologically moderate critique of American institutions. Perhaps more that the other magazines, *McClure's* was influenced by its editor's evangelical Protestant background that sought to infuse moral principles into the corrupt public sphere, to do battle with the selfish industrial plutocrats, just as the moral reformers of an earlier generation had done battle with the slave plutocracy. In addition, *McClure's* consistently presented the wonders of science and technology and was a leading journal of realism in both fiction and in its nonfiction "human interest" pieces. In their use of halftone photography and advertising, all three magazines helped to popularize the new visual culture that mugwump critics thought was so dangerous and subversive.

As we look back at this period from the vantage point of the late twentieth century, we may agree with Lincoln Steffens who in his *Autobiography* called the turn of the century "innocent days."[37] Who could today be so naively optimistic about the ease of creating a just social order or about the wonders of science and technology? After a century that has seen totalitarian regimes, who can think of the dream of a social order controlled by enlightened experts and not see in it the germs of a nightmare? By the 1920s the critique of consumer culture flowered as intellectuals, social critics, and novelists poked fun at standardization and shallow materialism, at the superficiality of defining oneself through one's possessions (Sinclair Lewis's *Babbitt* is one example). This critique of mass consumption or "consumer culture" continues today as we become increasingly aware of human and natural limitations and the dangers posed by a thoughtless flight from our responsibility to nature and to our fellow human beings. Does anyone talk anymore in terms similar to S. S. McClure when he said in a letter to his wife, "I want to study God in history"?[38] Wherever God may reside today, it is certainly not in history. We may admire the historical vision of intellectuals and reformers of the turn of the century, but the quest for meaning and certainty in history is foreign to a postmodern sensibility. We may rummage nostalgically through the past for sources of entertainment, but we have largely given up on grand utopian visions of history and we tend to mistrust thinking that does not acknowledge its own limited, socially constructed character. Like many people who do not remember their dreams because they fear what they might learn from them, as a culture we may be choosing to forget what we now find disturbing. But whatever the limitations of the cultural dreams of a previous age, these dreams have shaped the world we live in, and if we are to understand ourselves the dreams must be remembered.

In another sense the early popular magazines are quite relevant to contemporary late twentieth-century readers awaiting a new century and a new millennium. Much more than our predecessors in the late nineteenth and early twentieth centuries, we live in a society permeated by forms of mass culture—both the mass communications industries of television, newspapers, film, and popular music as well as the mass commercial culture of advertising, sports, videos, fashion, and the rest. There is a cynical, sophisticated, and ironic tone in contemporary mass culture that wasn't there earlier, but the modern dreams that appeared in the pages of *McClure's*, *Cosmopolitan*, and *Munsey's* are still with us even if the historical and evolutionary language has been shed and the enthusiasm replaced by a dry cynicism. The concern for health, both psychological and physical, has reached an intensity that overshadows anything expressed in the early popular magazines. The quest for "an imaginative release from institutional restraints" permeates the forms of mass culture which today are everywhere. The dream of abundance takes on new and more sophisticated forms but is still with us—from the luxurious urban and suburban shopping malls to modern advertising's fixation with style and personal appearance, and in many of the themes of popular psychology and therapy which depict the self as infinitely malleable and changeable. Moreover, we know from the recent history of the 1960s that the medium of television and "investigative journalism" played a central role in the social movements of this period just as magazines, newspapers, and muckraking journalism played a central role in the social movements of the Progressive era. In fact, part of the postmodern sensibility is the realization that the images and information flowing from mass culture have become so pervasive and influential that one cannot readily separate image from reality, that what we read and see doesn't so much reflect or express "real life" but defines for us and shapes the nature of what real life is. Reality and our representations of it are becoming more difficult to disentangle.

Today television has become the preeminent cultural form, the dominant medium through which issues, images, and ideas are given credibility by being presented to a national audience. While the debates of the Progressive era no longer dominate mass culture and it is fair to say that the fundamental relations between government, business, and society are well outside the sphere of public debate, mass communications continues to play a leading role as collective therapist, as an exposer of the system's corruption, and as a cheerleader for "progress." It is equally important today to discover the ways in which collective dreams and fears are expressed in the mass media, the complex ways in which mass culture contributes to our society's reproduction and transformation. But that is another story.

APPENDIX ONE

*Circulation in Thousands of the Leading General Interest Magazines from 1900 Through 1913**

	1900	1901	1902	1903	1904	1905	1906	1907	1908	1909	1910	1911	1912	1913
SEP	250	331	375	512	656	728	705	747	886	1124	1425	1739	1885	1986
MU	590	623	576	634	627	611	698	698	618	500	500	500	400	400
EV	100	150	150	250	500	700	600	550	500	500	508	632	600	600
COL	170	260	321	400	528	568	568	568	531	500	571	520	500	562
MC	369	360	377	370	375	375	414	472	440	425	450	450	400	500
COS	350	350	350	300	300	400	450	450	400	425	440	750	750	800
AM						300	250	280	267	287	313	275	300	320

Abbreviations:
SEP = *Saturday Evening Post*
MU = *Munsey's*
EV = *Everybody's*
COL = *Collier's*
MC = *McClure's*
COS = *Cosmopolitan*
AM = *American*

*From N.W. Ayer and Son's *Newspaper Annual* (Philadelphia: Ayer Press): reprinted in Theodore P. Greene, *America's Heroes: The Changing Models of Success in American Magazines* (New York: Oxford University Press, 1970).

APPENDIX TWO

Topics of Lead Cosmopolitan *Articles, 1893–1904**

	1893–1894	1895–1896	1897–1898	1899–1900	1901–1902	1903–1904
AL	7	6	2	2	4**	1
SP	0	5	0	2	4	4
ST	1	1	3	2	2	2
PC	2	1	10	8	6	10
FIC	2	1	2	0	0	0
ROY	1	0	0	3	2	1
TR	4	7	4	2	0	2
BIO	6	3	0	2	1	2
SF	1	0	2	0	0	0
ENT	0	0	0	1	1	0

Abbreviations:
AL = Art, Literature and High Culture
SP = Sports, Recreation, and Health
ST = Science and Technology
PC = Politics and Current Events (including expositions, current military articles)
FIC = Fiction
ROY = International Royalty and American "high society"
TR = Travel
BIO = Biography and History (excluding biographies of artists and writers who are including under AL).
SF = Self-Promotion (editorials longer than one page or promotions of the magazine other than advertising)
ENT = Popular entertainment including popular music, theater, circuses, film, amusement parks

*Volume 30 was missing in the Hillman Library *Cosmopolitan* collection and so November 1900 to April 1901 issues are not included in this table.

**A lead article by Lavinia Hart called "Motherhood" was hard to classify. Since the article did not place "motherhood" in historical or contemporary context and contained numerous illustrations of art work, it was included under "Art, Literature and Poetry."

APPENDIX THREE

Topics of Lead Cosmopolitan *Articles, 1905–1914**

	1905–1906	1907–1908	1909–1910	1911–1912	1913–1914#
AL	1	8	8	0	9
SP	3	0	0	0	2
ST	1	4	2	6	3
PC	12	6	6	8	0
FIC	1	1	1	6	2
ROY	3	4	3	0	0
TR	1	0	0	1	0
BIO	1	0	3	3	1
SF	0	0	0	0	0
ENT	1	0	1	0	0

Abbreviations:
AL = Art, Literature and High Culture
SP = Sports, Recreation, and Health
ST = Science and Technology
PC = Politics and Current Events (including expositions, current military articles)
FIC = Fiction
ROY = International Royalty and American "high society"
TR = Travel
BIO = Biography and History (excluding biographies of artists and writers who are including under AL)
SF = Self-Promotion (Editorials longer than one page or promotions of the magazine other than advertising)
ENT = Popular entertainment including popular music, theater, circuses, film, amusement parks

*This period roughly corresponds to time that Hearst bought the *Cosmopolitan* up to the end of this study.

#The last volume in the Hillman Library *Cosmopolitan* collection is Volume 50 (December 1913 to May 1914). June to December 1914 issues are not included in this table.

APPENDIX FOUR

Century Magazine *Articles, 1893–1900 (Percentage Distribution of Magazine Articles* by Category)*

	1893–1894	1895–1896	1897–1898	1899–1900
Fiction	28	36.6	25.9	28.7
Science and Technology	.9	2.5	4.6	3.9
Biography, History	12	18.5	19	16.2
Art, Literature, and Music	27	17.3	16.4	15.6
Sports, Leisure	5.2	3.7	2.9	2.5
Travel, Nature	9.3	8.6	13.3	16.2
Politics, Current Events	16.5	11.9	15.9	16
Royalty	.9	.8	1.4	.5
Number of Articles	406	243	347	351

*The unit of analysis here is the article rather than number of pages. Volume 49 (November 1894–April 1895) was missing from the University of Pittsburgh collection. *All* articles are included except for the "Topics of the Times" editorials, letters, and poetry.

APPENDIX FIVE

Cosmopolitan Magazine *Articles, 1893–1900 (Percentage Distribution of Magazine Articles by Category)*

	1893–1894	1895–1896	1897–1898	1899–1900
Fiction	24.0	31.1	27.8	27.8
Science and Technology	13.8	12.2	8.8	11.6
Biography, History	12.5	8.1	8.5	9.85
Art, Literature, and Music	13.8	14.4	12.4	6.7
Sports, Leisure	1.6	7.7	4.2	6.7
Travel, Nature	12.8	12.6	7.5	8.5
Politics, Current Events	19.0	12.6	27.1	26
Royalty	2.3	1.1	3.5	2.8
Number of Articles	304	270	306	284

APPENDIX SIX

Major Contributors to Walker's Cosmopolitan

Many of John Brisben Walker's leading contributors were active in independent journalism as well as being contributors to the "quality magazines." Murat Halstead wrote the "Review of Current Events" feature for *Cosmopolitan* in the 1890s. He was also the editor of the *Cincinnati Commercial*, a former Republican party newspaper that had become independent by the 1880s. Halstead's newspaper was part of "the communications network that nurtured liberal reform within the Republican party."[1] During the early 1890s, Edward Evert Hale wrote the "Social Problems" feature, which also explored topical issues from "The Danger of Cities," to "The Work of Women" and "The Promotion of Laborers." Hale was a well-known writer, editor, and social reformer. He was a "Boston man of letters" who edited a number of scholarly review journals with limited circulation in the New England area. He participated in the first "Nationalist Club" organized in support of Edward Bellamy's best-selling utopian reform novel, *Looking Backward* (1888). He was also a critic of orthodox Christianity and an advocate of a more socially conscious and reform-oriented Christianity. His popular novel, *If Jesus Came to Boston,* published in 1896, espoused many of these themes.

Along with Halstead and Hale, William Dean Howells was a regular contributor to the *Cosmopolitan* and, for a brief period after Walker purchased the publication, the joint editor along with Walker (Howells resigned because Walker's autocratic style made him difficult to work with). Prior to Howells, Walker offered the editorship to James Blaine, who could not accept because he had taken a position as Secretary of State in the Harrison administration. Howells, as we already know, was part of the Eastern literary establishment and an advocate of a domesticated form of realism in fiction.

Many of Murat Halstead's articles were devoted to the problems of "labor unrest" and the central political questions of the day—the money supply and the "free silver demands" of some in the Democratic party (later to become William Jennings Bryan's chief campaign issue in the 1896 election), and the tariff question. On these issues Halstead, who had been part of the liberal wing of the Republican party, maintained a nonpartisan tone. Walker was supporting the Democrats during the 1896 election, but little of his political preferences (at least in terms of electoral politics) made its way into the magazine. In keeping with American political trends, the popular magazine was issue-oriented not party-oriented. At any rate, given the level of education and likely Eastern-dominated readership of the *Cosmopolitan* during the 1890s, Walker's political orientation would not have made most of the subscribers happy.

Hale, Howells, and Halstead were solidly in the Eastern cultural establishment and were frequent contributors to the quality magazines as well. During the later years of the 1890s, Walker's editorial staff changed somewhat in composition, and Walker took a more active role as a contributor. Regular contributors included Elizabeth Bisland, Ella Wheeler Wilcox, Cleveland Moffett, Brander Mathews, Julian Hawthorne, Hjalmar Hjorth Boyesen, Elbert Hubbard, Lavinia Hart, Harry Thurston Peck, and Israel Zangwill,[2] among others. Many of these *Cosmopolitan* contributors also published in the quality magazines as well as the other popular magazines (they were established "magazinists," in other words).

Harry Thurston Peck was a professor of literature at Columbia and the editor of the *Bookman*,[3] a journal of criticism and commentary on literature. Ella Wheeler Wilcox grew up in Madison, Wisconsin. Her father was a music teacher and unsuccessful businessman and speculator. She described both her parents as "intellectual," and they encouraged her writing.[4] Wilcox had been a regular contributor to magazines and newspapers from the Kansas City–based weekly, the *Independent* to the short-lived New York weekly, *Truth*. She had written articles on women's issues for Edward Bok's "Syndicate Press," before Bok became editor of the *Ladies' Home Journal*.[5] She was a widely read poet whose *Poems of Passion* sold well in the 1880s, and she contributed a number of short stories to the *Ladies' Home Journal* and *Woman's Home Companion*. Along with Lavinia Hart, she contributed numerous articles on women's issues to the *Cosmopolitan* and represented, perhaps better than Hart, the views of the new generation of college-educated women who were becoming involved in the suffrage and settlement house movements and in other social reform efforts (Wilcox attended Madison University for a short period). Wilcox remained a regular *Cosmopolitan* contributor of verse and essays until her death in 1919.[6]

Hubbard, one of the regular contributors to "Men, Women and Events," was certainly an "interesting personality" as the title of an autobiographical article phrased it.[7] Before thirty he had founded J. D. Larkin and Company, a successful soap company, and was responsible for the development of innovative sales techniques. Like George Horace Lorimer, he was an Ivy League (Harvard) dropout who quit in order to write and travel. While in England he became enthralled by the work of William Morris and his experimental workers' cooperatives. This inspired him to set up in East Aurora, New York, a cooperative workshop and community of "Roycrofters" and a print shop that acquired worldwide fame for quality, "The Roycroft Shop." Hubbard claimed that he transformed "idle hoodlums" into self-respecting laborers and craftsmen through work and the joys of communal life.

Hubbard was best known for his little magazine, *The Philistine,* which appeared in June of 1895. In the opening issue Hubbard depicted the new journal as taking on the role of "Sancho Panza" in a satirical "belittling of lofty enterprise." His main objects of satire were the major publishing houses and the leaders of the literary establishment from Richard Watson Gilder of the *Century* to William Dean Howells (part of this may have been motivated by their continuous rejection of his work).[8] Hubbard's most famous essay was *A Message to Garcia,* which was eventually distributed as a pamphlet and became a publishing phenomenon. By 1938 it had sold eighty million copies worldwide. It was inspired by the true story of a youth who carried a message from President McKinley to the leader of the Cuban rebels during the Spanish-American War. Hubbard's theme was that real heroism lies in "the man who does the thing—does his work."[9] The man who displays loyalty to his commander or employer and steadfastness in carrying out his work was the real hero, not only the doer of great deeds.[10] This homespun, inspirational essay was not qualitatively different in substance than *Saturday Evening Post* editor George Horace Lorimer's best-selling *Letters of a Self-Made Merchant to His Son.* In substance and tone, Hubbard was a far cry from the gentility of Gilder or Cyrus Hermann Curtis. In fact, his enormous popularity and influence is good evidence of significant changes in American culture during this period.

NOTES

Introduction: A Power and a Pleasure

1. William Dean Howells, "Letters of an Alturian Traveller (Part 1)," *Cosmopolitan* 16 (November 1893): 113–14.

2. George Curtis, "Easy Chair," *Harper's Monthly* 18 (January 1874): 295.

3. For information on magazine circulation during the 1890s and a discussion of the "magazine revolution" see Frank Luther Mott, *A History of American Magazines,* vol. 4, *1885–1905* (Cambridge: Harvard University Press, 1957), 1–17.

4. Data on magazine circulation can be found in N. W. Ayer and Son's *Newspaper Annual* (Philadelphia: Ayer Press). Information on aggregate per-issue circulation is available starting in 1900. In 1900 the combined circulation of all 3,500 magazines was 65 million per issue. A useful discussion of the new popular magazines of the 1890s can be found in Theodore Peterson, *Magazines in the Twentieth Century* (Urbana: University of Illinois, 1964). The statistic cited is somewhat misleading since individuals typically had a subscription to more than one magazine.

5. Richard Ohmann, "Where Did Mass Culture Come From? The Case of Magazines," *Berkshire Review* 16 (1981): 85–101.

6. See Antonio Gramsci, *Selections from the Prison Notebooks* (New York: International Publishers, 1971), edited and translated by Quintin Hoare and Geoffrey Nowell Smith.

Three sympathetic discussions of Gramsci are Eugene Genovese, "On Antonio Gramsci," *Studies on the Left* 2 (1967): 83–107; Raymond Williams, "Base and Superstructure in Marxist Cultural Theory," *New Left Review* 82 (1973): 3–16; and T. Jackson Lears, "The Concept of Cultural Hegemony," *American Historical Review* 90 (1985): 567–93.

An interesting application of the concept of hegemony in mass communications research can be found in Todd Gitlin, "Prime Time Ideology: The Hegemonic Process in Television Entertainment," *Social Problems* 26 (February 1979): 250–65. Two critics of historians' use of Gramsci are Eric Foner, "Why Is There No Socialism in the United States?" *History Workshop* 17 (1984): 64; and Thomas Haskell, "Contention and Economic Interest in the Debate Over Antislavery," *American Historical Review* 92 (1987): 829–78.

7. Christopher P. Wilson, "The Rhetoric of Consumption: Mass-Market Magazines and the Demise of the Gentle Reader, 1880–1920," in Richard Wightman Fox and T. J. Lears, eds., *The Culture of Consumption: Critical Essays in American History, 1880–1980,* 39–64 (New York: Pantheon, 1983).

8. Jan Cohn, *Creating America: George Horace Lorimer and the Saturday Evening Post* (Pittsburgh: University of Pittsburgh Press, 1989).

9. Gabriel Kolko, *The Triumph of Conservatism* (New York: Free Press, 1963); Robert H. Wiebe, *The Search for Order, 1877–1920* (New York: Hill and Wang, 1967); James Weinstein, *The Corporate Ideal in the Liberal State, 1900–1918* (Boston: Beacon Press, 1968); Martin Sklar, *The Corporate Reconstruction of American Capitalism, 1890–1916* (Cambridge: Cambridge University Press, 1988).

10. Gramsci's use of the concept of hegemony is open to a variety of interpretations. I am rejecting the use of this term to imply manipulation and domination of the masses by an elite or ruling class. Instead, Gitlin in "Prime Time Ideology" tries to retain the notion of hegemony while being sensitive to variations within a hegemonic culture. He also explores the connections between "social developments" and how they are represented in mass culture. Raymond Williams, who has become a central theorist in cultural sociology, has also tried to develop Gramsci's concept of hegemony. In fact, Gitlin relies to a large extent on Williams's work. See Raymond Williams, *Marxism and Literature* (Oxford: Oxford University Press, 1977).

11. Theodore P. Greene, *America's Heroes: The Changing Models of Success in American Magazines* (New York: Oxford University Press, 1970), 288–97.

12. While Ohmann (see note 5, above) does not explicitly define "corporate capitalism," he suggests that it is characterized by the growing dominance of the corporate form of economic organization during the turn of the century. This involved not only the incorporation of noncorporate forms of property but also to a society-wide shift from competitive to "administered" or oligopolistic markets, vertical and horizontal integration of industries, and the growing reliance on advertising. Martin Sklar provides a useful definition of "corporate capitalism" in *The Corporate Reconstruction of American Capitalism,* 5*n*1.

13. Sklar argues that "it would be helpful to conceive of capitalism not simply as 'economics,' not simply as an 'economic aspect' of society, but as a system of social relations

expressed in characteristic class structures, modes of consciousness, patterns of authority, and relations of power." Sklar criticizes those who regard changes in the economy "as something that happens in the realm of 'objective' conditions, and then of movements and reforms as 'responses' by people." See Sklar, *The Corporate Reconstruction of American Capitalism,* 6 and 12. On struggles in the workplace see David Montgomery, *Workers Control in America* (Cambridge: Cambridge University Press, 1979).

14. Short sketches of all three magazines are in Mott, *A History of American Magazines,* vol. 4.

15. Greene, *America's Heroes,* 288–97.

16. Greene, *America's Heroes,* 339–41, discusses his sampling method. Reading only biographical articles, he selected four issues for each year between 1894 and 1919. But this sample was further reduced (one out of every three biographies) for the purposes of a "close reading." Jan Cohn, *Creating America,* claims to have read "or skimmed" every page of the *Saturday Evening Post* for a 39-year period. It is not clear which articles were read and which were skimmed.

17. Clifford Geertz, "Thick Description: Toward an Interpretive Theory of Culture," reprinted in Clifford Geertz, *The Interpretation of Cultures* (New York: Basic Books, 1973), chap. 1.

18. Michael Denning, "The End of Mass Culture," *International Labor and Working Class History* 37 (Spring 1990): 4–18. In addition to Denning's article, another interesting review of recent developments in cultural studies can be found in Chandra Mukerji and Michael Schudson, eds., *Rethinking Popular Culture: Contemporary Perspectives in Cultural Studies* (Berkeley: University of California Press, 1991), 1–61.

19. Wendy Griswold, *Renaissance Revivals, City Comedies and Revenge Tragedy in the London Theater, 1576–1980* (Chicago and London: University of Chicago Press, 1986), 6–8.

20. Two examples of the "poststructuralist" emphasis on the contexts of production and reception are by John Fiske, *Television Culture* (London and New York: Routledge, 1987), and Tony Bennett, ed., *Popular Fiction: Technology, Ideology, Production, Reading* (London and New York: Routledge, 1990).

21. This collection of articles includes some of the representative work of the sociological tradition of mass culture criticism and includes the Dwight MacDonald essay, "A Theory of Mass Culture." See Bernard Rosenberg and David Manning White, eds., *Mass Culture: The Popular Arts in America* (New York: Free Press, 1957). For a short but useful summary of the Frankfurt School's view of the "culture industry" see Theodore Adorno, "Culture Industry Reconsidered," *New German Critique* 6 (Fall 1975): 12–19. The classic statement is Max Horkheimer and Theodore Adorno, *The Dialectic of Enlightenment* (New York: Seabury Press, 1972), 120–67.

22. This famous essay is reprinted in Leo Lowenthal, *Literature, Popular Culture and Society* (Palo Alto, Calif.: Pacific Books, 1961), 109–36 (quoted extract from p. 116).

23. Simon Firth, *Sound Effects: Youth, Leisure and the Politics of Rock 'n' Roll* (New York: Pantheon, 1981), 39–57.

24. For a discussion of the popular appeal of Poe's stories for his contemporaries see Neil Harris's biography of P. T. Barnum, *Humbug: The Art of P. T. Barnum* (Boston: Little, Brown, 1973), 61–89.

25. A discussion of the socially constructed nature of the high-popular culture distinction and its connection to social class can be found in Pierre Bourdieu, *Distinction: A Social Critique of the Judgment of Taste* (Cambridge: Harvard University Press, 1984).

26. Peter Burke, "The Discovery of Popular Culture," in Raphael Samuel, ed., *People's History and Socialist Theory* (London: Routledge, 1981), 216–26.

27. Stuart Hall, "Notes on Deconstructing the Popular," in Samuel, ed., *People's History and Socialist Theory*, 233. See also Stuart Hall, "Cultural Studies: Two Paradigms," *Media, Culture and Society* 2 (1980): 57–72.

28. Fredric Jameson, "Reification and Utopia in Mass Culture," *Social Text* 1 (1979).

29. Denning, "The End of Mass Culture," 4.

30. Frank Munsey, *Munsey's* (April 1895): 104.

1. *The Family House Magazines and the Gospel of Culture*

1. These dates are important in terms of the development of the magazine. After 1865 there was such a rapid growth in magazine, book, and newspaper circulation that some historians call this a "communications revolution." Also, this was the period of highest circulation for the family house magazines. The year 1893 was the beginning of the "magazine revolution" and saw the publication of the first popular general interest magazines. That year was also the date of the Great Panic that economic historians consider a crucial turning point in the development of corporate capitalism, and it was the year of the World's Columbian Exposition in Chicago (popularly known as the World's Fair), which for cultural historians is significant as the culmination of late Victorian culture. The years from 1865 to 1893 are roughly consistent with the period included in "the Gilded Age" and constitute the mid to late Victorian era.

2. *Scribner's* became the *Century* in 1881 and the publishing firm of *Scribner's* started another magazine (also called *Scribner's*) in 1887. My focus is primarily on the *Century* and the pre-1881 *Scribner's*.

3. "Mugwump" was originally a derisive term used to refer to the New York Republicans who bolted the Republican party in 1884 over the nomination of James G. Blaine.

4. The word *liberal* here refers to classical liberalism, which emphasized laissez-faire economics and a broad political program that favored middle-class and business interests. It also refers to the reform-oriented campaigns that sought to limit the influence of the powerful political parties from various levels of government. From a contemporary point of view they hardly seem "liberal," and in their defense of high culture some of the mugwumps can be thought of as cultural conservatives. But in terms of politics they regarded themselves as liberal reformers who sought good government organized according to sound business principles. In this sense they began a long tradition of upper-class-directed reform.

5. Gerald W. McFarland, in *Mugwumps, Morals and Politics: 1884–1920* (Amherst:

University of Massachusetts Press, 1975), described the debate among historians concerning their influence and politics. What he called the "realist" school—represented by John G. Sproat, *"The Best Men": Liberal Reformers in the Progressive Age* (New York: Oxford University Press, 1968)—viewed the mugwumps as conservatives, if not reactionaries, whose political program was largely unsuccessful. The "idealist" school argued that the mugwumps were forerunners of Progressive Era reformers. McFarland sided with the "idealists" although he stressed the complex and contradictory nature of the ideas of the mugwumps and the reform wing of the Republican party.

6. While the general population doubled between 1870 and 1900, the industrial labor force increased to more than one-third of the population by the end of the 1890s. Moreover, the composition of the working class changed. A declining percentage were skilled artisans from English or German backgrounds and a higher percentage were unskilled and recent immigrants. By 1870 one out of every three industrial workers was an immigrant. See Alan Trachtenberg, *The Incorporation of America: Culture and Society in the Gilded Age* (New York: Hill and Wang, 1982), 87–88.

7. On nineteenth-century popular entertainments see Neil Harris, *Humbug: The Art of P. T. Barnum* as well as Alexander Saxton, "Blackface Minstrelsy and Jacksonian Ideology," *American Quarterly* 27 (March 1975): 3–28. The fear of popular amusements is clearly expressed in one of the "open letters" published in the *Century.* The author argued that "anyone who makes a study of the lower class theaters and resorts in our large cities must be convinced of the need of more wholesome popular amusement. . . . In these the chief elements of popular pleasure are eating, drinking, smoking, society of the other sex, with dancing, music of a noisy and lively character, spectacular shows, and athletic exhibitions. In fact we may define the 'masses' as those whose sole delight is in these things." See Hiram M. Stanley, "A Suggestion as to Popular Amusements," *Century* 47 (January 1894): 476.

8. By the term *middle class* I am referring to the "old middle class" of small businessmen, artisans, merchants, writers, and independent professionals as well as the "new middle class" of salaried professionals and white-collar employees. During this period readers of the "quality" magazines were most likely upper-income segments of the middle class. The cost of yearly subscriptions made these magazines prohibitive for lower-income groups. More importantly, the content was clearly oriented to a literate and educated subculture. *Atlantic Monthly* had a predominately Eastern readership as did *Harper's Monthly* during the 1870s. But *Harper's Monthly, Century,* and *Scribner's* as they increased their circulation appealed to regions outside the Eastern seaboard. For a useful review and discussion of the various meanings of "middle class" see Steven Mintz, *A Prison of Expectations: The Family in Victorian Culture* (New York and London: New York University Press, 1983), 203–206 (Appendix, "A Note on the Use of the Term 'Middle Class'").

9. Fears of immigration, working-class radicalism, and rural populism are discussed in Sproat, *"The Best Men,"* chap. 8 ("The Dangerous Classes"). Expressions like "lower orders" and "dangerous classes" were common in the independent press and in the genteel magazines.

10. George Santayana, "The Genteel Tradition in American Philosophy," in D. L.

Wilson, ed., *The Genteel Tradition* (Cambridge: Harvard University Press, 1967). The article was originally published in 1913.

11. Mark Twain and Charles Dudley Warner, *The Gilded Age: A Tale of Today* (originally published in 1873). It appears that Twain and Warner invented the designation "Gilded Age" for this period.

12. Neil Harris, *The Land of Contrasts, 1880–1901* (New York: George Braziller, 1970), 6.

13. Mark Twain in *Harper's Monthly* 80 (February 1890): 438.

14. Charles Eliot Norton in *Atlantic Monthly* 100 (November 1907): 580.

15. Articles espousing these positions in *Atlantic Monthly, Harper's Weekly, Harper's Monthly, Century,* and *Scribner's* were numerous. A representative example is Horatio C. Burchard, "Who Pays Protective Duties?" *Atlantic Monthly* 41 (May 1878): 607–15. Burchard reminded his readers that high tariffs were supposed to be temporary, to "build up infant industries." The saplings of 1816 are now "mighty oaks," he maintained, and do not need to be supported. Another example is Richard Watson Gilder, a strong advocate of "sound money." See Gilder, "Modern Cheap Money Panaceas," *Century* 42 (June 1891): 310–13. Mugwump thinking on economics is discussed in John Tomsich, *A Genteel Endeavor: American Culture and Politics in the Gilded Age* (Stanford: Stanford University Press, 1971), chap. 5.

16. Christopher Lasch, "The Moral and Intellectual Rehabilitation of the Ruling Class," *The World of Nations* (New York: Hill and Wang, 1967), 80. McFarland's data (*Mugwumps, Morals and Politics,* 30) seem to confirm the difference between the regionally oriented mugwumps and the new nationally oriented leaders of national corporations. Among the millionaire supporters of Republican James G. Blaine were Andrew Carnegie, Charles Crocker, Henry M. Flager, Jay Gould, and Russell Sage—representing Carnegie Steel, Standard Oil, Armour Brothers, Western Union Telegraph, and the Southern Pacific and Union Pacific railroads.

17. The quote is from William Dean Howells, *The Rise of Silas Lapham* (New York: Holt, Reinhart and Winston, 1949 [1885]), 66. Lapham is portrayed as a somewhat crude and uneducated industrialist who has made a fortune in the paint business. The heart of the novel is the relationship between Lapham and his family and a young "Boston Brahmin." Unlike his father, who is content to be a man of culture and learning, this young Eastern aristocrat is attracted to the "romance of money." He obtains a job in Lapham's business and becomes interested in marrying Lapham's daughter.

18. For a discussion of the mugwump fears of working-class unrest and immigration see Sproat, *"The Best Men,"* chap. 8.

19. For the relationship between American and English Victorians see David D. Hall, "The Victorian Connection," in Daniel Walker Howe, ed., *Victorian America* (Philadelphia: University of Pennsylvania Press, 1976). Tomsich, *A Genteel Endeavor,* also explores the "transatlantic connection" as well as the gospel of culture. Stow Persons argues that the cultural gentry had an implicit theory of mass culture in *The Decline of American Gentility* (New York: Columbia University Press, 1973). On the museum movement see Neil Harris,

"The Gilded Age Revisited: Boston and the Museum Movement," *American Quarterly* 14 (Winter 1962): 545–66, and Harris, "Museums, Merchandising, and Popular Taste: The Struggle for Influence," in Ian M. B. Quinby, ed., *Material Culture and the Study of American Life* (New York: W. W. Norton, 1978), 140–74.

The editors and publishers of the family house magazines can be thought of as a subgroup of the mugwumps. There were also mugwump businessmen, lawyers, doctors, ministers, social workers, and others. For a breakdown of New York mugwump occupations see McFarland, *Mugwumps, Morals and Politics,* 203–204. For a discussion of the "Boston Brahmins" and their role in the creation of elite cultural institutions in Boston see Paul DiMaggio, "Cultural Entrepreneurship in Nineteenth-Century Boston: The Creation of an Organizational Base for High Culture In America," *Media, Culture and Society* 4 (1982): 33–50.

20. McFarland demonstrated that mugwumps were active in the early professional associations and "learned societies" from the American Historical Association to the American Chemical Society. He argued that the theme that united mugwump professional and businessmen was "the idea that men trained in business or the professions were more fit to administer municipal affairs than were career politicians" (*Mugwumps, Morals and Politics,* 48). Fifty percent of New York mugwumps were in professions compared to 30 percent of his "regular Republican" sample. They were more likely to have completed college than the "regular Republican" sample, but there were fewer millionaires in the mugwump group (McFarland, 24–25).

21. Persons, *The Decline of American Gentility,* 103–109; Tomsich, *A Genteel Endeavor,* 1–26; and Burton J. Bledstein, *The Culture of Professionalism: The Middle Class and the Development of Higher Education in America* (New York: W. W. Norton, 1976). Also see Henry F. May, *The End of American Innocence: The First Years of Our Own Time, 1912–1917* (Oxford: Oxford University Press, 1959), part 1 ("The Nineteenth Century Intact").

22. Richard L. McCormick, *The Party Period and Public Policy: American Politics from the Age of Jackson to the Progressive Era* (New York: Oxford University Press, 1986), discusses the importance of political parties in the nineteenth century. On the party-dominated press of the mid-nineteenth century see Gerald J. Baldasty, *The Commercialization of News in the Nineteenth Century* (Madison: University of Wisconsin Press, 1992), 11–35.

23. Jonathan Baxter Harrison, quoted in Michael E. McGeer, *The Decline of Popular Politics* (New York: Oxford University Press, 1986), 59.

24. Even many liberal reformers (this was before the mugwump split) disagreed with proposals to limit the franchise. R. R. Bowker, "Political Responsibility of the Individual," *Atlantic Monthly* 46 (September 1880): 320, argued that the problem with the "failure of democratic government" was not with universal suffrage but with the individual voter "of intelligence and education."

25. A good example of antiparty sentiment expressed throughout the genteel magazines is Herbert Tuttle, "The Despotism of the Party," *Atlantic Monthly* 54 (September 1884): 374–84.

26. McGeer, *The Decline of Popular Politics,* 113.

27. For another discussion of the mugwumps role in civil service reform and the importance of their magazines see Stephen Skowronek, *Building a New American State* (New York: Cambridge University Press, 1982), 43–46. Skowronek mentions *Atlantic Monthly, Century, Forum, Harper's Weekly, Nation,* and *North American Review* as central in "creating a national community . . . and a national forum where positive and concrete proposals for institutional reform could be aired and debated" (43). Skowronek characterizes the magazines as a blend of the traditional ideal of the "virtuous gentleman" with the emerging ideal of the scientific expert. The mugwumps are discussed in a section of the chapter titled, "The New Intellectuals: America's State-Building Vanguard."

28. See McGeer, *The Decline of Popular Politics,* 80–81, and McFarland, *Mugwumps, Morals and Politics,* 126.

29. McFarland, *Mugwumps, Morals and Politics,* 180–99, lists all the "New York City Area mugwumps." The editors of *Scribner's, Century, Harper's Weekly,* and *Harper's Monthly* as well as *Atlantic Monthly* are all on this list with the single exception of William Dean Howells (who nevertheless was sympathetic to the mugwump reform effort). Compared to a sample of "regular Republicans," in the New York City area, the mugwumps had a much higher level of education than the regular Republicans and were more concentrated in the Episcopalian and Congregational denominations. McFarland uses the term *mugwump* in the specific sense of only those individuals who bolted the Republican party in 1884.

30. David Thelen, *The New Citizenship: Origins of Progressivism in Wisconsin, 1885–1900* (Columbia: University of Missouri Press, 1972), 9–32.

31. Tomsich, *A Genteel Endeavor,* refers to the late nineteenth-century cultural establishment as the "Victorian gentry" while others have specifically referred to the cultural elite of Boston as the "Boston Brahmins."

32. Lasch, "The Moral and Intellectual Rehabilitation of the Ruling Class," 83–87; McFarland, *Mugwumps, Morals and Politics,* 17 and 34. Popular magazine biographies of Theodore Roosevelt in 1901 (by Walker and William Allen White among others), after he assumed the Presidency, saw him as representing an ethic of public service combined with an assertion of the values of masculine vigor and willfulness. Henry Cabot Lodge also made a number of contributions to *McClure's.* Along with Brooks Adams and Roosevelt, Henry Cabot Lodge helped to defeat anti-imperialist elements in the upper class.

33. See Gordon Milne, *George William Curtis and the Genteel Tradition* (Bloomington: Indiana University Press, 1956). There is an entry on Curtis in the *Dictionary of American Biography* 4:614–16.

34. Tomsich, *A Genteel Endeavor,* 8.

35. I have included Howells in this group because he became one of the leading members of the literary establishment and an editor of *Atlantic Monthly.* But in terms of background he was not one of the "Boston Brahmins." Also, he became an advocate of a domesticated version of realism and a critic of sentimental literature. But he admired genteel poetry.

36. On the Victorian emphasis on order see Robert Wiebe, *The Search for Order, 1877–1920,* and Bledstein, *The Culture of Professionalism,* 46–79.

37. Daniel Walker Howe, "Victorian Culture in America," in Howe, ed., *Victorian America,* 3–28. For another discussion of American Victorian culture which contrasts it with "modernism" see Daniel Joseph Singal, "Toward a Definition of American Modernism," *American Quarterly* 39 (Spring 1987): 7–26.

38. See Paul Faler, "Cultural Aspects of the Industrial Revolution," *Labor History* 15 (Summer 1974): 367–94; Herbert Gutman, *Work, Culture and Society in Industrializing America* (New York: Knopf, 1976), 79–117; and Richard Schneirov, *Graft for Power: The Knights of Labor, Trade Unions and Politics in Late Nineteenth Century Chicago* (Urbana: University of Illinois Press, forthcoming).

39. Tomsich, *A Genteel Endeavor,* 73–93; and Milne, *George William Curtis.*

40. Tomsich, *A Genteel Endeavor,* 90.

41. Richard Watson Gilder, "Topics of the Time," *Century* 29 (February 1885): 636. In an 1890 editorial Gilder praised "New York's Reformed Electoral System," which, among other things, required a secret ballot in elections. He particularly praised the part of the Saxton Corrupt Practices Act that did not list party names above the names of the candidate. Gilder, "Topics of the Time," *Century* 40 (July 1890): 475.

Other "Topics of the Time" editorials that focused on civil service reform and attacked the party system included: "Some Practical Reforms" (February 1885): 635; "Abetting the Enemy" (June 1885): 327; "Extend the Merit System" (August 1885): 643; "The Outlook for Civil Service Reform" (November 1885): 150; "Legislative Inefficiency" (September 1886): 801; "A Tyranny That Cannot Live in America" (January 1887): 488; "The Management of Cities" (September 1890): 798; "Partisan Recognition of the Independent Voter" (October 1890): 950; and "The Merit System in the Fifty-first Congress" (October 1890): 953.

42. Gilder, "Topics of the Time," *Century* 36 (August 1888). Gilder expressed alarm at the growing class conflict throughout the country in a series of editorials; "A Readjustment of the Industrial Order" (May 1886): 163; "Two Kinds of Boycotting" (June 1886): 320; "The Falsehood of Extremes" (August 1886): 646: "The American Militia" (November 1886): 148; "The Eight Hour Working Day" (December 1886): 318; "The Injustice of Socialism" (April 1887): 967.

43. See Gilder, "The New Political Economy" ("Topics of the Time"), *Century* 31 (January 1886): 475. In this editorial Gilder informed his readers of the "new political economy" that was challenging the "orthodox" view of economics. Gilder devoted most of his attention to the scientific emphasis of the "new economic research" and their criticisms of classical economists who based their work on assumptions that "outran their data."

44. Gilder, "Topics of the Time," *Century* 40 (May 1890).

45. Gilder, "Topics of the Time," *Century* 31 (January 1886): 475.

46. Terry Eagleton, *Literary Theory: An Introduction* (Minneapolis: University of Minnesota Press, 1983), 24.

47. Charles Dudley Warner, "What Is Your Culture to Me?" *Scribner's* 4 (1872): 470–78.

48. Tomsich, *A Genteel Endeavor,* 174.

49. Curtis, "The Easy Chair," *Harper's Monthly* 48 (January 1874): 295.

50. Also see D. H. Meyer, "American Intellectuals and the Victorian Crisis of Faith," in Howe, *Victorian America*, 59–77.

51. W. D. Howells, *Atlantic Monthly* 100 (November 1907): 605.

52. Gilder expressed, implicitly, the genteel view of the editor when he talked about himself as an "old manuscript reader." In this short commentary Gilder observed that contributors were submitting more and higher quality work, but he wondered "whether the literary artist of our day has not caught somewhat of the hurry, the immediateness, of the time; whether the present age is not too present with us." Gilder, "Topics of the Time," *Century* 40 (June 1890): 313.

53. For a discussion of the genteel editing style see Robert Underwood Johnson (assistant to Gilder on the *Century*), *Remembered Yesterdays* (Boston: Little, Brown, 1923), 149. An excellent discussion of the editorial policies of genteel and popular magazines can be found in Christopher P. Wilson, "The Rhetoric of Consumption: Mass Market Magazines and the Demise of the Gentle Reader, 1880–1920." Also see Larzer Ziff, *The American 1890's: Life and Times of a Lost Generation* (New York: Viking, 1966), chap. 6.

54. Gilder announced, "The Authorized Life of Abraham Lincoln," *Century* 32 (October 1886): 956, the first installment of John George Nicolay and John Hay's biography of Lincoln. Nicolay and Hay were Lincoln's private secretaries. According to Gilder it was "the only authoritative life of Lincoln." In addition to the Civil War series and Nicolay and Hay's Lincoln series, the third "illustrated nonfiction serial" of the 1880s in *Century* was George Kennan's, "Siberia and the Exile System," which was a report on the condition of Siberian exiles who had participated in the revolutionary movement of the 1870s.

55. Arthur John, *The Best Years of the Century: Richard Watson Gilder, Scribner's Monthly and Century Magazine, 1870–1909* (Urbana, Chicago, and London: University of Illinois Press, 1981), 184.

56. John, *The Best Years of the Century*, 149. John points out that *North American Review* was the first journal to break with that policy, in 1868. But *Century* was the first "widely circulated magazine" to change the policy.

57. For Gilder's view of the importance of this series see "The 'Century' War Series" ("Topics of the Time"), *Century* 29 (March 1885): 788.

58. The Civil War series started in November 1884 and lasted until November 1877 (but other articles about the Civil War continued well after this date). Circulation doubled within six months after the series began. *Century*'s business manager Roswell Smith claimed the series made one million dollars for the magazine's publisher. See John, *The Best Years of the Century*, chap. 8.

59. Gilder, "Topics of the Time," *Century* 32 (October 1886): 956.

60. John, *The Best Years of the Century*, 122.

61. Ziff, *The American 1890's*, 123.

62. Ziff, *The American 1890's*, 124.

63. See M. A. DeWolfe Howe, *The Atlantic Magazine and Its Makers* (Boston: Atlantic Monthly Press, 1919), 77–92.

64. Gilder, "Topics of the Time," *Century* 30 (May 1885): 164.

65. See Richard Watson Gilder, "The Newspaper, the Magazine and the Public," *Outlook* 61 (February 4, 1899): 317.

66. The terms *highbrow* and *middlebrow* were coined by the famous literary critic Van Wyck Brooks in "The Culture of Industrialism," *Seven Arts* (April 1917): 655–66. The concept of "secondary audience" has been developed by mass communications researchers. The concept is similar to the sociological concept of "reference group."

2. The Victorian Reader and the Political Economy of the Magazine

1. For a discussion of imaginative literature uniting Americans and English in a common literary culture as well as transcending class see Steven Mintz, *A Prison of Expectations,* chap. 3; and Daniel Walker Howe, *Victorian America,* 23–25. On the importance of reading for Victorian Americans see Louise L. Stevenson, *The Victorian Homefront: American Thought and Culture, 1860–1880* (New York: Twayne, 1991), 30–47. On the school curricula see Richard D. Altick, *The English Common Reader: A Social History of the Mass Reading Public, 1800–1900* (Chicago: University of Chicago Press, 1957). The importance of words and the communications revolution is discussed by Burton J. Bledstein, *The Culture of Professionalism,* 65–79.

2. Bledstein, *The Culture of Professionalism,* 76.

3. Michael Gilmore, *American Romanticism and the Marketplace* (Chicago and London: University of Chicago Press, 1985).

4. On Louisa May Alcott see Mintz, *A Prison Of Expectations,* 23. On Catherine Beecher see Kathryn Kish Sklar, *Catherine Beecher: A Study in American Domesticity* (New York: W. W. Norton, 1973), 20.

5. *Atlantic Monthly* 100 (July 1907): 37.

6. On dime novels see Edmund Pearson, *Dime Novels, or Following an Old Trail in Popular Literature* (Port Washington, N.Y.: Kennikat Press, 1929). The latest work on dime novels is by Michael Denning, *Mechanic Accents: Dime Novels and Working-Class Culture in America* (London and New York: Verso, 1987).

7. For a discussion of Victorian concerns about the theater see Claudia Johnson, "The Guilty Third Tier: Prostitution in Nineteenth-Century American Theaters"; for a discussion of subversive literature see Dee Garrison, "Immoral Fiction in the Late Victorian Library." Both articles are in Daniel Walker Howe, *Victorian America,* 111–20 and 141–59, respectively.

8. Henry Seidel Canby, *The Age of Confidence: Life in the Nineties* (New York: Farrar and Rinehart, 1934), chap. 11.

9. Canby, *The Age of Confidence,* 193.

10. Norbert Elias, *The Civilizing Process: The History of Manners,* trans. Edmund Jephcott (New York: Pantheon, 1978), 1–29.

11. On *Godey's Ladies Book* and its editor Sarah Hale see Ann Douglas, *The Feminization of American Culture* (New York: Avon, 1977), 51. Also see Sklar, *Catherine Beecher,* 163 and

153–54; Ruth E. Finley, *The Lady of Godey's, Sarah Josepha Hale* (Philadelphia and London: J. B. Lippincott, 1931). *Godey's* continued publication until 1897, eighteen years after its original editor (Hale) died.

12. Persons, *The Decline of American Gentility*, 29–50.

13. Karen Halttunen, *Confidence Men and Painted Women: A Study of Middle-Class Culture in America, 1830–1870* (New Haven and London: Yale University Press, 1982), 114.

14. Sklar, *Catherine Beecher*, 152.

15. Quoted in Ziff, *The American 1890's*, 123.

16. For information on *Harper's Monthly* and *Century* during the 1865–1885 period see Frank Luther Mott, *A History of American Magazines*, vol. 3.

17. See Michael E. McGeer, *The Decline of Popular Politics*, chaps. 4 and 5; and Gerald J. Baldasty, *The Commercialization of News in the Nineteenth Century*, 11–35.

18. George Curtis, *Harper's Monthly* 49 (October 1874): 739.

19. F. B. Sanborn, *Atlantic Monthly* 34 (July 1874): 64–65.

20. James Parton, *Harper's Monthly* 49 (July 1874): 269–80.

21. E. L. Godkin, "Influence of the Press," *Nation* 65 (November 25, 1897): 410–11, and "New Political Force: Journalism," *Nation* 66 (May 5, 1898): 336.

22. Gilder, "Topics of the Time," *Century* 29 (January 1885): 461.

23. Gilder, "Topics of the Time," *Century* 40 (June 1890): 314.

24. Bledstein, *The Culture of Professionalism*, 107, discusses the popularization of American history "through textbooks and colorful narrative accounts" throughout the mid- to late Victorian period in America. He discusses this as part of the "vertical vision" of the middle class. On popular historical fiction during this period see Ernest Leisy, *The American Historical Novel* (Norman: University of Oklahoma Press, 1950).

25. Samuel McChord Crothers, *Atlantic Monthly* 86 (November 1900): 654–63.

26. Bliss Perry, *Atlantic Monthly* 89 (January 1902): 1–4.

27. Charles Eliot Norton, *Atlantic Monthly* 100 (November 1907): 581.

28. Kimball provided one of the better pieces of magazine research in his documentation of the trend toward the short story and away from serialized fiction during the 1872–1897 period. The trend continued in the 1890s with the "storiette," a two- or three-page story. See Arthur Reed Kimball, *Atlantic Monthly* 86 (July 1900): 124.

29. See Roy Rosenzweig, *Eight Hours for What We Will: Workers and Leisure in an Industrial City* (Cambridge: Cambridge University Press, 1983), on workers' struggles over leisure and popular recreation in Worcester between 1870 and 1920. He discusses the saloon, Fourth of July celebrations (chap. 6), parks and playgrounds, and movies.

30. See Arthur Reed Kimball, "The Invasion of Journalism," *Atlantic Monthly* 86 (July 1900): 119–24; "Tyranny of Timeliness," *Atlantic Monthly* 98 (August 1906): 285–87; "Wanted: A Retrospective Review," *Atlantic Monthly* 86 (September 1900): 428–30.

31. Henry Dwight Sedgwick, "The Mob Spirit in Literature," *Atlantic Monthly* 96 (July 1905): 9–15.

32. Henry Holt, "The Commercialization of Literature," *Atlantic Monthly* 96 (November 1905): 577–600.

33. Frederick Lewis Allen, "Fifty Years of Scribner's Magazine," *Scribner's* 101 (January 1937): 21.

34. Christopher Lasch argues that this "neo-regional" revival in literature "celebrated ways of life that were rapidly passing into memory." He argues that this revival was an important influence on architecture, theater, and music "at precisely the moment at which regionalism had ceased to be an important influence on politics" ("The Moral and Intellectual Rehabilitation of the Ruling Class," *The World of Nations,* 81).

35. Sarah Jewett's collected stories, *Tales of New England,* were first published in 1894; see Sarah Jewett, *The Best Stories of Sarah Orne Jewett* (Gloucester, Mass.: Peter Smith, Mayflower ed., 1965). Kate Chopin's stories are compiled in *Bayou Folk* (1894; rpt., Ridgewood, N.J.: Gregg Press, 1967); Chopin also wrote the then-scandalous *The Awakening* (1899; rpt., London: Women's Press, 1978). Hamlin Garland (who was also to write extensively for the mass-circulation magazines) published his *Main Travelled Roads,* a collection of short stories compiled in book form, in 1891 (rpt., New York: New American Library, 1962).

For a discussion of the local color writers see Warner Berthoff, *The Ferment of Realism* (Cambridge: Cambridge University Press, 1965), 90–103. While I mentioned that local color fiction paved the way for realism, historical romances were far more popular than realism in the magazine fiction of the 1890s.

36. A few examples from *Harper's Monthly* include Z. L. White, "Western Journalism" (October 1888): 678–97; "City Athletics" (January 1884): 297–305; "The Education of Women" (July 1883): 292–96; and "Civil Service Reform in New York" (May 1880): 899–905.

37. The categories used for this comparison were travel and exploration, poetry, short fiction, serialized fiction, topical and descriptive articles, editorial features, and miscellaneous. The percentage of pages in each category were counted for four issues in *Harper's Monthly* of 1854 and 1874.

38. Arthur John, *The Best Years of the Century: Richard Watson Gilder, Scribner's Monthly and Century Magazine, 1870–1909,* chap. 3.

39. Some examples from *Harper's Monthly* include "The Columbia River" (December 1882): 3–14; "Across Arizona" (March 1883): 489–514; "San Francisco" (May 1883): 813–32; "Cincinnati" (July 1883): 245–65; "Saunterings in Utah" (October 1883): 705–14; "St. Louis" (March 1884): 497–517; Charles Dudley Warner, "Studies of the Great West, Part 4: Chicago" (June 1888): 116–27.

40. On the overall trends in *Harper's Monthly* in terms of fiction see Mott, *A History of American Magazines* 3:383–405. On the *Century* see John, *The Best Years of the Century,* as well as Theodore P. Greene, *America's Heroes: The Changing Models of Success in American Magazines,* 73–81. Changes in content and editorial policy at *Harper's Monthly* in the 1890s

is discussed by Henry Alden, the editor in "Editor's Study," *Harper's Monthly* 112 (April 1906): 800–802; also see Alden, "Fifty Years of Harper's Magazine," *Harper's Monthly* 101 (May 1900): 950. A retrospective on *Scribner's* (the one established in 1887) was written by Frederick Lewis Allen, "Fifty Years of Scribner's Magazine," 19–23.

41. Mott, *A History of American Magazines* 3:391.

42. John, *The Best Years of the Century*, 153.

43. For an interesting discussion of the question of women in college as well as the controversy over Dr. Edward Clarke's book *Sex in Education: Or, A Fair Chance for Girls* (1873), see "Editor's Literary Record," *Harper's Monthly* 49 (July 1874): 287–88. Also see "The Easy Chair" (May 1874): 895, and (July 1874): 286, which discussed, among many other matters, women's rights.

44. Rosalind Rosenberg, *Beyond Separate Spheres: Intellectual Roots of Modern Feminism* (New Haven: Yale University Press, 1982), chaps. 2 and 3.

45. Mott, *A History of American Magazines* 3:5–7.

46. Bledstein, *The Culture of Professionalism*, 33.

47. For the data on the growth of the new middle class see Richard Hofstadter, *The Age of Reform*, 217–18.

48. *The Dial* (May 1, 1900): 351.

49. For a discussion of the "industrialization of printing" during the antebellum period see Ronald J. Zboray, "Antebellum Reading and the Ironies of Technological Innovation," *American Quarterly* 40 (March 1988): 65–82.

50. Michael Schudson, in *Discovering the News; A Social History of American Newspapers* (New York: Basic Books, 1978), developed this argument in accounting for the development of the penny press in the 1830s. Another discussion of literacy in industrializing America is Harvey J. Graff, *The Legacy of Literacy* (Bloomington and Indianapolis: Indiana University Press, 1987), 340–72.

51. Pearson, *Dime Novels*, 4 and 8–13.

52. Merle Curti, "Dime Novels and the American Tradition," in Curti, *Probing Our Past* (New York: Harper, 1955), 172–88. Michael Denning in *Mechanic Accents* has a somewhat different view of the dime novel, emphasizing its contradictory nature.

53. An interesting discussion of the difference between formula publishing and the traditional model that emphasized specialized markets can be found in Janice Radway, *Reading the Romance: Women, Patriarchy and Popular Literature* (Chapel Hill and London: University of North Carolina Press, 1984), 19–45.

54. See Douglas, *The Feminization of American Culture*, for a critique of female novelists in the nineteenth century. Mary Kelly, in *Private Woman, Public Stage: Literary Domesticity in Nineteenth-Century America* (New York: Oxford University Press, 1984), provides a more positive assessment. Henry Nash Smith, "The Scribbling Women and the Cosmic Success Story," *Critical Inquiry* 1 (September 1974): 47–70, is also somewhat contemptuous of the first female bestsellers, characterizing them as escapist, crude, and expressing an "ethos of

conformity." For a comprehensive treatment see Herbert Ross Brown, *The Sentimental Novel in America, 1769–1860* (Durham, N.C.: Duke University Press, 1940).

55. For a discussion of the bestsellers of the 1850s see James D. Hart, *The Popular Book* (Berkeley: University of California Press, 1950), 85–124.

56. While the penny papers were an important development, some scholars have argued that their significance has been overestimated. The penny papers were free of party control and developed the concept of "news," but they were in the distinct minority among newspapers. Most newspapers were still partisan papers, dependent on political parties for subsidies. For a discussion of the penny press see John C. Nerone, "The Mythology of the Penny Press," in *Jean Folkerts, Media Voices: An Historical Perspective* (New York and Toronto: Macmillan, 1992), 157–82. Also see Baldasty, *The Commercialization of News*, 46–48.

57. Richard Zboray, "Antebellum Reading and the Ironies of Technological Innovation," 79; and Stevenson, *The Victorian Homefront*, 30–47.

58. M. A. DeWolfe Howe, *The Atlantic Magazine and Its Makers*, 61–64.

59. Tomsich, *A Genteel Endeavor*, 22.

60. Mott, *A History of American Magazines* 3:386.

61. *National Republic* 1 (June 1877): 574.

62. John, *The Best Years of the Century*, 68.

63. Peterson, *Magazines in the Twentieth Century*, 1–18.

64. Mott, *A History of American Magazines* 3:3–24; and Peterson, *Magazines in the Twentieth Century*, 18–29.

65. An article by William A. Coffin, in *Scribner's* 11 (January 1892): 106–17, discussed developments in American illustration. Also see "Illustration of Books and Newspapers," *Century* 27 (February 1890): 213.

66. *Munsey's* 13 (May 1895): 152–53.

67. *Nation* 56 (May 4, 1893): 325–26. Also see "Over- Illustration," *Harper's Weekly* 55 (July 29, 1911), and "A Growl for the Picturesque," *Atlantic Monthly* 98 (July 1906): 141–42.

68. See E. L. Godkin, "Newspaper Pictures," *Nation* 56 (April 27, 1893): 306–307.

69. Neil Harris, "Pictorial Perils: The Rise of American Illustration," from Harris, *Cultural Excursions: Marketing Appetites and Cultural Tastes in Modern America* (Chicago and London: University of Chicago Press, 1990), 337–48. According to Harris, genteel critics worried that "the importance of the reading experience and the author's vision were both threatened" by illustrations (341). Harris's discussion of picture postcards and comic strips, both of which attracted widespread attention in the 1890s, is also of interest (345–46). For a discussion of the interest in postcards see Julian Ralph, "The Post-Card Craze," *Cosmopolitan* 32 (January 1902): 421.

70. *Bookman* 1 (January 1895): 312.

71. See Neil Harris, "Iconography and Intellectual History: The Half-Tone Effect," in

John Higham and Paul Conklin, eds., *New Directions in American Intellectual History* (Baltimore: Johns Hopkins University Press, 1979), 196–211.

72. Harris, "Iconography and Intellectual History," 198.

73. Gilder, "Topics of the Time," *Century* 50 (October 1895).

74. John, *The Best Years of the Century*, 237.

75. John, *The Best Years of the Century*, 234.

76. Rupert Hughes, *Cosmopolitan* 26 (December 1898): 123.

77. For a discussion of the Victorian conception of photography and how it changed in the twentieth century see Miles Orvell, *The Real Thing: Imitation and Authenticity in American Culture, 1880–1940* (Chapel Hill and London: University of North Carolina Press, 1989), chaps. 3 and 6. Also see Lawrence W. Levine, *Highbrow, Lowbrow: The Emergence of Cultural Hierarchy in America* (Cambridge: Harvard University Press, 1988), 160–63.

78. Harris, "Pictorial Perils," 343.

79. Walter Benjamin, in contrast to Adorno's mass culture critique, believed that the mass reproduction of art could have progressive consequences. The result of the mass reproduction of art would be to demystify art and deprive it of its aura that separated the elite artist from the masses. It could also democratize art and make possible collective authorship. See Walter Benjamin, *Illuminations* (New York: Schocken, 1968) and his essay in this collection, "The Work of Art in the Age of Mechanical Reproduction," 217–51.

80. See Orvell, *The Real Thing*, 92. Also see "Are Composite Photographs Typical Pictures?" in *McClure's* 3 (September 1894): 331–42.

81. Speed, *North American Review* 163 (July 1896): 64–74.

82. Benjamin, "The Work of Art in the Age of Mechanical Reproduction," 221.

83. William Allen White, *The Autobiography of William Allen White* (Lawrence: University Press of Kansas: 1990 [1946]), 198–99.

84. *Independent* 47 (June 27, 1895), page unknown.

3. *The Magazine Revolution of the 1890s*

1. "Publisher's Desk," *Munsey's* 13 (April 1895).

2. S. S. McClure, *My Autobiography* (New York: Ungar, 1914; rpt., 1963), 207–208.

3. Excellent discussions of the development of the popular magazines in the 1890s can be found in Theodore Peterson, *Magazines in the Twentieth Century*; John Tebbel, *The American Magazine: A Compact History* (New York: Hawthorn Books, 1969); James Playsted Wood, *Magazines in the United States* (New York: Ronald Press, 1956); and Frank Luther Mott, *A History of American Magazines*, vol. 4.

4. The *Review of Reviews* commented that "one examines the *Cosmopolitan* for July with an interest to see if the reduction of 50 per cent in its price, which has created quite a breeze in the magazine world, means contraction and lowering of quality. But on the contrary it is one of the best Mr. Walker has yet published." *Review of Reviews* 8 (August 1893): 218.

5. Walker was not the sole editor for this entire period. W. D. Howells accepted the joint

editorship in 1892 but left shortly thereafter. Arthur Sherburne Hardy became a coeditor (with Walker) in 1893 and stayed for two years. J. Wilson Hart was Walker's first managing editor, followed by George R. Miner, George Casamajor, and Samuel G. Blythe. All commentators said that Walker exerted complete control over the publication. See Mott, *A History of American Magazines* 4:484.

6. Arthur John, *The Best Years of the Century,* chap. 12. John characterized the 1890s as the beginning of a "loss of preeminence" for the *Century* but acknowledged that it remained the leading genteel magazine and retained its position as one of the leaders in circulation. Theodore P. Greene, *America's Heroes,* in his discussion of magazines of the 1890s, also mentioned the *Century* as one of the leading publications during this period.

7. Mott, *A History of the American Magazine* 4:9.

8. Arthur Kimball, *Atlantic Monthly* 86 (July 1900): 124.

9. On Hearst see W. A. Swanberg, *Citizen Hearst* (New York: Scribner's, 1961), 100–49. On Pulitzer and sensational or "yellow journalism" see Michael E. McGeer, *The Decline of Popular Politics,* chap. 5; Michael Schudson, *Discovering the News,* 91–106; and Joseph Juergens, *Joseph Pulitzer and the New York World* (Princeton: Princeton University Press, 1966).

10. A discussion of the Sunday supplements can be found in Frank Luther Mott, *American Journalism: A History 1690–1960* (New York: Macmillan, 1962), 480–82. H. L. Mencken believed that the "real father [of the popular magazine] was the unknown originator of the Sunday Supplement." See Mott, *A History of American Magazines* 4:6.

11. Mott, Peterson, and Wood all focus on the technological and social conditions that made the new mass-circulation magazines possible. Mott focuses on changes in middle-class culture as well as well as the development of national marketing and national advertising. Peterson and Wood focus on technological changes as well as the development of the new halftone method of reproducing photographs.

12. This exchange between Gilder and McClure has appeared in quite a few accounts of the famous editor and his magazine. See Peter Lyon, *Success Story: The Life and Times of S. S. McClure* (New York: Scribner's, 1963), 135, for one account. John, *The Best Years of the Century,* in his last chapter also discusses the rivalry between the *Century* and *McClure's.*

13. Baker, "Capture, Death and Burial of J. Wilkes Booth," *McClure's* 9 (May 1897): 574–85.

14. See Harold S. Wilson, *McClure's Magazine and the Muckrakers* (Princeton: Princeton University Press, 1970), 109. Wilson's study of the Index to *McClure's Magazine:* vols. 1–18 (New York, 1903), issues from 1893 to 1903, shows that close to 10 percent of all *McClure's* articles explored Civil War themes—from accounts of battles to a biography of Lincoln by Ida Tarbell and twenty-six articles on General Grant. These articles were highly successful in increasing circulation.

15. An article that received the attention of *Review of Reviews* was Cleveland Moffett's account of his journey on a New York locomotive called the "World's Fair Flyer," which went eighty miles an hour on a route from New York to Chicago. While expressing

admiration at this technological marvel, Moffett also observed "that this great speed is obtained only by a complete physical and nervous exhaustion of the engineers who drive the locomotives." *Review of Reviews* 8 (October 1893): 477.

16. H. J. W. Dam's article on the Maxim "air-ship" appeared in *McClure's* January 1894 issue. The author tried to provide the "point of view of a prospective passenger" and described his visit to Maxim's workshop. See the account of this article in *Review of Reviews* 9 (February 1894): 234.

17. Richard Hofstadter in *The Age of Reform,* 198–214, argued that fundamental to the realism and the "new journalism" of the 1890s was a desire to get the "inside story" and to expose what was "behind the scenes" of the corporation, the big-city machine, urban poverty and vice, the new amusements, and so on.

18. Garland managed to get into the Homestead steel mill with the help of *McClure's* staff member (and chief partner of S. S. McClure) John Phillips, who had a relative who worked in the Homestead blast furnace. See Wilson, *McClure's Magazine and the Muckrakers*, 112.

19. *McClure's* 3 (July 1894): 163.

20. The *Review of Reviews* highlighted this feature of *McClure's* for attention. These interviews as well as the "Human Documents" feature were mentioned as "distinctive features of *McClure's.*" *Review of Reviews* 8 (July 1893): 106.

21. Circulation rose from 60,000 in the fall of 1894 to 166,000 by July 1895. Much of this has been attributed to Ida Tarbell's series on Napoleon.

22. A discussion of the early history of *Cosmopolitan* can be found in Mott, *A History of American Magazines* 4:480–82.

23. This comment appeared in *Journalist* 23 (September 1897): 475.

24. Some examples from *Cosmopolitan* include "Recent Developments in Gun-Making" (February 1890); "The Militia" (March 1890); "National Guard Camps of Instruction, and Their Faults" (August 1890); "Desertion and the Military Prison" (November 1890).

25. Examples of these *Cosmopolitan* articles include "Sugar-Cane and Sugar-Cane Making," "The Development of Our Modern Costume, Part 1: The Coat and Waistcoat," "A Cruise Around Antigua: In the Sailing Canoe 'Caribee,' Part 1" (January 1890); "The Romance of a Great Corporation: The Hudson's Bay Trading Company, Part 2" (February 1890); "The Evolution of the Gondola," "Browning's Place in Literature," "Royal Authors" (March 1890).

26. Historical pieces in *Cosmopolitan* included "The Coaching Era," "A Dark Page of Russian History" (June 1890); "Historical Illustrations of the Confederacy" (August 1890). Articles on journalism, Wall Street, and education included "Georgetown University" (February 1890); "Princeton University" (April 1890); "The Gymnasium of a Great University" (May 1890); "Reporters" (June 1890); "The Ethics of Wall Street" (September 1890).

27. Appendices 4 and 5 show a much smaller percentage of articles on art/literature and history/biography in *Cosmopolitan* during the 1890s compared to the *Century.* It also shows a higher percentage of articles on science/technology and current events. Starting in 1895 we also see an increase in articles on sports/leisure and health.

28. *Review of Reviews* 5 (June 1892): 609.

29. Schurz, *McClure's* 23 (October 1904): 614.

30. Examples from *Cosmopolitan* include John Brisben Walker, "Public Baths for the Poor," "Co-Operative Public Laundries" (August 1890); Katherine Pearson Woods, "Queens of the Shop, the Workroom and the Tenement" (November 1890); "What Society Offers Mary Drew" (a discussion of the problems of working women) (June 1893); and "How to Make a City Cholera Proof" (August 1893).

31. Brooks Adams, *McClure's* 12 (April 1899): 558.

32. Theodore Roosevelt, "Taking the New York Police Out of Politics," *Cosmopolitan* 20 (November 1895): 40–52. Other articles written by Roosevelt about municipal reform during this year include "Six Years of Civil Service Reform," *Scribner's* 18 (August 1895): 238–47; "Present Status of Civil Service Reform," *Atlantic Monthly* 75 (February 1895): 239–46; "Higher Life of American Cities," *Outlook* 52 (December 21, 1895): 1083–1085; and "Latitude and Longitude Among Reformers," *Century* 60 (June 1900): 211–16.

33. Robert Stinson, "McClure's Road to *McClure's:* How Revolutionary Were the 1890's Magazines?" *Journalism Quarterly* 47 (Summer 1970): 256–62.

34. The emphasis on entertainment was associated with the "yellow" journalism of Pulitzer and Hearst. The emphasis on information was associated with the *New York Times* and the independent journalism tradition. Both forms of journalism had replaced the partisan press by the 1870s. See Schudson, *Discovering the News,* chap. 3; and Gunther Barth, *City People: The Rise of the Modern City* (New York: Oxford University Press, 1980), 58–109. Also see Larzer Ziff, *The American 1890's,* chaps. 7, 8, and 9.

35. These comments can be found in the "Publisher's Desk" department in *Munsey's.* The November issue (one month after the price reduction) identified *Munsey's* with "the best" of daily journalism. In the same issue, Munsey discussed his conception of the "fin de siècle" magazine. "There is no excuse for a magazine being dull—being heavy and technical. . . . People want to be entertained—to feel their blood stirred by a bit of healthy adventure." The comment on "live magazines" for "living people" was in the January 1894 "Publisher's Desk" department.

36. The "Impressions by the Way" department in *Munsey's* contained more extended discussions of fiction. See the October 1894 issue ("Is the Literary Field Exhausted?"). The famous comment by Munsey on wanting "strong stories" can be found in the April 1895 "Publisher's Desk."

37. Advertisement appearing in the July 1894 issue of *McClure's.*

38. In addition to Civil War stories, the largest number of articles published during the ten-year period form 1893 to 1903 were on science and technology. Articles discussed developments in photography, the telegraph, X-rays, medical advances (including anesthetics and inoculations for poisons), the automobile, trains, developments in astronomy, and volcanoes, to name a few of the topics. More stories by Rudyard Kipling were published (twenty-eight) than by any other author. Stories and serials by Booth Tarkington, Jack London, and Stephen Crane were also published. See "Index to *McClure's* for Vols. 1 to 18."

39. The motto for Walker's *Cosmopolitan,* an expression of the publisher's liberal prolabor politics, was "From Each According to His Ability, To Everyone According to His Needs." In addition to the 1897 article, there were other editorial features that promoted the magazine. See "The Making of an Illustrated Magazine," *Cosmopolitan* 14 (January 1893): 259–72, and "The Cosmopolitan's New Home," *Cosmopolitan* 17 (September 1894): 551–55.

40. Susan Waugh McDonald, "From Kipling to Kitsch: Two Popular Editors of the Gilded Age: Mass Culture, Magazines and Correspondence Universities," *Journal of Popular Culture* 15 (Fall 1981): 50–61.

41. *Cosmopolitan* 23 (September 1897): 465–80.

42. Discussions of advertising in the "Publisher's Desk" department can be found in *Munsey's* (December 1894): 332; (May 1895): 209; (June 1895): 319; (July 1895): 438.

43. *Munsey's* 20 (December 1898): 476–86. Two more articles by Frank Munsey that discuss these issues are "Something More About Advertising," *Munsey's* 20 (January 1899): 656), and "The Making and Marketing of Munsey's Magazine," *Munsey's* 22 (November 1899): 323.

44. John Brisben Walker, "Beauty in Advertising Illustration," *Cosmopolitan* 33 (September 1902): 491–500.

45. On *Munsey's* price reduction see "Publisher's Desk" (October and November 1893), and on illustrations see "Publisher's Desk" (February 1894); a discussion of the conflict with the American News Company is in "Publisher's Desk" (April 1895 issue).

46. "Publisher's Desk," *Munsey's* 19 (May 1898): 317–18.

47. Frank Munsey, "Advertising in Some of Its Phases," *Munsey's* 20 (December 1898): 482.

48. Brady, "The Story of *McClure's,*" *Profitable Advertising* (October 15, 1897): 143. Mott, *A History of American Magazines* 4:21, also discusses *McClure's* business policies.

49. See Alan Trachtenberg, *The Incorporation of America,* chap. 1.

50. Peter Finley Dunne was the creator of the famous "Mr. Dooley" newspaper column (based on the observations of an Irish saloon keeper) that earned him a national reputation. Dunne started off as a journalist on the *Chicago Evening Post* and later became a regular contributor to popular magazines. He was also a staff member of *McClure's.* See Barbara C. Schaaf, *Mr. Dooley's Chicago* (Garden City, N.Y.: Doubleday-Anchor, 1977).

51. On the shift from New York to Chicago as the cultural center of the country see Ziff, *The American 1890's,* 111–14 and 161–63.

52. *Review of Reviews* 5 (June 1892): 609.

53. Trachtenberg, *The Incorporation of America,* 145.

54. The references by many contributors and editors of the popular magazines to "real life" and the words associated with "real life" ("blood," "vitality," "energy," "process") point to a larger cultural phenomenon. Theodore Dreiser's *Sister Carrie* (1900) and even Henry James's *The Ambassadors* (1903) expressed the same desire for experience and belief that life could not be reduced to formulas. This emphasis on process and indeterminacy was

expressed by the pragmatic philosophy of William James. Intellectual historians have argued that there was a "revolt against formalism" in law, economics, history, and throughout intellectual culture. See Morton White, *Social Thought in America: The Revolt Against Formalism* (Boston: Beacon Press, 1964).

55. Ann Douglas, *The Feminization of American Culture,* 397–400.

56. John Higham, "The Reorientation of American Culture in the 1890's," in John Weiss, ed., *The Origins of Modern Consciousness* (Detroit: Wayne State University Press, 1965), 24–48. This essay, along with Henry May's *The End of American Innocence,* are among the seminal historical works that highlight the importance of this period in terms of cultural history. The Higham essay will be discussed in chapter 5.

57. See Jackson Lears, *No Place of Grace: Antimodernism and the Transformation of American Culture, 1880–1920* (New York: Pantheon, 1981), 4–58.

58. Christopher Lasch, "The Moral and Intellectual Rehabilitation of the Ruling Class," in *The World of Nations,* 86–87.

59. Mott traced the human interest story to Charles Dana's *New York Sun,* purchased by Dana in 1868. The *Sun* carried a feature that it called "the human interest story" (Mott, *A History of American Journalism* 4:376). Also see Barth, *City People,* 74–75.

60. Hofstadter, *The Age of Reform,* 189–90.

61. The muckraking exposés that will be discussed in chapter 7 are an obvious example, but as early as 1890 *Cosmopolitan* printed an account of conditions of working women and other glimpses into the lives of the poor. See Woods, "Queens of the Shop, the Workroom and the Tenement," *Cosmopolitan* 10 (November 1890): 99–106. But there were few such human interest stories about the poor in *Cosmopolitan* until the early 1900s. *McClure's* articles on conditions among workers at Homestead are also examples.

62. The word *sensational* here is meant to refer to the "yellow" journalism popularized by Pulitzer and Hearst. These papers focused on sports, women's features, cartoons, and titillating crime and sex stories.

63. Juergens provided a useful and amusing comparison between the headlines in Pulitzer's *New York World* and the *New York Times* during one week of March 1884. Some examples of the *World's* headlines included "A Brutal Negro Whips His Nephew to Death in South Carolina," "An Entire Family Annihilated by Its Murderous Head," "A Lady Gagged in a Flat." The *New York Times* was somewhat more restrained: "Representative Potter's Refunding Bill," "The Anti-Confirmation Bill Passed by the Senate," "A Motion to Consider the Bonded Period Bill Lost." Juergens discussed some of the *New York World*'s puns, "its delight with plays on words." One example was a notice on the death of industrialist Cyrus H. McCormick: "Cyrus H. McCormick invented a great reaper, but the Reaper whose name is Death cut him down, and now he is no mower." See Juergens, *Joseph Pulitzer and the New York World,* 67–69 and 36.

64. For an interesting discussion of the differences between the "two journalisms" represented by Pulitzer's *New York World* and Adolph Ochs's *New York Times* see Schudson,

Discovering the News, 88–120. Schudson argues that the *New York World* emphasized the "story" that was "the genre of self indulgence" while the *New York Times* emphasized information that was the "genre of self denial."

65. *Cosmopolitan* had a reputation for its quality halftone illustrations and photographs. One reviewer, in commenting on the Chicago World's Fair issue of *Cosmopolitan,* asserted that "this number of the *Cosmopolitan* fully exploits the magazine's reputation for beautiful, clear, half-tone pictures." *Review of Reviews* 9 (January 1894): 106.

66. *Munsey's* 18 (1895): 565.

67. *Munsey's* 20 (1899): 73.

68. *Munsey's* 21 (1899): 124.

69. Wilson, *McClure's Magazine and the Muckrakers,* 105, argued that *McClure's* "carried articles pointed towards special groups such as women, workers, children."

70. Pulitzer, quoted in Juergens, *Joseph Pulitzer and the New York World,* 32.

71. See George Horace Lorimer, "The Unpopular Editor of the Popular Magazine," *Bookman* 60 (December 1924): 396–97. Lorimer, editor of the *Post,* complained about the criticisms of popular magazines as appealing to "popular tastes" and excluding a higher quality of literature.

72. Richard Ohmann, "Where Did Mass Culture Come From?" 91.

73. William Allen White, *Autobiography,* 157.

74. Salme Harju Steinberg, *Reformer in the Marketplace: Edward Bok and the Ladies' Home Journal* (Baton Rouge and London: Louisiana State University Press, 1979), 6.

75. Steinberg, *Reformer in the Marketplace,* 6.

76. A good summary of reader reception theory can be found in Terry Eagleton, *Literary Theory,* 54–91. For a leading proponent of this perspective see Wolfgang Iser, *The Implied Reader* (Baltimore: Johns Hopkins University Press, 1974).

77. The literature on "subjectivity and address" is discussed in John Fiske, *Television Culture,* 48–61.

78. See Barth, *City People,* 81.

79. Robert E. Park, "The Natural History of the Newspaper," *American Journal of Sociology* 29 (November 1923): 273–89.

80. See Juergens, *Joseph Pulitzer and the New York World,* 39, and Schudson, *Discovering the News,* 91–106.

81. *Cosmopolitan* 40 (February 1906): 466.

82. Theodore Dreiser, *Sister Carrie* (Middlesex, Eng.: Penguin, 1981 [1900]), 22.

83. See Louis Wirth, "Urbanism as a Way of Life," *American Journal of Sociology* 44 (July 1938): 21.

84. By the 1920s advertisers would adopt the same "therapeutic" stance, counseling readers on how to cope with modern life. The given product became the magical solution to an assortment of insecurities, while advertising copy presented the company as a wise and kindly ally to the reader in his or her struggles. See Roland Marchland, *Advertising and the*

American Dream: Making the Way for Modernity, 1920–1940 (Berkeley: University of California Press, 1986), 13–16.

85. Alvin W. Gouldner, *The Dialectic of Ideology and Technology* (New York and Toronto: Oxford University Press, 1976), 95. For another discussion of "the public sphere" see Jurgens Habermas, "The Public Sphere," in Chandra Mukerji and Michael Schudson, eds., *Rethinking Popular Culture,* 398–404. Habermas defines "public sphere" as a "domain of our social life in which such a thing as public opinion can be formed. Citizens act as a public when they deal with matters of general interest without being subject to coercion."

86. S. S. McClure, "Concerning Three Articles in This Number of *McClure's,* and a Coincidence That May Set Us Thinking," *McClure's* 20 (January 1903).

87. Lincoln Steffens, "The Shame of Minneapolis," *McClure's* 20 (January 1903).

4. "The Whirlpool of Real Life": The Popular Magazine Project

1. In David Thelen's excellent study of Progressivism in Wisconsin between 1885 and 1900, he cites a Milwaukee newspaper editor who, a few years after the 1893 depression, worried about the need to "save our social system from the destruction into the *vortex* of which it is fast traveling." See Thelen, *The New Citizenship,* 80.

2. For biographical information on Walker see the *Dictionary of American Biography* 19:347–48; *Who Was Who in America: 1897–1942,* 1290; Flora Mai Holly, "Notes on Some American Magazine Editors," *Bookman* 7 (December 1900): 359; and Mott, *A History of American Magazines* 4:482–91.

3. "The Cosmopolitan Magazine—Its Methods and Its Editors," *Review of Reviews* 5 (June 1892): 609. Bisland's articles appeared in *Cosmopolitan* 8 and 9 (1890).

4. Pulitzer's defense of himself from charges of practicing sensational journalism and appealing to more "base" human emotions is discussed in Joseph Juergens, *Joseph Pulitzer and the New York World,* 43–92.

5. According to one commentator, "There has been some criticism of the audacious journalistic methods which Mr. Walker has found useful in bringing his pet before the public. He answers that he has convinced himself that the *Cosmopolitan* is a good magazine and worthy to be introduced into the homes of our American People; that there isn't a particle use of its being good if people don't read it, and that, consequently, he considers justifiable any honest means of bringing before their eyes until such time as it has the assured audience it deserves." See "The Cosmopolitan Magazine—Its Methods and Its Editors," 608.

6. W. A. Swanberg, *Citizen Hearst,* 85–90. One of the guests at Walker's house when he entertained Bryan was Hearst. Eventually Walker, who had been neglecting *Cosmopolitan* because of other business ventures, sold *Cosmopolitan* to Hearst in 1905.

7. See Walker's biography of Theodore Roosevelt, particularly the introductory article, "A Working Man in the Presidency," *Cosmopolitan* 32 (November 1901): 25–29.

8. In Walker's introduction to a series on "The Use of Money in Elections," *Cosmopolitan* 26 (January 1899): 288, he argued that the "spending of millions to influence an election" by the political parties is "a new problem in a republican form of government." In the April 1898 issue, Walker interviewed the Hon. Thomas B. Reed of Maine, then Speaker of the House. The interview was somewhat hostile as Walker made it clear that he disapproved of the Speaker's partisanship.

9. Ellery Sedgwick, *The Happy Profession* (Boston: Little, Brown, 1946), 113.

10. A comment on Walker's essay in *Review of Reviews* 6 (October 1892): 335, was titled, "A Capitalist's Sympathetic View of the Strike." The author of the article observed that "the weight of [Walker's] words is especially great, from the fact that he himself is a prominent exponent of the monied class, which he criticizes with such remarkable freedom and vigor." It should also be noted that W. D. Howells, for a short time the editor of *Cosmopolitan,* also departed from the strident antilabor rhetoric that was common among the upper class during this period.

11. *Cosmopolitan* 13 (October 1892): 575.

12. *Cosmopolitan* 33 (May 1902): 114.

13. Susan Waugh McDonald, "From Kipling to Kitsch," provides a valuable and sympathetic account of Walker's *Cosmopolitan* University.

14. The January 1898 issue presented a detailed "General Plan of the University," including a curriculum (334–40). Walker's breakdown of the applications for admission is in the August 1897 issue (99–101). By 1899 (vol. 26) Walker had defined the project as a success because it had demonstrated the public's interest in a correspondence school. He estimated that "close to a million people" were anxious for an education that "the state does not provide." The one-page article ended with a discussion of legislation that would be presented in Congress for a National Correspondence University under government control but "free from personal interest and entirely removed from politics."

15. Michael E. McGeer, *The Decline of Popular Politics,* 53.

16. See Walker's June 1905 editorial (vol. 39), "The Magazine as an Educator" and "The High Privilege of the Voter," *Cosmopolitan* 37 (August 1904).

17. See the editorial by Walker, "Should Young Men Enter Political Life and How?" *Cosmopolitan* 38 (November 1904). Walker argued that any young man who enters New York State politics, no matter how well intentioned, would end up being controlled by a political "boss." He urged young men interested in politics to go into business and "give up your spare moments to taking an interest in affairs." Walker hoped that the right time would come when young men interested in serving the public could go into politics. Also see his August 1904 editorial "The High Privilege of the Voter."

18. John Brisben Walker, "What Is Education? The Studies Most Important for the Modern Man. Who Should Study Science," *Cosmopolitan* 37 (1904): 401–403.

19. In the opening of this essay Walker made reference to reports that Princeton had decided to emphasize classical studies and deemphasize science. Walker proceeded to make fun of these old-fashioned Princeton professors. Woodrow Wilson, then president of

Princeton, was not amused. He regarded the article as a "gross injustice to Princeton." Wilson implied that Walker had set up a straw man to attack. "No man in his senses or with any real learning would in our day wish to create a reaction against science." Walker reprinted the letter and his response to it in, "Men, Women and Events" (October 1904): 741.

20. John Brisben Walker, "What You Can Do for Your Children and Grandchildren," *Cosmopolitan* 38 (January 1905): opening editorial.

21. *Cosmopolitan* 38 (January 1905).

22. "Great Problems in Organization: Recent Developments in Industrial Organization" (with editorial comments in the magazine), *Cosmopolitan* 26 (March 1899): 617–24.

23. John Brisben Walker, "The Trusts and the End," *Cosmopolitan* 29 (July 1900): 310–312.

24. This comment is from Walker's essay on the 1892 Homestead strike, "The Homestead Object Lesson," discussed in this chapter (see note 10, above).

25. *Cosmopolitan* 32 (November 1901): 28.

26. See Walker's editorial, "The First Essential for Prosperity," *Cosmopolitan* 22 (March 1897), in which he advocated a "regulated system of money" that would automatically expand during periods of commercial and financial crisis. The article is discussed in *Review of Reviews* 15 (March 1897): 328.

27. Harold S. Wilson, *McClure's Magazine and the Muckrakers*, chaps. 1 and 15.

28. S. S. McClure, *My Autobiography*, 149.

29. A good discussion of McClure's literary syndicate is in "Mr. McClure and His Magazine," *Review of Reviews* 8 (July 1893): 98. The author claimed that McClure "has within the past ten years made the acquaintance of more authors of standing in different countries than any other man knows or ever knew." Later in the essay the author observed that "the first number throbs with actuality from beginning to end."

30. McClure, *My Autobiography*, 168. During his years as proprietor of the literary syndicate (called "The Associated Literary Press"), McClure helped to popularize the fiction of Robert Louis Stevenson in the United States (although Stevenson was also under contract to *Scribner's*) as well as A. Conan Doyle and Rudyard Kipling. His syndicate contributed (along with the *Century*) to the revival of Lincoln literature as well. Large numbers of articles on "trusts, prohibition and civil service reform" were sold as well as stories by New England authors like Harriet Prescott Spofford, Sarah Orne Jewett, Elizabeth Sturat Phelps, and Julian Hawthorne.

According to Wilson, McClure's material appealed to "rural households" (*McClure's Magazine and the Muckrakers*, 42; also see McClure, *My Autobiography*, 170–85). Also according to Wilson (ibid.), *McClure's* literary syndicate eventually became successful because it supplied a valuable service in a highly competitive newspaper industry. Newspapers could purchase fiction and nonfiction material from a variety of literary syndicates at a far lower cost than it would take for them to purchase the material directly from the author.

31. This account is based primarily on Robert Stinson, "McClure's Road to *McClure's*."

32. The quote about editing for his readers comes from *Profitable Advertising* (October 15, 1897). The staff speech is discussed in Wilson, *McClure's Magazine and the Muckrakers*, 105.

33. Juergens, *Joseph Pulitzer and the New York World*, 175.

34. See Wilson, *McClure's Magazine and the Muckrakers*, 105. According to Wilson, "Most of the fifteen hundred articles published during the first decade sprang from McClure's creativity. Years later, as if they were his children, he could name them and recall the history of each."

35. For a discussion of McClure's staff see Wilson, *McClure's Magazine and the Muckrakers*, 81–103. On the development of the magazine's "staff system" see George Jean Nathan, "The Magazine in the Making," *Bookman* 34 (December 1911): 414–16.

36. See Jan Cohn, *Creating America*, chap. 2, for a discussion of Lorimer's staff.

37. See Mott, *A History of American Magazines* 4:590–91, for a description of McClure's meetings with Tarbell (also see Peter Lyon, *Success Story*, 130–32). In America there was a revival of interest in Napoleon as a result of the centennial celebrations of Napoleon's military successes in France. More than forty years earlier in the popular magazines, there had been a wave of interest in Napoleon. The new "Napoleon cult" was even more intense and was reflected in every American magazine, both the quality publications and the new popular magazines.

38. According to the *Independent* (originally a religious weekly magazine that became an advocate of the Social Gospel movement and reform in politics): "Newspaper editorials are casual comments, neutral and inoffensive. But there is no doubt what magazines are trying to accomplish. . . . The modern editor does not sit in his easy chair, writing essays and sorting over the manuscripts that are sent in by his contributors. He goes hunting for things. The magazine staff is coming to be a group of specialists of similar views, but diverse talents who are assigned to work up a particular subject, perhaps for a year or two before anything is published and who spend that time in travel and research among the printed and living sources of information." See "An Editorial to Order," *Independent* 65 (October 1, 1908): 797.

39. Lincoln Steffens, *The Autobiography of Lincoln Steffens* (New York: Harcourt, 1931), 362–63.

40. William Allen White, *Autobiography*, 200.

41. Sedgwick, *The Happy Profession*, 142–43.

42. *McClure's* muckraking social reform perspective evolved over the 1893–1911 period. *McClure's* did not have a clearly defined reform perspective during its first decade. See Wilson, *McClure's Magazine and the Muckrakers*, chaps. 4 and 8.

43. S. S. McClure, "Concerning Three Articles in This Number of McClure's and a Coincidence That May Set Us Thinking," *McClure's* 20 (January 1903): 336.

44. Theodore P. Greene, *America's Heroes*, 176.

45. Frank Munsey, *The Story of the Founding and Development of the Frank Munsey Publishing House* (New York, 1907), 10.

46. Munsey emphasized this "rags to riches" probusiness theme throughout his publica-

tions, including, of course, *Munsey's*. For a discussion of this issue see George Britt, *Forty Years—Forty Millions: The Career of Frank A. Munsey* (New York: Kennikat Press, 1972 [1935]).

47. Mott, *A History of American Magazines* 4:418.

48. McGeer, *The Decline of Popular Politics*, 68–106, and Britt, *Forty Years—Forty Millions*, 70–71.

49. *Dictionary of American Biography* 13:334–35.

50. Mott, *A History of American Magazines* 4:540. According to Mott, Bok, then a bachelor, was embarrassed about having to respond to these personal letters written by young girls to the *Ladies' Home Journal* and got Isabel A. Mallon to write this feature.

51. Holly, "Notes on Some American Magazine Editors," 358.

52. Roland Marchland, *Advertising and the American Dream*, 13–16.

53. *Review of Reviews* 5 (June 1892): 609.

54. Wilson described *McClure's* first decade (1893–1903) as having "operated free of any ideological matrix. Its contents were pluralistic, each article shaped by a different set of hands." See Wilson, *McClure's Magazine and the Muckrakers*, 105.

55. The fact that the popular magazine could be all things to all people is indicated by the range of contradictory comments on these magazines during the 1890s. H. L. Mencken thought that McClure had brought sensational journalism to the magazine world while others saw *McClure's* as a cheaper version of the *Century* (like the English *Strand*). Walker and *Cosmopolitan* were thought of as part of the literary establishment by Elbert Hubbard of *The Philistine*, but *Review of Reviews* focused on Walker's departures from the genteel model and his "dignified sensationalism."

56. Frank Munsey was not highly thought of by reporters, writers, or other magazine publishers and editors. Highbrow critics did not think much of *Munsey's*, in part because of its reputation for "naughty pictures." *Review of Reviews* made little mention of *Munsey's* even though it was the circulation leader during the 1890s. William Allen White wrote of Frank Munsey after his death, "Frank Munsey contributed to the journalism of his day the morals of a money changer and the manner of an undertaker. He and his kind have succeeded in transforming a once-noble profession into an 8 per cent security. May he rest in trust" (George Britt, *Forty Years—Forty Millions*, 17).

57. For an interesting discussion of the Horatio Alger stories and the reaction of genteel critics to this new genre of adolescent literature see Daniel T. Rodgers, *The Work Ethic in Industrial America, 1850–1920* (Chicago and London; University of Chicago Press, 1978), 140–43.

58. Christopher Wilson makes this argument in "The Rhetoric of Consumption." Larry May makes a similar argument about the movie industry in *Screening Out the Past: The Birth of Mass Culture and the Motion Picture Industry* (Chicago and London: University of Chicago Press, 1980), 169–99.

59. Josiah Holland, the first editor of *Scribner's*, was a descendent of John and Judith Holland, who had settled in New England in 1630. Henry Adams, editor of the *North*

American Review, was of course the great grandson of John Adams and the grandson of John Quincy Adams. His father was reputed to be the wealthiest man in Boston. Henry Mills Alden, editor of *Harper's Magazine,* was the son of Ira Alden, eighth in descent from John Alden the Pilgrim. Thomas Bailey Aldrich, editor of *Atlantic Monthly,* was descended on his father's side from George Aldrich, who came to Massachusetts Bay in 1631. These are just a few examples. The twelve editors and publishers of genteel magazines used in this comparison were, by and large, of "old stock" New England ancestry and college-educated. All were born between 1819 and 1844. The biographical information comes from the *Dictionary of American Biography.*

60. Christopher Wilson, "The Rhetoric of Consumption," 45.

61. A good discussion of the sense of estrangement from Protestant culture of middle-class intellectuals and writers can be found in Christopher Lasch, *The New Radicalism in America: 1889–1963* (New York: Vintage, 1965), and Larzer Ziff, *The American 1890's,* 206–29.

62. Jackson Lears called the quest for "real life" the "psychic project" of the age. See T. Jackson Lears, "From Salvation to Self-Realization: Advertising and the Therapeutic Roots of Consumer Culture, 1880–1930," in Richard Wightman Fox and T. J. Lears, eds., *The Culture of Consumption,* 1–38.

63. Steffens, *Autobiography,* 244.

64. This aspect of Steffens's life, particularly his fascination with urban immigrants, is discussed in Patrick F. Palermo, *Lincoln Steffens* (Boston: Twayne, 1978), 23–24.

65. On "overcivilization" see Ziff, *The American 1890's,* 206–29, and T. Jackson Lears, *No Place of Grace,* 4–58.

66. Steffens, quoted in Justin Kaplan, *Lincoln Steffens* (New York: Simon and Schuster, 1974), 58.

67. William Allen White, *Autobiography,* 157.

68. The data for this comparison comes from biographies of the eighteen popular magazine editors and publishers: Ray Stannard Baker (*McClure's, American*), Edward Bok (*Ladies' Home Journal*), S. S. Chamberlain (*Cosmopolitan* editor), Cyrus Hermann Curtis (publisher of the *Ladies' Home Journal* and the *Saturday Evening Post*), Norman Hapgood (*Collier's*), Sewell Hapgood (*McClure's, Cosmopolitan*), Arthur Sherburne Hardy (editor, *Cosmopolitan*), William Randolph Hearst (*Cosmopolitan,* after 1905), George Horace Lorimer (*Saturday Evening Post* editor), S. S. McClure, Bailey Millard (*Cosmopolitan*), Frank Munsey, Lincoln Steffens (*McClure's, American*), Ida Tarbell (*McClure's, American*), James Adams Thayer (*Everybody's* publisher), Arthur Turner Vance (*Woman's Home Companion*), John Brisben Walker, and William Allen White (*McClure's, American*).

5. *The New Secular Religion of Health*

1. John Higham, "The Reorientation of American Culture in the 1890's," 27.

2. In addition to Higham's classic article see Donald J. Mrozek, *Sport and American*

Mentality, 1880–1910 (Knoxville: University of Tennessee Press, 1983), 3–27; and T. Jackson Lears, *No Place of Grace.*

3. Some examples of articles in family house magazines that focused on neurasthenia, degeneration, or overcivilization include "The Penalty of the Systematic Life," *Scribner's* 35 (February 1904): 249–50; William Blaikie, "Is American Stamina Declining?" *Harper's Monthly* 79 (July 1899): 241–44; Henry Childs Merwin, "On Being Civilized Too Much," *Atlantic Monthly* 79 (June 1897): 838–46; Charles L. Dana, "Are We Degenerating?" *Forum* 19 (June 1895): 458–65; Max Nordau, "A Reply to My Critics," *Century* 50 (August 1895): 546–51; Cesare Lombroso, "Nordau's Degeneracy: Its Value and Its Errors," *Century* 50 (October 1895): 936–40; Francis A. Walker, "Immigration and Degeneration," *Forum* 11 (August 1891): 634–44; Philip Coombs Knapp, "Are Nervous Diseases Increasing?" *Century* 52 (May 1896): 146–53.

4. John H. Girdner, M.D., worried about the "serious damage to health" caused by the noise of cities. See John H. Girdner, M.D., "Noise and Health," *Munsey's* 25 (June 1901): 323–26. Also, on the problem of suicide, see "A Blot on Modern Civilization," *Munsey's* 16 (October 1896): 128.

5. George M. Beard, *American Nervousness: Its Causes and Consequences* (New York: G. P. Putnam, 1881), 96–113 and 133–38. These passages were reprinted in Alan Trachtenberg, *Democratic Vistas, 1860–1880* (New York: George Braziller, 1970), 238–47.

6. Mitchell was an associate editor of the *Journal of Nervous and Mental Disease.* His coeditor was Edward Hammond Clarke, whose *Sex in Education; Or a Fair Chance for Girls* (1873) claimed to prove that women's physiology made too much "brain-work" dangerous. Julia Ward Howe responded to Clarke's book in *Sex and Education: A Reply to E. H. Clarke's "Sex in Education"* (1874). Howe argued that the bad health of women was not a result of their physiology but a result of lack of physical education and training. Rather than more rest Howe urged more physical activity. For an interesting discussion of nineteenth-century attitudes toward the body see Roberta J. Park, "Physiology and Anatomy Are Destiny!? Brains, Bodies and Exercise in Nineteenth-Century American Thought," *Journal of Sport History* 18 (Spring 1991), no. 1: 31–63. Mitchell was also a popular author of historical fiction and a contributor to magazines, especially the *Century.* For a short biographical sketch see Talcott Williams, "Dr. S. Weir Mitchell: Physician, Scientist and Author," *Century* 57 (November 1898): 136–40.

7. Edward Wakefield, "Nervousness: The National Disease of America," *McClure's* 2 (February 1894): 303–307.

8. Harold Frederic's best-selling book of the 1890s, *The Damnation of Theron Ware,* revolves around the theme of overcivilization. In many of Edith Wharton's short stories and in Kate Chopin's *The Awakening,* neurasthenia and overcivilization are associated with the lifeless homogeneity of small-town life and traditional gender roles. Theodore Roosevelt in a number of his essays equated overcivilization with "narrow materialism" and a loss of transcendent purpose.

9. See Nilola Tresla, "The Problem of Increasing Human Energy," *Century* 60 (June 1900): 175–211.

10. See Anson Rabinbach, *The Human Motor: Energy, Fatigue and the Origins of Modernity* (Berkeley and Los Angeles: University of California Press, 1992); Park, "Physiology and Anatomy Are Destiny!?"; William James, "The Energies of Men," in *William James: Writings 1902–1910* (New York, N.Y.: Library of America), 1223–1241. This essay was originally delivered as the Presidential Address before the American Philosophical Association at Columbia University, December 28, 1906. It was published in *Philosophical Review* (January 1907).

11. Anna C. Bracket, "The Technique of Rest," *Harper's Monthly* 83 (June 1891): 46–55 (the quote is on p. 50).

12. Frederic W. Burry, "The Fear of Failure," *Cosmopolitan* 35 (June 1903): 233.

13. Frank Morgan, "Getting and Spending," *Cosmopolitan* 23 (June 1897): 193–200.

14. Upton Sinclair, "What Life Means to Me," *Cosmopolitan* 41 (October 1906): 592.

15. Louis Filler, *Crusaders for American Liberalism* (Yellow Springs, Ohio: Antioch Press, 1950 [1939]), 121–24.

16. Upton Sinclair, "Starving for Health's Sake," *Cosmopolitan* 48 (May 1910): 739–46. The editor's introduction to this series informed *Cosmopolitan* readers, "This is the first of a unique series of articles on gaining and keeping perfect health." Also see "What Do I Fear?" *Cosmopolitan* 26 (December 1898): 216–28.

17. Howard Pyle, "A Modern Magian," *Cosmopolitan* 17 (August 1894): 461.

18. Edgar Saltris, "The Princess of the Golden Isles," *Cosmopolitan* 33 (July 1902).

19. Adele Marie Shaw, "The Survival," *Cosmopolitan* 40 (February 1906): 401.

20. Bret Harte, "Zut-ski, the Problem of a Wicked Feme Sole," *Cosmopolitan* 32 (April 1902).

21. Charles D. Lanier, "The World's Sporting Impulse," *Review of Reviews* 14 (July 1896): 58–63. For similar discussions of the nation's growing interest in athleticism see James E. Sullivan, "Athletics and the Stadium," *Cosmopolitan* 31 (September 1901): 501; Helmet Stag Archer, "Sports with Which We Are Unfamiliar," *Cosmopolitan* 37 (May 1904): 109–16, and in the same volume H. H. Boyesen 2d, "The Most Athletic Nation in the World," 83.

22. The word *discourse* has been defined in many ways, but a definition that fits the way this concept is being used here comes from Graeme Turner: "socially produced groups of ideas or ways of thinking that can be tracked in individual texts or groups of texts, but also demand to be located within wider historical and social structures or relations." See Graeme Turner, *British Cultural Studies: An Introduction* (Boston: Unwin Hyman, 1990), 32- 33.

23. Walter Germain Robinson, "Diversions of Some Millionaires," *Cosmopolitan* 33 (August 1902): 384–92.

24. Cleveland Moffett, "Luxurious Newport," *Cosmopolitan* 43 (August 1907): 349–58.

25. Clinton Van Horne, "Ball Giving in New York," *Munsey's* 21 (April 1899): 124–28. On another popular upper-class amusement see Vance Thompson, "The Roof-Gardens of New York," *Cosmopolitan* 27 (August 1899): 503–14.

26. Robert Stewart, "The Hotels of New York," *Munsey's* 22 (November 1899): 287–95, and Stewart, "Clubs and Club Life in New York," *Munsey's* 22 (October 1899): 105–22. It should be noted here that articles on entertainment drew not only from the new upper-class subculture but also from black and immigrant subcultures. For example, Walter Creedmoor in "The Real Coney Island," *Munsey's* 21 (August 1899): 745–49, opposed efforts to tear down the famous "watering place" or turn it into a public park. Creedmoor argued, "Let us tear down one or two of those gaudy fashionable hotels which do so much to shelter and encourage vulgarity in every form and to create for the rising generation of American standards of taste that are not only false but vicious."

Also see Reginald de Koven, "Music Halls and Popular Songs," *Cosmopolitan* 23 (September 1897): 531–40 (the article discussed the influence of "Afro-American music" on popular music among other topics); Ernest Jarrold, "The Makers of Popular Songs," *Munsey's* 13 (June 1895): 289, as well as the monthly department in *Munsey's* called "In the World of Music," which began in September 1895. On vaudeville and the music hall see Charles Reginald Sherlock, "From Breakdown to Rag-time," *Cosmopolitan* 31 (October 1901): 631–39, and Sherlock, "Where Vaudeville Holds the Boards," *Cosmopolitan* 32 (February 1902): 411–20; Israel Zangwill, "The Future of Vaudeville," *Cosmopolitan* 38 (April 1905): 639–46.

27. Mrs. Reginald de Koven, "Bicycling for Women," *Cosmopolitan* 19 (August 1895): 392–94.

28. Richard Watson Gilder, "The Influence of Athletics," *Century* 40 (June 1900): 314.

29. Theodore Roosevelt, "True American Ideals," *Forum* 18 (February 1895): 743–50.

30. John Brisben Walker, "Athletics and Health: The Department of Physical Culture," *Cosmopolitan* 37 (September 1904): 594.

31. J. I. C. Clarke, "The Brotherhood of Strenuosity," *Cosmopolitan* 32 (March 1902): 569.

32. An article on hunting horses and steeplechases was accompanied by a full-page photograph of Theodore Roosevelt on his horse with the caption, "President Roosevelt Taking a Three Bar Fence on His Favorite Hunter." See Belmont Purdy, "The High-Jumping Horse," *Cosmopolitan* 42 (January 1907): 269–75.

33. Higham, "The Reorientation of American Culture," 26.

34. Elbert Hubbard, "A Gladiatorial Renaissance," *Cosmopolitan* 34 (March 1903): 597.

35. Walker, "Athletics and Health," 593.

36. Hubbard, "A Gladiatorial Renaissance," 599. John S. White took a moderate position on football, arguing that it should continue to be played on the college level only if new rules were adopted to eliminate the excessive violence. See White, "The Education of the Foot," *Cosmopolitan* 14 (February 1894): 508–509.

37. See Mrozek, *Sport and American Mentality,* 67–102. On changing beliefs about the body and exercise see Park, "Physiology and Anatomy Are Destiny!?"

38. Mrozek, *Sport and American Mentality,* 189–235.

39. See James C. Whorton, "Eating to Win: Popular Concepts of Diet, Strength and Energy in the Early Twentieth Century," in Kathryn Grover, ed., *Fitness in American*

Culture: Images of Health, Sport, and the Body, 1830–1940 (Rochester, N.Y.: University of Massachusetts Press and the Margaret Strong Museum, 1989), 86–122.

40. Mrozek reports that E. L. Godkin, while recognizing the benefits of sports for society, was not happy about the vast sums of money spent for college athletics. He preferred the ideal of amateur sports rather than the increasingly specialized and competitive male sports developing on college campuses (Mrozek, *Sport and American Mentality*, 98). Bernarr MacFadden, editor of *Physical Culture*, was not particularly interested in character building or nation building but instead focused on the health and well-being of the individual (see Grover, *Fitness in American Culture*, 11).

41. Few articles explicitly addressing health issues appeared in the 1890s, but they became more common after 1900.

42. Elbert Hubbard, "How To Keep Well," *Cosmopolitan* 40 (November 1905): 80.

43. Julian Ralph, "Famous Cures and Humbugs of Europe," *Cosmopolitan* 34 (April 1903): 665–72.

44. Bernarr MacFadden, "Health Made and Preserved by Daily Exercise," *Cosmopolitan* 34 (April 1903): 705–12.

45. Woods Hutchinson, M.D., "Exercise That Rests," *Cosmopolitan* 46 (May 1909): 698.

46. By 1912 an article in *McClure's* commented on the rapid growth of baseball as a big business and a spectator sport. See Edward Mott Woolley, "The Business of Baseball," *McClure's* 39 (July 1912): 241–56. Also see Frederick Courtnoy Barber, "The Star Ball-Players and Their Earnings," *Munsey's* 49 (May 1913): 213–21.

47. For an example see Stoddard Goodhire, M.D., "Adding Years to Your Health," *Cosmopolitan* 55 (September 1913): 434–42.

48. One indication of the growing interest in the outdoors and sports was that after 1896 sports-related articles began to be placed first in the issue. Two examples were Price Collier, "A Word About Golfers and Golf-Links in England and Scotland," *Cosmopolitan* 20 (April 1896): 575–82; and John R. Spears, "The America's Cup," *Cosmopolitan* 27 (September 1899): 459–72. Also see appendixes 2 and 3 in this volume.

49. Orrin E. Dunlap, "Niagara—The Scene of Perilous Feats," *Cosmopolitan* 32 (February 1902): 358–70.

50. Mrs. Aubrey Le Blond, "The Perils of High Peaks," *Cosmopolitan* 37 (July 1904): 245–52. Another article on mountain climbing appeared a year later with George D. Abraham's "Most Daring of All Mountain Climbers," *Cosmopolitan* 39 (July 1905): 365.

51. P. T. McGrath, "Wonderful Whale-Hunting by Steam," *Cosmopolitan* 37 (May 1904): 49–56.

52. "Winter Sports," *Cosmopolitan* 32 (January 1902): 235–43. Other articles on winter sports and activities included Harry L. Wells, "Coasting Down Some Great Mountains," *Cosmopolitan* 20 (January 1896): 240–48; Orrin E. Dunlap (lead article), "The Niagara in Winter," *Cosmopolitan* 28 (April 1900): 593–604; Harry Thomas Clinton and P. T. McGrath, "Adventures in the Ice-Floes," *Cosmopolitan* 36 (November 1903): 3–12.

53. In this article the editors announced a "round the world voyage" along with a series

of articles on his trip written exclusively for *Cosmopolitan.* See Jack London, "The Voyage of the Snark," *Cosmopolitan* 42 (November 1906): 115–22.

54. Frederic Remington, "The Way of an Indian" (Part 7), *Cosmopolitan* 40 (February 1906): 378.

55. Leo Crane, "East of Eden: The Story of a Man's Fight with Death in the Snow," *Cosmopolitan* 48 (May 1910): 697.

56. See Mabel Osgood Wright, "Our Neighbors the Birds," *Cosmopolitan* 27 (June 1899): 143–48; and a lead article, Katherine V. C. Matthews, "The Rose of Yesterday and Today," *Cosmopolitan* 35 (June 1903): 119–28.

57. For an example of this position see "Modern Self Consciousness," *Atlantic Monthly* 86 (October 1900): 573–74.

58. Hjalmar Hjorth Boyesen, "A Glacier Excursion in Norway," *Cosmopolitan* 23 (October 1897): 625–32. For another example of a story that depicts the therapeutic value of the outdoors, see Robert E. Strahorn, "A Summer Outing on Northwestern Waters," *Cosmopolitan* 21 (September 1896): 473–83.

59. Helen Lukens Jones, "The Music of Nature," *Cosmopolitan* 34 (January 1903): 259–68.

60. Well-known naturalist John Muir wrote for and was the feature of a number of articles in both family house magazines like Gilder's *Century* and popular magazines like *Cosmopolitan.* This was the period when national parks were established, reflecting a desire to preserve the environment as well as the resurgence of nationalistic feeling. Even among those who advocated national parks there were disagreements among those who favored a contemplative, passive stance toward nature and those who held the more dominant active view in which parks would provide recreational "activities" to entertain visitors. See Mrozek, *Sport and American Mentality,* 182–88.

61. Edgar L. Larkin, "Wonderful New Inland Sea," *Cosmopolitan* 41 (October 1906).

62. Dictated to George R. McIntyre by Ellery S. Scott, Chief Officer of the lost steamship *Roraima,* "The Eruption of Mont Pelee," *Cosmopolitan* 33 (July 1902): 242–52.

63. B. F. Fisher, "Vesuvius, Destroyer of Cities," *Cosmopolitan* 32 (April 1902): 575–84.

64. Mary Elizabeth Jennings, "Frozen Mountains of the Sea," *Cosmopolitan* 15 (August 1893): 405–10.

65. Harry Thurston Peck, in "The Woman of Fascination," *Cosmopolitan* 26 (November 1898): 71, observed that "American periodicals have been devoting an enormous amount of space to the discussion of what may be called the psychological side of the social world." For discussion of the "new psychology" see John Burnham, "The New Psychology: From Narcissism to Social Control," in John Braeman, Robert H. Bremner, and David Brody, eds., *Change and Continuity in Twentieth-Century America: The 1920's* (Columbus: Ohio State University Press, 1968), 361–91.

66. On the mind cure movement and the interest in spiritualism, especially among the educated middle class, see Donald Meyer, *The Positive Thinkers: Religion as Pop Psychology from Mary Baker Eddy to Oral Roberts* (New York: Pantheon, 1965), 73–129; and Ann

Braude, *Radical Spirits: Spiritualism and Women's Rights in Nineteenth-Century America* (Boston: Beacon Press, 1989). Also see Howard Kerr, *Mediums and Spirit Rappers and Roaring Radicals: Spiritualism in American Literature, 1850–1900* (Urbana: University of Illinois Press, 1972); R. Lawrence Moore, "Spiritualism and Science: Reflections on the First Decade of the Spirit Rappings," *American Quarterly* 24 (October 1972): 474–500, and Moore, "The Spiritualist Medium in a Study of Female Professionalism in Victorian America," *American Quarterly* 27 (May 1975): 200–21.

67. *Munsey's* and *Cosmopolitan* carried many more articles on women and athletics and on women's colleges than did *McClure's*. A few examples from *Munsey's* included Leonora Beck, "Women on Horseback," *Munsey's* 15 (April 1896): 23 (opening article); Jean Pardee-Clark, "In a Girls' Gymnasium," *Munsey's* 15 (September 1896): 737; Anne O'Hagan, "The Athletic Girl," *Munsey's* 25 (August 1901): 729–38; Elizabeth York Miller, "Should Women Ride Astride?" *Munsey's* 25 (July 1901): 553–57; Alice Katherine Fallows, "The Girl Freshmen," *Munsey's* 25 (September 1901): 818–28.

68. Harry Thurston Peck expressed the view of most male members of the medical profession on the dangers of education for women in "The Overtaught Woman," *Cosmopolitan* 26 (January 1899): 329. Later in the year Peck critically reviewed a book sympathetic to women's rights. He asserted that the movement for women's rights was a dangerous symptom of the age's growing discontent and contrary to human nature. Charlotte Perkins Stetson responded forcefully in the following issue. See Harry Thurston Peck, "The Woman of Today and To-Morrow," *Cosmopolitan* 27 (June 1899): 149–62, and Charlotte Perkins Stetson, "Woman's Economic Place: In Reply to the Article of Professor Peck in the June Cosmopolitan," *Cosmopolitan* 27 (July 1899): 309–33. Walker commented on this debate in the October issue: "The Intellectual Duel in the Cosmopolitan between Mrs. Charlotte Perkins Stetson and Harry Thurston Peck on that omnipresent and overshadowing problem, the Woman Question, attracted much attention, not only in this country but abroad. Hundreds of letters and manuscripts replying to both writers have been sent to this office." See "The Woman Question," *Cosmopolitan* 27 (October 1899): 664. The same volume carried a number of articles on these larger political questions as well as "The Art of Buying Food for a Family," and "The Delightful Art of Cooking," *Cosmopolitan* 27 (June 1899).

69. Dimest T. S. Denison, "Woman's Need of Leisure," *Woman's Home Companion* 31 (April 1904): 50.

70. Christopher Lasch, "The Snare of Preparation," in Lasch, ed., *The Social Thought of Jane Addams* (New York: Irvington, 1982), 1–43.

71. Ella Wheeler Wilcox, "The Restlessness of the Modern Woman," *Cosmopolitan* 31 (July 1901): 314–17.

72. Mark Twain, *The Adventures of Huckleberry Finn* (New York: New American Library, 1959), chap. 17.

73. Higham, "The Reorientation of American Culture," 31.

74. Kathryn Kish Sklar, *Catherine Beecher: A Study in American Domesticity*, 203.

75. An advertisement for a series of stories to appear in *Woman's Home Companion* alerted

readers to "Thrilling True Stories of Modern Heroines." "This is without a doubt the most thrilling and fascinating series of articles that has ever appeared in any magazine. They are true stories of the most wonderful deeds of valor and adventure in the face of appalling danger—deeds performed at unheard of risk by American women in the ordinary walks of life." *Woman's Home Companion* 31 (January 1904): 50–51.

76. Daniel T. Rodgers, *The Work Ethic in Industrializing America, 1850–1920,* 204.

77. Sheila M. Rothman, *Woman's Proper Place: A History of Changing Ideals and Practices, 1870 to the Present* (New York: Basic Books, 1978), 106.

78. A number of authors expressed some concern or reported on the growing number of "Bachelor Maids," educated women who chose not to marry. Two articles that discussed this issue was Juliet Wilbor Tompkins, "Why Women Do. Marry," *Cosmopolitan* 42 (February 1907): 468–71, and Elizabeth Meriwether Gilmer, "The Unglorified Spinster," *Cosmopolitan* 43 (May 1907): 42–43. Also see Winfred Sothern, "The Truth About the Bachelor Girl," *Munsey's* 25 (June 1901): 282–88.

79. On changes in sexual morality and women's roles during the Progressive era see James R. McGovern, "The American Woman's Pre–World War I Freedom in Manners and Morals," *Journal of American History* 55 (September 1968): 315–33.

80. Eleanor Gates, "The Woman Who Travels Alone" (Part 2), *Cosmopolitan* 42 (December 1906): 169.

81. Eleanor Gates, "The Girl Who Travels Alone" (Part 1), *Cosmopolitan* 42 (November 1906): 1.

82. Gates, "The Girl Who Travels Alone" (Part 3), *Cosmopolitan* 42 (January 1907): 308.

83. Carroll Smith-Rosenberg, "The New Woman as Androgyne: Social Disorder and Gender Crisis, 1870–1936," in Smith-Rosenberg, *Disorderly Conduct* (New York: Basic Books, 1978), 245–96.

84. The quote appeared in "Shop Talk," *Cosmopolitan* 48 (November 1909): 259. The first installment in Harold Bolce's series on women in higher education, "The Crusade Invisible," appeared in the February 1910 issue.

85. Harold Bolce, "Away from Ancient Alters," *Cosmopolitan* 48 (March 1910): 519–28.

86. Lavinia Hart, "A Girl's College Life," *Cosmopolitan* 31 (June 1901): 188–95. See also by the same author, "Women as College Presidents," *Cosmopolitan* 33 (May 1902): 72.

87. Mrozek, *Sport and American Mentality,* 136–60; Park, "Physiology and Anatomy Are Destiny!?" 40–60.

88. Mrs. Reginald de Koven, "The New Woman and Golf Playing," *Cosmopolitan* 21 (August 1896): 352–61.

89. Anna Wentworth Sears, "The Modern Woman Out-of-Doors," *Cosmopolitan* 21 (October 1896): 630–40.

90. O'Hagan, "The Athletic Girl," 729–38.

91. Gertrude Lynch, "Yachtswomen of America," *Cosmopolitan* 41 (May 1906): 73.

92. "Vacations: Sixteen *Woman's Home Companion* Readers Explain to Us How They Enjoyed Themselves Last Summer," *Woman's Home Companion* 36 (June 1909): 21–23.

93. See the February, March, and April 1904 issues of *Woman's Home Companion.*

94. Julius Henri Browne, "Are Women Companionable to Men?" *Cosmopolitan* 4 (January 1888): 452.

95. Elizabeth Cady Stanton, "Is Marriage a Failure?" *Cosmopolitan* 6 (November 1888): 93.

96. Rafford Pyke, "The Woman's Side," *Cosmopolitan* 33 (July 1902): 323.

97. Lavinia Hart, "When Woman's Ideals Fall," *Cosmopolitan* 33 (October 1902): 695.

98. Anthony Hope, "Double Harness" (Part 1), *Munsey's* 30 (December 1903): 331.

99. Charles Michael Williams, "A Man of Success," *Munsey's* 30 (October 1903).

100. Mary and Rosalie Dawson, "The Burton House Beautiful," *Munsey's* 28 (February 1903): 763.

101. Juliet Wilbor Tompkins, "Bertha's Mr. Wentworth," *Munsey's* 28 (November 1902): 241.

102. Emma Lee Walton, "A Symphony in Two Flats," *Munsey's* 14 (March 1896): 698.

103. Ella Wheeler Wilcox, "Parenthood," *Cosmopolitan* 32 (December 1901): 175.

104. Lavinia Hart, "Motherhood," *Cosmopolitan* 32 (March 1902): 469.

105. John Brisben Walker, "On the Choice of a Profession—Motherhood," *Cosmopolitan* 25 (May 1898): 89.

106. Anna Leach, in "Science in the Modern Kitchen," *Cosmopolitan* 27 (May 1899): 95–104, told her readers about the latest scientific discoveries concerning nutrition, ventilation, how to equip a modern kitchen, the need to expose the kitchen to sunlight, and other matters.

107. Many of the leading writers, scientists, and intellectuals of the period were interested in these movements. Neil Harris comments, "In both Britain and the United States spiritualist societies enjoyed a resurgence. Hundreds of mediums held seances to stimulate direct communication with the spirits. . . . Novelists of the period—Howells, James, Harold Frederic, Richard Harding Davis—treated the phenomenon as a major social issue. University commissions held hearings to determine fraudulence; distinguished scholars like William James in America and Henry Sidgwick in England, celebrities like Houdini and Sir Arthur Conan Doyle, paid their respects to this quest for certainty." See Neil Harris, "Utopian Fiction and Its Discontents," in *Cultural Excursions, Marketing Appetites and Cultural Tastes in Modern America,* 172.

108. Lavinia Hart, "To Love or to Be Loved," *Cosmopolitan* 34 (April 1903): 638.

109. Ella Wheeler Wilcox, "My Autobiography," *Cosmopolitan* 31 (August 1901): 419.

110. The *Arena*'s (founded in 1889) first editor was B. O. Flower, the son of an Illinois minister, who became interested in a variety of social reform causes during the 1890s. Louis Filler called the magazine one of the most influential of all "radical journals" and, during the 1890s, "the direct forerunner of the muckraking magazines." See Filler, *Crusaders for American Liberalism,* 39–42.

111. Ella Wheeler Wilcox, "Spiritual Phenomena from a Theosophical View," *Arena* 8 (September 1893): 472–76.

112. Ella Wheeler Wilcox, "What Life Means to Me," *Cosmopolitan* 42 (December 1906): 203–207.

113. Mark Twain, "Christian Science and the Book of Mrs. Eddy," *Cosmopolitan* 27 (October 1899): 585.

114. Charles Klein, "Christian Science: An Impartial Estimate," *Cosmopolitan* 42 (February 1907): 458–63; and Earl of Dunmire, "The Truth About Christian Science," *Cosmopolitan* 42 (March 1907): 535–44. Not long after, there was an explicit rebuttal to Twain's article by a "prominent Christian Science author." See Edward Kimball, "Mark Twain, Mrs. Eddy, and Christian Science," *Cosmopolitan* 43 (May 1907): 35–41; and Joel Rufus Mosley, "Christian Science Idealism," *Cosmopolitan* 43 (July 1907): 330–34. Mrs. Eddy was interviewed in another article by Arthur Brisbane, "An Interview with Mrs. Eddy," *Cosmopolitan* 43 (October 1907): 451–58. An article on Eddy appeared a few years later, Frederick Dixon's "Mary Barker Eddy," *Cosmopolitan* 50 (February 1911): 363.

In addition to articles on Christian Science, Edmund Wilson Roberts discussed "Successful Attempts at Scientific Mind-Reading," *Cosmopolitan* 26 (March 1899): 561; and Joseph Jastrow reported on "Mesmer, Animal Magnetism and Hypnotism," *Cosmopolitan* 20 (January 1896): 360. A muckraking article in *McClure's* also contributed to the controversy concerning Christian Science. See *McClure's* 27 (December 1906): 211.

115. Harold Bolce, "Polygots in Temples of Babel" (Part 2), *Cosmopolitan* 47 (June 1909): 52.

116. Bolce, "Polygots in Temples of Babel" (Part 3), *Cosmopolitan* 47 (July 1909): 209.

117. Bolce, "Polygots in Temples of Babel" (Part 3), 217.

118. On religious developments during this period, including the new Social Gospel movement, see William McLoughlin, *Revivals, Awakenings, and Reform* (Chicago: University of Chicago Press, 1978), 141–78. An article in the *Atlantic Monthly* summarized some of the new religious developments (of which the author approved); see George Hodges, "The Religion of the Spirit," *Atlantic Monthly* 95 (May 1905): 701–707.

119. James H. Canfield, "The Philosophy of Staying in Harness" (lead article), *Cosmopolitan* 39 (May 1905): 3–14 (the quote is on pp. 9–10).

120. Camille Flammarion, "Omega: The Last Days of the World" (conclusion), *Cosmopolitan* 15 (August 1893): 472.

121. *Cosmopolitan* 50 (February 1911): 296.

122. Higham, "The Reorientation of American Culture," 31.

123. This series appeared throughout *Cosmopolitan*'s 1894 issues. Between 1900 and 1910 *Cosmopolitan* carried a number of major biographical series, among which were Andrew Jackson and Charlemagne.

124. For an interpretation of these magazine biographies see Richard Ohmann, "Advertising and the New Discourse of Mass Culture," in Ohmann, *Politics of Letters* (Middletown, Conn.: Wesleyan University Press, 1987), 164; and Theodore P. Greene, *America's Heroes* ("The Hero as Napoleon").

125. Mrozek, *Sport and American Mentality*, 51–61.

126. Theodore Roosevelt, "Military Preparedness and Unpreparedness," *Century* 59 (November 1899): 149–53. A number of other articles on related themes by Roosevelt also appeared in the *Century* during 1900: "Fellow Feeling as a Political Factor," *Century* 59 (January 1900): 466–71; "Civic Helpfulness," *Century* 60 (October 1900): 939–44; "Latitude and Longitude Among Reformers," *Century* 60 (June 1900): 211–16.

127. Theodore Roosevelt, "True American Ideals."

128. Christopher Lasch, "The Moral and Intellectual Rehabilitation of the Ruling Class," in *The World of Nations,* 86.

129. Some of Henry Cabot Lodge's publications during the 1890s included "Political Issues of 1892," *Forum* 12 (September 1892): 98–105; "Our Blundering Foreign Policy," *Forum* 19 (March 1895): 8–17; "Our Duty to Cuba," *Forum* 21 (May 1896): 278–87. On the war with Spain see *Harper's Monthly* 99 (October 1899): 820.

130. Also see John P. Mallan, "Roosevelt, Brooks Adams, and Lea: The Warrior Critique of the Business Civilization," *American Quarterly* 8 (1956): 216–30.

131. Brooks Adams, "The New Struggle for life Among Nations," *McClure's* 6 (April 1899): 558–64.

132. Christopher Lasch, "The Moral and Intellectual Rehabilitation of the Ruling Class," in *The World of Nations,* 83–87. For a broad overview of American foreign policy and the era of empire building, see Walter Lafeber, *The New Empire: An Interpretation of American Expansion, 1860–1898* (Ithaca, N.Y.: Cornell University Press, 1963).

133. Walker did not support, at least in 1896, the proposals for a naval buildup. In an 1896 article, Walker argued that a large navy is an offensive weapon and those that advocate a naval buildup are supported by a "large and powerful class of armor manufacturers." Nevertheless, he believed that military preparedness was important. See John Brisben Walker, "In Case of War with England—What?" *Cosmopolitan* 21 (June 1896): 149–51.

134. W. A. Swanberg, *Citizen Hearst,* 119–93.

135. John Brisben Walker, "Republic of the United States of Great Britain," *Cosmopolitan* 29 (August 1900): 403.

136. John Brisben Walker, "China and the Powers," *Cosmopolitan* 29 (September 1900): 469–75.

137. Morton Keller mentioned "the publisher Frank Munsey" as one of a number of leading politicians, officers, and businessmen who were "advocates of imperialism." Other individuals mentioned were Brooks Adams, Alfred Thayer Mahan, Henry Cabot Lodge, Robert M. La Follette, Albert J. Beveridge, and George Perkins (insurance company executive). See Morton Keller, *Affairs of State: Public Life in Late Nineteenth-Century America* (Cambridge: Harvard University Press, 1977), 593.

Frank Munsey's enthusiasm for imperial expansion was reflected in a high percentage of enthusiastic articles on the war with Spain, more than in *Cosmopolitan.*

138. Richard H. Titherington, "Our War with Spain," *Munsey's* 21 (August 1899): 750 (eleventh and last installment).

139. Edwin Wildman, "The Filipinos," *Munsey's* 21 (April 1899): 32–39 (the quote is on p. 32).

140. Walstein Root, "Cuba Under American Rule," *Munsey's* 21 (July 1899): 561–74 (the quote is on p. 561).

141. John Barrett, "The Value of the Philippines," *Munsey's* 21 (August 1899): 689–703 (the quote is on p. 694).

142. "A Dangerous Mission To Spain," *Cosmopolitan* 26 (November 1898): 3.

143. Frank R. Roberson, "After the Capture of Manilla," *Cosmopolitan* 26 (January 1899): 379.

144. Grant Lynd, "In Southern Spain During the War," *Cosmopolitan* 26 (March 1899): 549.

145. Stephen Crane, "The Woof of Thin Red Threads," *Cosmopolitan* 26 (December 1898): 164–73.

146. For a discussion of current developments see Benjamin G. Rader, "The Quest for Self-Sufficiency and the New Strenuosity: Reflections on the Strenuous Life of the 1970's and 1980's," *Journal of Sport History* 18 (Summer 1991), no. 2: 255–66.

147. The concept of "structure of feeling" comes from Raymond Williams in *Marxism and Literature,* 128–135. Williams argues that this concept fixes our attention on social and cultural forms that are not "fixed and finished" but are "active, more flexible, less singular." Williams seems to associate "structures of feeling" with "practical consciousness" rather than "official consciousness." Practical consciousness is "what is actually being lived, and not only what is thought is being lived."

6. *"New Worlds To Conquer": The Dreams of Progress*

1. John G. Cawelti, "America on Display: The World's Fairs of 1876, 1893, 1933," in Frederic Cople Jaher, ed., *The Age of Industrialism in America: Essays in Social Structure and Cultural Values* (New York: Free Press, 1968), 323. Also see Robert W. Rydell, *All the World's a Fair: Vision of Empire at American International Expositions, 1876–1916* (Chicago and London: University of Chicago Press, 1984), 8.

2. *Century* articles on the Columbian Exposition in Chicago include Mrs. Schuler van Rensselaer, "At the Fair"; Gustav Kobbé, "Sights at the Fair"; W. Lewis Fraser, "Decorative Painting at the Fair"; Richard Watson Gilder, "The Vanishing City"; and "Do Not Miss the World's Fair" (editorial). All appeared in vol. 46 (May–October 1893). Eight articles appeared in vol. 45 (November 1892–April 1893), including Henry C. Potter, "Some Exposition Uses of Sunday," and Washington Gladden, "Sunday in Chicago."

3. Candace Wheeler, "A Dream City," *Harper's Monthly* 86 (May 1893): 830. The same issue contained the fifth part of a series of articles by Thomas A. Janvier called "The Evolution of New York."

4. The *Nation* was a weekly magazine founded in 1865 by E. L. Godkin, who was also

the editor of the *New York Evening Post* and a prominent advocate of civil service reform. The magazine during the late nineteenth century has been called "among the major guardians of traditional culture" (Henry F. May, *The End of American Innocence,* 72). The articles on the Chicago Columbian Exposition in the *Nation* included William A. Coffin, "The Columbian Exposition (Part 2): Fine Arts: The United States Section," *Nation* 57 (August 10, 1893): 96–96, and Coffin, Part 3, "Fine Arts: Pictures by American artists: Sculptural and Pictorial Decoration," *Nation* 57 (August 17, 1893): 114–16; Part 4 (signed "S.K."), "The Ensemble," *Nation* 57 (August 24, 1893): 132–33. Also see the article on "Science" (Part 7 in the series, by "W.H.D"), *Nation* 57 (September 14, 1893): 186–87.

5. Henry Van Brunt, *Atlantic Monthly* 71 (May 1893): 577–88.

6. *McClure's* did not cover the exposition, perhaps because *McClure's* first issue was a month after the exposition opened and, being short on capital, S. S. McClure used material from his literary syndicate for his first few issues. *Munsey's* provided limited coverage, but again, its "ten cent" revolution occurred at roughly the same time as the exposition. Of the leading popular magazines, *Cosmopolitan* was the only one that had been in existence a number of years before the 1893 Columbian Exposition.

7. M. H. Young, *Cosmopolitan* 12 (March 1892): 599–611.

8. Neil Harris, "Great American Fairs and Cities: The Role of Chicago's Columbian Exposition," in *Cultural Excursions, Marketing Appetites and Cultural Tastes in Modern America,* 119–23.

9. John Brisben Walker, "The World's College of Democracy," *Cosmopolitan* 15 (September 1893): 517–27.

10. John Brisben Walker, "The City of the Future—A Prophecy," *Cosmopolitan* 31 (September 1901): 473–75.

11. John Brisben Walker, "Preface—Why and How," *Cosmopolitan* 37 (September 1904): preface to issue. Walker's emphasis on urban planning was echoed by Albert Shaw (editor of the English *Review of Reviews*) in "The Real Value of the Fair, *Cosmopolitan* 31 (September 1901): 462.

12. This is Harris's argument in "Great American Fairs and Cities," 112.

13. Frederick Howe, "The World's Fair at St. Louis, 1904," *Cosmopolitan* 35 (July 1903): 281.

14. The *Cosmopolitan* pieces by Howells were part of a larger work, *A Traveller from Alturia* and *Through the Eye of the Needle.* Both were published later as *The Alturian Romances.*

15. William Dean Howells, "Letters of an Alturian Traveller (Part 3)," *Cosmopolitan* 16 (January 1894): 259–77.

16. Howells, "Letters of an Alturian Traveller (Part 2)," *Cosmopolitan* 16 (December 1893): 218–32 (the quote is on pp. 222–23).

17. Howells, "Letters of an Alturian Traveller (Part 1)," *Cosmopolitan* 16 (November 1893): 110–16.

18. Howells, "Letters of an Alturian Traveller (Part 2)," 226.

19. *Cosmopolitan* carried many pieces on the Midway. One example is Julian Hawthorne, "Foreign Folk at the Fair," *Cosmopolitan* 15 (September 1893): 567–76.

20. Walter Bessant, "A First Impression," *Cosmopolitan* 15 (September 1893): 533.

21. Murat Halstead, "Electricity at the Fair," *Cosmopolitan* 15 (September 1893): 577–78.

22. Paul Bouget, "A Farewell to the White City," *Cosmopolitan* 16 (December 1893): 133–40.

23. Octave Thanet, "The Trans-Mississippi Exposition," *Cosmopolitan* 25 (October 1898): 599–614. The *Century* published a number of articles on the exposition including Albert Shaw's "The Trans-Mississippian and Their Fair at Omaha," *Century* 56 (September 1898): 836–52.

24. See Moses P. Handy (U.S. Commissioner to the Paris Exposition), "The Paris Exposition of 1900," *Munsey's* 20 (October 1898): 90–98; Captain A. H. Mattox (presidential representative of the U.S. Commission), "Sights of the Paris Fair," *Munsey's* 22 (February 1900): 784–91; Charles A. Towne, "Plans for the Paris World's Fair," *Cosmopolitan* 28 (January 1900): 149–61; F. A. Kidder, "First View of the Exposition of 1900," *Cosmopolitan* 29 (July 1900): 228; and William Stead, "The Paris Exposition," *Cosmopolitan* 29 (August 1900): 339–55. The *Century* carried a number of articles on the Paris Exposition including Baron Pierre de Coubertin, "Building Up a World's Fair in France," *Century* 57 (November 1898): 115–26; and Jean Schopfler, "Amusements of the Paris Exposition," *Century* 60 (August 1900): 483–95 (lead article).

25. While Walker devoted an entire issue to the St. Louis exposition, *McClure's* completely neglected it. The reason seemed to be that *McClure's* had already entered its muckraking phase (it led the way in this area). While *Cosmopolitan* devoted all its September 1904 issue to the fair, *McClure's* was printing, in its September issue, Louis Wigfall Wright's "Memoirs of the Beginning and End of the Southern Confederacy" (another account of a Civil War battle), serialized fiction by Francis Hodgson Burnett and George Madden Martin, a muckraking exposé by William Allen White, "Roosevelt and the Postal Frauds," and part two of Ida Tarbell's "History of Standard Oil" (to be discussed in chapter 7). The October issue of *McClure's* contained an installment of Lincoln Steffens's "Enemies of the Republic" (on corruption in the state of Wisconsin and La Follette's reform campaign).

26. Robert Grant, "Notes on the Pan-American Exhibition," *Cosmopolitan* 31 (September 1901): 451–60. Also see Julian Hawthorne, "Some Novelties at Buffalo Fair," *Cosmopolitan* 31 (September 1901): 484.

27. Howells, "Letters of an Alturian Traveller (Part 2)," 223.

28. Hawthorne, "Some Novelties at Buffalo Fair," 492.

29. William Dean Howells wrote a number of articles on American cities from the point of view of an "Alturian traveller." See Howells, "A Bit of Alturia in New York," *Cosmopolitan* 17 (January 1894): 260–77; "Letters of an Alturian Traveller: Aspects and Impressions of a Plutocratic City," *Cosmopolitan* 16 (February 1894): 415–25; and a discussion of the Columbian Exposition in Chicago in *Cosmopolitan* 16 (December 1893): 218–32. Murat Halstead, in a lead article, wrote about "The City of Brooklyn," *Cosmopolitan* 15 (June 1893): 131–44.

30. See Ray Stannard Baker, "The Modern Skyscraper," *Munsey's* 22 (October 1899): 48–58. The editor's introduction of the article reads, "The architectural revolution brought about by the American invention of the steel frame building—some interesting facts about the vast modern structures that overtip the pyramids." A few years earlier Ernest Flagg had worried about "The Dangers of High Buildings." This article complained about "the disfigurement of the streets," the "damage to adjoining property and the many dangers which buildings of such height engender," *Cosmopolitan* 21 (May 1896): 70.

31. A few examples of articles advocating greater urban planning, municipal ownership, and professionalism in local government are Hazen S. Pingree (governor of Michigan), "Municipal Ownership of Street Railways," *Munsey's* 22 (November 1899): 220–25; and Charles Edward Russell, "Socialistic Government of London," *Cosmopolitan* 40 (February 1906): 368. The former mayor of San Francisco wrote about the "Rise of the New San Francisco," *Cosmopolitan* 41 (October 1906): 575–84. A series of satirical articles with a social reform focus appeared in *Cosmopolitan* 42 (November 1906–April 1907): see James L. Ford, "Seeing the Real New York, from the Deck of the Rubberneck Coach." Also see Robert Harton's fictional series (based on Howells's work), "The Discovery of Alturia," *Cosmopolitan* 20 (November 1895–April 1896): 85–93, 219–24, 321–25, 437–41, 544–47. Harton constructed a middle-class utopia based on enlightened planning and the Social Gospel movement. Another futuristic piece inspired by Howells was Julian Hawthorne's "June 1993," *Cosmopolitan* 14 (February 1893): 450–58.

32. Howells, "Letters of an Alturian Traveller (Part 4)," *Cosmopolitan* 16 (February 1894): 415–25.

33. John Brisben Walker, "The Wonders of New York," *Cosmopolitan* 36 (December 1903): 143–60.

34. Rosalind H. Williams, *Dream Worlds: Mass Consumption in Late Nineteenth-Century France* (Berkeley: University of California Press, 1982), 70.

35. Much of the above information comes from Frank Luther Mott, *A History of American Magazines* 4:20–34. For an interesting discussion of magazine advertising in the 1890s and its relationship to magazine content, see Richard Ohmann, "Advertising and the New Discourse of Mass Culture," in Ohmann, *Politics of Letters,* 152–70.

36. See Theodore Peterson, *Magazines in the Twentieth Century,* 18–22.

37. Roland Marchland, *Advertising and the American Dream,* 9.

38. A. E. Dolbear, "An Electric Comparison," *Cosmopolitan* 15 (September 1893): 623.

39. John Brisben Walker, "Electricity Up to 1904," *Cosmopolitan* 37 (September 1904): 555–65.

40. Curtis Brown, "The Diversion of the Niagara," *Cosmopolitan* 17 (September 1894): 527–45.

41. A. E. Dolbear, "The Electrical Utilization of Niagara," *Cosmopolitan* 17 (May 1894): 125.

42. E. J. Edwards, "The Capture of Niagara," *McClure's* 3 (October 1894): 423–35.

43. Walter C. Hamm, "Great Engineering Projects," *Cosmopolitan* 28 (December 1899): 163–70.

44. Theodore Waters, "Guarding the Highways of the Sea," *McClure's* 13 (September 1899): 434–47.

45. Alexander O. Brodie, "Reclaiming of the Arid West," *Cosmopolitan* 37 (October 1904): 715–22.

46. Henry Muir, "The Making and Laying of an Atlantic Cable," *McClure's* 8 (January 1897): 255–62.

47. Cleveland Moffett, "Marconi's Wireless Telegraph," *McClure's* 13 (June 1899): 99–112.

48. Edward Hungerford, "The Great Catskill Aqueduct, New York's New Water Supply—A Tremendous Engineering Work Nearing Completion," *Munsey's* 49 (July 1913): 747–57.

49. Walter Wellman, "The Race for the North Pole," *McClure's* 14 (February 1900): 318–28.

50. Milton Ailes, "Adventure and Death in the Far North," *Cosmopolitan* 27 (May 1899): 25.

51. Vernon, "The Flying Man," *McClure's* 3 (September 1894): 323–31.

52. Jacques Boyer, "The Modern Aeronaut," *Cosmopolitan* 32 (November 1901).

53. John Brisben Walker, "The Final Conquest of the Air," *Cosmopolitan* 36 (March 1904): 501–16.

54. Augustine Post, "The Man-Bird and His Wings," *Cosmopolitan* 48 (May 1910): 683.

55. T. R. MacMechen and Carl Dienstbach, "The Wonderful Wizards of the Air," *Cosmopolitan* 50 (April 1911): 582–93.

56. W. D. Kelley, "The Intercontinental Railway," *Cosmopolitan* 15 (August 1893): 389–404.

57. Sydney H. Short, "The Coming Electric Railroad," *Cosmopolitan* 26 (1899): 269–76.

58. Cy Warmer, "A Thousand Mile Ride on the Engine of the Swiftest Train in the World; From New York to Chicago in the Cab of the Exposition Flyer," *McClure's* 2 (January 1894): 164–84.

59. H. G. Prout, "The Fastest Trains," *Munsey's* 22 (October 1899): 93–97, and (November 1899): 264–67.

60. William J. Lampton, *Cosmopolitan* 33 (June 1902): 123.

61. John Brisben Walker, *Cosmopolitan* 23 (1897): 339–40.

62. John Gilmer Speed, "The Modern Chariot," *Cosmopolitan* 29 (June 1900): 139–52.

63. Edwin Wildman, *Munsey's* 22 (February 1900): 704–12.

64. According to Miles Orvell, "In the nineteenth century, the machine was used predominately to create consumer objects that enthusiastically mimicked handcrafted things (furniture, household objects, clothing and accessories); in the twentieth century it was used increasingly to manufacture objects that were themselves machines" (see Orvell, *The Real Thing*, 142).

65. Ray Stannard Baker, *McClure's* 13 (July 1899): 195–208.

66. For a useful discussion of this subject as well as the more general point about the presentation of technology in the popular magazines, see Cecelia Tichi, *Shifting Gears; Technology, Literature, Culture in Modernist America.* Chapel Hill and London: University of North Carolina Press, 1987), 19–26.

67. "Out with a Moving-Picture Camera," *Cosmopolitan* 40 (January 1906).

68. Some articles that explicitly focused on photography in *Cosmopolitan* included Clarence Moore, "The Leading Amateurs in Photography," *Cosmopolitan* 12 (February 1892): 421; W. S. Hargood, "Amateur Photography of Today," *Cosmopolitan* 20 (December 1895): 249; Walter Devereaux Pinkus, "Photographic Story of a Boy's Trip to Europe," *Cosmopolitan* 22 (March 1897): 541; Robert Hughes, "Art in Portrait Photography," *Cosmopolitan* 26 (December 1898): 123; Richard Stearns, "Picture Photography," *Cosmopolitan* 32 (January 1902): 257; Mrs. Wilson Woodrow, "The Fascination of Being Photographed," *Cosmopolitan* 35 (October 1903): 675; Bailey Millard, "In the Darkroom," *Cosmopolitan* 40 (December 1905): 171–78; Arthur Hoeber, "The Triumph of the Camera," *Cosmopolitan* 47 (June 1909): 3.

69. Some examples from *Munsey's* between October 1894 and March 1896 included Richard H. Titherington, "The British Peerage," *Munsey's* 11 (p. 128), and "The English Dukes and Duchesses," *Munsey's* 11 (p. 15); Margaret Field "A Future Emperor and Empress," *Munsey's* 11 (p. 629); Arthur Hornblow, "Contemporary French Novelists," *Munsey's* 12 (p. 483); Henry W. Fischer, "The Kaiser and His Family," *Munsey's* 12 (p. 45); Fischer, "The Kaiser as Sportsman," *Munsey's* 13 (p. 637); "The Prince of Whales and His Set" (by "Ex-Diplomat"), *Munsey's* 13 (p. 164); Fischer, "The Summer Homes of Royalty," *Munsey's* 13 (p. 406); Fischer, "The Royal Family of Sweden," *Munsey's* 14 (p. 202); George Holme, "Some Unhappy Queens," *Munsey's* 14 (p. 164).

70. In addition to "The Brotherhood of Strenuosity," *Cosmopolitan* 32 (March 1902): 569, there were many other articles on the German monarch. Other examples were "The Emperor William in the Holy Land," *Cosmopolitan* 26 (February 1899): 363, and John Brisben Walker, "A Clever Emperor and a Confederation of Nations," *Cosmopolitan* 32 (April 1902); C. Frank Dewey, "The German Emperor," *Cosmopolitan* 25 (July 1898): 235–54 (lead article), and Dewey, "Francis Joseph—The Beloved Monarch," *Cosmopolitan* 25 (August 1898): 377–84.

71. See "Dying Words of Autocracy: Written by the Chief Upholder of the Iron Hand in Russia and Answered by a Plain American," *Cosmopolitan* 40 (February 1906): 407. A year before the 1905 war between Japan and Russia, Walker in a lead article expressed alarm over the expansion of Russia into Asia and asserted that a possible war between Japan and Russia might lead to a "great war." See John Brisben Walker, "The Conquest of Asia by Russia," *Cosmopolitan* 36 (February 1904): 381–86. A few months later Walker authored another opening piece, "If Europe Should Go to War," *Cosmopolitan* 36 (April 1904).

72. Charles Edward Russell, "Germanizing the World," *Cosmopolitan* 40 (January 1906): 274–82.

73. See Williams, *Dream Worlds,* 19–57.

74. Stead, "The Paris Exposition," 339.

75. Towne, "Plans for the Paris World's Fair," 153.

76. Alexander Harvey, "By Trolley to the Sphinx," *Cosmopolitan* 27 (August 1899): 339–49.

77. Saunders Norvell, "A Nineteenth Century Daughter of Pharaoh," *Cosmopolitan* 27 (November 1899): 114–24.

78. Alexander Harvey, "Some Types of Egyptian Women," *Cosmopolitan* 27 (January 1900): 276–82.

79. Alice Nielsen, "Geisha Girls," *Cosmopolitan* 26 (December 1898): 145.

80. George Francis Bird, "Fan-Fan," *Cosmopolitan* 32 (January 1902).

81. Theodore Wore, "The Wistaria Shrine of Kameido," *Cosmopolitan* 25 (May 1898): 15–22.

82. Laura B. Starr, "Through Oriental Doorways," *Cosmopolitan* 22 (November 1896): 21–28.

83. General Edward Forester, "Personal Recollections of the Tai-Ping Rebellion," *Cosmopolitan* 22 (November 1896): 34–38.

84. Ednah Aiken, "The Cross and the Dragon," *Cosmopolitan* 41 (October 1906): 611.

85. Gertrude Bailey Tredick, "An Arab Fete in the Desert," *Cosmopolitan* 22 (April 1897): 587–98.

86. John Brisben Walker, *Cosmopolitan* 27 (May 1899): 59–70. Walker's interest in empire building was also illustrated in a multipart series called "The Dramatic History of South America." The first installment described Pizarro's conquest of the Peruvian empire. These articles were in volumes 35 and 36 (1903–1904).

87. Vance Thompson, "The Fate of the Brown Empire," *Cosmopolitan* 40 (November 1905): 79–86.

88. Lawrence Harris, "Morocco—A New El Dorado for American Enterprise," *Cosmopolitan* 49 (June 1910): 3.

89. William R. Draper, "The Last of the Red Race," *Cosmopolitan* 32 (December 1901): 244–46.

90. Lewis Lindsay Dyche, "Walrus Hunting in the Arctic Regions," *Cosmopolitan* 20 (February 1896): 347–59.

91. Lewis Lindsay Dyche, "The Curious Race of Arctic Highlanders," *Cosmopolitan* 21 (July 1896): 228–37.

92. William Crocker Duxbury, "A Legend of the Navajos," *Cosmopolitan* 22 (November 1896): 73–79.

93. Major Edmund G. Fechet, "The True Story of the Death of Sitting Bull," *Cosmopolitan* 20 (March 1896): 493–501.

94. Mrs. D. B. Dyer, "Some Types in Dixieland," *Cosmopolitan* 22 (January 1897): 235–46. It should be noted that this particular article was a somewhat extreme expression of the range of popular magazine depictions of African-Americans. Reflecting the more progres-

sive stance of many reformers, Mrs. Van Rensselier Cruger (who occasionally used the pseudonym Julian Gordon) compared the struggle of African-Americans to the struggle of women for the right to vote and of subjugated nations for independence. See Mrs. Van Rensselier Cruger, *Cosmopolitan* 36 (February 1904): 464–65. Ray Stannard Baker's muckraking articles on racial bigotry in the South made a significant contribution to raising national consciousness about this issue. He wrote a number of articles for *McClure's* and later with *American* in 1906, he wrote "Following the Color Line." This explored the causes of the 1906 race riot in Atlanta. *McClure's* published Carl Schurz's "Can the South Solve the Negro Problem," in January 1904.

95. Theodore P. Greene, *America's Heroes,* 98.

96. One example of the numerous *Cosmopolitan* articles on Napoleon was the series called "Autobiography of Napoleon." Walker explained, in some detail, why he believed the manuscript was authentic, although he left room for contrary claims. See John Brisben Walker, "The Autobiography of Napoleon: The Story of a Manuscript," *Cosmopolitan* 25 (August 1898): 440–47. The series ran throughout this volume (pp. 83–88, 143–48, 325–30, 440–47).

97. *Cosmopolitan* 33 (May 1902): 33.

98. The individuals covered in this series included many of the leading industrialists, financiers, and inventors of the period. Some examples are John Pierpont Morgan, Thomas Alva Edison, John Wanamaker, Charles Cramp, John William MacKay, Alexander Graham Bell, James Gordon Bennett, William Randolph Hearst, Joseph Pulitzer, Albert Augustus Pope: *Cosmopolitan* 33, Part 1 (May 1902): 33–55; Marcus Alonzo Hanna, Claus Spreckels, John Davison Rockefeller, James Ben Ali Haggin: *Cosmopolitan* 33, Part 2 (June 1902): 153–65; Charles Michael Schwab, Darus Ogden Mills, Charles Frohman, Andrew Carnegie, John Augustine McCall: *Cosmopolitan* 33, Part 3 (July 1903): 284; Gustavus Franklin Swift, Clement Acton Griscom, George Jay Gould: *Cosmopolitan* 35, Part 13, (May 1903): 55–61; Norton Goddard, Francis Hector Clergue: *Cosmopolitan* 36, Part 20, (December 1903): 176; William Ellis Corey, George Cadbury: *Cosmopolitan* 36, Part 22, (March 1904): 479–87; William Kissam Vanderbilt, Peter Cooper Hewitt: *Cosmopolitan* 36, Part 23, (March 1904): 553–58.

99. *Cosmopolitan* 33 (May 1902): 43.

100. *Cosmopolitan* 33 (June 1902): 160.

101. *Cosmopolitan* 33 (May 1902): 48.

102. *Cosmopolitan* 33 (May 1902): 33.

103. *Cosmopolitan* 33 (June 1902): 153.

104. *Cosmopolitan* 33 (May 1902): 41.

105. *Cosmopolitan* 36 (March 1904): 479.

106. See John G. Cawelti, *Apostles of the Self-Made Man: Changing Concepts of Success in America* (Chicago: University of Chicago Press, 1965); and Irvin G. Wyllie, *The Self-Made Man in America* (New Brunswick, N.J.: Rutgers University Press, 1954).

107. *Cosmopolitan* 33 (May 1902): 46–47.

108. John Brisben Walker, "Dreamers in the Business World," *Cosmopolitan* 29 (May 1900): 107–108.

109. See David Noble, *America by Design: Science, Technology and the Rise of Corporate Capitalism* (Oxford: Oxford University Press, 1977), 8–9; and Larry May, *Screening Out the Past*, 23–24.

110. Theodore Dreiser, "The Chicago Packing Industry," *Cosmopolitan* 25 (October 1908): 615–26.

111. See Gilder's editorial called "The Civic Revival," *Century* 50 (July 1895). This editorial discussed the interest in religious reform as part of a "religious awakening."

112. Talcott Williams, "The Kindergarten Movement," "Kindergarten Not a Fad" (editorial), W. T. Harris, "The Kindergarten in a Nutshell," Angeline Brooks, "The Possibilities of the Kindergarten," Mary Katherine Young, "The Philanthropic Side of Kindergarten Work," Alice H. Putnam, "The Kindergarten Movement in Chicago," and Carrie P. Farnsworth, "The Kindergarten in Turkey." All appeared in the *Century*, vol. 45 (November 1892–April 1893).

113. Other articles on urban reform published during the 1890s include George E. Parker, "An Object Lesson in Municipal Government: Showing How Public Affairs Are Conducted in the City of Birmingham," *Century* 53 (November 1896): 71–89; Albert Shaw, "The Government of German Cities: The Municipal Framework," *Century* 48 (June 1894): 296–305; "Stamping Out the London Slums: By the Secretary of the New York Tenement-House Commission," *Century* 51 (March 1896): 700–706; Richard Ely, "Fraternalism and Paternalism in Government," *Century* 55 (March 1898): 780–788; Theodore Roosevelt, "Civic Helpfulness," *Century* 60 (October 1900): 939–44.

114. A number of articles by Jacob Riis were printed by Gilder's *Century*. See "Merry Christmas in the Tenements," *Century* 55 (December 1897): 163–82 (lead article).

115. W. D. Howells, "Who Are Our Brethren?" *Century* 51 (April 1896): 932–35. Other articles written by Howells during this period include "Equality the Basis for a Good Society," *Century* 29 (November 1895): 63–67, and "Are We a Plutocracy?" *North American Review* 158 (1894): 185–96. In terms of his literary criticism Howells's most famous work was published in his "Editor's Study" series in *Harper's Monthly*, starting in January 1886 up to 1891 in which he became the leading advocate of realism in fiction. Between 1894 and 1896 Howells was also active in the populist movement.

116. Fred Woodrow, "Plain Words to Working Men by One of Them," *Century* 45 (November 1892): 134.

117. Archibald Forbes, "What I Saw of the Paris Commune," *Century* 45 (November 1892): 48–60; and C. W. T., "What an American Girl Saw of the Commune," *Century* 45 (November 1892): 61. Also see Judge Joseph Gary's defense of the Haymarket trial (he was the presiding judge), "The Chicago Anarchists of 1886: The Crime, the Trial and the Punishment," *Century* 45 (April 1893): 803–37.

118. Henry Cabot Lodge, "The Census and Immigration," *Century* 46 (September 1893): 737–39.

119. Washington Gladden, "The Anti-Catholic Crusade," *Century* 47 (March 1894): 789–95.

120. "The Story of the Captains" (May 1899).

121. For example, John Muir, "The Alaska Trip," *Century* 54 (August 1897): 513–26. Also see Henry Fairfield Osborn, "A Great Naturalist: Edward Drinker Cope," *Century* 55 (November 1897): 10–15.

122. Some examples of the *Century*'s articles on science, technology, and exploration include Frederic Courtland Penfield, "Harnessing the Nile," *Century* 57 (February 1899): 483–92; Walter Wellman, "On the Way to the North Pole; The Wellman Polar Expedition," *Century* 57 (February 1899): 531–37; John R. Porter (geologist), "The Mammoth Cave of Kentucky," *Century* 55 (March 1898): 643–58 (lead article); and E. L. Snell, "Dr. Morton's Discovery of Anesthesia," *Century* 48 (August 1894): 584–91.

123. Warren Susman discussed the widespread use of the word *dream* in the late nineteenth century in *Culture as History: The Transformation of American Society in the Twentieth Century* (New York: Pantheon, 1973), xxvi–xxvii.

124. *Cosmopolitan* 38 (March 1905): 603–608.

125. On Lester Ward and the new sociology see Thomas Haskell, *The Emergence of Professional Social Science* (Urbana: University of Illinois Press, 1977), introduction, and Richard Hofstadter, *Social Darwinism in American Thought* (Boston: Beacon Press, 1944), 156–61.

126. Anne O'Hagan, *Munsey's* 22 (January 1900): 528–37.

127. See Richard Schneirov, *Graft for Power,* chap. 12.

128. David Burnham, planner of the White City, was the founder of the "city beautiful" movement based on his proposal of an ideal city. On the "new town" movement see Ebenezer Howard, *Garden Cities of To-morrow* (Cambridge: MIT Press, 1965 [1898]).

7. *Muckraking, Realism, and the Dream of Social Justice*

1. The name *muckraker* came from a speech given by Roosevelt on April 14, 1906, at the Gridiron Club in Washington, D.C. Roosevelt was close to the *McClure's* group, especially Lincoln Steffens (for a period), Ray Stannard Baker, and William Allen White. But he thought that David Graham Phillips went too far in the Hearst *Cosmopolitan* "Treason of the Senate" series. Steffens was upset by the speech and told the President the next day, "Well Mr. President, you have put an end to all these journalistic investigations that have made you." Roosevelt responded by saying that halting all muckraking was not his intention and that he wasn't referring to Steffens but to David Graham Phillips for his series. See Arthur and Lila Weinberg, eds., *The Muckrakers* (New York: G. P. Putnam's, 1964), 56–65. The quote from Steffens is in his *Autobiography*, 581.

2. Louis Filler, *Crusaders for American Liberalism,* 357–58.

3. For a discussion of the "agenda setting" function of urban newspapers in the 1890s in

contributing to urban reform movements, as well as the contribution of these newspapers to the "new politics," see David Paul Nord, *Newspapers and the New Politics: Midwestern Municipal Reform, 1890–1900* (Ann Arbor, Mich.: UMI Research Press, 1981).

4. Richard L. McCormick argues that "Progressivism's national reach and mass base vastly exceeded that of Jacksonian reform several generations before. And its dependence on the people for its shape and timing has no comparison in the later executive-dominated New Deal and Great Society. Wars and depressions had previously engaged the whole nation, but never reform." See Richard L. McCormick, "Progressivism: A Contemporary Reassessment," in *The Party Period and Public Policy,* 272.

5. An examination of issues of *Munsey's* from 1903 to 1907 shows a continuation of the earlier emphasis on the glamour of urban life, royalty, new scientific and technological developments, biographies, further commentaries on the Philippines and other military issues, sports, short fiction, and departments on "the stage" and current events as well as editorial comments by Munsey. One of the few articles that even acknowledged the reform movement in the country was Herbert N. Casson's "The Wave of Reform," *Munsey's* 34 (October 1905): 17–46. The month that *Cosmopolitan* ran the "Treason of the Senate" series saw *Munsey's* lead with Anne O'Hagan's "The Treasures of Feenway Court" on "the wonderful Venetian palace that Mrs. Gardner, of Boston has built" *Munsey's* 34 (March 1906): 2.

6. The reason for choosing the 1903 date as the beginning of the muckraking period is that this was the year of *McClure's* decisive turn to the "literature of exposure." Shortly after 1903 *McClure's* became known for these features. The important date is January 1903 when S. S. McClure wrote about the "pattern of lawlessness" identified in the muckraking work of Steffens, Tarbell, and Baker.

I am using the term *muckraking* in the specific sense of a genre of journalism, developed systematically during the first decade of the twentieth century, that focused on the "widespread corruption of society by the forces of wealth." While reform-oriented journalism existed previous to 1903, what made the 1903–1910 period significant is that these reform journalists developed a coherent social philosophy, saw themselves as part of a common social and intellectual movement, and were eventually thought of by others as representatives of a distinct political perspective and style of writing. In addition, the muckrakers were part of a larger social movement. Such a phenomenon did not exist in the 1890s or earlier. While muckraking has become a permanent feature of modern journalism, this is when it all began. Overall, according to David Mark Chalmers in *The Social and Political Ideas of the Muckrakers* (New York: Citadel, 1964), 15–20, more than two thousand magazine muckraking articles were written during this period. Close to a third of them were written by a small group of twelve journalists: Samuel Hopkins Adams, Ray Stannard Baker, Christopher P. Connolly, Burton J. Hendrick, Will Irwin, Thomas W. Lawson, Alfred Henry Lewis, David Graham Phillips, Charles Edward Russell, Upton Sinclair, Lincoln Steffens, Ida Tarbell, and George Kibbe Turner.

7. The first part of Baker's eight-part series, "The Right to Work," appeared in the famous January 1903 issue of *McClure's* along with the second installment of Steffens's "Shame of the Cities" and the second part of Tarbell's "History of Standard Oil."

8. See Harold S. Wilson, *McClure's Magazine and the Muckrakers,* 253–83, and Justin Kaplan, *Lincoln Steffens,* 165.

9. Some of Russell's contributions included a four-part series comparing the caste system in various countries with the conspicuous consumption of the rich in America. The series ran throughout vol. 42 (November 1906–April 1906). See the first article in the series, "The Growth of Caste in America," *Cosmopolitan* 42 (March 1907): 524–34. Also see Russell, "Socialist Government of London" (opening article), *Cosmopolitan* 40 (February 1906), and Russell's multipart biography of Charlemagne that appeared throughout 1910 (vol. 48). Russell also wrote one of the last of the muckraking series to appear in the *Cosmopolitan.* The series, "What Are You Going to Do About It?" appeared in the 1910 *Cosmopolitan* and exposed corruption in state legislatures.

10. Filler, *Crusaders for American Liberalism,* 115; and W. A. Swanberg, *Citizen Hearst,* 229. A valuable sketch of the socialist perspectives of Upton Sinclair and Charles Edward Russell can be found in Chalmers, *The Social and Political Ideas of the Muckrakers,* 88–103.

11. "The Day of Discontent: First of the Series of Cosmopolitan Table-Talks in Which Vital Problems Are Discussed in a Vital Way" (opening article), *Cosmopolitan* 40 (March 1906).

12. *Cosmopolitan* published an article by Robert Hunter in which he described working conditions, many of which were said to be "injurious to health," for the five million American women wage earners. See Robert Hunter, "Burdens Borne by Women," *Cosmopolitan* 40 (December 1905): 155.

13. Bierce was one of the nation's leading journalists when Hearst took over his father's newspaper, the *San Francisco Examiner.* Before his employment with Hearst, he was the author of a very popular column for the San Francisco newspaper the *Argonaut* called "Prattle: A Transient Record of Individual Opinion." For the Hearst papers Bierce's column was called "The Passing Show: A Record of Personal Opinion and Dissent." He was a regular contributor to the *Cosmopolitan* from 1905 to 1909. See Lawrence I. Berkove, "The Man with the Burning Pen: Ambrose Bierce as Journalist," *Journal of Popular Culture* 15 (Fall 1981): 34–40.

14. "The Social Unrest," *Cosmopolitan* 41 (July 1906): 297–302.

15. A discussion of George Horace Lorimer's *Saturday Evening Post* during this period can be found in Jan Cohn, *Creating America,* 21–99, and Theodore P. Greene, *America's Heroes,* 177–219. Both Greene and Cohn argue that the *Post* was not a "muckraking" magazine although it did reflect the social reform spirit of this period in some ways, publishing the work of David Graham Phillips (author of *Cosmopolitan*'s "Treason of the Senate" series) and the work of Republican reform senator Albert J. Beveridge.

16. Mott, *A History of American Magazines* 4:457–62.

17. Filler, *Crusaders for American Liberalism,* 85; and Wilson, *McClure's Magazine and the Muckrakers,* 168–89.

18. Filler, *Crusaders for American Liberalism,* 271–72.

19. Salme Harju Steinberg, *Reformer in the Marketplace,* 97–106. In 1905 the issue of the dangers of unregulated medicines and dangerous preservatives in food were taken up with far more effectiveness by *Collier's.* See Samuel Hopkins Adams, "The Great American Fraud," *Collier's* (October 28, 1905).

20. Jane Addams, *Democracy and Social Ethics* (Cambridge and London: Belknap Press of Harvard University Press, 1964 [1907]), 139 and 178.

21. See Filler, *Crusaders for American Liberalism,* 260–74.

22. Bailey Millard, "Lackeys Out of Livery," *Cosmopolitan* 40 (January 1906): 364.

23. Bailey Millard, "When Alturia Awoke," *Cosmopolitan* 41 (June 1906): 237.

24. Filler, *Crusaders for American Liberalism,* 57–58.

25. Huntington, quoted in Swanberg, *Citizen Hearst,* 209.

26. *McClure's* 13 (May 1899): 15–16.

27. Edwin Markham, "What Life Means to Me," *Cosmopolitan* 41 (June 1906): 186.

28. Bailey Millard, "What Life Means to Me," *Cosmopolitan* 41 (September 1906): 512–16.

29. Upton Sinclair, "What Life Means to Me," *Cosmopolitan* 41 (October 1906): 591–95.

30. Jack London, "What Life Means to Me," *Cosmopolitan* 40 (March 1906): 526–29. *Cosmopolitan*'s "Shop Talk" department commented on the large order of reprints requested for London's contribution to this series; see *Cosmopolitan* 41 (September 1906): 560.

31. Jack London, "What Life Means To Me," p. 528.

32. Steffens, in his *Autobiography,* 359; and William Allan White, *Autobiography,* 148–58. Ray Stannard Baker had a series of mystical experiences in which he felt in the presence of God. This divine presence became personified in the form of another personality, a "religiously oriented alter ego" whom Baker called David Grayson. Baker wrote a series of articles under this name as well as a number of novels. Baker believed that it was this other personality doing the writing. See Wilson, *McClure's Magazine and the Muckrakers,* 300–301.

33. Steffens, *Autobiography,* 358.

34. Steffens, *Autobiography,* 169–291.

35. Kaplan, *Lincoln Steffens,* 58–59.

36. Steffens, *Autobiography,* 364.

37. Steffens, *Autobiography,* 368. The reformer Frederick Howe (who wrote the article for *Cosmopolitan* on the St. Louis World's Fair discussed in chapter 6, note 13, and who was one of the founders of the Progressive party in 1912) had written a complimentary article on Joseph W. Folk a number of years before the Steffens series. See Frederick Howe, "Men of Honor and Stamina Who Make the Real Successes in Life—Joseph W. Folk," *Cosmopolitan* 25 (April 1899): 619–24.

38. See McCormick, "The Discovery That Business Corrupts Politics: A Reappraisal of the Origins of Progressivism," in *The Party Period and Public Policy,* 311–56.

39. In his autobiography Steffens supplied a sketch of the corrupt invisible government of American cities, which showed the connections between the "political boss," "business boss," and the "vice and crime" sectors (*Autobiography,* 596).

40. Lincoln Steffens, *The Shame of the Cities* (New York: Sagamore Press, 1957), 2. Steffens's book, which was a collection of all the original *McClure's* articles without revision, was first published in 1904 by McClure, Phillips.

41. Steffens, *The Shame of the Cities,* 9.

42. Kaplan, *Lincoln Steffens,* 132–39.

43. An interesting discussion of Steffens's implicit theory of urban corruption can be found in Patrick E. Palermo, *Lincoln Steffens,* 37–70.

44. Steffens, *The Shame of the Cities,* 10–11.

45. Steffens, *The Shame of the Cities,* 74. The St. Louis "boodling system" was described by Steffens in the second article on St. Louis, which focused on the business rather than the political side of the process. This article, "The Shamelessness of St. Louis," appeared in *McClure's* 20 (March 1903).

46. Steffens, *The Shame of the Cities,* 42–68. The article originally appeared as, "The Shame of Minneapolis" in the famous *McClure's* 20 (January 1903) issue.

47. See Steffens, *Autobiography,* 247, on the Lexow investigations. Steffens discusses "The Shame of Minneapolis" article on 374–84.

48. Steffens, *Autobiography,* 379.

49. See Steffens, *Autobiography,* 402–406, on Steffens's anxiety about being on his own in Pittsburgh and his discovery of two sources of inside information.

50. Steffens, *The Shame of the Cities,* 101. The original article, "Pittsburgh: A City Ashamed," appeared in *McClure's* 20 (May 1903).

51. Steffens, *Autobiography,* 416. Steffens explained how "reformers, business men, politicians, teachers and professors, newspaper men with tips, and ordinary citizens with grievances" sought him out in his hotel room in Philadelphia.

52. Steffens, *Autobiography,* 407–15. The Durham interview is discussed on 411–15. Also see the following chapter, "The Dying Boss" (416–21). The full account of Steffens's remarkable relationship with Durham (who Steffens discovered had a fatal disease) was published as fiction in Steffens, *The Dying Boss.* The novel was serialized in *McClure's* beginning in May 1914.

53. Steffens, *The Shame of the Cities,* 134–61. The article on Philadelphia ("Philadelphia: Corrupt and Contented") originally appeared in *McClure's* 21 (July 1903).

54. After Philadelphia Steffens wanted to go to Boston, but S. S. McClure had other ideas. He sent Steffens to Chicago in order to end the series on an upbeat note with an article on the reform movement there. See Kaplan, *Lincoln Steffens,* 125.

55. Steffens, *Autobiography,* 422–29.

56. A useful summary of nineteenth century Chicago newspapers can be found in Willis J. Abbot, "Chicago and Their Makers," *Review of Reviews* 11 (June 1895): 646–665.

57. In addition to the two factors that Steffens believed accounted for the success of the

Chicago reformers—the help of the newspapers and the reformers' willingness to use machine methods for reform ends—recent historical research has shown that elements of the increasingly organized and politically active Chicago working class supported the reform movement. In a forthcoming issue of *International Labor and Working Class History*, Richard Schneirov demonstrates that "workers in the less tightly organized and less powerful trades and industries, workers from immigrant groups not well situated in party politics, especially recent German immigrants, and workers imbued with causes that required state action—particularly socialists and single taxers" were the ones likely to support the Chicago reform movement. These were the groups that formed the Chicago Federation of Labor in 1895. See Richard Schneirov, "The Rise of Labor and the Transformation of Urban Politics in Late Nineteenth-Century Chicago," *International Labor and Working Class History* 46 (Fall 1994).

58. Steffens, *The Shame of the Cities*. 162–94. The discussion of Fischer as a "reform boss" is on p. 184. The original article, "Half Free and Fighting On," appeared in *McClure's* 21 (October 1903).

59. Nord, *Newspapers and the New Politics*, 5–19.

60. Thelen, *The New Citizenship*, 55–85.

61. Steffens, *The Shame of the Cities*, 12.

62. Steffens, *Autobiography*, 407.

63. See Thomas Haskell, *The Emergence of Professional Social Science*, chap. 1.

64. Steffens, *Autobiography*, 419.

65. Steffens, *Autobiography*, 417.

66. In a *McClure's* editorial William Allen White argued that the value of Steffens's work was that for the first time Americans learned about the "real government" of American cities, not the ones described in "classes in civil government." White argued that Steffens's series "has made an important step in the scientific study of city government," that "it merely presented the facts without trying to form a theory about them." He claimed that "the book has done for American cities what De Tocqueville did for the country a hundred years ago." The following three pages consisted of enthusiastic letters sent to *McClure's* from public officials, educators, ministers, and "our readers." See *McClure's* 23 (June 1904): 220–24.

67. Ida Tarbell discussed the writing of this book in her autobiography, *All in a Day's Work* (New York: Macmillan, 1939).

68. S. S. McClure, *My Autobiography*, 237.

69. Ida Tarbell, *The History of Standard Oil*, 2 vols. (New York: Macmillan, November 1904; rpt., New York: Peter Smith, 1950: two volumes in one).

70. See Wilson, *McClure's Magazine and the Muckrakers*, 140–41; and Filler, *Crusaders for American Liberalism*, 106–107.

71. Tarbell, *The History of Standard Oil* 1:34. The first chapter of the book originally appeared as the first installment of the series in *McClure's* 20 (November 1902).

72. Tarbell, *The History of Standard Oil* 1:37.

73. Tarbell, *The History of Standard Oil* 2:31–62 (chap. 10).

74. Tarbell, *The History of Standard Oil* 2:111–28 (chap. 13).

75. Tarbell, *The History of Standard Oil* 2:231–55.

76. Tarbell, *The History of Standard Oil* 2:253–54.

77. Tarbell, *The History of Standard Oil* 2:285, 287.

78. This last quote is from an essay by Elbert Hubbard in 1910 in *The Standard Oil Co.* (East Aurora, N.Y.: Roycroft Shop, 1910).The essay was a hymn of praise for Standard Oil (Hubbard had come along way from his early prosocialist leanings).

79. Steffens interviewed Hearst for a lead article in the *American* (after the split with *McClure's*) that appeared in November 1906. The article was largely sympathetic. Upton Sinclair's comment on Hearst as the first socialist president appeared in his *The Industrial Republic* (1907). Steffens also discussed his view of Hearst in his *Autobiography*, 539–40.

80. While bringing in new editors and writers, Hearst was wise enough to keep many of Walker's most popular contributors, including Ella Wilcox and Elbert Hubbard.

81. Filler, *Crusaders for American Liberalism*, 133.

82. Charles Edward Russell, perhaps the most prolific of all muckrakers, exposed the beef trust in "The Greatest Trust in the World," which ran early in 1905 in *Everybody's*. Of course, Upton Sinclair's *The Jungle* (1906), originally serialized in the socialist newspaper *Appeal to Reason*, helped to create a national movement for pure-food laws. For a discussion of Hearst's campaign against the beef trust see Filler, *Crusaders for American Liberalism*, 136.

83. On Hearst's political career see Swanberg, *Citizen Hearst*, 205–340.

84. Steffens's "Enemies of the Republic" article on Wisconsin told the story of corruption on the state level and Robert M. La Follette's reform movement. See Steffens, "Enemies of the Republic: Wisconsin: A State Where the People Have Restored Representative Government—The Story of Governor La Follette," *McClure's* 23 (October 1904): 563.

85. Filler, *Crusaders for American Liberalism*, 245–59.

86. "The Treason of the Senate: An Editorial Foreward," *Cosmopolitan* 40 (February 1906): 477–80.

87. David Graham Phillips, "The Treason of the Senate (Part 1)," *Cosmopolitan* 40 (March 1906): 487–502.

88. Phillips, "The Treason of the Senate (Part 1)," 486 and 490–91 (Depew's residences).

89. Phillips, "The Treason of the Senate (Part 2)," *Cosmopolitan* 40 (April 1906): 628–45.

90. Phillips, "The Treason of the Senate (Part 2)," 632.

91. Phillips, "The Treason of the Senate (Part 3)," *Cosmopolitan* 41 (May 1906): 3–12.

92. Phillips, "The Treason of the Senate (Part 4)," *Cosmopolitan* 41 (June 1906): 123–32.

93. Phillips, "The Treason of the Senate (Part 5)," *Cosmopolitan* 41 (July 1906): 267–76.

94. Filler, *Crusaders for American Liberalism*, 250 and 253–54.

95. "Shop Talk," *Cosmopolitan* 40 (February 1906): 481–82.

96. "Shop Talk," *Cosmopolitan* 40 (March 1906): 598–602 (the quotes are on 598).

97. "Shop Talk," *Cosmopolitan* 40 (May 1906): 113–15.

98. "Careful Consideration of the 'Constructive' and 'Destructive' Policies of Modern Magazines," *Cosmopolitan* 40 (August 1906): 442–44.

99. *Hampton's,* under the editorship of Ben Hampton, was known for its exposés concerning children and its espousal of women's rights. *Hampton's* printed a series of articles by Rheta Dorr which were later published as *What Eight Million Women Want,* an account of the work of women's clubs and a passionate statement of the goals of the women's movement. In 1907 the *Saturday Evening Post* printed a series on child labor by Mrs. John Van Vorst, and *Woman's Home Companion* sponsored the Anti–Child Slavery League. See Filler, *Crusaders for American Liberalism,* 260–73.

100. "Shop Talk," *Cosmopolitan* 41 (October 1906): 677–78.

101. "Shop Talk," *Cosmopolitan* 42 (December 1906): 233–34.

102. "Shop Talk," *Cosmopolitan* 42 (January 1907): 349–50.

103. Edwin Markham, "The Hoe-Man in the Making: The Child at the Loom," *Cosmopolitan* 41 (September 1906): 480–87.

104. Markham, "The Hoe-Man in the Making: Child-Wrecking in the Glass-Factories," *Cosmopolitan* 41 (October 1906): 567–74.

105. Markham, "The Hoe-Man in the Making: Little Slaves of the Coal-Mines," *Cosmopolitan* 42 (November 1906): 21–22.

106. Markham, "The Hoe-Man in the Making: The Grind Behind the Holidays," *Cosmopolitan* 42 (December 1906): 143–50 (the quote is on p. 149).

107. Markham, "The Hoe-Man in the Making: The Blight of the Easter Lilies," *Cosmopolitan* 42 (April 1907): 667–73 (the quote is on p. 673).

108. Markham, "The Hoe-Man in the Making; The Sweat-Shop Inferno," *Cosmopolitan* 42 (January 1907): 327–33.

109. Markham "The Hoe-Man in the Making; The Smoke of Sacrifice," *Cosmopolitan* 42 (February 1907): 391–97. The account of his visit to the tobacco factory is on p. 397.

110. See Alfred Henry Lewis, "What Life Means to Me," *Cosmopolitan* 42 (January 1907): 293–98. Also see Chalmers, *The Social and Political Ideas of the Muckrakers,* 33–41.

111. Filler, *Crusaders for American Liberalism,* 119–21.

112. Alfred Henry Lewis, "Owners of America (Part 1): Andrew Carnegie," *Cosmopolitan* 45 (June 1908): 3–16.

113. Alfred Henry Lewis, "Owners of America: J. Pierpont Morgan," *Cosmopolitan* 45 (August 1908): 250–62.

114. Alfred Henry Lewis, "Owners of America; John D. Rockefeller," *Cosmopolitan* 45 (November 1908): 610–21.

115. Filler, *Crusaders for American Liberalism,* 68–79.

116. Josiah Flynt, "The Pool-Room Vampire and Its Money-Mad Victims," *Cosmopolitan* 42 (February 1907): 359–71. The other four articles in the series were: "The Pool-Room Spider and the Gambling Fly," "The Men Behind the Pool-Rooms," "Allies of the Criminal

Pool-Rooms," and "Partners of the Criminal Pool-Rooms." The last two articles appeared in vol. 43 (May–October 1907). Flynt died on January 20, 1907, before the first article in the series was printed.

117. In addition to sketches of immigrant life, another important genre of literary realism was the detective story. *McClure's* helped to popularize the Sherlock Holmes stories of Arthur Conan Doyle. These stories were clearly centered around the mysteries of city life. Holmes, the scientist-detective, was able in each episode to unmask the false appearances of the increasingly opaque world of nineteenth-century urban life. In the process, he encountered many unusual urban types.

118. Jack London, "My Life in the Underground; A Reminiscence and a Confession," *Cosmopolitan* 43 (May 1907): 17–22.

119. Jack London, "My Life in the Underworld: 'Holding Her Down'," *Cosmopolitan* 43 (June 1907): 142–50.

120. Jack London, My Life in the Underworld: Pinched, a Prison Experience," *Cosmopolitan* 43 (July 1907): 263–70.

121. Jack London, "My Life in the Underground: Long Days in a County Penitentiary," *Cosmopolitan* 43 (August 1907): 374.

122. Jack London, "Pictures, Stray Memories of Life in the Underworld," *Cosmopolitan* 43 (September 1907): 513–18.

123. Three short stories by Lessing provide a good sample of his work: "The Parrot of Uncle Hurwitz," *Cosmopolitan* 41 (October 1906): 584; "A Priscilla of Hester Street," *Cosmopolitan* 42 (November 1906): 85–92; "The Waiter, a Lucky Stemming of the Tide of Fortune," *Cosmopolitan* 48 (May 1910): 706.

124. See Martin Sklar, *The Corporate Reconstruction of American Capitalism,* 334–63 (this section discusses Theodore Roosevelt's political views).

125. Martin J. Sklar, "Some Political and Cultural Consequences of the Disaccumulation of Capital: Origins of Postindustrial Development in the 1920's," in Sklar, *The United States as a Developing Country: Essays in U.S. History in the Progressive Era and the 1920's* (Cambridge: Cambridge University Press, 1992), 170–76.

126. Ray Stannard Baker, quoted in Wilson, *McClure's Magazine and the Muckrakers,* 285. For a discussion of some of Baker's beliefs see Chalmers, *The Social and Political Ideas of the Muckrakers,* 66–74.

127. Wilson, *McClure's and the Muckrakers,* 285.

8. *The Dream of a New Social Order*

1. Arthur John, *The Best Years of the Century,* 244.
2. "Ethics in the Heart," *Century* 71 (March 1906): 814–15.
3. "Two Views of the Situation," *Century* 72 (September 1906): 795–95.
4. "The Corruption of Public Opinion," *Century* 73 (January 1907): 480–81. Theodore

Roosevelt called Hearst "a sinister agitator" and "the most potent single force for evil we have in our life." See Justin Kaplan, *Lincoln Steffens,* 144.

5. Alice Katherine Fallows, "Fair Play for Wayward Children," *Century* 73 (December 1907): 253–63.

6. Andrew Carnegie, "My Experience with Railway Rates and Rebates," *Century* 75 (March 1908): 722–28.

7. Ray Stannard Baker, "Destiny and the Western Railroad," *Century* 75 (April 1908): 892.

8. Ray Morris, "Federal Rate Regulation," *Atlantic Monthly* 95 (June 1905): 737–47.

9. William Z. Ripley, "President Roosevelt's Railway Policy," *Atlantic Monthly* 96 (September 1905): 377–85.

10. Edward Alsworth Ross, "New Varieties of Sin," *Atlantic Monthly* 95 (May 1905): 594–98.

11. J. Laurence Loughlin, "Large Fortunes," *Atlantic Monthly* 96 (July 1905): 40–46.

12. George W. Alger, "The Literature of Exposure," *Atlantic Monthly* 96 (August 1905): 210–13. During the same year *Cosmopolitan* printed a number of "Shop Talk" editorials that may have been intended, at least in part, as a response to this article (see chapter 7). A vigorous defense of muckraking written by an English journalist appeared five years later in the pages of the respectable *Bookman:* C. M. Francis, "The Fighting Magazines," *Bookman* 31 (July 1910): 474–77.

13. Ellery Sedgwick III, "The American Genteel Tradition in the Early Twentieth Century," *American Studies* 25 (Spring 1984): 49–67.

14. Joan Shelly Rubin, *The Making of Middlebrow Culture* (Chapel Hill and London: University of North Carolina Press, 1992).

15. It seems justifiable to call this strand of thought "mugwump" since these more progressive thinkers came from social backgrounds quite similar to the other mugwump thinkers. Dorothy Ross described the founders of the American Economics Association as from New England families and from highly religious, evangelical homes. See Dorothy Ross, "Socialism and American Liberalism: Academic Social Thought in the 1880's," in *Perspectives in American History* 11 (1977–78): 16. For a similar discussion of the "younger social scientists of the 1880's" who "advocated ideas which would undergird progressivism," see David P. Thelen, "Social Tensions and the Origins of Progressivism," *Journal of American History* 56 (1969): 323–41 (quotes are from pp. 335, 337).

16. In a widely discussed article, Richard Ely criticized the paternalism of Pullman's industrial community. The article is a good summary of Ely's thinking and outlook during this period. See Ely, "Pullman: A Social Study," *Harper's Monthly* 70 (February 1885): 452–66.

17. Ross, "Socialism and American Liberalism," 13.

18. The consumer cooperative movement was a far more important development in France than in the United States during the turn of the century. An interesting discussion of

this movement and its intellectual leaders can be found in Rosalind H. Williams, *Dream Worlds,* 276–321.

19. "Shop Talk," *Cosmopolitan* 50 (January 1911): 289.

20. "Shop Talk," *Cosmopolitan* 53 (November 1912): 721.

21. For a discussion of London's contribution to *Cosmopolitan* see "Shop Talk," *Cosmopolitan* 50 (April 1911): 720.

22. Mott, *A History of American Magazines* 4:496.

23. Mott, *A History of American Magazines* 4:602–603.

24. Mott, *A History of American Magazines* 4:617.

25. A valuable series of essays on muckraking can be found in John M. Harrison and Harry H. Stein, eds., *Muckraking: Past, Present and Future* (University Park and London: Pennsylvania State University Press, 1973). An essay by Louis Filler, "The Muckrakers and Middle America" (25–41), explores the reasons for the appeal of muckraking during the turn of the century. John Cawelti examines the relationship between muckraking fiction and the contemporary bestseller in "Blockbusters and Muckraking: Some Reflections on Muckraking in the Contemporary Best Seller" (84–99). Carey McWilliams focuses on the waves of reform and reform journalism throughout the twentieth century in "The Continuing Tradition of Reform Journalism" (118–34). Jay Martin discusses the aesthetics of muckraking in "The Literature of Argument and the Arguments of Literature" (100–15).

26. Filler, *Crusaders for American Liberalism,* 365. The quote is originally from Margaret Connolly's biography of Orison Swett Marden, the editor of *Success* magazine. Filler relies heavily on Connolly's account of *Success*'s bankers curtailing loans to the magazine because of its muckraking. But it isn't clear what evidence Connolly has for this claim.

27. Harold Wilson in his study of *McClure's* briefly refers to Ray Stannard Baker's remark that muckraking magazines were undergoing a "Morganization" and Walter Lippman's claim that he had been told that there was a scheme by financiers to eliminate muckraking magazines. Wilson, though, does not evaluate the validity of these claims. See Wilson, *McClure's Magazine and the Muckrakers,* 320.

28. Theodore P. Greene, *America's Heroes,* 288–91.

29. Carey McWilliams in "The Continuing Tradition of Reform Journalism," 118–20, attributes the decline of muckraking to the merger of the Progressive movement with the Progressive party in 1912 as well as to World War I and the growing domination of magazines by national advertising.

30. In addition to this legislation, which established the basis for the American regulatory state in terms of the economy, other bills passed during the Wilson years expanded the state's role in foreign investment, in regulating aspects of social life, and in extending its distributive functions. The Adamson Act established the eight-hour day for railroad workers, the first child labor act was passed, new legislation established federal farmland banks, and there were new taxes on upper-income groups, estates, and corporations.

31. For an in-depth discussion of the debates leading up to the passage of the Interstate Commerce Commission Act in 1914, see Martin Sklar, *The Corporate Reconstruction of*

American Capitalism, 228–332. Harold Wilson discusses the evolving economic views of Baker, Tarbell, and William Allen White, in *McClure's Magazine and the Muckrakers,* 253–83. Baker, along with S. S. McClure and William Allen White, sided in 1912 with Roosevelt and his "New Nationalism," which saw the corporation as inevitable and sought a regulatory commission with strong powers of regulation that went well beyond publicity and oversight. Tarbell supported Wilson's "New Freedom," which also saw the corporation as inevitable but did not want to challenge the rights of property and the autonomy of the market as directly as Roosevelt. Steffens by this period had moved far to the left of his former colleagues and public opinion in advocating nationalization of most corporations.

32. Filler, *Crusaders for American Liberalism,* 374–75.

33. Sklar, *The Corporate Reconstruction of American Capitalism,* 1–40. On page 439, Sklar argues that there "was in the period 1890–1916 a widespread and highly charged sense of the emergence of a new era in American history among capitalists, politicians, and intellectuals—a sense of an evolutionary outcome that marked a distinct break with the past, comparable to that of the Revolutionary and Civil War eras."

34. George Lipsitz, *Time Passages: Collective Memory and American Popular Culture* (Minneapolis: University of Minnesota Press, 1990), 16–17.

35. Sigmund Freud, *The Interpretation of Dreams.* New York: Avon, 1965 [1900].

36. Henry Adams, *The Education of Henry Adams* (Boston: Houghton Mifflin, 1961 [1918]), 380.

37. Lincoln Steffens, *Autobiography,* 357.

38. S. S. McClure, quoted in Harold Wilson, *McClure's Magazine and the Muckrakers,* 285.

Appendix 6: Major Contributors to Walker's Cosmopolitan

1. Michael E. McGeer, *The Decline of Popular Politics,* 113.

2. Zangwill was an English novelist whose first work, *The Children of the Ghetto,* depicted life in the Jewish quarter of London. A biographical sketch in *Review of Reviews* praised Zangwill as "the Dickens of the ghetto," whose descriptions provided a "living photograph," and whose pictures "are wonderful in their fidelity." Zangwill wrote "The Turkish Messiah," a serialized novel published by *Cosmopolitan* about a Turkish Jew who declares himself the Messiah in 1648 (*Cosmopolitan* 23 [May 1897]: 40). Zangwill also wrote commentaries on literature for *Cosmopolitan* and was a contributor to *McClure's.* See "The Dickens of the Ghetto," *Review of Reviews* 12 (November 1895): 604–605.

3. The *Bookman* was a magazine of reviews and commentary with some fiction as well. According to Mott, "The early success of the *Bookman* was due mainly to the literary and editorial genius of Professor Peck." One of the *Bookman's* most famous features was a list of books "in the order of demand in various cities, a forerunner of best-seller lists" (Mott, *A History of American Magazines* 4:432).

4. Ella Wheeler Wilcox, "My Autobiography," *Cosmopolitan* 31 (August 1901): 414–20.

5. See the entry on Edward Bok in *Encyclopedia of American Biography,* 113.

6. Mott, *A History of American Magazines* 4:84, 98, 120, 537, and 765.

7. *Cosmopolitan* 32 (March 1902): 309.

8. In the June 1895 issue of *The Philistine,* Edward Bok, Richard Watson Gilder, and John Brisben Walker were attacked as part of a "Mutual Admiration Society" for reading "lucubrations of the contributors to the dreary masses of inanities they edit." While Elbert Hubbard did not write this passage, it does reflect the biting, though somewhat humorous attacks on the Eastern literary establishment that characterized this journal. Clearly, Walker not only did not take this personally but thought well enough of Hubbard to make him a regular contributor to *Cosmopolitan,* which he remained throughout the Hearst period as well. See Bruce A. White, *The Philistine: A Periodical of Protest (1895—1915): A Major American "Little Magazine"* (Lanham, Md.: University Press of America, 1989), 111.

9. *Cosmopolitan* 32 (January 1902): 316.

10. Some scholars consider Hubbard's essay a "showpiece" of inspirational literature and as the "gospel of the new order of things." See White, *The Philistine: A Periodical of Protest,* 128. White also characterized Hubbard as an "advertising pioneer."

BIBLIOGRAPHY

Adams, Brooks. *Law of Civilization and Decay* (1896). Rpt., New York: A. A. Knopf, 1943.

Adams, Henry. *The Education of Henry Adams* (1918). Rpt., Boston: Houghton Mifflin, 1961.

Addams, Jane. *Democracy and Social Ethics* (1907). Rpt., Cambridge and London: Belknap Press of Harvard University Press, 1964.

Adorno, Theodore. "Culture Industry Reconsidered." *New German Critique* 6 (Fall 1975): 12–19.

Altick, Richard D. *The English Common Reader: A Social History of the Mass Reading Public, 1800–1900.* Chicago: University of Chicago Press, 1957.

Baker, Ray Stannard. *American Chronicle: The Autobiography of Ray Stannard Baker.* New York: Scribner's, 1945.

Baldasty, Gerald J. *The Commercialization of News in the Nineteenth Century.* Madison: University of Wisconsin Press, 1992.

Barth, Gunther. *City People: The Rise of the Modern City.* New York: Oxford University Press, 1980.

Beard, George M. *American Nervousness: Its Causes and Consequences: A Supplement to Nervous Exhaustion.* New York: G. P. Putnam, 1881.

Bellamy, Edward. *Looking Backward* (1888). Rpt., New York: Modern Library, 1982.

Benjamin, Walter. "The Work of Art in the Age of Mechanical Reproduction." Reprinted in Benjamin, *Illuminations*, 217–51. New York: Schocken, 1968.

Bennett, Tony, ed. *Popular Fiction: Technology, Ideology, Production, Reading*. London and New York: Routledge, 1990.

Berkove, Lawrence I. "The Man with the Burning Pen: Ambrose Bierce as Journalist," *Journal of Popular Culture* 15 (Fall 1981): 34–40.

Berthoff, Warner. *The Ferment of Realism*. Cambridge: Cambridge University Press, 1965.

Bledstein, Burton J. *The Culture of Professionalism: The Middle Class and the Development of Higher Education in America*. New York: W. W. Norton, 1976.

Bok, Edward. *The Americanization of Edward Bok*. New York: Scribner, 1920.

Bourdieu, Pierre. *Distinction: A Social Critique of the Judgment of Taste*. Cambridge: Cambridge University Press, 1984.

Brady, Kathleen. *Ida Tarbell: Portrait of a Muckraker*. New York: Seaview-Putnam, 1984.

Braeman, John, Robert H. Bremner, and David Brody, eds., *Change and Continuity in Twentieth-Century America: The 1920's*. Columbus: Ohio State University Press, 1968.

Braude, Ann. *Radical Spirits: Spiritualism and Women's Rights in Nineteenth-Century America*. Boston: Beacon Press, 1989.

Britt, George. *Forty Years—Forty Millions: The Career of Frank A. Munsey* (1935). Rpt., New York: Kennikat Press, 1972.

Brooks, Van Wyck. "The Culture of Industrialism." *Seven Arts* (April 1917): 655–66.

Brown, Herbert Ross. *The Sentimental Novel in America, 1769–1860*. Durham, N.C.: Duke University Press, 1940).

Buenker, John D. "The Progressive Era: A Search for a Synthesis." *Mid-America* 51 (1969): 175–93.

Burke, Peter. "The Discovery of Popular Culture." Reprinted in Raphael Samuel, ed., *People's History and Socialist Theory*, 216–26.

Burnham, John. "The New Psychology: From Narcissism to Social Control." Reprinted in John Braeman, Robert H. Bremner, and David Brody, eds., *Continuity and Change in Twentieth-Century Culture: The 1920's*.

Burnham, Walter Dean. *Critical Elections and the Mainsprings of American Politics*. New York: W. W. Norton, 1970.

Canby, Henry Seidel. *The Age of Confidence: Life in the Nineties*. New York: Farrar and Rinehart, 1934.

Cawelti, John G. "America on Display: The World's Fairs of 1876, 1893, 1933." Reprinted in Frederic Cople Jaher, ed., *The Age of Industrialism in America: Essays in Social Structure and Cultural Values*, 317–46.

——. *Apostles of the Self-Made Man: Changing Concepts of Success in America*. Chicago: University of Chicago Press, 1965.

——. "Blockbusters and Muckraking: Some Reflections on Muckraking in the Contemporary Best Seller." Reprinted in John M. Harrison and Harry H. Stein, eds., *Muckraking: Past, Present and Future*, 84–99.

Chalmers, David Mark. *The Social and Political Ideas of the Muckrakers.* New York: Citadel, 1964.

Chandler, Alfred D. Jr. *The Visible Hand: The Managerial Revolution in American Business.* Cambridge: Harvard University Press, 1977.

Cohn, Jan. *Creating America: George Horace Lorimer and the Saturday Evening Post.* Pittsburgh: University of Pittsburgh Press, 1989.

Crane, Stephen. *Maggie: A Girl of the Streets: A Story of New York* (1893, 1896). Reprinted in Joseph Katz, ed., *The Portable Stephen Crane,* 3–75. Middlesex, Eng.: Penguin, 1969.

——. *The Red Badge of Courage* (1895). Rpt., New York: New American Classic, 1960.

Croly, Herbert. *The Promise of American Life* (1909). Rpt., New York: Dutton, 1963.

Curran, James, Michael Gurevitch, and Janet Woollacott. "The Study of the Media: Theoretical Approaches." Reprinted in Michael Gurevitch, Tony Bennett, James Curran, and Janet Woollacott, eds., *Culture, Society and the Media,* 11–29. London and New York: Methuen, 1982.

Curti, Merle. "Dime Novels and the American Tradition." Reprinted in Curti, *Probing Our Past.* New York: Harper, 1955.

Davis Allen F. *Spearheads for Reform: The Social Settlements and the Progressive Movement, 1890–1914.* New Brunswick, N.J.: Rutgers University Press, 1984.

Denning, Michael. "The End of Mass Culture." *International Labor and Working Class History* 37 (Spring 1990): 4–18.

——. *Mechanic Accents: Dime Novels and Working-Class Culture in America.* London and New York: Verso, 1987.

DiMaggio, Paul. "Cultural Entrepreneurship in Nineteenth-Century Boston: The Creation of an Organizational Base for High Culture in America." *Media, Culture and Society* 4 (1982): 33–50.

Douglas, Ann. *The Feminization of American Culture.* New York: Avon, 1977.

Dreiser, Theodore. *Sister Carrie* (1900). Rpt., Middlesex, Eng.: Penguin, 1981.

Eagleton, Terry. *Literary Theory: An Introduction.* Minneapolis: University of Minnesota Press, 1983.

Elias, Norbert. *The Civilizing Process: The History of Manners.* Translated by Edmund Jephcott. New York: Pantheon, 1978.

Emery, Michael C. *The Press in America: An Interpretive History of the Mass Media.* 7th ed. Englewood Cliff, N.J.: Prentice Hall, 1992.

Erenberg, Lewis A. *Steppin' Out: New York Nightlife and the Transformation of American Culture, 1890–1930.* Chicago and London: University of Chicago Press, 1981.

Ewen, Stuart. *Captains of Consciousness: Advertising and the Social Roots of Consumer Culture.* New York: McGraw-Hill, 1976.

Faler, Paul. "Cultural Aspects of the Industrial Revolution." *Labor History* 15 (Summer 1974): 367–94.

Filene, Peter. "An Obituary for the 'Progressive Movement.'" *American Quarterly* 22 (1970): 20–34.

Filler, Louis. *Crusaders for American Liberalism* (1939). Rpt., Yellow Springs, Ohio: Antioch Press, 1950.

——. "The Muckrakers and Middle America." Reprinted in John M. Harrison and Harry H. Stein, eds., *Muckraking: Past, Present and Future*, 25–41.

Finley, Ruth E. *The Lady of Godey's, Sarah Josepha Hale*. Philadelphia and London: J. B. Lippincott, 1931.

Firth, Simon. *Sound Effects: Youth, Leisure and the Politics of Rock 'n' Roll*. New York: Pantheon, 1981.

Fiske, John. *Television Culture*. London and New York: Routledge, 1987.

Folkerts, Jean. *Media Voices: An Historical Perspective*. New York and Toronto: Macmillan, 1992.

Foner, Eric. "Why Is There No Socialism in the United States?" *History Workshop* 17 (1984).

Fox, Richard Wightman, and T. J. Lears, eds. *The Culture of Consumption: Critical Essays in American History, 1880–1980*. New York: Pantheon, 1983.

Freud, Sigmund. *The Interpretation of Dreams* (1900). Rpt., New York: Avon, 1965.

Garland, Hamlin. *Main Travelled Roads* (1891). Rpt., New York: New American Library, 1962.

Garrison, Dee. "Immoral Fiction in the Late Victorian Library." Reprinted in Daniel Walker Howe, ed., *Victorian America*, 141–59.

Geertz, Clifford. "Thick Description: Toward an Interpretive Theory of Culture." In Geertz, *The Interpretation of Cultures*, chap. 1. New York: Basic Books, 1973.

Genovese, Eugene. "On Antonio Gramsci." *Studies on the Left* 2 (1967): 83–107.

Gilmore, Michael. *American Romanticism and the Marketplace*. Chicago and London: University of Chicago Press, 1985.

Gitlin, Todd. "Prime Time Ideology: The Hegemonic Process in Television Entertainment." *Social Problems* 26 (February 1979): 250–65.

Gouldner, Alvin W. *The Dialectic of Ideology and Technology*. New York and Toronto: Oxford University Press, 1976.

Graff, Harvey J. *The Legacy of Literacy*. Bloomington and Indianapolis: Indiana University Press, 1987.

Greene, Theodore P. *America's Heroes: The Changing Models of Success in American Magazines*. New York: Oxford University Press, 1970.

Griswold, Wendy. *Renaissance Revivals: City Comedy and Revenge Tragedy in the London Theater, 1576–1980*. Chicago and London: University of Chicago Press, 1986.

Grover, Kathryn, ed. *Fitness in American Culture: Images of Health, Sport, and the Body, 1830–1940*. Rochester, N.Y.: University of Massachusetts Press and the Margaret Strong Museum, 1989.

Gurevitch, Michael, Tony Bennett, James Curran, and Janet Woollacott, eds., *Culture, Society and the Media*. London and New York: Methuen, 1982.

Gutman, Herbert. *Work, Culture and Society in Industrializing America*. New York: A. A. Knopf, 1976).

Habermas, Jurgens. "The Public Sphere." Reprinted in Chandra Mukerji and Michael Schudson, eds., *Rethinking Popular Culture: Contemporary Perspectives in Cultural Studies,* 398–404.

Hall, David D. "The Victorian Connection." Reprinted in Daniel Walker Howe, ed., *Victorian America,* 81–94.

Hall, Stuart. "Cultural Studies: Two Paradigms." *Media, Culture and Society* 2 (1980): 57–72.

——. "Notes on Deconstructing the Popular." In Raphael Samuel, ed., *People's History and Socialist Theory.*

Halttunen, Karen. *Confidence Men and Painted Women: A Study of Middle-Class Culture in America, 1830–1870.* New Haven and London: Yale University Press, 1982.

Harris, Neil. *Cultural Excursions: Marketing Appetites and Cultural Tastes in Modern America.* Chicago and London: University of Chicago Press, 1990.

——. "The Gilded Age Revisited: Boston and the Museum Movement." *American Quarterly* (Winter 1962): 545–66.

——. *Humbug: The Art of P. T. Barnum.* Boston: Little, Brown, 1973.

——. "Iconography and Intellectual History: The Half-Tone Effect." Reprinted in John Higham, Paul Conklin, and Neil Harris, eds., *New Directions in American Intellectual History,* 196–211.

——. *The Land of Contrasts, 1880–1901.* New York: George Braziller, 1970.

——. "Museums, Merchandising, and Popular Taste: The Struggle for Influence." In Ian M. B. Quinby, ed., *Material Culture and the Study of American Life,* 140–74. New York: W. W. Norton, 1978.

Harrison, John M., and Harry H. Stein, eds., *Muckraking: Past, Present and Future.* University Park and London: Pennsylvania State University Press, 1973.

Hart, James D. *The Popular Book.* Berkeley: University of California Press, 1950.

Haskell, Thomas. "Contention and Economic Interest in the Debate Over Antislavery." *American Historical Review* 92 (1987): 829–78.

——. *The Emergence of Professional Social Science.* Urbana: University of Illinois Press, 1977.

Hays, Samuel. *The Response to Industrialism: 1885–1914.* Chicago: University of Chicago Press, 1957.

——. *Conservation and the Gospel of Efficiency: The Progressive Conservation Movement, 1890–1920.* Cambridge: Harvard University Press, 1959.

Higham, John. *From Boundlessness to Consolidation: The Transformation of American Culture, 1848–1860.* Ann Arbor, Mich.: William L. Clements Library, 1967.

——. "The Reorientation of American Culture in the 1890's." Reprinted in John Weiss, ed., *The Origins of Modern Consciousness,* 24–48. Detroit: Wayne State University Press, 1965.

Higham, John, Paul Conklin, and Neil Harris, eds. *New Directions in Intellectual History.* Baltimore: Johns Hopkins University Press, 1979.

Hoare, Quintin, and Geoffrey Nowell Smith, eds. *Antonio Gramsci: Selections from the Prison Notebooks.* New York: International Publishing, 1971.

Hofstadter, Richard. *The Age of Reform.* New York: Random House, 1955.

——. *The Progressive Historians: Turner, Beard, Parrington.* New York: A. A. Knopf, 1968.

——. *Social Darwinism in American Thought.* Boston: Beacon Press, 1944.

Hofstadter, Richard, ed. *The Progressive Movement, 1900–1915.* Englewood Cliffs, N.J.: Prentice-Hall, 1963.

Horkheimer, Max, and Theodore Adorno. *The Dialectic of Enlightenment.* New York: Seabury Press, 1972.

Howard, Ebenezer. *Garden Cities of To-morrow* (1898). Rpt., Cambridge: MIT Press, 1965.

Howe, Daniel Walker, ed. *Victorian America.* Philadelphia: University of Pennsylvania Press, 1976.

Howe, M. A. DeWolfe. *The Atlantic Magazine and Its Makers.* Boston: Atlantic Monthly Press, 1919.

Howells, William Dean. *The Rise of Silas Lapham* (1885). Rpt., New York: Holt, Rinehart and Winston, 1949.

Iser, Wolfgang. *The Implied Reader.* Baltimore: Johns Hopkins University Press, 1974.

Jaher, Frederic Cople, ed., *The Age of Industrialism in America: Essays in Social Structure and Cultural Values.* New York: Free Press, 1968.

James, William. *The Varieties of Religious Experience* (1902). Rpt., New York: New American Library, 1957.

——. *William James: Writings 1902–1910.* New York: Library of America, 1987.

Jameson, Fredric. "Reification and Utopia in Mass Culture." *Social Text* 1 (1979).

John, Arthur. *The Best Years of the Century: Richard Watson Gilder, Scribner's Monthly and Century Magazine, 1870–1909.* Urbana, Chicago, and London: University of Illinois Press, 1981.

Johnson, Claudia. "The Guilty Third Tier: Prostitution in Nineteenth-Century American Theaters." Reprinted in Daniel Walker Howe, ed., *Victorian America,* 111–20.

Johnson, Robert Underwood. *Remembered Yesterdays.* Boston: Little, Brown, 1923.

Juergens, Joseph. *Joseph Pulitzer and the New York World.* Princeton: Princeton University Press, 1966.

Kaplan, Justin. *Lincoln Steffens.* New York: Simon and Schuster, 1974.

Keller, Morton. *Affairs of State: Public Life in Late Nineteenth-Century America.* Cambridge: Harvard University Press, 1977.

Kelly, Mary. *Private Women, Public Stage: Literary Domesticity in Nineteenth-Century America.* New York: Oxford University Press, 1984.

Kerr, Howard. *Mediums and Spirit Rappers and Roaring Radicals: Spiritualism in American Literature, 1850–1890.* Urbana: University of Illinois Press, 1972.

Kolko, Gabriel. *The Triumph of Conservatism.* New York: Free Press, 1963.

Lafeber, Walter. *The New Empire: An Interpretation of American Expansion, 1860–1898.* Ithaca, N.Y.: Cornell University Press, 1963.

Lasch, Christopher. *The New Radicalism in America: 1889–1963.* New York: Vintage, 1965.

——. *The World of Nations.* New York: Hill and Wang, 1967.

Lasch, Christopher, ed. *The Social Thought of Jane Addams.* New York: Irvington, 1982.

Lears, T. Jackson. "The Concept of Cultural Hegemony." *American Historical Review* 90 (1985): 567–93.

——. "From Salvation to Self-Realization: Advertising and the Therapeutic Roots of Consumer Culture, 1880–1930." Reprinted in Richard Wightman Fox and T. J. Lears, eds., *The Culture of Consumption*, 1–38.

——. *No Place of Grace: Antimodernism and the Transformation of American Culture, 1880–1920*. New York: Pantheon, 1981.

Leisy, Ernest. *The American Historical Novel*. Norman: University of Oklahoma Press, 1950.

Levine, Lawrence W. *Highbrow, Lowbrow: The Emergence of Cultural Hierarchy in America*. Cambridge: Harvard University Press, 1988.

Lewis, R. W. B. *The American Adam: Innocence, Tragedy and Tradition in the Nineteenth Century*. Chicago and London: University of Chicago Press, 1955.

Lipsitz, George. *Time Passages: Collective Memory and American Popular Culture*. Minneapolis: University of Minnesota Press, 1990.

Lorimer, George Horace. *Letters from a Self-Made Merchant to His Son*. Toronto: William Briggs, 1902.

Lowenthal, Leo. *Literature, Popular Culture and Society*. Palo Alto, Calif.: Pacific Books, 1961.

Luckhurst, K. W. *The Story of Exhibitions*. London and New York: Studio Publications, 1951.

Lutz, Tom. *American Nervousness: 1903*. Ithaca and London: Cornell University Press, 1991.

Lyon, Peter. *Success Story: The Life and Times of S. S. McClure*. New York: Scribner's, 1963.

MacDonald, Dwight. "A Theory of Mass Culture." Reprinted in Bernard Rosenberg and David Manning White, eds., *Mass Culture: The Popular Arts in America*, 59–73.

Mallan, John P. "Roosevelt, Brooks Adams and Lea: The Warrior Critique of the Business Civilization." *American Quarterly* 8 (1956): 216–30.

Marchland, Roland. *Advertising and the American Dream: Making the Way for Modernity, 1920–1940*. Berkeley: University of California Press, 1986.

Martin, Jay. "The Literature of Argument and the Arguments of Literature." Reprinted in John M. Harrison and Harry H. Stein, eds., *Muckraking: Past, Present and Future*, 100–15.

May, Henry F. *The End of American Innocence: The First Years of Our Own Time, 1912–1917*. Oxford: Oxford University Press, 1959.

May, Larry. *Screening Out the Past: The Birth of Mass Culture and the Motion Picture Industry*. Chicago and London: University of Chicago Press, 1980.

McCloskey, Robert Green. *American Conservatism in the Age of Enterprise, 1865–1910: A Study of William Graham Sumner, Stephen J. Field and Andrew Carnegie*. Cambridge: Harvard University Press, 1951.

McClure, S. S. *My Autobiography* (1914). Rpt., New York: Ungar, 1963.

McCormick, Richard L. *The Party Period and Public Policy: American Politics from the Age of Jackson to the Progressive Era*. New York: Oxford University Press, 1986.

McDonald, Susan Waugh. "From Kipling to Kitsch: Two Popular Editors of the Gilded

Age: Mass Culture, Magazines and Correspondence Universities." *Journal of Popular Culture* 15 (Fall 1981): 50–61.

McFarland, Gerald W. *Mugwumps, Morals and Politics: 1884–1920.* Amherst: University of Massachusetts Press, 1975.

McGeer, Michael E. *The Decline of Popular Politics.* New York: Oxford University Press, 1986.

McGovern, James R. "The American Woman's Pre–World War I Freedom in Manners and Morals." *Journal of American History* 55 (September 1968): 315–33.

McLoughlin, William. *Revivals, Awakenings and Reform.* Chicago: University of Chicago Press, 1978.

McWilliams, Carey. "The Continuing Tradition of Reform Journalism." Reprinted in John M. Harrison and Harry H. Stein, eds., *Muckraking: Past, Present and Future,* 118-34.

Meyer, D. H. "American Intellectuals and the Victorian Crisis of Faith." Reprinted in Daniel Walker Howe, ed., *Victorian America,* 59–77.

Meyer, Donald. *The Positive Thinkers: Religion as Pop Psychology from Mary Baker Eddy to Oral Roberts.* New York: Pantheon, 1965.

Milne, Gordon. *George William Curtis and the Genteel Tradition.* Bloomington: Indiana University Press, 1956.

Mintz, Steven. *A Prison of Expectations: The Family in Victorian Culture.* New York and London: New York University Press, 1983.

Montgomery, David. *Workers Control in America.* Cambridge: Cambridge University Press, 1979.

Moore, Lawrence R. "Spiritualism and Science: Reflections on the First Decade of the Spirit Rappings." *American Quarterly* 24 (October 1972): 474–500.

——. "The Spiritualist Medium in a Study of Female Professionalism in Victorian America." *American Quarterly* 27 (May 1975): 200–21.

Mott, Frank Luther. *A History of American Magazines.* 5 vols. Cambridge: Harvard University Press, 1930–68.

——. *American Journalism: A History 1690–1960.* New York: Macmillan, 1962.

Mrozek, Donald J. *Sport and American Mentality, 1880–1910.* Knoxville: University of Tennessee Press, 1983.

Mukerji, Chandra, and Michael Schudson, eds. *Rethinking Popular Culture: Contemporary Perspectives in Cultural Studies.* Berkeley: University of California Press, 1991.

Munsey, Frank. *The Story of the Founding and Development of the Frank Munsey Publishing House.* New York, 1907.

Nerone, John C. "The Mythology of the Penny Press." Reprinted in *Jean Folkerts, Media Voices: An Historical Perspective,* 157–82. New York and Toronto: Macmillan, 1992.

Noble, David. *America by Design: Science, Technology and the Rise of Corporate Capitalism.* Oxford: Oxford University Press, 1977.

Nord, David Paul. *Newspapers and the New Politics: Midwestern Municipal Reform, 1890–1900.* Ann Arbor, Mich.: UMI Research Press, 1981.

Ohmann, Richard. "Where Did Mass Culture Come From? The Case of the Magazines." *Berkshire Review* 16 (1981): 85–101.

——. *Politics of Letters.* Middletown, Conn.: Wesleyan University Press, 1987.

O'Neill, William. *Everyone Was Brave: A History of Feminism in America.* New York: Quadrangle Books, 1969.

Orvell, Miles. *The Real Thing: Imitation and Authenticity in American Culture, 1880–1940.* Chapel Hill and London: University of North Carolina Press, 1989.

Palermo, Patrick E. *Lincoln Steffens.* Boston: Twayne, 1978.

Park, Robert E. "The Natural History of the Newspaper." *American Journal of Sociology* 29 (November 1923): 273–89.

Park, Roberta J. "Physiology and Anatomy Are Destiny!? Brains, Bodies and Exercise in Nineteenth-Century American Thought." *Journal of Sport History* 18 (Spring 1991), no. 1: 31–63.

Parrini, Carl P., and Martin J. Sklar. "New Thinking About the Market, 1896–1904: Some American Economists on Investment and the Theory of Surplus Capital." *Journal of Economic History* 43 (September 3, 1983): 559–78.

Pearson, Edmund. *Dime Novels, or Following an Old Trail in Popular Literature.* Port Washington, N.Y.: Kennikat Press, 1929.

Persons, Stow. *The Decline of American Gentility.* New York: Columbia University Press, 1973.

Peterson, Theodore. *Magazines in the Twentieth Century.* Urbana: University of Illinois Press, 1964.

Pfaelzer, Jean. *The Utopian Novel in America, 1886–1896.* Pittsburgh: University of Pittsburgh Press, 1984.

Rabinbach, Anson. *The Human Motor: Energy, Fatigue and the Origins of Modernity.* Berkeley and Los Angeles: University of California Press, 1992.

Rader, Benjamin G. "The Quest for Self-Sufficiency and the New Strenuosity: Reflections on the Strenuous Life of the 1970's and 1980's." *Journal of Sport History* 18:2 (Summer 1991): 255–66.

Radway, Janice. *Reading the Romance: Women, Patriarchy and Popular Literature.* Chapel Hill and London: University of North Carolina Press, 1984.

Riis Jacob A. *How the Other Half Lives: Studies Among the Tenements of New York* (1890). Rpt., New York: Charles Scribner's, 1939.

Rodgers, Daniel T. *The Work Ethic in Industrial America, 1850–1920.* Chicago and London: University of Chicago Press, 1978.

Rosenberg, Bernard, and David Manning White, eds. *Mass Culture: The Popular Arts in America.* New York: Free Press, 1957.

Rosenberg, Rosalind. *Beyond Separate Spheres: Intellectual Roots of Modern Feminism.* New Haven: Yale University Press, 1982.

Rosenzweig, Roy. *Eight Hours for What We Will: Workers and Leisure in an Industrial City.* Cambridge: Cambridge University Press, 1983.

Ross, Dorothy. *The Origins of American Social Science.* Cambridge: Cambridge University Press, 1991.

——. "Socialism and American Liberalism: Academic Social Thought in the 1880's." *Perspectives in American History* 11 (1977–78): 5–79.

Rothman, Sheila M. *Woman's Proper Place: A History of Changing Ideals and Practices, 1870 to the Present.* New York: Basic Books, 1978.

Rubin, Joan Shelly. *The Making of Middlebrow Culture.* Chapel Hill and London: University of North Carolina Press, 1992.

Rydell, Robert W. *All the World's a Fair: Vision of Empire at American International Expositions, 1876–1916.* Chicago and London: University of Chicago Press, 1984.

Samuel, Raphael, ed. *People's History and Socialist Theory.* London: Routledge, 1981.

Santayana, George. "The Genteel Tradition in American Philosophy" (1913). Reprinted in D. L. Wilson, ed., *The Genteel Tradition.* Cambridge: Harvard University Press, 1967.

Saxton, Alexander. "Blackfaced Minstrelsy and Jacksonian Ideology." *American Quarterly* 27 (March 1975): 3–28.

Schaaf, Barbara C. *Mr. Dooley's Chicago.* Garden City, N.Y.: Doubleday-Anchor, 1977.

Schneirov, Richard. *Graft for Power: The Knights of Labor, Trade Unions and Politics in Late Nineteenth Century Chicago.* University of Illinois University Press, forthcoming.

——. "The Rise of Labor and the Transformation of Urban Politics in Late Nineteenth-Century Chicago." *International Labor and Working Class History* 46 (Fall 1994).

Schudson, Michael. *Advertising and the Uneasy Persuasion: Its Dubious Impact on American Society.* New York: Basic Books, 1984.

——. *Discovering the News: A Social History of American Newspapers.* New York: Basic Books, 1978.

Sedgwick, Ellery. *The Happy Profession.* Boston: Little, Brown, 1946.

Sedgwick, Ellery III. "The American Genteel Tradition in the Early Twentieth Century." *American Studies* 25 (Spring 1984): 49–76.

Sinclair, Upton. *The Jungle* (1906). Rpt., New York and Toronto: Bantam, 1981.

Singal, Daniel Joseph. "Toward a Definition of American Modernism." *American Quarterly* 39 (Spring 1987): 7–26.

Sklar, Kathryn Kish. *Catherine Beecher: A Study in American Domesticity.* New York: W. W. Norton, 1973.

Sklar, Martin. *The Corporate Reconstruction of American Capitalism, 1890–1916.* Cambridge: Cambridge University Press, 1988.

——. *The United States as a Developing Country: Studies in U.S. History in the Progressive Era and the 1920's.* Cambridge: Cambridge University Press, 1992.

Skowronek, Stephen. *Building a New American State.* New York: Cambridge University Press, 1982.

Smith-Rosenberg, Carroll. "The New Woman as Androgyne: Social Disorder and Gender Crisis, 1870–1936." Reprinted in Smith-Rosenberg, *Disorderly Conduct,* 245–96. New York: Basic Books, 1978.

Smith, Henry Nash. "The Scribbling Women and the Cosmic Success Story." *Critical Inquiry* 1 (September 1974): 47–70.

——. *Virgin Land: The American West as Symbol and Myth.* Cambridge: Harvard University Press, 1950.

Sproat, John G. *"The Best Men": Liberal Reformers in the Progressive Age.* New York: Oxford University Press, 1968.

Steffens, Lincoln. *The Autobiography of Lincoln Steffens.* New York: Harcourt, 1931.

——-. *The Letters of Lincoln Steffens; Volume 1: 1889–1919.* New York: Harcourt, 1938.

——. *The Shame of the Cities* (1904). Rpt., New York: Sagamore Press, 1957.

Steinberg, Salme Harju. *Reformer in the Marketplace: Edward Bok and the Ladies' Home Journal.* Baton Rouge and London: Louisiana State University Press, 1979.

Stevenson, Louise. *The Victorian Homefront: American Thought and Culture, 1860–1880.* New York: Twayne, 1991.

Stinson, Robert. "McClure's Road to *McClure's:* How Revolutionary Were the 1890's Magazines?" *Journalism Quarterly* 47 (Summer 1970): 256–62.

Susman, Warren. *Culture as History: The Transformation of American Society in the Twentieth Century.* New York: Pantheon, 1973.

Swanberg, W. A. *Citizen Hearst.* New York: Scribner's, 1961.

Tarbell, Ida. *All in a Day's Work.* New York: Macmillan, 1939.

——. *The History of Standard Oil,* 2 vols. (1904). Rpt., New York: Peter Smith, 1950 (two volumes in one).

Tebbel, John. *The American Magazine: A Compact History.* New York: Hawthorn Books, 1969.

——. *George Horace Lorimer and the Saturday Evening Post: The Biography of a Great Editor* (Garden City, N.Y.: Doubleday, 1948.

Thelen, David. *The New Citizenship: Origins of Progressivism in Wisconsin, 1885–1900.* Columbia: University of Missouri Press, 1972.

——. *Robert La Follette and the Insurgent Spirit.* Boston: Little, Brown, 1976.

——. "Social Tensions and the Origins of Progressivism." *Journal of American History* 56 (1969): 323–41.

Tichi, Cecelia. *Shifting Gears: Technology, Literature, Culture in Modernist America.* Chapel Hill and London: University of North Carolina Press, 1987.

Tomsich, John. *A Genteel Endeavor: American Culture and Politics in the Gilded Age.* Stanford: Stanford University Press, 1971.

Trachtenberg, Alan. *Democratic Vistas, 1860–1880.* New York: George Braziller, 1970.

——. *The Incorporation of America: Culture and Society in the Gilded Age.* New York: Hill and Wang, 1982.

Trachtenberg, Alan, ed. *Critics of Culture: Literature and Society in the Early Twentieth Century.* New York: John Wiley, 1976.

Turner, Graeme. *British Cultural Studies: An Introduction.* Boston: Unwin Hyman, 1990.

Twain, Mark, and Charles Dudley Warner. *The Gilded Age: A Tale of Today* (1873). Rpt., New York: New American Library, 1980.

Weinberg, Arthur, and Lila Weinberg, eds. *The Muckrakers.* New York: G. P. Putnam's, 1964.

Weinstein, James. *The Corporate Ideal in the Liberal State, 1900–1918.* Boston: Beacon Press, 1968.

White, Bruce. *The Philistine: A Periodical of Protest (1895–1915): A Major American "Little Magazine."* Lanham, Md.: University Press of America, 1989.

White, Morton. *Social Thought in America: The Revolt Against Formalism.* Boston: Beacon Press, 1964.

White, William Allen. *The Autobiography of William Allen White* (1946). Rpt., Lawrence: University Press of Kansas, 1990.

Whorton, James C. "Eating to Win: Popular Concepts of Diet, Strength, and Energy in the Early Twentieth Century." Reprinted in Kathryn Grover, ed., *Fitness in American Culture: Images of Health, Sport, and the Body, 1830–1940,* 86–122.

Wiebe, Robert H. *The Search for Order, 1877–1920.* New York: Hill and Wang, 1967.

Williams, Raymond. "Base and Superstructure in Marxist Cultural Theory." *New Left Review* 82 (1973): 3–16.

——. *Marxism and Literature.* Oxford: Oxford University Press, 1977.

Williams, Rosalind H. *Dream Worlds: Mass Consumption in Late Nineteenth-Century France.* Berkeley: University of California Press, 1982.

Wilson, Christopher P. "The Era of the Reporter Reconsidered: The Case of Lincoln Steffens," *Journal of Popular Culture* 15 (Fall 1981): 41–49.

——. "The Rhetoric of Consumption: Mass-Market Magazines and the Demise of the Gentle Reader, 1880–1920." In Richard Wightman Fox and T. J. Lears, eds., *The Culture of Consumption: Critical Essays in American History, 1880–1980,* 39–64.

Wilson, D. L. *The Genteel Tradition.* Cambridge: Harvard University Press, 1967.

Wilson, Harold S. *McClure's Magazine and the Muckrakers.* Princeton: Princeton University Press, 1970.

Wirth, Louis. "Urbanism as a Way of Life." *American Journal of Sociology* 44 (July 1938): 21.

Woollacott, Janet. "Messages and Meanings." In Michael Gurevitch, Tony Bennett, James Curran, and Janet Woollacott, eds., *Culture, Society and the Media.*

Wood, James Playsted. *Magazines in the United States.* New York: Ronald Press, 1956.

Wyllie, Irvin G. *The Self-Made Man in America.* New Brunswick, N.J.: Rutgers University Press, 1954.

Zboray, Ronald J. "Antebellum Reading and the Ironies of Technological Innovation." *American Quarterly* 40 (March 1988): 65–82.

Ziff, Larzer. *The American 1890's: Life and Times of a Lost Generation.* New York: Viking, 1966.

INDEX